Japan-SAARC Partnership
A Way Ahead

Japan-SAARC Partnership
A Way Ahead

Edited by

Srabani Roy Choudhury

PENTAGON PRESS

Japan-SAARC Partnership: A Way Ahead
Srabani Roy Choudhury (Ed)

First Published in 2014

ISBN 978-81-8274-784-5

Published by
PENTAGON PRESS
206, Peacock Lane, Shahpur Jat,
New Delhi-110049
Phones: 011-64706243, 26491568
Telefax: 011-26490600
email: rajan@pentagonpress.in
website: www.pentagonpress.in

Branch:
Prime Arcade
Office #11
1154 Saifee Street
Opp. M.G. Road, Camp
Pune-411001
Email: pentagonpresspune@gmail.com

Printed at Aegean Offset Printers, Greater Noida, U.P.

CONTENTS

PREFACE

This book is the end product of discussions from an international conference held on "Japan-SAARC Partnership: A Way Ahead" by the Centre for East Asian Studies, School of International Studies, Jawaharlal Nehru University and Sasakawa Peace Foundation on November 14 and 15, 2013 in New Delhi.

With globalization, there has been an upsurge of regionalism and as action in international relations shift to Asia, there has been a growing interest in the South Asian region. Strategically placed between South East Asia and West Asia, some of the South Asian Association of Regional Cooperation (SAARC) nations have become critical for energy security as Sea Lines of Communication weave around them. The importance of this region and the interest of the world to use the platform of SAARC to enhance their relationship with it can be gleaned from the fact that all major powers of the world have gained Observer status in this forum with many more aspiring to it.

In his inaugural speech at the 17th SAARC Summit held from 10-11 of November 2011 in Addu City, President Mohammed Nasheed of Maldives called on SAARC leaders to "deepen economic integration and build bridges of co-operation between their countries and people". He ended his speech on an upbeat note: "The fundamentals of our region (SAARC) are strong. We have young, energetic populations. We live in a region of vibrant democracies, with strong civil societies."

SAARC as an organization has had a tremulous past. The issues between the member countries are driven by the history of this region and paradoxically, this often has been a stumbling block for a constructive progress. Despite this, since its inception, SAARC has plodded along often tentatively, cautiously and guardedly but diligently; towards creating an environment of cooperation and cordiality between the member nations. The current changes in the international arena and the progress made by other regional entities has provided positive impetus towards this very goal of co-prosperity and today, each of the member states of SAARC realise the significance of this entity and are willing to reap benefits collectively as well as bilaterally from it.

The 14th Summit of SAARC, held on 3 and 4 April 2007, welcomed Japan along with China, the European Union, the Republic of Korea and the

United States of America, as Observers. It was a momentous decision indicating that the leaders of the SAARC nations had collectively become conscious of the significance of the region and were willing to drive SAARC as an entity into new realms of activity. Giving Japan Observer status was not only the recognition that Japan as the most advanced Asian economy could be a resource of funds, technology and skill development; but also for a country like India, an offset to the influence of China.

For Japan on the other hand, due to growing tensions in the East Asia region, securing the Sea Lines of Communication for its energy needs and with the growing influence of China, promoting peace and co-prosperity in the SAARC region has gained considerable relevance. With a relatively young population, a growing economy and slow emergence of political stability, Japan perceives that by engaging with SAARC, it would not only benefit economically but also look to counterbalance the growing influence of China in the region.

For a long time, keeping in focus the potential of this region, Japan has contributed by creating special funds for stability and progress of the countries in this region and programmes like Japan-East Asia Network of Exchange for Students and Youths (JENESYS) to develop human resource. While the help extended by Japan is well appreciated by the quarters that have benefited from it, little efforts have been made towards exchanging views between the SAARC nations on how each of them has harnessed their relationship with Japan. The purpose of the international conference was to promote understanding of contemporary Japan in India and other SAARC countries; to facilitate exchange of researchers/experts/scholars interested in regionalism; to encourage specialists on SAARC nations to study and understand Japan-SAARC relations; to motivate young scholars to develop interest in the concerns of Japan vis-a-vis South Asia and to increase the research and educational level of contemporary Japan in India and other SAARC countries.

The outcome of this conference is this volume in which we have twenty one contributors of whom eighteen, participated in the conference. While the discussions during conference were vibrant, the papers have been a culmination of each author's understanding and their reflection of how this region will shape up in the future. While many of the authors are veterans on the subject, it is a pleasure to see few young scholars making their presence felt by contributing to this book.

This book, "Japan-SAARC Partnership: A Way Ahead" reflects on the role of Japan in this region from various perspectives. Broadly speaking, regionalism, politics, security, economics and use of soft power have been the spectrum on which the authors have contributed. It has been enriched by the contributions of authors from not only India and Japan but also from

Bangladesh, Nepal and Sri Lanka. Discussion of SAARC region is incomplete without gaining some understanding of the China perspective, which has been ably delved into by experts on China.

As the authors began submitting their papers, it was evident that two distinct streams were emerging- ones that looked at the whole region, drawing the interest of all the member states and seeking to understand Japan's role and contribution; and others that looked at bilateral relations between Japan and one of the member nations in either the political, economic or cultural aspect. Two of the authors bring out China's perspective in its engagement with SAARC. The volume has thus been sequenced from the broader perspective of the region and then moving towards bilateral relations between member nations and Japan.

The opening chapter by Lalima Varma titled "Japan's Approach to Regionalism with Reference to SAARC" refers to Japan's foreign policy and its economic and strategic objectives during the Cold War period and after; and reasons for its visible interest and participation in the existing regional groupings such as the ASEAN. Japan's keenness was propelled largely by its interest in protecting its economic interests. Fluctuations in its relations with the neighbouring countries especially China; and most importantly, maritime security called for diverting its attention to look beyond East Asia, and thus spreading to South Asia and SAARC. In playing a meaningful role in SAARC, what kind of challenges and limitations Japan is confronted with, or will be in the future is discussed in detail.

Japan has taken a number of measures for 'peace building' in Afghanistan and Sri Lanka and has assisted Bangladesh, Maldives, Nepal and Pakistan in consolidating democracy. Even so, critics have pointed out that Japan places low emphasis on civil society assistance. When it comes to security concerns, securing Sea Lines of Communications from piracy and other non-state actors remains one of the priority areas for Japan. Constitutional limitations prevent Japan from playing a full-fledged security role for regional peace, and therefore Japan has adopted means other than hard power to promote peace and stability. How Japan has used both hard and soft powers for the security and stability of the SAARC countries is discussed extensively in the second chapter of this book by Shamshad A Khan titled, "Japan-SAARC Relations: Tokyo's Initiatives for Regional Peace, Prosperity and Stability".

While relationship between Japan and any country or region is pivoted on economic exchange, with the SAARC nations, it has the added advantage of a strong cultural linkage, in form of Buddhism. The third chapter by Takenori Horimoto titled "Japan-SAARC Relations: The Political Dimension" draws upon this deep seeded relationship which began by the spread of

Buddhism and extensively explores the specifics of the relationship between Japan and the SAARC region and the various dimensions that currently govern it.

The fourth chapter by H.S. Prabhakar, titled "Extra-Regional Powers in SAARC: Japan" examines Japan's involvement in SAARC nations and then compares it to the level of its involvement in ASEAN. It reflects that in the recent attempt of reviving the Japanese economy through investment in foreign shores as part of 'Abenomics", more investment is flowing into Vietnam, Philippines and Myanmar and eluding the SAARC region. The paper focuses on the strengths and opportunities that exist for Japan in deepening its engagement with the SAARC nations.

While Japan-SAARC partnership is driven by its own strategic and economic considerations, it has progressively involved itself into the realms of SAARC in the turn of the century albeit to counter China's rising influence in the region. As China surged ahead to the second position in the world economic order and sought a place in the international order, within SAARC nations too, there was a clear divergence between those who welcomed it and those who felt challenged. China's claim for an Observer status in SAARC was then suitably countered with Japan also being made an Observer. The current move by China to claim membership in SAARC has put India in a very unsettling position, given the plethora of issues between the two nations. Alka Acharya in her paper titled "Perspectives on 'China's Engagement with SAARC' in India" which forms the fifth chapter in this book, brings out the tension, strain and pressures that engulf India due to China's engagement in SAARC. The chapter explains how China can actually benefit the region as a SAARC member and how that will only draw Japan into a more committed role.

In order to secure its Sea Lines of Communication, and more importantly to secure its oil, Japan has drawn closer to the South Asian region and is engaging bilaterally not only in the area of economics but also strategically. The current issues of Takeshima islands and Air Defence Identification Zone have only furthered Japan's interest in spreading itself strategically beyond its backwaters of the South China Sea. Given the importance that security is gaining in Japan's perception of international relations, the sixth and seventh chapters: Tomoko Kiyota's "Japan's Security Cooperation with SAARC Countries" and Joshy M. Paul's "Japan-SAARC Security Relations: A Maritime Perspective" give the reader a comprehensive understanding of Japan's interest in aligning itself strategically with the littoral countries of the region. Kiyota claims that it "clearly mirrors the imperatives of the changing balance of power in Asia" and infers that over time influence of Japan will expand to countries like Sri Lanka which is geo-strategically situated in the Sea Lines of Communication. Paul concurs that Japan's interest in this region is derived from the acts of piracy and other crimes in the Indian Ocean and that while the current engagement in security in this region is pivoted on India-Japan relations, its expansion to other nations of this region especially the littoral states of Sri Lanka and Maldives is imperative.

Srikanth Kondapalli brings in China's engagement in SAARC from the perspective of China's western development campaign and "go west" policy in his paper "Knocking at the Himalayan Gates - China's Perspectives on SAARC". He proclaims that "securing Xinjiang against Uighur activism, going beyond the current Tibet imbroglio, and reshaping the regional order, China needs to associate with the SAARC process". It is in China's interest, both in view of its security concern and economic opportunities that "China's official position indicates towards pragmatic and effective cooperation with the SAARC."

No book on Japan's relations with a region or a country is complete without looking into economic relationships. Economic relationship of Japan has always been two pronged. The Official Development Assistance (ODA) which the Government of Japan gives to the developing economies to help better lives and living environment of its people and its investment through private business to help the process of economic development. The growing economy of India, Sri Lanka, and emerging economies of Bangladesh and Pakistan, resulted in rising consumerism providing a huge market of opportunity for Japanese businesses which until now have shied away for a lack of understanding of the pluralistic social structure and a vastly diverse customer base. Srabani Roy Choudhury in her paper "SAARC Nations' Markets: Opportunities for Japanese Business" addresses in detail the opportunities for Japanese companies in the consumer sector, across different sectors while asserting that it requires a substantial understanding of the uniqueness of the sector in which the company operates and also the changing dynamics that the market throws-up regularly. Similarly, Makoto Kojima's paper on "New Dimensions of Japan-India Economic Partnership" is almost a case in point to show-case how India has benefited from its strong alliance with Japan. The paper delves into how the policy of Comprehensive Economic Partnership Agreement (CEPA) has helped attract investment into India and discusses at length projects like the Delhi Mumbai Industrial Corridor (DMIC) and Delhi Freight Corridor. He attempts to draw on the new dimensions of Japan-India bilateral relations and Japanese commitment through analysis of these mega projects and IT off-shoring by Japan into India. Needless to say, this paper can help other member states of SAARC to create road maps for harnessing Japanese investment.

The next two papers touch upon developmental support given by Japan to two member nations, namely Nepal and Bangladesh. In chapter eleven by Ram Chandra Dhakal and Ram Kumar Phuyal titled " An Overview of Japan's Support for SAARC Member States: With Reference to Nepal" the authors outline the major contribution of Japanese official development assistance to SAARC countries; and its role in the process of their economic development, especially of Nepal, by adapting from available literature of last four decades. The paper then explores and examines the ways in which Japan has been established as one of the major donors to Nepal and concludes that shortcomings of the development process in Nepal, even after receiving Japanese assistance are not only because of the terms of the donor's aid policy, but also due to the political interventions and fluctuations, and socio-economic environment of Nepal. In the case of aid to Bangladesh, chapter twelve by M. Abul Kashem Mozumder and Abdullah Al Mamun titled "Japan's Contribution Towards Economic Development and Stability of Bangladesh" gives details of the various contributions of Japanese aid to Bangladesh and how it benefits that country because the aid policy is specifically oriented to the country's needs. The authors conclude that for Bangladesh to accomplish its vision of becoming a middle income country by 2021, technical and financial assistance from Japan would be indispensable.

On similar lines, chapter thirteen by Mayumi Murayama titled "Shifting Images of Bangladesh in Japan–Bangladesh Relationship" explains that Japan's interest in Bangladesh has gone through two 'booms'. The current boom is two-fold: first as a business investment destination, and second as a philanthropic destination especially for the younger generation, who aspire to contribute to social causes. The paper also gives added perspective on the subject of Japan-Bangladesh relations by giving example of the Japanese support to Bangladesh's garment industry, a critical industry for Bangladesh, being the biggest employer as well as the highest earning sector from exports.

In the next chapter: "Japan-SAARC Relations: Addressing Challenges of Afghan Women" Mondira Dutta provides portraiture of the status of women in Afghanistan and Japan's commitment to the development process in that country. In her concluding section, she suggests steps that can be taken by Japan, as a member of the international community, to improve the status of women in Afghanistan.

The above chapters have probed into Japan-SAARC relations from regional, political, international and economic points of view. Japan has always had to counter its constitutional weakness of "pacifism" with strong cultural networking. The contribution to betterment of its equation with SAARC nations utilizing its soft power in various forms has been extensively documented. The fifteenth chapter by Sushila Narsimhan titled "Buddhism: Japan's Soft Power Tool Towards India" highlights how respect for Buddhism has prompted the people of Japan to give aid or donate generously for many projects on restoration, and how it has cultivated tourism and helped in local development. The revival of the Nalanda University Project by India which has brought together divergent and hostile players of the Asia-Pacific and become a conduit of international cooperation has only furthered the cause of Japan as it generously donates for this activity and promotes its image of a peace loving nation.

While dissemination of knowledge, language and other forms of culture and the absence of any historical baggage helps both countries reflect a positive image of the other, according to Madhuchanda Ghosh in her paper "India-Japan Relations: The Dividend of Cultural Affinity", the current spate of engagement between India and Japan in other realms of activity, necessitates 'greater flow of cultural exchanges' which would then provide 'an edifice for deepening and for the expansion of India-Japan relations'.

A major source of disseminating Japanese culture is by popularizing its language as it becomes the conduit for people to people exchange not only in language learning but also in other educational fields. Given the importance of the role of the Japanese language in the broader view of bilateral relations, the chapter on "Japanese Language as Soft Power", by Janashruti Chandra looks at length at the issue of language as a soft power and the advantages of using this soft power to enhance relationship. The last chapter in the book "Japan's Influence on Sri Lankan Higher Education" by Nanda Gunawardhana and Shanthini Shanmugarajah infers that Japanese language as a tool can help Japan in "supporting democratization and peace building measures" and that "such initiatives will be stepping stones to internationalization from the inward-orientation of its culture". Apart from discussing the various forms of assistance given by Japan to the higher education sector of Sri Lanka and the growing level of Sri Lankan youth travelling for higher education to Japan, the authors use the Sri Lanka Japan Study Centre as an example of a flourishing relationship. They then go on to prescribe how Japan can employ a more comprehensive engagement in higher education in SAARC nations.

This book has been possible because of the commitment of the authors who have all adhered to the deadlines in spite of their busy schedules. The generous financial assistance by the Sasakawa Peace Foundation for conducting the conference and publishing of this book has been the major reason how we could accomplish our goal. Rani Bopanna with her timely editorial help, contributed immensely towards its successful conclusion. While the above were core contributors to the book, a large number of students who silently but enthusiastically and tirelessly worked for the conference must be acknowledged. While the list is endless, credits are especially due Debendra Sahu, Pravhat Lama, Titli Basu, Santosh Kumar, P. Prakash, Nengneithem Kipgen, Arnab Dasgupta, Karuna Amy Guria, Keisha Kashyap and P.T. Shahana without whose unstinted support the conference would not have achieved an unprecedented level of success. Grateful acknowledgement is also due to the Pentagon Press for their support and diligence in processing the book.

The book has a variety of perspectives as it has contributions from scholars from Japan and the South Asian region. It is hoped that the view and observations that this book brings out will contribute to enrich future literature on the subject.

April 2014 **Srabani Roy Choudhury**

ABOUT THE CONTRIBUTORS

Dr. Lalima Varma is a senior Professor of Japanese Studies in the Centre for East Asian Studies, School of International Studies, Jawaharlal Nehru University. Prof. Varma received commendation in 2013 by the Ministry of Foreign Affairs, Japan, for her distinguished service in promoting understanding between Japan and India, contributing to promoting friendly relations between Japan and other countries. She has been a recipient of Japan Foundation Professional Fellowship twice, 1987-1988 and 2005-2006. She was Visiting Scholar to University of Tokyo. She has authored a book entitled 'Making of Japan's China Policy' and edited volumes, one among them being, "India-Japan Relations in Emerging Asia" [2013].

Dr. Shamshad Ahmad Khan is a Research Fellow at the ICWA. He completed his M.Phil and Ph.D from Japanese Studies Division, Centre for East Asian Studies, School of International Studies, JNU, New Delhi. He was Government of Japan's Mombusho Fellow and was affiliated with Waseda University, Tokyo, as research student during his fellowship. He was Visiting Research Fellow at the Slavic Research Centre, Hokkaido University, Japan. He was also a Visiting Research Fellow at the Institute of Developing Economies, Japan. In 2011, he got Nakasone Award from Japan's former Prime Minister Nakasone Yasuhiro for his contribution to Japanese studies in India. His research interests include Japan's foreign policy, Japan's role in international security, debates on Japanese constitutional revision and internal politics, India-Japan relations and Japan's relations with its neighbours.

Dr. Takenori Horimoto is a specialist in Contemporary South Asian Politics. He has authored and edited eleven books⁻*India: The Big Elephant Globalizes*, Iwanami Shoten, 2007 (Japanese), co-ed with Prof. Masashi Nishihara) *India as a Rising Military Power*, Askishobo, 2010 (Japanese), co-ed with Prof. Lalima Varma *India-Japan Relations in Emerging Asia*, Manohar, Feb. 2013. He has to his credit over one hundred and twenty four articles and is a frequent speaker in many forums in Japan on South Asia politics and India-Japan relations.

Dr. H.S. Prabhakar, Associate Professor, Centre for East Asian Studies, School of International Studies at the Jawaharlal Nehru University in New Delhi. He has been teaching here since 1985. Prabhakar holds Masters, M.Phil and Doctoral degrees. Areas of his teaching and research interests are: Political Economy of Japan, Government and Politics in Japan, Business Organisation and Management in Japan. He had been a Visiting Foreign Researcher in many Japanese universities at different times. A recipient of Japan Foundation fellowship, he was till recently on a year's sabbatical affiliated to the Institute of Asia- Pacific Studies, Waseda University, Tokyo. He has participated and presented research papers at many Japanese universities (in Honshu, Hokkaido and Shikoku) and in several Indian universities, institutions and think tanks. He has extensively published on different areas covering India-Japan relations, besides many aspects of contemporary Japan—foreign relations, development assistance, policy, problems, process, domestic politics, political economy, welfare state, society and the like. He is a familiar commentator in Indian media on contemporary Japanese and East Asian affairs.

Dr. Alka Acharya is currently on deputation as Director and Senior Fellow of the Institute of Chinese Studies, Delhi, from the Centre for East Asian Studies (Chinese Studies) School of International Studies, Jawaharlal Nehru University (JNU) where she is Professor and former Chairperson. She has been teaching courses on Chinese Foreign Policy and Political Economy to the Masters and M.Phil students and guiding doctoral research since 1993. Ten scholars have so far been awarded a doctoral degree under her supervision. She is the joint editor of the book *Crossing A Bridge of Dreams: 50 years of India-China*, published in 2002, has contributed chapters to many books and regularly features in the *Economic and Political Weekly*, published from Mumbai, India. She was nominated by the Indian government as a member of the India-China Eminent Persons Group (2006-2008) and member of the National Security Advisory Board (2006-2008) of the Government of India. She has authored a book *China & India: Politics of Incremental Engagement*, published in 2008. She was reappointed for a second term on the National Security Advisory Board (2011-2012). Her current research focuses on India-China-Russia Trilateral Cooperation and the Chinese strategic response to the post-cold war regional architecture, with special reference to China's neighborhood.

Ms. Tomoko Kiyota is a Ph.D. candidate at the Graduate School of International Cooperation Studies, Takushoku University, Tokyo. She was a Visiting Fellow at the Department of Geopolitics and International Relations, Manipal University, Karnataka from April 2012 to February 2014. She taught a course to the post graduate students on *India and the Great Powers in the Asia-Pacific*. She used to work at the Ministry of Foreign Affairs of Japan as a Political Analyst from April 2010 to September 2011. She was a Research Intern at the Institute of Peace and Conflict Studies (Nov 2008 to May 2009), and a Visiting Fellow at the Institute for Defence Studies Analyses (Jul 2009 to Jan 2010). Her doctoral thesis explores India's arms development and the Military-Industrial Complex. She also contributed her papers on the India-Japan relations and Japanese national security to several international conferences. Her recent publications are: "Japan's South China Sea Conundrum," Kaushiva and Singh eds., *Geopolitics of the Indo-Pacific* "India's Defence Budget and Arms Procurement Decision-making Process," *Kaigaijijo [Journal of World Affairs]* (June 2013, pp. 122-138); "The Return of Shinzo Abe: Implications for Indo-Japanese Relations," (RSIS Commentary, January 2013).

Dr. Joshy M. Paul is an Associate Fellow at the National Maritime Foundation, New Delhi. He has a Ph.D. in International Politics from School of International Studies, Jawaharlal Nehru University, New Delhi. His research areas are Asian Security, Japan's Foreign Policy, China's Grand Strategy, India's Look-East Policy, and Maritime Security. He has been MacArthur Visiting Associate Fellow at S. Rajaratnam School of International Studies (RSIS), Nanyang Technological University, Singapore in 2010, and Visiting Research Fellow at the National Institute for Defence Studies, Tokyo in 2011. His latest articles include; "Emerging Powers and Cooperative Security in Asia", RSIS Working Paper 221 (December 2010), "India and Japan Reluctant Idealism to Practical Realism", South Asian Survey (Sage), Summer 2008;"Territorial Dispute in the East China Sea and its Effects on China-Japan Relations" Maritime Affairs (Routledge), Summer, 2008; "Energy Security in China's Foreign Policy : A Maritime Perspective", Maritime Affairs, Winter, 2010; "Emerging Security Architecture in the Indian Ocean Region: Policy Options for India", Maritime Affairs, Summer 2011 and India-Japan Security Cooperation: A New Era of Partnership in Asia, Maritime Affairs, Summer, 2012; and "Cooperative Balancing: Emerging Security Order in Asia", International Studies, Vol. 49, Nos.1 & 2, 2012. He has also written many commentaries and articles to various newspapers and web-journals on Asian security.

Dr. Srikanth Kondapalli is Professor in Chinese Studies at Jawaharlal Nehru University. He was Chairman of the Centre for East Asian Studies, SIS, JNU twice from 2008 to 2010 and 2012 to 2014. He is educated in Chinese studies in India and China with a Ph.D. in Chinese Studies. He learnt

Chinese language at Beijing Language & Culture University and was a post-Doctoral Visiting Fellow at People's University, Beijing from 1996-98. He was a Visiting Professor at National Chengchi University, Taipei in 2004, a Visiting Fellow at China Institute of Contemporary International Relations, Beijing in May 2007, an Honorary Professor at Shandong University, Jinan in 2009, 2011 and 2013 and a Fellow at Salzburg Global Seminar in 2010. He wrote two books (*China's Military: The PLA in Transition* in 1999 & *China's Naval Power* in 2001), two monographs, co-edited three volumes (*Asian Security & China* in 2004; *China and its Neighbours* in 2010 & *China's Military and India* in 2012) and a number of articles in journals and edited volumes – all on China. He received the *K. Subramanyam Award* in 2010 for *Excellence in Research in Strategic and Security Studies.*

Dr. Srabani Roy Choudhury is an Associate Professor in Japanese Studies, in the Centre for East Asian Studies, School of International Studies at the Jawaharlal Nehru University in New Delhi. A recipient of Japan Foundation Fellowship in 1996-1997 affiliated to Tokyo University and a Ph.D. from Jawaharlal Nehru University, her research interest lies in the area of Japanese investment in India. Her recent publications are centered on Japan-India economic relations and Japanese Multinationals' experiences in India; their entry strategies and their expansion. She has also been a Visiting Scholar to the Keizai Koho Centre, through Japan's Ministry of Economics and Industry, in January 2012. In the summer of the same year, and given her expertise on the subject, Japan's Ministry of Finance assigned her to the Policy Research Institute, Tokyo outcome of which resulted in a paper titled "Understanding the Impact of the Comprehensive Economic Partnership Agreement and the Ensuing Prospects for Japanese Companies in India". In 2008, she was commissioned by ICRIER to study "Japanese Investment in India: A Firm Level Survey", in which eight companies were studied to identify the issues that confront them and also to throw light on how operating in India has improved over the two decades. She is often invited to discussion in the electronic media in India, and her articles frequently appear in the print media.

Dr. Makoto Kojima is Professor of Indian economic studies in the Faculty of International Studies at Takushoku University. He served as the Chairman of Study Group on India at the Ministry of Finance, Japan in 2004-05, and as a Government-designated Member of Japan-India Joint Study Group in 2005-06. He holds his Bachelor Degree, Master Degree and Ph.D. (Economics) from Keio University. Dr. Kojima is author of *Analysis of Modern Indian Economy* (Keiso Shobo, 1993), *The Indian Economy in a Changing Asia*

(PHP Institute, 1995), *The Indian Software Industry* (Toyo Keizai Shimposha, 2004), and *The Tata Group* (Toyo Keizai Shimposha, 2008). He contributed many articles, including "Industrialisation, Income Distribution and Labour Migration: the Case of India", in Sukhamoy Chakravarty (ed.) *The Balance between Industry and Agriculture in Economic Development*, vol.3 (London: Macmillan Press, 1989), and "Power Sector Reform in India and the Japanese Experience", in K.V. Kesavan (ed.) *Economic Liberalization in India: Japanese & Indian Perspectives* (New Delhi: Indian Council of Social Science Research).

Dr. Ram Chandra Dhakal has been an Executive Director of Centre for Economic Development (CEDA), Tribhuvan University since 2012. Prior to this appointment, he was Associate Professor of Economics at Central Department of Economics, Tribhuvan University. Dr. Dhakal has earned his Ph.D. Degree with specialization on Labour Economics from the Lucknow University in 2009. He obtained his M.A in Economics from Tribhuvan University in 1986 and then he joined Birendra Multiple Campus, Chitwan as a faculty of economics of post-graduate level in 1988 and served there for about twenty years. Over the last five years, he was involved in teaching economics in M.Phil and supervised Ph.D. scholars in Central Department of Economics. To his credit, he has also supervised more than two dozens of M.A. theses, evaluated half dozen of Ph.D. dissertations of national and foreign universities, authored a couple of text books and successfully conducted a number of research projects. Besides, he has over dozens of articles published in different peer review national and international journals. He is now the Chief Editor of the Journal of Development and Administrative Studies (JODAS) published by CEDA. Dr. Dhakal has attended many national and international seminars, workshops and conferences and has gained extensive contact and knowledge. He is also associated in various capacities with the different Ministries of Government of Nepal in its different activities.

Dr. Ram Kumar Phuyal obtained his M.A in Economics from Tribhuvan University (TU.) in 2000, and joined as a faculty of Economics in Patan Multiple Campus, TU. After teaching for five years in post-graduate level, he was awarded Scholarship to pursue his Ph.D. in Economics in Korea. He was at Chonnam National University (CNU), South Korea from 2006 to 2011 for his Ph.D. and he worked as a Post Doctoral Researcher at the Centre for Regional Development, CNU, for one year (2011 to 2012) and then on his return, was appointed Associate Professor at the Centre for Economic Development and Administration (CEDA), TU. Prior to this appointment, he was also involved as a guest faculty in domestic and foreign universities.

His academic areas of research interest are on Industrial Organization and International Trade, and worked intensively with game theoretical modeling, micro-simulation and micro-econometrics tools on his research. Dr. Phuyal has published his research outcomes in top ranking journals of Tribhuvan University He presented academic papers in more than a dozen of international conferences in different parts of the world. He also contributed number of news articles on economics, and public policy issues in international newspapers as a columnist.

Dr. M. Abul Kashem Mozumder completed BA (Hons.) and MA in Public Administration from Dhaka University. He completed another MA in Political Science from Waterloo University, Canada and Ph.D. in Political Science from Melbourne University, Australia. He had a stint as post-doctoral fellow in the Faculty of Law, Tokyo University. He started his career as lecturer in Political Science Department of Chittagong University in 1980 and later on, he joined in Public Administration Department of the same university. Thereafter, he joined as an Assistant Professor in the Government and Politics Department of Jahangirnagar University in 1992 and became Associate Professor and Professor in 1994 and 1998 respectively. Apart from discharging the responsibilities of Chairmanship (2000–2003) of the Department, he also chaired its Higher Studies Committee for several years. He led the establishment of a full-fledged Public Administration Department in Jahangirnagar University and became its founding Chairman (2006-2011). He has 87 publications in recognized journals from home and abroad. He edited and authored several books, and also supervised more than 20 completed Ph.D. and M.Phil researches. In addition, he submitted 13 reports to relevant authorities as requirements of consultancy work.

Mr. Abdullah-Al-Mamun is currently working as Assistant Professor in the Japan Study Centre (JSC) of the University of Dhaka, Bangladesh. Having completed MSS in Sociology from the University of Dhaka with excellent academic record, he joined as a lecturer in JSC in 2006. Mr. Mamun is a MBA and has completed Diploma in Japanese Studies from the University of Dhaka. He has produced a variety of research works including 2 books on Japanese Government and Politics and Japanese Society and Culture, seven journal articles in local and international journals. His research area includes transnational security, population and environment also.

Ms. Mayumi Murayama is Senior Research Fellow at the Institute of Developing Economies (IDE-JETRO), a governmental research institute under the Ministry of Economy, Trade and Industry in Japan. Murayama's interests cover labour and gender issues as well as regional relationship around India and Bangladesh. Her publications include *Gender and Development: The Japanese Experience in Comparative Perspective*, 2005 (Editor, Palgrave Macmillan), *Globalization, Employment and Mobility: South Asian Experience*, 2008 (Co-editor, Palgrave Macmillan). 'Borders, Migration and Sub-regional Cooperation in Eastern South Asia', *Economic and Political Weekly*, Vol. 41, No.14, 2006. 'Revisiting Labour and Gender Issues in Export Processing Zones: Cases of South Korea, Bangladesh and India', *Economic and Political Weekly*, Vol.44, No.22, 2009 (Co-author), 'Challenges for Inclusive Sustained Employment: An Attempt to Organise Female Embroidery Home workers in Delhi,' in Hirashima, Shigemochi, et al eds. *Inclusiveness in India: A Strategy for Growth and Equality*, 2011 (Palgrave MacMillan) and 'Problems of Youth Employment in India and Japan: A Call for a Joint Comparative Study,' in Horimoto, Takenori and Lalima Varma eds., *India-Japan Relations in Emerging Asia*, 2013 (Manohar).

Dr. Mondira Dutta, M.A., M.Phil., Ph.D., is currently the Chairperson of the Centre for Inner Asian Studies, School of International Studies, Jawaharlal Nehru University. With 34 years of experience her fields of specialization include Gender Studies, Violence against Women, Human Security with particular reference to India, Afghanistan and Central Asia. She was awarded the Lifetime Achievement Award by the United Nations Information Centre for India and Bhutan and the Govt of India in New Delhi on 7th March 2009. She has worked as a consultant with international organizations such as the UN Women, Human Rights Commission-Maldives, the British Council, The Ford Foundation, Human Rights Commission-Geneva, etc. Some of her important publications include an impact study on the 'Indian Initiatives for Afghan Women' completed by her in 2010 based on primary survey in Afghanistan and was sponsored by the Ministry of External Affairs, Government of India. Some of her books published by Pentagon Press include "Gender and Human Development in Central and South Asia" (2013) and "Capturing Women's Work" (2010) besides many articles. She has been a Senior Advisor to the Ministry of Women and Child Development, Government of India for developing the National Strategy on anti–trafficking measures, from Aug 2011 to Dec 2011. Her study on 'Mapping Vulnerability to Trafficking of Women and Children in India', sponsored by UN Women and the National Commission for Women was completed in 2011. She was a guest researcher at the Stockholm University, Sweden, in 2012.

Dr. Sushila Narsimhan, Professor of Japanese Studies, began her career in 1964 in Daulat Ram College, University of Delhi, and later moved to the Department of East Asian Studies where she taught until her retirement in October 2007. She continues teaching as Guest Faculty in the same department. She is recipient of the Japan Foundation Fellowship in 1987-1988 for doctoral dissertation, and in 2001 for post-doctoral research and, on both the occasions, was affiliated with the University of Tokyo, Japan. In 2002, she got UGC field trip grant to work in Stanford University, California, USA. Her specialization is Japan's Meiji period and 19th century Sino-Japanese relations. Her major publications include: *Nineteenth Century Japanese Perceptions of China: Influence of Fukuzawa Yukichi* (New Delhi: 1999) and several research papers. She has also co-edited five books, namely *India and East Asia: Learning from Each Other* (New Delhi: 2004), *Korea and India: A Forging Relationship* (New Delhi: 2005), *Korea in Search of a Global Role* (New Delhi: 2006), *India and Korea: Bridging the Gaps* (New Delhi: 2007), and *Growing Synergy between India and Korea* (New Delhi: 2014). Her academic interests also include the study of plants that changed the course of human history and world civilization.

Dr. Madhuchanda Ghosh has done her Ph.D. in the area study of India-Japan relations. She has done her doctoral research based at Jadavpur University and Waseda University, Tokyo, under the Tokyo Foundation's collaborative research programme. She was a SYLFF Fellow of Nippon Foundation at the doctoral level. She has learnt Japanese and conducted research for extended spells in Japan. She was a Visiting Fellow of Waseda University. She has published three books and a monograph and contributed many articles and research papers in refereed journals of national and international repute, including a publication in the journal of Asian Survey. She has been engaged in post doctoral research under the Japan Foundation fellowship on India's foreign policy with a focus on Japan. She has presented papers in conferences in India, Japan, China, South Korea, Cambodia and Germany, the most recent one being Salzburg Global conference held in Japan by Nippon Foundation in Tokyo, and Kyoto. Her areas of research interest include foreign policy studies, Asia Pacific security, area studies with a focus on East Asia, Southeast Asia and South Asia.

Ms. Janashruti Chandra, teaches Japanese Language at Centre for Japanese Studies, Jawaharlal Nehru University (JNU), New Delhi as an Assistant Professor since 2002. She completed M.A (Japanese) from JNU in 2000, and M.A in Japanese Language and Society from Osaka University of Foreign Studies, Japan in 2002. She is currently pursuing Ph.D. in Sociolinguistics from JNU. Her research interests lie in the fields of sociolinguistics, teaching methodology, Japanese culture studies and children's literature. She was engaged in drafting of school textbooks of Japanese language in collaboration with Japan Foundation. She has also prepared the course material for Distance Education Program of Haldwani University.

Dr. Nanda Gunawardhana works as the Director of the International Research Centre in the University of Peradeniya. Prior to that, he was a JSPS postdoctoral Fellow and research scientist in Saga University and Fukuoka Industry and Science Foundation, Japan. Dr. Gunawardhana received his bachelor's degree from the University of Peradeniya, Sri Lanka and doctoral degree from Baylor University, USA. He is passionate about creating cross-national, multi-disciplinary collaborative research among staff members of University of Peradeniya with intentional scholars. He has played an important role in establishing the Sri Lanka Japan Study Centre in the University of Peradeniya. His research interests are diverse and expand from basic science to the social sciences.

Ms. Shanthini Shanmugarajah completed her B.Sc (Hons) and M.Sc in Forensic Science with a specialization in Toxicology and Forensic Chemistry from Amity University in Noida, India. She worked in the forensic field briefly before being appointed as the Project Manager at the International Research Centre of the University of Peradeniya where she is currently employed. Her work consists of developing international relations and coordinating agreements and collaborative programs between the University of Peradeniya and other higher education institutes around the world. She has coordinated activities with Japanese students and scholars at the University of Peradeniya during the course of her work. Her current areas of interest are process management and architecture, especially in its application towards reforming the administrative processes in the Higher Education network of Sri Lanka; and in the development and coordination of International Relations and Collaborations in Higher Education Institutes. She is interested in public speaking, linguistics, reportage and creative writing, and cross cultural communication.

1

Japan's Approach to Regionalism with Reference to SAARC

Lalima Varma

Japan's Approach to Regional Groupings: Cold War Era

For almost three decades after Japan regained its sovereignty in 1952 it was more inclined towards maintaining a low profile in international affairs. Japan's position in the world and in the East and Southeast Asian region was rather precarious. Relations with its neighbors, mainly People's Republic of China (China) and Republic of Korea (ROK) and the Southeast Asian countries was far from cordial due to the bitter history which it shared with them. Japan's main focus in the post World War II years was to rebuild its economy which was shattered during the war period. A stable, peaceful and friendly neighborhood was essential for beneficial economic activity. Japan was keen to convince its neighbors that it was aware of its past behavior and would not repeat it. Time and again Japan expressed its determination, 'not to follow the road to becoming a big military power' even though it was economically capable of doing so.[1] Consequently, Japan refrained from taking any initiative which would suggest that it was again reviving its pre war ambition of playing a leadership role in the region. During the pre war period Japan had tried to promote the idea of a 'Greater East Asia Co Prosperity Sphere' by assuming a position of leadership. Japan's prewar expansionist and aggressive foreign policy has not been completely forgotten by the neighboring countries till date. Thus, Japan refrained from supporting or suggesting the formation of any regional organization. Any such idea emanating from Japan would have been received with suspicion by its neighboring countries in Asia.

Another important factor which prevented Japan from being interested in regional organizations was that it was closely aligned with United States of America. During the Cold War era with most countries belonging to one of the two blocs led by the two super powers i.e. one by erstwhile Soviet Union and the other by US, it was difficult for regional powers to form regional groupings. There were very few regional organizations during the Cold War era. Most notable are the European Community (EU) formed in 1957 and the Association of Southeast Asian Nations (ASEAN) in 1967. Being part of either of the two blocs meant adhering to certain guidelines set by the super powers. With the conclusion of the 'Treaty of Mutual Cooperation and Security between Japan and United States' in 1951 Japan was dependent on the US for its security. Economically too, the US was Japan's most important partner. Thus, Japan's foreign policy during the Cold War era in particular tended to follow the US guidelines. Japan to a great extent tried to avoid any foreign policy decisions which would upset its equation with the US or suggest that it was trying to tread a path in foreign affairs which was not in tune with that of the US.

Another important consideration as mentioned earlier was to protect and promote its economic interests. Japan has been and is acutely aware of the fact that it lacks raw materials and needs markets for its manufactured goods. This vulnerability "seems to have been deeply embedded in the national pysche".[2] Encouraging formation of regional groupings would mean promoting protectionism and conflict. Yet Japan did not want to be excluded from other regions which could have a negative impact on its economy.

Shift in Japan's Approach towards Regionalism: Early Indications

During the Cold War era although Japan was hesitant to belong to a regional group or promote the idea of a formation of a regional organization, several developments even as early as in the 1970s indicated that Japan had begun to realize the advantages of being a member of regional organizations. Irritants in its relations with the US which had begun to surface since the close of the 1960s and the oil crisis of 1972-73 created an environment which called for review of its foreign policy objectives. Necessity of strengthening ties with neighboring countries became more crucial for Japan. In 1977, summit talks were held between Japan and ASEAN. Soon after that the then Prime Minister of Japan, Fukuda Takeo visited six Southeast Asian countries. In his speech at Manila, Philippines, in August 1977 he spelled out three principles on which Japan's basic attitude towards Southeast Asia would be based: 1. Japan is committed to peace, and rejects the role of a military power; 2. Japan will do its best to consolidate the relationship of mutual confidence and trust based on "heart-to-heart" understanding with nations of Southeast Asia; 3. Japan will cooperate positively with ASEAN.[3]

At home also opinions on the need for Japan being part of regional organizations were being expressed. Politicians, bureaucrats and the academia were gradually realizing the benefits of being part of a regional organization. Well known economists like Okita Saburo and Kojima Kiyoshi gave positive support to Japan belonging to a regional group. Kojima was a professor at Hitotsubashi University. Okita Saburo held many important positions; one of them was as international Chairman of the Pacific Economic Cooperation Council, from 1986-88. He also served as a foreign minister (1979-80) in Prime Minister Ohira Masayoshi's Cabinet (1978-80). In 1979 Ohira and Australian Prime Minister Malcolm Fraser agreed to form a Non-Governmental Pacific Basin Cooperation Council.

By the late 1980s Japan was one of the leading aid giving country and major investor in most of the East and Southeast Asian countries. It was clear that Japan's deep involvement in the region called for a forum where the countries of the region could meet at regular intervals to discuss issues and interact with each other. Despite this Japan was still hesitant to take any bold step which may suggest that its ambitions of assuming a leadership role in the region were reviving. In 1990, Malaysian Prime Minister Mahathir Mohammad floated the idea of an East Asian grouping which later was renamed East Asia Economic Caucus (EAEC), and suggested that Japan play a lead role but Japan did not respond to this suggestion enthusiastically. Even though by now Japan had emerged as the second largest economy it was still not confident to be a part of an organization which did not include the US. The idea of EAEC did not include US, Canada, Australia and New Zealand. Japan was more comfortable with the broader based organizations such as Asia-Pacific Economic Council (APEC) which was established in 1989. The twenty one members of APEC are the Pacific Rim economies. APEC represents more than half of the global economic output. The main objective of APEC is to promote Free trade and economic cooperation throughout the Asia-Pacific region.

Japan's Changed Perception on Regional Groupings: The 1990s

With the end of the Cold War the obligation on the part of a particular country to abide by the guidelines of the bloc to which they belonged in pursuing its foreign policy almost disappeared. The relevance and advantages of being a part of one of the blocs in the East–West rivalry diminished. Japan, like most countries, felt the need to review its foreign policy goals.

Japan's relations with its close ally the US were undergoing some important changes. Japan was not very confident as to how much it could rely on the US for its security.[4] It was important that it adopt policies which served its interests best and not rely on any one country for protecting its national interests. A network of strong bilateral relations with various countries and membership to multilateral organizations was the best option in the changed international and regional environment. An important development was that the power of the two superpowers had declined considerably.

The influence of the two superpowers was to some extent also reduced due to the rise of other powers. Western European countries were gaining in economic strength. Japan itself was an economic power. Besides Newly Industrialized Countries (NICs) such as Republic of Korea, Hong Kong, Singapore and Republic of China were also posing challenges to the countries of the region as well as to the world. The rise of these powers consequently reduced US dominance in various international organizations and forums. Basically the situation at the international and regional level was fluid. Most countries were concerned about their status and role in the region and the world.

Growing Support for Regional Organizations: Domestic Factors

There were several economic and political developments at the domestic level also which led to the realization that regional organizations were necessary. Most important was that Japan's economic growth since the 'bubble burst' in 1991 had started to decline. On the other hand, during the 1990s many of the Southeast Asian countries including China and India's economy had started to grow at a fast pace. The urgency of having a regional level organization became most apparent after the financial crisis of 1997. Decline in Japan's economic growth affected Japan's position in the region as well. Japanese business community were hesitant to increase foreign investments since many banks and trading companies either closed down their branches or reduced their presence abroad. At home there was criticism regarding providing Official Development Assistance (ODA) to developing countries when there was need to invest at home in important sectors such as education, social security etc.

By the beginning of the 1990s there seemed to be a convergence of views among the political parties on the need to support and be part of multilateral organizations. The reasons for each political party to support or to be part of regional groups were different but the main point is that there was general agreement that Japan needs to be a member of larger organizations. The Left parties for example considered it to be a means to distant itself from the US on whom Japan depended for its security. Other democratic parties' position was that belonging to a regional group provided an opportunity to be part of a collective security system and play an effective role in the region. Japan, due to constitutional constraints, cannot possess and use hard power to settle issues outside of its own territory. Diplomacy and use of 'soft' power were the tools by which Japan could sustain and maintain its position in the region and at the global level.

One of the important realizations on the part of Japan was that its stature in the region as a leader for economic growth was affected after the 'bubble burst' in 1991. Japan realized that it was important to be active as one of the members of the region. Declining economic growth had a negative impact on Japan's bargaining position. Japan had to find alternatives to play a more active role in the region by showing more political initiative.

Establishment of a number of regional organizations the world over also became a cause of concern for Japan. Major developed countries formed regional organizations such as North American Free Trade Association (NAFTA), a more well structured European Union in 1993, and Mercosur in South America were few of them. With the existence of so many regional organizations Japan was worried that its economic activity in these regions would be restricted. Close ties with countries of the region assured a secure environment to promote economic and political interests.

Japan actively participated in the ASEAN Post Ministerial Conference in 1991 and suggested the idea of a regional security forum. However, it was only in 1994 that the first formal ASEAN Regional Forum (ARF) was held in Brunei. Japan joined as a dialogue partner. The turning point in Japan's effort to be part of a multilateral dialogue in the region was provided by the financial crisis of 1997-98 which hit a number of Southeast Asian countries. Japan along with China and ROK became a part of ASEAN+3. Acceptance of Japan as part of ASEAN+3 also indicated that the countries of the region acknowledged that Japan was a major economic power in the region and that its participation in resolving the economic issues confronting the region was necessary. The crisis brought forth the fact that the East and Southeast Asian countries were economically closely integrated and culturally there was more similarity and familiarity. It was the impact of the financial crisis which led to the Chiang Mai Initiative (CMI) in 2000. The CMI is a multilateral currency swap arrangement to which the ASEAN, Japan, China and ROC agreed upon. The idea was to prevent the repetition of another Asian financial crisis of 1997-98. APEC it was clear was too huge and could not play a decisive role in a situation such as the 1997 financial crisis.

After the 1997 financial crisis the idea of East Asian Community gained momentum. The East Asia Summit (EAS) was first held in December 2005. It's members include; ten ASEAN countries, New Zealand, Australia, Japan, South Korea, India and China. Japan took a keen interest in the formation and proceedings of East Asian Summit. Informal consultations and ministerial meetings are held regularly. The discussions are not only limited to economic matters but other important issues are also discussed. The eighth EAS Summit was held in October 2013 in Brunei

However, one important point to be noted is that Japan's main effort till the beginning of the twenty first century was mainly directed towards being involved in organizations which included East and Southeast Asian Regions. In 2009 in a speech in Singapore, the then Prime Minister of Japan Hatoyama Yukio stated that the most important key to promote an East Asian Community initiative is 'person –to person contact' which is the only way to truly understand each other.[5] He talked of how Japan would make the East Asia Community concept the key pillar of its policy.

Twenty First Century: Moving Focus Towards South Asia

Japan's enhanced interest in actively participating and promoting regional forums was also propelled by the rapidly changing nature of its relations with China. The year 2005 can be regarded as a watershed in Japan's urgent need to develop close relations with South Asia countries. Wide spread anti-Japan movement in China in 2005 upset the Japanese immensely. Japan was convinced that maintaining a low profile will not serve its national interests. This fact has increasingly become more apparent than ever especially since the confrontation between the Chinese fishing boats and a Japanese coast guard vessel near the waters of Senkaku/Diaoyu islands in the East China Sea in September 2010. Relations have been on the downslide since then.[6] The situation worsened when the Japanese government purchased the disputed islands in 2012. Demonstrations were held in China and several Japanese owned shopping malls and factories were vandalized. Visits by Japanese leaders to Yasukuni Shrine which enshrines the Japanese war dead, including the fourteen World War II military leaders who were pronounced guilty for war atrocities has further vitiated the relations between the two countries.

Japan has to balance China's influence in Southeast Asia and also increasingly in South Asia. Outright confrontation with China is not possible for Japan not only because China is an important economic partner but also because Japan is not in a position to manage a variety of challenges posed by China's growing stature in the region both politically and militarily. The total trade between the two countries is more than $300 billion. However, after the relations between the two countries began to deteriorate since 2010, Japan is keen to diversify its economic interests to other countries which is popularly known as its 'Plus One' strategy. Japan, henceforth, aims to develop its strategic and economic interests with the Southeast and South Asian countries. It is in keeping with this strategy that Shinzo Abe visited several Southeast Asian countries soon after he became Prime Minister in December 2012. Here both Japan and India's economic and strategic interests seem to be similar. India has defense agreements with Indonesia, Malaysia, Mongolia, Vietnam, South Korea and Thailand. India, since the beginning of the twenty first century has given a definite boost to its 'Look East' policy.

An important development which has become a cause of concern for Japan is that during the 1970s and 1980s when its economy was booming there was not much of a threat from other countries for markets or raw materials, However, with the economies of several countries in the Asian region rising, including that of China and India since the 1990s, the competition for markets and energy resources has become more severe. Thus, the vested interest of all the countries in the region in the security of the sea lanes passing through the India Ocean, Southeast Asia, Malacca straits, South China sea through which pass the tankers and other cargo ships is also growing. It is important for each country to see that no one country becomes very dominant in the region. It is also in the interest of all the countries that there should be forums which should discuss the problems confronting the region.

Challenges to the security need not emanate from any one country alone. There are some problems which have to be resolved collectively like the problem of increasing number of cases of piracy in the seas of the region. According to Chamber of Commerce's International Maritime Bureau (London) there were 199 pirate attacks on vessels in the subcontinent's waters between 2006 and 2012. The Bureau's 2012 report stated that seas and oceans around Africa top the chart with 1,228 cases; while the Indian waters came third after the Southeast Asian waters.[7] Strategically, the importance of South Asia has increased greatly.

Japan's Interest in SAARC

One important fact which has come forth in this era of globalization is that the countries of the world have become more interdependent than ever before. Consequently, most countries even if they are not geographically located in the region would not like to be totally disassociated from any regional organization of a particular region. South Asian Association for Regional Cooperation (SAARC) is one such organization with which several countries seek to be associated. SAARC was founded in December 1985. At present it has eight members. However, there are nine countries which enjoy Observers status in SAARC. Japan and China were granted Observer status in 2005. The others are US, EU, ROK, Iran, Mauritius, Myanmar and Australia. One of the topics of discussions at SAARC meetings is that there are more

Observers than members. There are other countries as well which are keen to be Observers of SAARC like Turkey. In the 2008 meeting at Colombo in Sri Lanka, SAARC countries had decided on a moratorium on the admission of Observers. This enthusiasm of many countries wanting to be associated with SAARC is a commentary on the growing importance of the region. The 17th SAARC meeting in Maldives in 2011 reviewed the matters relating to its engagement with Observers countries including the question of dialogue partnership. Decision regarding the role of the Observer became necessary since China with the support of Pakistan expressed keenness to have a more interactive partnership with SAARC.[8] Initially Observers did not have much say in the proceedings. However, even though their role has not expanded much, now Observers are given an opportunity to express their opinion. Since the New Delhi meeting in 2007 Observers are able to attend the opening and closing ceremonies

Japan's interest in SAARC dates back to 1993 when Japan supported the activities of the organization through the Japan-SAARC Fund. However, since South Asia did not figure as topmost in Japan's foreign policy priority at that point of time, its involvement in the region was also limited. Japan's policy towards this region began to change effectively since the turn of the twenty first century. South Asia for several economic, political and strategic reasons has acquired immense importance for Japan.

The importance of the region was clearly spelled out by Japan's former Foreign Minister Aso Taro in his address to the 14th SAARC summit held in India in 2007. He stated in his address that "Japan was advancing a new initiative to create an arc of freedom and prosperity. The outer rim of the Eurasian continent has seen historic transitions in many countries. A new frontier of arc has emerged. It is a growth region, more stable than ever committed to universal values. South Asia indeed makes a central pillar of the arc".[9]

In his address he also pointed out the three areas in which Japan would like to contribute to the region. 1. Democracy and stability in the region; 2. Improve regional connectivity; and 3. Promote person to person exchanges.[10]

Japan-SAARC: Exploring Areas of Cooperation

Japan, through SAARC, is trying to explore areas of cooperation with the South Asian region. Efforts are being made to improve bilateral relations with each of the South Asian countries but participation in SAARC would provide an opportunity to address all the countries on a common platform and also acquaint itself with the problems confronting the region. It is crucial for Japan to understand the problems of the South Asian countries if it has to play an important role in the region. Its task of building close ties with the South Asian countries is somewhat made easier considering that it shares a cordial past with all the countries of SAARC and they do not feel mutually threatened.

One of the priority areas of Japanese cooperation with SAARC is to improve the region's connectivity, address such challenges as infrastructure development and harmonization of systems. The exact projects and areas in which Japan should invest or extend support could be possible by observing or participating in the meetings and seminars organized by SAARC Chambers of Commerce and Industry (SAARC CCI). The South Asian countries are making an effort to develop and promote economic ties with each other. The SAARC CCI is active in providing opportunities to the business community of the SAARC countries to meet and have dialogue. SAARC CCI was established in 1985. However, core economic issues were not included in its agenda. It was only in December 1992 that SAARC CCI was officially recognized as the apex body of all the SAARC nations' Federation of Chambers of Commerce and Industry. The secretariat of SAARC CCI is located in Islamabad. SAARC CCI regularly organizes events on varied themes such as climate, environment, youth meetings on energy; trade etc. In January 2014 the fifth SAARC Business Leaders Conclave was held in New Delhi, India. The objectives spelled out are basically to encourage and safeguard the economic interests of the countries of the region; exchange commercial, technical, industrial management and scientific education and know how among member countries.[11]

The increasing focus of SAARC countries in enhancing their economic capability provides an opportunity to the Observer countries like Japan to participate in the endeavor of the countries of this region to improve the environment for economic development individually as well as collectively. China is active in this area. In June 2011 the sixth China-South Asia Business Forum was held in Kunming through SAARC CCI and China Council for Promotion of International Trade (CCPIT). Financial contributions to SAARC Development Fund, headquartered in Bhutan was approved in 2008. China has contributed generously to this fund. Japan has also encouraged such meetings. One SAARC business delegation visited Japan through the initiation of Japan. However, Japan needs to have many more such meetings if it has to understand the problems and needs of region and the areas where it can cooperate to strengthen the economic base of these countries.

ODA is one of the tools by which Japan hopes to achieve its objectives in South Asia. India is the largest recipient of Japanese ODA since 2004-5. India was the first country to receive ODA from Japan in 1958. Pakistan received technical assistance in accordance with the Colombo Plan. It was in

1961 that Pakistan received ODA from Japan for the first time. Japan considers Pakistan's role as crucial as a front line state in the fight against terrorism. UK and Asia Development Bank (ADB) are the second and third largest partners. In the South Asian region close relationship between China and Pakistan is an important fact which Japan needs to take into consideration and balance out to make the region stable for economic activity. China is rapidly becoming the largest trading partner of the SAARC countries. Japan is a major contributor to Asia Development Bank. ADB extends support to SAARC. Consequently Japan is also indirectly in a position to support developmental projects in South Asia.

Though Japan is strengthening ties with all the South Asian countries, undoubtedly relations with India are very important bilaterally and even as a member of SAARC. Compared to other regional organizations like European Union or ASEAN, in none of these groups does one country dominate as India does in SAARC. India is the largest country in terms of land mass, population and economy. Japan and India relations have strengthened significantly since 2000. Yoshiro Mori's historic visit in March 2000 was a turning point in the relations between India and Japan. The two countries concluded a "Global Partnership for the Twenty First Century". Japan's close ties with India can facilitate its further involvement in SAARC.

Japan-SAARC: Mutually Beneficial Relations

Japan's importance and role in the world and the region has been determined largely due to its economic power. Since 1991 the pace of its economic growth has been slow. The situation has only worsened after the March 2011 tsunami and earthquake and nuclear leakages. So far Japan was dependent on the outside world for raw material and markets but now Japan aims to benefit from its relationship with other countries including the South Asian countries in other areas as well. Given the present trend of low birth rate and aging population, challenges confronting Japan are numerous. Shortage of skilled labour, problems confronting institutions of higher learning, and health care are few of them. Now is the opportune time for Japan to expand its area of interest in the South Asian region. There seems be many areas in which Japan and South Asian countries can cooperate and benefit mutually.

One area in which both Japan and South Asian countries stand to benefit from each other is in education. In Japan due to low birth rate there is a fall in admissions to most universities. Fall in admissions leads to financial problems in the universities which in turn affects several aspects of the society. Japan has more than 600 universities. The Japanese government has adopted several policies to deal with the problems affecting the universities. One of the ways by which the problem of lack of enrollment to universities can be at least partially resolved is by attracting foreign students. In Japan at present, the largest numbers of foreign students studying are mainly from China and South Korea. The number of students from other countries is very small. The number of Indian students studying in Japan is only about 500.[12] Contrary to Japan's aging population, the youth form majority of the population in the South Asian countries, especially in India.

There are several reasons for students from South Asian countries not opting to study in Japan. One of the important reasons is language. Studying Japanese language is difficult and time consuming. It is hence, not surprising that most students from these countries prefer to study in countries where English is the medium of instruction like the US, United Kingdom and Australia. India's student community has been one of the largest in the US since the end of World War II. There are about 100,000 Indian students in US. In addition to other advantages the fact that a student does not have to invest time in learning the language is definitely an important reason.

The Japanese government has taken some initiatives to make the academic environment in Japan attractive enough for foreign students to opt to study in Japanese institutions of higher learning. Ministry of Education, Culture, Sports, Science and Technology (MEXT) has started a 'Global 30' Project. According to this project 30 universities have been identified to offer courses in English.[13] Prime Minister Abe Shinzo has established the Education Rebuilding Implementation Council with the objective of bringing out reforms in the universities and the development of global human resources. Another advantage of these reforms will be that Japanese students will have more opportunity to interact with foreigners. Japanese students are often shy to interact with foreign students partly due to their of lack knowledge of the English language. In a globalized world a populace conversant in an international language like English is an asset for any country.

Youth in most countries are facing numerous problems. In Japan too there are several problems confronting the young which the Japanese government has to address. One such problem is a trend known as 'hikikomori' or 'withdrawal'. Hikikomori refers to people who distance themselves from the society and tend to confine themselves in a room or in their houses for prolonged period of time. This development has become a cause of concern for the Japanese. According to the Cabinet office survey nearly 700,000 Japanese all over the country were shut-ins.[14] The cause for this are several including bullying at school; problems at the work place and interpersonal relations in addition to other reasons. One of the attempts made to deal with this problem is to get such people together for interactive sessions. These gatherings are called 'Hikikomori University'. Another manner by which this problem could be overcome is by providing opportunities to young Japanese students to interact and mingle with foreign students.

Contributions made by foreign students to the host country are varied. Valuable contributions made by the large number of Indian students who continued to stay in the US after completing their studies in various fields such as medicine, science, engineering and other fields is well known. In its 2008 study released by Harvard Business School, immigrants comprised nearly half of all scientists and engineers in the US who have a doctorate and accounted for 67 per cent of the increase in the US science and engineering work force between 1995-2006.[15] Not only the US but also China is benefitting from the best minds around the world. As a editorial in Japan Times stated "Chinese government seems acutely aware of the commitment that it takes to lure the best minds from halfway around the world."[16] Japan can also utilize talent of foreign students in face of reduced number of Japanese youth.

As mentioned earlier in this paper, in Japan due to the fall in admission to institutions of higher learning, universities are confronted with financial problems. Attracting foreign students can to some extent resolve this problem as well. According to the US Department of Commerce international students contributed more than $24 billion to the US economy.[17] The 2013, the Open Door Report on International Educational Exchange stated that about 72 per cent of international students received majority of their funds from sources outside of the US including personal and family resources as well as from the home country or universities.[18] Similarly Japan can also benefit by making it more attractive for foreign students to join Japanese universities. It is often claimed that higher institutions of learning in many other countries such as the US and UK also survive because of the foreign students from India, China and other countries.

Since Japan's position in the world has primarily been due to its economic status it is imperative that it taps the human resources from other countries including South Asia. This will not only give an opportunity to attract skilled and capable workers but it will also help in improving people-to-people relations between Japan and the South Asian countries. Japanese government is also legislating to make it easier for firms to hire foreign workers for highly skilled positions and as trainees to offset a declining workforce and accelerate economic growth.[19]

Japan has to work at various levels to consolidate relations with the South Asian countries. It must promote mobility among the youth and support the economic growth of these countries. In March 2013, Japan contributed Yen

623,500,000,00 to the SAARC Secretariat for the Japan–East Asia Network of Exchange for Students and Youth (JENEYS) program.[20]

The SAARC Fund has two components: first is used to finance projects in order to encourage cooperation in activities between member states of SAARC. (The SAARC Secretariat determines how this is used). The second component of the fund is used to promote intellectual exchanges between Japan and SAARC member countries. (This is decided by the Japanese government). This is very useful because it helps in understanding controversial issues at various levels and to understand different aspects of the same problem. It also helps to bring together non state actors and contributes to creating a friendly environment in the region. Japan is aware that improvement in bilateral relations among the South Asian countries is necessary for peace and stability in the region. It also realizes that the Japanese need to be more familiar with the diversity of the region and the numerous problems confronting the region if it has to play an important role in the South Asian region.

END NOTES

1. Ministry of Foreign Affairs, Public Information Bureau, Japan, "Review of Foreign Relations: April 1971-March 1972, July 1972, p.103.
2. Kawashima Yutaka, Japanese Foreign policy at the Crossroads: Challenges and Options for the Twenty First Century", Printed: R.R. Donnelley, Harrisonburg, Virginiam, 2003, p.18.
3. Ministry of Foreign Affairs, Diplomatic Bluebook for 1977, Published: Foreign Press Center, Japan, p.30.
4. Lalima Varma, "Japan-United States Security Arrangements and Northeast Asia: Its Relevance in the Post-Cold War Period", China Report, (Sage Pub., New Delhi) vol.15, no, 1, 1999, pp.84-85.
5. Address by H.E. Yukio Hatoyama Prime Minister of Japan, "Japan's New Commitment to Asia-Toward the Realization of an East Asian Community", 15 November 2009, Singapore.www.kantei.go.jp/foreign/hatoyama/statement/200911/15 singapore_e.html. Accessed on 26 February 2014.
6. Lalima Varma, "Enhancing Strategic Ties between Japan and India: Japan-China Relations as a Factor," in Takenori Horimoto/and Lalima Varma (Eds), India-Japan Relations in Emerging Asia, Manohar Publishers and Distributors, Delhi, 2013, pp.44-46.
7. V. Narayan, 'Piracy: India Waters among worst – hit" Times of India, 23 December 2013).
8. "SAARC to review role of Observers, dialogue partners option", http://www.India-forums.com/news/Maldives/370694-saarc-to-review. Accessed on 27 February 2014.
9. *The Economic Times*, on-line, PTI, 3 April, 2007, Accessed on 17 October 2013.
10. Ministry of Foreign Affairs of Japan, 'The South Asian Association for Regional Cooperation (SAARC) and Japan', June 2009, http://www.mofa.go.jp/regional/asia-paci/saarc/overview.html. Accessed on 28 October, 2013.
11. South Asian Association for Regional Cooperation/Areas of Cooperation, http;//saarc-sec.org/areaof cooperation/detail.php?activity_id==39. Accessed on 5 February 2014.
12. Lalima Varma, "Japan's Policy towards South Asia: Shifting Paradigms", in Uno Takao (Edt), Changing Perceptions of Japan in South Asia in the New Asian Era: The State of Japanese Studies in India and Other Countries, International Research Center for Japanese Studies, Kyoto, Japan, 2009, p.238.

13. Hakubun Shimomura (Minister of Education) Making Japanese higher education more international", *Japan Times*, 2 September 2013.
14. *Japan Times*, 'Shut-ins use a 'university' to get out", 13 December 2013.
15. Immigration Policy Center: American Immigration Council, on-line, 30 March 2011, "The US Economy Still Needs Highly Skilled Foreign Workers"//www.immigrationpolicy. Org/ just-facts, Accessed on 21 January 2014.
16. *Japan Times*, "Higher =education stimulus would be sure bet for Japan, 13 December 2013.
17. *Times of India*, on-line, 11 November 2013, Chidanand Rajghatta, "Indian Students Count in US Drops Below 100,000", Accessed on 21 January 2014.
18. Ibid.
19. *Japan Today*, 21 January 2014, "Japan to Open Door Further to Skilled Foreign Workers"www.japantoday.com/category/politics, Accessed on 21 January 2014).
20. SAARC Secretariat on-line, March 2013, www.saarc-sec.org/2013/news/.. Accessed on 5 January 2014.

REFERENCES

Beauchamp, Edward, "East Asia: History, Politics, Sociology, Culture" (Routledge, New York, 2002).

Green, Michael Jonathan, "Japan's Reluctant Realism: Foreign Policy Challenges in an Era of Uncertain Future", Palgrave Macmillan, 2003, New York, USA.

Kato, Ryozo, "The Shifting Landscape of Japan-US Ties', *Japan Echo*, Vol. 35, No. 6, December 2008.

Kawashima, Yutaka, "Japanese Foreign Policy at the Crossroads: Challenges and Options for the Twenty First Century", (Published by R.R. Donnelly, Harrisonburg, Virginia, 2003.)

Rahman, Ataur (Eds), "Japan-SAARC Cooperation" (Japan Study Center, University of Dhaka, Bangladesh, 2006.)

Shirashim Takashi, " 'Crafting Japan's Asia policy in a Multipolar World", *Japan Echo*, Vol. 35, No, 4, August 2008.

Sing, Lim Hua, "Japan and China: In East Asian Integration", Institute of Southeast Asian Studies, Singapore, 2008.

Takenori, Horimoto and Lalima Varma (Eds), "India-Japan Relations in Emerging Asia' (Manohar Publishers and Distributors, Delhi, 2013.)

Varma, Lalima, "Japan's Policy towards South Asia: Shifting Paradigms", in Uno, Takao, (eds.), Changing Perceptions of Japan in South Asia in the New Asian Era: The State of Japanese Studies in India and other SAARC Countries", International Center for Japanese Studies, Kyoto, Japan, 2009.

Yasutomo, Dennis, T., The New Multilateralism in Japan's Foreign Policy (Macmillan, London, 1995)

2

Japan-SAARC Relations: Tokyo's Initiatives for Regional Peace, Prosperity and Stability

Shamshad A. Khan

Introduction

The stability and development in South Asia directly affects the peace and stability of the international society.[1] Japan is dependent on the outside world to sustain its economic growth and therefore it strives for a stable international political and economic order. Keeping this in mind, Japan,—an Observer member of SAARC, has been engaging itself in the political, security, economic and development process of the region. It is a fact that Japan has played an important role in economic development of Southeast Asian nations through its development assistance and ODA loans and thus helped them achieving peace, stability and prosperity.[2] A close look of Japan's aid to SAARC countries, especially after the 1990s, suggests that Japan has a similar agenda for the South Asian region.

Constitutional limitations prevent Japan from playing a full-fledged security role for regional peace; so it has adopted means other than hard power to promote peace and stability. It has taken a number of measures for 'peace building' in Afghanistan and Sri Lanka and has assisted Bangladesh, Maldives, Nepal and Pakistan for consolidating democracy. But since most of the aid for democratic assistance has been channelized through the governments of recipient countries, critics have pointed out that Japan had placed low emphasis on civil society assistance.[3]

When it comes to security concerns, securing Sea Lines of Communications (SLOCs) from piracy and other non-state actors remains one of the priority areas of Japan. Keeping this in mind, Japan has enhanced its security cooperation with India, Sri Lanka and other littoral states of the

SAARC. To increase its profile as 'security provider', it has sent its Air Self Defense Forces to Pakistan in the aftermath of heavy floods as well as quakes to participate in rescue missions. Therefore, it can be said that Japan has used both hard power and soft powers for the security and stability of the SAARC countries. Against this context, the paper examines Japan's initiatives for regional peace and security.

Japanese Aid Towards Asia: Assessing the Strategic Objectives

In the post war period, Japan had limited options to contribute to the international community's efforts towards peace and stability as it was stripped off of its military power. It chose non-military contribution; aid and economic cooperation to achieve peace and stability in its immediate neighbourhood including the South East Asian region. It granted big loans as part of its Official Development Assistance (ODA) and undertook various infrastructure works in South East Asian countries which remarkably changed the landscape of the recipient countries. Japan did not acknowledge strategic motives of its aid policy. Critics, however, construed that Japanese aid disbursement was motivated to promote its exports in the recipient countries and its primary aim was to assist its own industries.

Criticism of Japanese aid policy yet again came to the fore, especially from its ally the US, when Soviets invaded Afghanistan and communism gained ground in Vietnam and Cambodia. Japan's western allies argued that Japanese aid has failed to achieve peace and stability in the world. This led Japan to revisit its aid policy and make it goal oriented. To assuage concerns of its western allies, Japan announced aid to countries considered important for western interest. Prime Minister Masayoshi Ohira announced aid for Pakistan, Thailand and Turkey. Japan tried to create employment opportunities and alleviate poverty from these countries. By doing so, Tokyo tried to check the spread of communism from Afghanistan to Pakistan and from Vietnam to Thailand and create an atmosphere conducive for free and open economies, a system amenable to its western allies. Dennis Yasutomo, interprets this policy as "burden sharing through non-military means." He opines:

> "The Japanese held to their pledge to remain a non-military power and proposed a Japanese definition of burden sharing: Tokyo would support the military role of the US through non-military contribution, whether increased financial support for American troops on Japanese soil or increased aid to strategic nations and regions."[4]

By adopting a targeted aid policy towards countries and regions prone to conflicts, Japan tried to refute the charges that its policy of pacifism is a calculated strategy of "disengagement from the world" and that Japan's aid "offers no concrete program for international contribution."[5] Because of Japan's consistent efforts to utilise aid as a strategic tool of its Foreign Policy, Dennis terms Japan as an aid great power. He states:

> "An aid great power is not a military power; non-military statecraft substitutes for military diplomacy. Aid thus inherits the pacifist sprit of the post war era, which has moulded aid into a concrete, activist, global foreign policy tool for a *heiwa kokka*, a peace loving Japan."[6]

Japanese Aid: Shifting Focus from South East Asia to South Asia

Japan turned its attention towards South Asia during Toshiki Kaifu's regime. During his sojourn of South Asian countries, Kaifu stated that "peace and stability in Asia is a matter of great concern for Japan... we must be engaged with multifaceted efforts that suits the region."[7] His announcement was in sync with his policy of making Japan a 'bridge' between the East and the West. His predecessors on the contrary, had tried to project Japan as an international country and a member of the West. In a clear departure from the policy of his predecessors, he announced a policy for Japan's re-association with Asia and stated that he would like to "pronounce Japan's intent to continue vigorous support for the economic redevelopment and stability of South Asia by engaging in dialogue and cooperation."[8] He announced a South Asia initiative which was based on three pillars; (a) promotion of political and economic dialogue, (b) expansion of ODA, and (c) increased cultural exchange with South Asian countries. Most importantly, during his visit to India, he announced Japan's intention to extend cooperation to the SAARC which around that time was still in the stage of infancy. During his address to the Indian Parliament, he said that "should SAARC as an organisation desire to receive cooperation from outside region.... Japan will be prepared to extend appropriate support."[9] India was most forthright in welcoming Japan's support to the region. In an apparent reference to Japan's desire to contribute to regional peace and stability, Prime Minister Narsimha Rao during his visit to Japan stated:

> "We (India and Japan) share a common interest in Asian peace and security which will enable India and other countries to concentrate on economic development. India has welcomed Japan's constructive engagement in the world because we see this buttressing India's own peace, stability and development."[10]

Because of Japan's consistent engagement with the South Asian region, SAARC invited Japan to join the regional block as an Observer in 2007 and with this, Japan's desire to play a role for the peace and prosperity of the regional countries, enunciated by Prime Minister Kaifu, was fulfilled. From an outside player of SAARC, Japan became an insider to a certain extent.

It has channelized its aid and assistance towards SAARC more actively ever since it has joined the regional block as an Observer. Japan's aid agencies, however, have been reluctant to go into areas having 'law and order' problems. For example, Japan's International Cooperation Agency (JICA) has no footprint in the Indian states of Jammu and Kashmir, Chhattisgarh, Jharkhand[11] etc. which are relatively underdeveloped and hit by militancy. Japan gave its nod to support construction of a new branch of Indian Institute of Technology in Bihar, one of the least developed states of India but later it withdrew support citing law and order problems there.[12] These states need more development assistance both from India and other external aid agencies to usher in development and overcome the problem of militancy. The external aid agencies can outsource the development projects in the states having law and order problems. But bold steps are needed to bring them back to the mainstream and wean them away from the militancy through development and prosperity.

Japanese Peace Offensive vis-à-vis SAARC Countries

The purpose of Japanese aid for the SAARC countries varies from politico-economic engagement to building peace and creating infrastructure for recipient countries. It would be difficult to analyse all the Japanese aid projects for the region. Therefore, this section discuses salient aspects of Japanese aid focussing on key projects in the recipient countries.

Among the SAARC countries, Japan has paid utmost focus to bring peace and stability in Afghanistan. Interestingly, Afghanistan is a test case where Japan has exercised its soft power as well as hard power. When Afghanistan witnessed internal strife as a result of fights among the warlords and the Taliban to control Kabul, Japan tried to bring the "warring parties together" to broker peace. But Japan's efforts did not materialise.[13] The September 11 attack on US's World trade towers and US's war on terrorism turned world attention back to Afghanistan. Japan, in close alliance with the US took various measures including the adoption of the Anti-terrorism Measures Law (ATSML) which authorised its Self Defense Force (SDF) vessels to provide a steady supply of fuel to the coalition forces in the Indian Ocean. Sadako Ogata argues that Japan's action was in the realm of peace and reconstruction.[14] However, Japan's rear area support to the US led operation in Afghanistan did not earn much diplomatic dividend and when the Democratic Party of Japan (DPJ) wrested power from the Liberal Democratic Party (LDP), it did not renew the ASTML bill beyond 2010 and the bill lapsed. According to the estimate issued by the Japanese government, the cost of fuel provided to foreign vessels during the mission since fiscal 2001 totalled ¥24.4 billion and expenses for the entire refuelling mission amounted to ¥71.5 billion.[15] In total, around 13,300 MSDF members took part in the mission. The new government decided a new course of action and decided to use the money directly for the betterment of Afghanistan.

For reconstruction of war ravaged Afghanistan, Japan committed five billion US dollars. A section of the Japanese media was critical of this policy. Regarding the Japanese aid pledge to Afghanistan, the *Yomiuri* daily in its editorial stated that "calculated in terms of the aid provided per fiscal year, this sum represents about four times the average aid provided up until now."[16] It termed this move as resorting to "check book diplomacy." stating that Japan has "once again resorted to the so-called check book diplomacy approach, in which it provides economic aid and investment but no security personnel." The then Japanese Foreign Minister Katsuya Okada, however, justified this strategy and stated that "sending troops is not necessarily the only way you can provide support."[17] Japan did send a small team of SDF to Kabul to inspect medical and other facilities. The United States had called for its allies to provide more physical support and Japan decided to send a ten member SDF team to meet American expectations.[18]

The critics, however, viewed this step as "far too little" in light of Afghanistan's daunting needs.[19]. The critics were upset that a mere ten SDF personnel were sent to Afghanistan in response to the US' request for assistance and support in reconstruction. In an opinion piece in *Yomiuri Shimbun*, American commentators, Newsham and Elbridge stated:

> "There is no reason why Japan, often aloof and indifferent to world events, should continue to stand aside or limit its role to 10 doctors and nurses—about a vanload—especially after Gates reportedly requested more than 2-$^1/_2$ years ago that the Japanese government send SDF personnel to Afghanistan for reconstruction and logistic support. Japan never sent its forces. Meanwhile, needs continue to grow in Afghanistan."[20]

The US scholars, quoted above, were of the view that by not getting directly involved in Afghanistan it is "punching well below its weight" on the international stage and advised Japan to "pay attention to its international image" Further they added that "direct involvement in the Afghan mission will do much for Japan in this regard, and we note there is no substitute for contributing manpower in these sorts of operations."[21] The criticism by the US's analysts of Japan's role in Afghanistan is reflective of the fact that a section of Americans wanted more active and direct involvement of Japanese troops in the country.

Japan, however, continued to play an active role without using its troops on the ground in Afghanistan. Apart from taking up reconstruction projects, it has undertaken vocational training programmes for surrendered Taliban militants through its NGOs. It has been training Afghan police forces as well as paying part salaries of some 800,000 police personnel.[22] Japan's programme to reintegrate surrendered Taliban into the society had a limited impact. It has offered vocational training, teaching them skills such as carpentry etc to a limited number of Taliban, roughly 2000 to 3000. But this has not been sufficient to "keep them off the field."[23] However, Japan's "generous support"[24] to Afghanistan has been welcomed by the authorities in Kabul. The Japanese aid has helped improve Japan's healthcare sector, education and reconstruction. Since Japanese are not so much on the ground and route their assistance through United Nation Development Programme and various other international agencies, they are unable to assess how their assistance are delivering.[25]

More importantly, Tokyo has organised two international donors' conferences on Afghanistan in 2002 and 2012. Why has Japan gone beyond its traditional check book diplomacy in Afghanistan? Japan seems committed to remain engaged in Afghanistan as they fear that if a consistent political commitment to Afghanistan is stopped, the country may be pushed once again into instability. One of the Japanese observers notes that "when Soviet Union troops were ejected by mujahideens, the international community failed to help the Afghans get back on their feet and instead, effectively abandoned them.... This sorry state of affairs led to the Taliban's rise to power. The Bonn Agreement and Tokyo Conference signify the conviction of the international community that it cannot allow the past to repeat itself."[26] Japan's engagement in Afghanistan is reflective of the fact that it has moved beyond the check book diplomacy.

Similarly, Japan through its ODA has undertaken various development projects in SAARC countries. It has earmarked a SAARC-Japan Special Fund to implement variety of programmes in Bangladesh, Nepal, Pakistan, Sri Lanka and other SAARC member countries.[27] With India, Japan has established a special relationship within SAARC, the only country in the SAARC group with which Japan has institutionalised annual meetings at the prime ministerial level. When they institutionalised their relationship they acknowledged that "a strong prosperous and dynamic India is in the interest of Japan and vice versa." To help India realise this goal, Japan has diversified its loan from China to India. Thereafter, India has become the largest recipient of Japanese aid. By fiscal 2012, Japan has allocated 349 billion yen loan to India under its ODA program which has been used in various development and infrastructure projects. One project that has become a landmark of India-Japan cooperation in development is the Delhi Mumbai Industrial Corridor (DMIC). This dedicated freight corridor is based on the Tokyo-Osaka expressway model along which several industrial zones would be set up. This 1483 kilometres long mega project will start from Delhi National Capital Region and will link to the Mumbai port in Maharashtra crossing through six Indian states viz. Uttar Pradesh, Haryana, Rajasthan, Madhya Pradesh, Gujarat and Maharashtra.[28] India has floated the Delhi Mumbai Industrial Corridor and Development Cooperation (DMIDC), a public enterprise to complete this project. The company has identified a band of 150 km (Influence region) on both sides of the Freight corridor to be developed as the Delhi-Mumbai Industrial Corridor. The vision for DMIC is to create a strong economic base in this band with globally competitive environment and state-of-the-art infrastructure to activate local commerce, enhance foreign investments, real-estate investments and attain sustainable development. In addition to the influence region, DMIC would also include development of requisite feeder rail and road connectivity to the hinterland and markets and select ports along the western coast. Yet another aim of the project is to ensure faster movement of goods. Construction of new eco-friendly cities along both the sides of the DMIC has been planned, with world class infrastructure including airports. It will incorporate 11 investment regions and 13 industrial areas. If this materialises, this project will give an entirely new look to India's economic landscape.[29]

The cost of the project has been estimated at USD 90 billion, part of which would be covered by Japanese funding and loans. India is making all efforts to clear political obstacles to provide a 26 per cent equity stake to Japan in the DMIDC. Indian government has moved a cabinet note for the participation of the Japanese government in DMIC.[30] Japan has already established a "Japanese Zone" in Neemrana in Rajasthan where Japanese companies have started setting up their industries.

Similarly, Japanese companies are eager to introduce the "bullet train technology" to India. India is interested in introducing the high-speed bullet trains on seven routes including between Ahmedabad and Mumbai. Japanese companies have already started promoting the Japanese Shinkaken technology and there are reports that the first such bullet train will run between Mumbai and Ahmedabad. The project is predicted to cost some 1 trillion yen and would be undertaken by East Japan Railway Company and Kawasaki Heavy Industries Limited. When completed, the Shinkansen line would shorten the 500-kilometer trip between Mumbai to Ahmedabad to two hours from the current 10 hours.[31]

The Japanese projects mentioned above have helped improve infrastructure and generated huge employment opportunities in recipient countries. Though there has been various internal factors that has propelled growth in South Asian countries, but Japan's role in these countries economic stability and prosperity cannot be negated.

Japan's Peace and Security Initiatives post the Cold War

As has been mentioned above, due to restriction imposed by its Constitution, Japan could not use its defence forces in any operations outside the country. It tried to use its soft power (aid and donations) to keep itself engaged with the world. However, it combined its soft and hard powers for achieving the goals of international peace and stability. This was triggered by criticism of Japan for its non-participation in 1990s Gulf War to liberate Kuwait from Iraqi occupation. It tried to save the situation by contributing 13.5 billion US dollars for the war fund. But this act was interpreted as cheque book diplomacy and equating blood with money. Following these criticism, Japan re-interpreted its constitution and allowed its troops to participate in the UN mandated peacekeeping operations as well as reconstruction efforts in the event of natural calamities. It has sent its Self Defense Forces for disaster relief operations to Pakistan.

Fortunately, the SAARC region has not faced any untoward developments which could force the UN to sanction use of force to resolve the issue. Since the UN has not authorised invasion of Afghanistan to oust the Taliban government there following the September 11 attack on US's world trade towers, Japan did not send its troops there. Japan has sent its troops to non-combat zones in Iraq in 2003 and offered rear area support to combat forces of other countries' troops participating in UN led Peace Keeping Operation. A section of Japanese politicians including the then DPJ Secretary General Ichiro Ozawa argued for sending Japanese troops for participation in International Security Assistance Force (ISAF) deployed in Afghanistan. But a consensus could not emerge within Japan as the security operation in Afghanistan was not mandated by the UN. Japan, however, sent its vessels to Indian Ocean on a refuelling mission and provided refuelling to NATO and ISAF forces there.

Japan has been very forthcoming in sending its troops on ground in relief and rescue operations where ever the disaster has struck. As regards South Asia is concerned, Pakistan has been forthcoming to invite Japanese troops on its ground. When a devastating earthquake struck Pakistan in 2005 it sent its troops to this South Asian country to assist rescue and reconstruction efforts there. In 2010, it sent its troops on the request of Pakistani government, mainly

Ground Self Defense Forces,[32] when a large part of the country faced deluge due to heavy downpour. Japanese initiative was backed by both soft and hard power. Japan announced an immediate US dollar 13 million emergency grant[33] to Pakistan followed by commitment to send its troops to participate in rescue and relief activities. The Japanese contingent airlifted flood affected Pakistani residents and provided relief goods and medicine. A total 210 GSDF personnel participated in relief activity in and around Multan, central Pakistan for over a month.[34] Though the most affected area of flood were parts of Southern Punjab, hit by militancy, Japan chose a relatively peaceful area of Pakistan and worked under the security cover provided by Pakistani forces. However, its relief mission was hailed and appreciated by the United Nations and the United States.[35]

Japan's Participation in Anti-piracy and SLOC

With the incidents of sea piracy and attacks on merchant vessels, Japan realised that its Sea Lines of Communication (SLOC), the life line of its economy, is threatened. Japan utilised this opportunity to send its vessels to Gulf of Aden and established a permanent naval base in Djibuti. It has also been supporting various littoral states to enhance their capabilities to check piracy, including South Asian countries, Sri Lanka and India. A major chunk of Japan's imports and exports pass through the Indian Ocean, and Japan has institutionalized a maritime dialogue with India in order to protect its SLOC. However, neither India nor Japan harbours ambition to hegemonies regional maritime domain. During a visit to New Delhi, the then Japanese Foreign Minister Yoriko Kawaguchi has stated that maintenance of maritime traffic between Indian Ocean and the Straits of Malacca are among the "security and defense issues which deserves our increased attention."[36] Similarly, Shigeru Ishiba, the then Defense Agency Chief of Japan stated that the democracies in Asia "should have a candid exchange of views and then try to make a contribution to formulate rules for international society."[37] India has also ensured that it will stand by Japan in it's strive to secure hassle free passage of vessels carrying goods and will ensure freedom of navigation and thereby achieving peace and stability of the region. Indian Foreign Minister Salman Khurshid while visiting Tokyo in March 2013 stated that "Countries like India and Japan must cooperate in ensuring the security of global commons including freedom of navigations on the high seas that is critical to both our countries which imports large amounts of oil and gas."[38]

Japan and India have been participating in naval drills on a regular basis. A close look at Japan's participation in anti-piracy and SLOCs suggest that it has proved a dual edge for Japan; on the one hand it helps Japan secure its vital economic life line and on the other hand it has helped re-establish itself as a naval power.

Conclusion and Assessment

Though various factors have led to the economic growth of Asia and particularly South Asia, role of Japan's infrastructure and developmental projects in the growth story of this region cannot be negated. Its mega projects in various South Asian countries have helped transform the economic landscape and have created a huge rise in employment, thereby contributing to stability and prosperity of the recipient nations.

As regards Japan's role in reconstruction and peace building, its role is laudable. These efforts have certainly helped Japan enhance its diplomatic stature. But Japan needs to be more proactive and enhance its peace building role in Asia. For example, it undertook reconstruction work in Afghanistan following US's invasion of the country. After Iraq, Japan has been reconstructing Afghanistan following destruction of these countries during US led operations. Japan would do well to maintain its efforts at peacekeeping through aid and diplomacy beyond just disaster and relief operations, and it will serve Japan well not to be tagged as one who reconstructs countries out rubble and debris created by the US.

END NOTES

1. "Japan's support to SAARC: Priority Areas and Policies," Ministry of Foreign Affairs, Japan, available online at http://www.mofa.go.jp/region/asia-paci/saarc/pdfs/support1004.pdf (accessed February 4, 2014)
2. For detail analysis of Japan's ODA towards Southeast Asia see, Mitsuya Araki, "Japan's Official Development Assistance: The Japan ODA model that began life in Southeast Asia," *Asia Pacific Review*, volume 14, issue 2, November 2007, pp. 17-29.
3. Makiko Ichihara, "Understanding Japanese democracy assistance," *The Carnegie Papers*, 2013, available at http://carnegieendowment.org/2013/03/25/understanding-japanese-democracy-assistance/ftcg (Accessed January 29, 2014).
4. Dennis T. Yasutomo, "Why aid? Japan as an Aid great power," *Pacific Affairs*, Vol. 62, No. 4 winter 1989-1990, p. 494.
5. Ibid.
6. Ibid.
7. Toshiki Kaifu, "Japan and South Asia: In pursuit of dialogue and co-operation," April 30, 1990, Text of Prime Minister Kishi's address to Indian Parliament. For details see, PA Narsimha Murthy, "India and Japan: Dimension of their relations, Appendix II, pp. 434-448, Lancer Book, New Delhi, 1992.
8. Ibid.
9. Ibid.
10. P.V. Narsimha Rao, "Towards an India-Japan partnership in the Twenty-first Century," *Japan Review of International Affairs*, Volume 6, No.2, 1992, pp.195-202.

11. "Map of ongoing JICA projects", in Operation and Activities in India, *Japan International Cooperation Agency*, hand out of JICA India Office, April 2013, p.10.
12. "Japan ditches Bihar IIT plan," *The Times of India*, April 10, 2008.
13. Sadako Ogata, "Rebuilding Afghanistan and Japan's Role," *Japan Society*, March 14, 2002, available at http://www.japansociety.org/page/multimedia/articles/imported_corporate_notes/rebuilding_afghanistan__japans_role_1 (Accessed January 26, 2014)
14. Ibid.
15. "US calmly accept end of MSDF refueling mission", *The Japan Times*, January 17, 2010.
16. "Is government returning to Checkbook diplomacy" (Editorial), *The Yomiuri Shimbun*, November 11, 2009.
17. Foreign Minister Okada makes surprise visit to Kabul, *Mainichi Japan*, October 11, 2009.
18. "Japan plans to send its SDF medical staff to Afghanistan", *Mainichi Japan*, October 15, 2010.
19. Grant Newsham and Robert D. Eldridge, "Time for Japan to step up in Afghanistan," *The Daily Yomiuri*, January 13, 2011.
20. Ibid.
21. Ibid.
22. "Japan to train Afghan police in Turkey," *The Yomiuri Shimbun*, August 16, 2010.
23. Author's interview with M. Ashraf Haidari, Deputy Ambassador, The embassy of Afghanistan, New Delhi, dated February 25, 2014.
24. Ibid.
25. Ibid.
26. Kenzo Oshima, "Aid for Afghanistan: Immediate needs and long term Considerations," *Japan Review of International Affairs*, Vol. 16, No.1, 2002,
27. "Japan's Support to SAARC," op. cit. n.1.
28. Amitabh K. Kanth, "Delhi Mumbai Industrial Corridor: Challenges and Prospects," lecture delivered at the Observer Research Foundation, New Delhi on October 11, 2012.
29. Ibid.
30. "Government moves cabinet note on 26% stake of Japanese government in DMIDC", *The Indian Express*, May 1, 2012.
31. "India near deal to use Shinkansen", *The Yomiuri Shimbun*, March 11, 2013.
32. GSDF helicopter unit ordered to Pakistan, *Japan Times*, August 11, 2010.
33. Japan readies SDF mission to Pakistan, *The Asahi Shimbun*, August 21, 2010.
34. GSDF Unit to end Pakistan flood relief, *The Japan Times*, October 6, 2010.
35. Ibid.
36. Madhuchanda Ghosh, "India and Japan's Growing Synergy: From a Political to Strategic Focus", *Asian Survey*, Vol. XLVIII, No. 2, March/April 2008, p. 87.
37. Indo-Japan Dialogue on Ocean Security, Keynote address by Honorable Mr. Shigeru Ishiba, *Journal of Indian Ocean Studies*, New Delhi, Vol. 13, No.1, April 2005, pp 6-10.
38. "We stand by Japan on freedom of navigation: Khurshid", *The Hindu*, March 27, 2013.

3

Japan–SAARC Relations: The Political Dimension

Takenori Horimoto

Japanese Perception of the Subcontinent

Historical Affinity

When discussing any relationship, historical memories constitute a basic foundation. This perspective is applicable also to assess such foreign relations as those between Japan and the Subcontinent. That is particularly true for Japanese people. The Japanese as Buddhists have historically held a strong affinity to the Subcontinent as the cradle of Buddhism, which arrived in Japan during the middle of the sixth century.

In those days in Japan, the Subcontinent was called *Tenjiku* from the Chinese word: Tianzhu. For the Japanese, Tenjiku was the birthplace of Buddha and the place of yearning among Buddhists. The Japanese image of the entire world long consisted of three countries or regions: Japan, Mainland China, and Tenjiku. Such a world view persists today.[1] Although few Japanese have visited Tenjiku, it has become an integral part of the Japanese global image.

Modern Japanese people feel a sense of closeness for Sri Lanka and Bhutan as Buddhist countries, and even for Pakistan, Bangladesh, Nepal, and the Maldives, which some of them mistakenly regard as Buddhist countries.

Aside from Buddhism and Tenjiku, there have been visits between Japan and the Subcontinent. The most famous event was a visit of Bodhisena (बोधिसेन), a Buddhist monk who came to Japan in 752 to perform the eye-opening ceremony for the newly constructed Buddha statute of the Todai temple, located in present day Nara prefecture. The Japanese have also travelled to the Subcontinent. Japan's young Christian delegates stayed in Goa on their way to Rome for an audience with the Pope in Rome in 1583 and stayed there again in 1587 on their way back. They were the first official Japanese emissaries dispatched to Europe. These incipient exchanges would have been expanded further if the closed door policy by the Tokugawa feudal government had not been introduced in the seventeenth century.

After two hundred years, the Tokugawa government collapsed and the period called Meiji in Japan began in 1868. The Meiji government tackled the initiation of Japan's modernization to catch up with the advanced European countries. The slogan of the government was "Rich country and Strong army": a policy of increasing national prosperity (wealth) and military power.

To become a rich country, the cotton industry was placed as the main engine of Japan's industrial development in the economic field. The industry was sustained mainly by raw cotton imported from the Subcontinent. In 1892, raw cotton accounted for half of major manufacturers' inputs. Because of such tremendous contributions, "rapid development of Japanese cotton industries which reached the highest standard before the World War II brought about the import of Indian raw cotton.[2]

After the World War II, the Japanese economy gradually recovered and then entered its high economic growth period during the mid-1950s. The driving force behind it was steel industries. Here again iron ore imported from the Subcontinent contributed substantially to the rapid development of its industries.

The Japanese economy has benefitted by the presence of its automobile industry in India and also in Pakistan. Consequently, Japan's economic development has been derived greatly from its contact with the Subcontinent during the past two centuries. It is possible to summarize that Japan has benefited by its close ties with the Subcontinent through B+CIA: B (Buddhism), C (cotton), I (iron ore), and A (automobiles).

Geographical Views of South Asia

Aside from these historical circumstances, there are additional perceptions among the Japanese in relation to the Subcontinent.

First, the Subcontinent has enjoyed geographical advantages. It is situated at the centre of the world, occupying a central place on the Eurasian continent whereas Japan is at its periphery. China and South Korea might be said to be in a similar position.

Second, another point closely associated with the first point is the fact that the Subcontinent lords over the great seas: the Bay of Bengal, the Indian Ocean, and the Arabian Sea. These seas are maritime highways for commodities and energy resource transportation. In the case of Japan, half of its energy resources are oil, 90 per cent of which comes from the Middle East through these seas.

From the 1990s onward, the Indian Ocean has attracted broad strategic attention from various countries[3] for its Sea Lines of Communications (SLOC). A typical case could be the so-called "Indo-Pacific"[4] proposed by the U.S. administration. It says in its 2010 QDR "The United States has a substantial interest in the stability of the Indian Ocean region as a whole, which will play an ever more important role in the global economy. The Indian Ocean provides vital Sea Lines of Communication that are essential to global commerce, international energy security, and regional stability. Ensuring open access to the Indian Ocean will need a more integrated approach to the region across military and civilian organizations."[5]

Current South Asia from Japan's Perspective

MOFA's View of South Asia

In view of Japan's historical affinity, economic relations, and geographical merits, to say the least of recent economic developments in India, Bangladesh, and Sri Lanka, it would be quite natural for Japan to show a passionate gaze at South Asia.

The Japanese Government has started emphasizing relations with South Asia. The Ministry of Foreign Affairs explains ties to South Asia favourably in its recent annual report.[6]

With a large population of approximately 1.6 billion and its geopolitical importance, South Asia has been increasing its weight in the international arena, while many countries in the region continue high economic growth. Japan will further strengthen its economic relations with countries in the region and continue to cooperate with their own efforts in such areas as national reconciliation and promotion and consolidation of democracy.

The South Asian countries might have identical motivations to foster closer relations with Japan. From their perspective, Japan might be regarded as a *major safe card.* Japan is a formidable economic power with adequate defence capabilities, but it is geographically distant from the South Asian countries. Historically very little negative baggage has been shouldered by Japan from South Asian countries.

Hope for Economic Connectivity of South Asian Countries

As an analysis of the Ministry's report has shown, South Asia has sufficient economic potentialities, although they have been only insufficiently explored in the past. In addition to developmental endeavours of individual countries, vigorous pursuits of intra-regional trade can be expected to turn out to be a positive and helpful factor of South Asian development.

Intra-regional trade in South Asia was around 4 percent in 2007.[7] The South Asian Association for Regional Cooperation (SAARC) has already reached an agreement of the *South Asian Free Trade Area or SAFTA*. SAFTA is expected to be effective in reducing customs duties of all traded goods to zero by 2016. As the agreement comes into effect, the intra-regional trade of the Subcontinent would gradually expand to the level of ASEAN's 25 percent and to the future EU's 55 percent.[8]

Although an ambitious appraisal of an ASEAN level of 25 percent might sound like daydreaming, one should remember this figure was a reality before the time of the Partition of India and Pakistan in 1947.[9] Considering the geographical connectivity of South Asian countries, it is not at all unrealistic. Ambassador Humayun Kabir opined that *Bangladesh and other small neighbours in South Asia are likely to benefit from that matrix of growing interdependence.*[10]

In the backdrop of such a view, it would be necessary to take note of policy changes in South Asian countries. In the past, particularly during the Cold War period, these countries were characterized by their unstable domestic politics and turbulent bilateral relations. Economic policies of these countries tended to resemble populist slogans. However, from the 1990s onward, each country has been compelled to conform to globalization and a market-oriented world economy in their implementation of economic policies.

Moreover, higher economic growth has been ubiquitous in Asia, starting in Southeast Asian countries during the 1980s and then China in the 1990s. Such phenomena have stimulated peoples of the Subcontinent countries to strive for greater economic performance. In short, they want to have adequate governance of their countries.

A typical case would be India. India has been maintaining high economic growth since its economic liberalization in 1991 and is now seen as the second country to emulate the Chinese precedent. The Indian economy has been placed in the high growth orbit in the 2000s (2000–09), particularly since the Congress government came to power in 2004, it has accelerated growth further. Its successful policy has produced good dividends for the Congress Party to win the 2009 general election.

That is true not only at the national level: similar trends can be found at the state level. Probably the best case is the State of Gujarat and its Chief Minister, Narendra Modi of the BJP. Under Modi's economic policies, Gujarat has marked a higher than 10 percent economic growth rate since 2001. Mainly because of that high rate, the BJP has won the state assembly elections for three consecutive terms. Because of its performance, he has been elected as BJP's Prime Ministerial candidate in 2013.

Perhaps the important key for intra-regional economic integration is already in the hands of the three South Asian countries: India, Pakistan, and Bangladesh. India holds its position as a super economic power and Pakistan and Bangladesh are the middle powers in the South Asian region. The three countries were integral parts of British India, constituting a single market. How these countries are able to become united as a single economic entity could determine the manner in which SAARC can attain 25 percent intra-regional trade.

To achieve such integration, a fundamental question is whether they can move to a North American model. In 1994, the three countries of North America established the North America Free Trade Agreement (NAFTA). Under the NAFTA regime, Canada and Mexico have been linked to the economic giant of U.S. and have benefitted greatly in terms of their economic development, as the U.S. has.[11]

Aside from the three South Asian countries, Sri Lanka is poised to achieve higher economic growth since the end of its civil war on May 2009. Sri Lanka's economic growth rate has been 6–8 percent, with per-capita income reaching US $3000 after 2009. It is expected to serve as an economic hub of the Indian Ocean because of its geographical location.[12]

Attempts at Rapprochement

The realization of economic integration in the South Asian region is not necessarily optimistic thinking. In fact, various attempts at it have been made in the past. It is particularly interesting that there have been attempts between India and Pakistan, despite their continuing antagonistic relations over the past six decades.

The latest olive branch was extended by Pakistani President Zardari in 2012. During informal luncheon talks with the Indian Prime Minister Singh on April 8, 2012 the Zardari broached the Indo–China model of a pragmatic approach, which has been followed by India and China, advancing mutually beneficial economic interests while pursuing contentious issues of long standing separately.[13] This India–China model under the agreement and related documents was, in short, an expansion of bilateral economic relations while shelving the border issues. This framework is being fundamentally observed by India and China even today.

Although Zardari's proposal has not come to fruition, it is worthwhile to take note of it. A similar undertaking in the field of politics between Prime Minister Singh and President Musharraf around 2007 was reported between

India and Pakistan to solve the Kashmir issue. However, because Musharraf slipped into a political death spiral and resigned in August of 2008, that effort died a natural death.[14]

If these attempts were to take shape and bear concrete results, they might be regarded as major breakthroughs between the two countries, bringing about an amicable atmosphere in the South Asian region. However, because of antagonistic relationships over the past six decades caused by lack of credibility because of the Partition, three Wars, and numerous terrorist activities, it might take some more time to reach peaceful situations.[15]

Hope for the future: Beyond Antagonism

Historic precedents tell us that immediate neighbours tend to be antagonistic. An example from modern history would be Germany and France. They needed more than one century to get over their animosities. Franco–German co-operation is now widely regarded as the engine of European integration.

In our twenty-first century, international relations are more globalized. Every country's foremost priority and people's main concerns centre upon good governance anchored in good economic circumstances. Moreover, without economic relations, bilateral relations tend to be trapped easily in critical ones and ultimately in wars. Close economic relations would somehow restrain a worsening overall relationship to extreme phases, although hasty closure of bilateral economic relations is not a recipe for avoiding a war. Probably Japan–China relations represent a case in point: without economic relations serving as something like an umbilical cord, bilateral relations might have already turned into a physical struggle between the nations.

Special situations have prevailed in South Asia, where a combination of such volatile factors as democratization, multi-ethnicism, Islamization, and nationalism have been causing considerable difficulties in nation building and have been jeopardizing the creation of peaceful international relations in the South Asian region. Nevertheless, regional situations of South Asia appear to be gradually changing for the better in the past two decades and are poised to catch up to that of Southeast Asia.

Japan and South Asia

Paradigm Shift in Asia with Emerging China

If economic situations of the Subcontinent countries become much improved and if closer economic relations among the countries are to be realized, and noticing that such realization is underway, how should relations between Japan and South Asian countries be moulded, considering contemporary international relations in Asia?

There are two points to bear in mind. One is transmutation of the geopolitical map of the world. No one might object to the argument that three political and economic centres now exist in the world: the U.S., Europe (EU), and Asia. Clearly, a shift is occurring in favour of Asia. Second, emerging Asia presents an important phenomenon of power transition among the related countries associated with the shift. If one were to apply a yardstick of status quo powers and revisionist powers to the contemporary Asian scene, then the U.S., Japan, and Australia belong to the former and China and to some extent India, both emerging powers, belong to the latter.

When we regard China as a revisionist power, we must ascertain whether China is moving to a revisionist policy orientation. According to Ronald L. Tammen and Jacek Kugler, when a challenger has over eighty percent of the capabilities of a dominant nation, it moves to challenge.[16] Presuming that the challenger is China and that the dominant nation is the U.S., particularly in Asia, application of the eighty percent benchmark to the case of the U.S. and China, in terms of GDP and defence expenditure, China is incompatible to the U.S at the moment as the chart shows.

GDP and Defence Expenditure of U.S. and China

	U.S.	China
GDP of 2012 trillion US$*	16.24	8.23
Defence Expenditure in 2012 Billion US$**	682.0	166.0

*GDP (current US$)
Source: The World Bank (http://data.worldbank.org/indicator/NY.GDP.MKTP.CD)
**Military Expenditure (US$)
Source: The SIPRI Military Expenditure Database
http://www.sipri.org/research/armaments/milex/milex_database/milexdata1988-2012v2.xsls/view

However, as Joseph Nye points out, one must make a clear distinction between "power as resources" and "power as a behavioural outcome."[17] He explains "For example, when people speak of the rising power of China or India, they tend to point to the large populations and increased economic or military resources of those countries. However, whether the capacity that those resources imply can actually be converted into preferred outcomes will depend upon the contexts and the country's skill in converting resources into strategies that will produce preferred outcomes."[18]

Hedging in the Indo-Pacific

Although China might not yet rival the U.S. in terms of national power, it looks to practice power as behavioural outcome. A case in point could be its military activism such as advancing its military build-up without much transparency and endeavouring to change the status quo unilaterally by force in the East China Sea and the South China Sea.

The U.S. has been trying to cope with the assertive China, which is making inroads into the Western Pacific region. Its strategy is Rebalancing to Asia—a slight shift from the so-called "Pivot" to Asia. As a more concrete policy, the U.S. has propounded the Indo-Pacific idea with Former Secretary of State, Hillary Clinton.[19] Her colleague, Secretary of Defense Panetta, announced in June 2012 that 60 percent of US navy forces would be deployed in the Pacific by 2020.

And as to the Indian Ocean, Clinton said "The United States has a substantial interest in the stability of the Indian Ocean region as a whole, which will play an ever more important role in the global economy. The Indian Ocean provides vital sea lines of communication that are essential to global commerce, international energy security, and regional stability. Ensuring open access to the Indian Ocean will require a more integrated approach to the region across military and civilian organizations."[20]

At the moment, a tussle in Asia seems to be underway between the U.S., Japan, Australia and to a certain extent India and the Southeast Asian countries, and China. The U.S. and other countries are fundamentally implementing a so-called quadrilateral or trilateral approach of combinations of the U.S., Japan, Australia, and India,[21] hedging the emerging China particularly in the Indo-Pacific region. China has also been implementing various policies such as the PLAN's expansion, the 'String of Pearls' operation, and the Island Chain strategy in the Pacific.

For Japan and South Asian countries, the U.S. could be designated as an indispensable ally to a greater or lesser degree. The U.S. has an intention to be a part of multilateral formations, as advocated clearly by a cable of 5 May 2006 from the US Embassy in New Delhi to its home office.[22] Fundamentally, it is only barely possible to maintain an Asian balance of power without the U.S., as ex-Minister mentor of Singapore, Lee Kuan Yew pointed out.[23]

Under the engagement and hedging policy orientation, one must bear in mind how to involve ASEAN countries. The countries have shown their anxiety over China in terms of security and economy. For them, the US annual defence cut from 600 billion US dollars to 500 billion US dollars in the coming decade has presented the largest headache in the field of security.[24]

Additionally, ASEAN countries have been anxious about the omnipresence of China's goods and people in their respective countries, with the fear that their economies would be engulfed by the Chinese economy. Such concerns have come to constitute a major factor for Singapore and Brunei (both original signatories) and Malaysia and Vietnam (both under negotiations to join) to be member countries of the 'Trans-Pacific Partnership' (TPP) framework. These four countries face China's large and looming economic might, although economic interactions with China are an inescapable reality.

Moreover, ASEAN countries such as Vietnam, Malaysia, Brunei, and the Philippines are facing standoffs with China over various disputes in the South China Sea. They include not only the maritime boundaries and the territorial claims of the Spratly Islands and the Paracel Islands but also fishing zones, the potential exploitation of crude oil and natural gas, and the strategic control of important shipping lanes.

Engagement and a New Mechanism

However, the hedging policy and China's countermeasures would tend to result in more confrontational atmospheres in Asia.

When one country grows stronger, its relationships with other countries tend to evolve imperceptibly, reflecting their relative power shift and such a tendency that allows a new order to emerge, absorbing an emerging country's ambition without conscious efforts of adjustments and concessions with concerned countries. Perhaps the world is now watching such a transformation without a clear image of what is going to happen. This view would be applicable to Asia as a whole.

Additionally, one must bear in mind the internal policy process of China, which consists of three major organs: The Communist Party, the PLAN, and the Government. Among the triad, there are moderates and hardliners. A hedging policy would tend to give much ammunition for the latter to pursue harder policies without giving space to take into account moderate policy orientations of the former.

Therefore, twofold orientations are simultaneously necessary: hedging and engagement. A hedging-only policy would turn out to be antagonistic; engagement alone would yield elusive results. By combining these two policies, one might expect an effective and sustainable situation in Asia.

China is a country with an extremely long cultural history of more than two thousand years. It is a predominant power in Asia. China might quite naturally seek to establish a preponderant position in the region. A popular proverb in China is that two tigers are not necessary on one mountain. China aspires to establish a hierarchical power structure: first in Asia and then in the remainder of the world.[25] After all, as Kondapalli and Mifune point out "Asian vicissitudes to a large extent are dependent on how China evolves its relations with its neighbours—in mutually beneficial interdependence or ending and costly conflicts.[26]

In this connection, Indian Prime Minister Manmohan Singh's remarks would be pertinent to bear in mind. He remarked to the Japanese media on November 14, 2012 immediately before his official visit to Japan[27] that *Japan and India have to work with China to ensure that the peaceful rise of China takes place in a manner which will be conducive to Asian security, Asian prosperity.*

To put into practice what Prime Minister Singh said is the engagement and the hedging policy framework, which should be pursued in a multilateral fashion. In such a framework, the basic concept should not be exclusive but inclusive. China must be included. Therefore, any strategic co-operation between Japan and South Asian countries should be so oriented as to create an Asian environment in which any country would find it difficult to become a hegemony and would instead accept co-operation for a regional framework.

At present, multilateral and regional mechanisms exist in Asia. In South Asian and the Indian Ocean regions, there are the Bay of Bengal Initiative for Multi-Sectoral Technical and Economic Cooperation (BIMSTEC), the Indian Ocean Rim Association for Regional Co-operation (IOR-ARC), and the Indian Ocean Navy Symposium (IONS) aside from SAARC. Their basic characteristics are inclusive. It can be expected that these organizations can develop into more full-fledged mechanisms.

However, in the Southeast Asian region are the Association of Southeast Asian Nations (AEAN), the ASEAN Regional Forum (ARF), and the East Asia Summit (EAS). EAS is more or less moribund these days. In the East Asian region, no entity except the Six-Party Talks aims to find a peaceful solution to security concerns as a result of the North Korean nuclear weapons program.

Whatever organizations and associations exist, ways and means must be found to operationalize them for more solid and effective mechanisms for Asian stability and peace. This is particularly so in the Western Pacific, where the concerned Southeast Asian countries and China are confronting each other, not to mention the East China Sea. The Western Pacific has now turned into the main stage of concern and rivalry for the U.S. (Rebalancing Asia policy[28]), Japan (under the active defence policy under the Abe government), China, and India, which are metamorphosing into nations with land and sea power in the past two decades, from being land powers,[29] not to mention the Southeast Asian countries. The Western Pacific, and to a certain degree, the Indian Ocean, have become the new main stage of naval activities in the world now that the pirate-infested Arabian Sea has been gradually fading from popular attention.

Conclusion

What should be the future relations between Japan and the South Asian countries? How should the relations be moulded? The relations should be formulated toward making a *public property* of Asia.[30]

Now would be an opportune time for Japan and South Asia to look forward to the future to consider their relationship as public property and not simply to promote bilateral benefits as private property. They can render a public good by providing appropriate services through their mutual relationships. Both should apply the present closest relationship for institutionalizing an inclusive mechanism for Asia's prosperity, peace, and stability.

END NOTES

1. When guests want to praise a bride in a marriage party, they say "the best bride in the three countries" which means the best bride.
2. Toshio Yamazaki & Mitsuru Takahasi (ed.), Japan and India history of intercourse (in Japanese), Sanseido, 1993, p.49.
3. See Robert D. Kaplan, Monsoon: *The Indian Ocean and the Future of Power*, 2011. He analyzes the Indian Ocean as a new center of power in the global politics and the stage for the new Great Game.
4. See C. Raja Mohan, *Samudra Manthan Sino–Indian Rivalry in the Indo–Pacific*, 2012 has also assigns great importance to the Indian Ocean, p. 60.
5. Department of Defense, Quadrennial al Defense Review Report, February 2012, p. 60. http://www.defense.gov/qdr/images/QDR_as_of_12Feb10_1000.pdf accessed on January 14, 2014.
6. Ministry of Foreign Affairs, Diplomatic Bluebook 2012 Summary. http://www.mofa.go.jp/policy/other/bluebook/2012/html/h2/h2_01.html
   It continues *"In particular, Japan will further deepen its Strategic and Global Partnership and enhance cooperation in various fields with India, where Prime Minister Noda visited for the Annual Summit meeting in December 2011, as India has been increasing its influence in the international community as an emerging country. With regard to Pakistan, which has a key role in counter-terrorism, Japan encourages its own efforts towards the peace and stability of the region and the entire international community, as well as continues its cooperation mainly in economic areas."*
7. Asian Development Bank, *Study on intraregional trade and investment in South Asia*, 2009, p.2. (http://www.adb.org/sites/default/files/intraregional-trade-investment.pdf). According to this study, the trade volume of $517.5 billion in 2007, only 4% was intraregional trade in South Asia.
8. Takenori Horimoto, India Globalizing Big Elephant (in Japanese), Iwanami-Shoten, 2007, p.96.
9. Muhammad F. Khan (Minister of Commerce), *Inaugural Address at Regional Symposium on "Improving Trade Flows in and from South Asia: Overcoming logistic challenges,* June 22, 2011, Bangladesh Enterprise Institute.
10. Humayun Kabir, "Bangladesh-India relations", *Daily Sun*, Sept.10, 2011. Prime Minister

Manmohan Singh similarly remarked *I have always believed that the destinies of the nations of South Asia are interlinked* (Dhaka University Speech in September 7, 2011). http://pib.nic.in/newsite/PrintRelease.aspx?relid=75700 (Accessed n January 11, 2014).

11. According to the U.S. Department of Commerce, U.S.–Mexico trade has increased 153% and U.S. –Canada trade 153% between 1993 and 2004 (the Ministry of Foreign Affairs, Outline of NAFTA (http://www.mofa.go.jp/mofaj/area/usa/keizai/nafta.html accessed on January 12, 2014). Particularly in the case of Mexico, it would surpass Brazil in the near future due to the NAFTA ("Mexico vs. Brazil: Who's winning?," *Global Post*, June 19, 2012)
12. "Sri Lanka after the Civil War occupies Strategic Point of the Indian Ocean," *The Nikkei Shimbun*, January 12, 2014.
13. Hemant Krishan Singh, "India–Pakistan Trade Diplomacy-Sustaining Hope," *ICRIER ISSUE BRIEF*, Vol. 2, Issue 5, Apr. 18, 2012. http://www.icrier.org/icrier_wadhwani/Index_files/icrierwadhwan_issuebrief5apr2012.pdf accessed on January 12, 2014.
14. Steve Coll, A Reporter at Large, "The Back Channel," *The New Yorker*, March 2, 2009.
15. Natwar Singh (former Foreign Secretary of India) has underlined Pakistan as a main negative factor "For the past 10 years, he has been trying to go to Pakistan and has not succeeded because the Pakistanis have repeatedly acted against our interests. Each time Manmohan Singh wanted to visit Pakistan, an anti-Indian incident was enacted." (Natwar Singh, "We have no foreign policy," MailOnline, January 8, 2014. http://www.dailymail.co.uk/indiahome/indianews/article-2536125/We-no-foreign-policy-Natwar-Singh-launches-devastating-attack-PMs-legacy-claims-Government-crutches.html: accessed on January 12, 2014.
16. Ronald L. Tammen & Jacek Kugler, "Power Transition and China–US Conflicts," *The Chinese Journal of International Politics*, Summer 2006. http://cjip.oxfordjournals.org/content/1/1/35.full accessed January 13, 2014. More concretely they argue that the conditions for parity are met when a challenger has over 80% of the capabilities of the dominant nation and cease when the challenger has exceeded the dominant nation's capability by 20%—when it becomes the dominant nation. Previous research strongly suggests that the period of greatest danger is when the challenger manages to overtake the dominant nation and traverses the region between 100% and 120%.
17. Joseph S. Nye, The Future of Power, 2011, pp. 9-10.
18. Ibid.
19. Hillary Clinton, "America's," The Foreign Policy, October 11, 2011. She stated that the future of politics will be decided in Asia, not in Afghanistan or Iraq, and that the United States will be right at the center of the action.
20. Ibid.
21. Takenori Horimoto, "Strategic Convergence of Japan–India Relations and China's Emergence," in Lalima Varma (ed.), *India–Japan Relations in Emerging Asia,* Manohar, p.60.
22. The cable pointed out that the stars had aligned for closer trilateral relations among the US, Japan, and India. *The Hindu*, 23 April 2010.
23. *The Asahi Shimbun*, 11 May 2010.
24. 'Asian Anxiety', *The New York Times*, 25 October 2011.
25. An Indian expert on China interviewed in New Delhi on September 6, 2011.
26. Srikant Kondapalli and Emi Mifune, "Introduction," in Srikant Kondapalli and Emi Mifune (ed.), China and its Neighbours, New Delhi, Pentagon Press, 2010, p. xiii.
27. His trip had been cancelled because of the dissolution of Japan's parliament on November 16, 2013.
28. U.S. global policy has shifted from *War on Terror* to *Counter to China. National Strategy for Counterterrorism* was made on June 28, 2011. Osama bin Laden was killed on May 2, 2011.

29. Takenori Horimoto, 'Major Country of South Asia and Japan', in Nishihara and Horimoto (eds.), *India as a Rising Military Power*, Askishobo, 2010 (in Japanese), pp. 22-32.
30. In the past, Japan–US relations have been compared to public property of Asia, which has said to be contributing to stabilize the Asian political environment. In other words, this relation is not meant for beneficial bilateral relations, as private property, but for Asia as a whole. In contrast, the Japan–US relationship has tended to be seen as a relationship of senior partner and junior partner. Therefore, the discourse of the Japan–U.S relationship as public property has not been readily acceptable in Asia in the past. This has been especially so in India. Satu Limaye pointed out that India had basically written off Japan as an American surrogate in Asia during the Cold War period: an attitude persisting even today. (Satu Limaye, "Japan and India after the Cold War," in Yoichiro Sato & Satu Limaye (ed.), *Jan in a Dynamic Asia Coping with the New Security Challenges*, Lexington Books, 2006, pp. 226-227).

REFERENCES

Coll, Steve Coll [2009], "The Back Channel," *The New Yorker*, March 2.

Hemant Krishan Singh [2012], "India–Pakistan Trade Diplomacy-Sustaining Hope," *ICRIER ISSUE BRIEF*, Vol. 2, Issue 5, Apr. 18.

http://www.icrier.org/icrier_wadhwani/Index_files/icrierwadhwan_issuebrief5apr2012.pdf. Accessed on January 12, 2014.

Horimoto, Takenori [2007], *India Globalizing Big Elephant* (in Japanese), Iwanami-Shoten.

Horimoto, Takenori & Varma, Lalima [2013], *India–Japan Relations in Emerging Asia*, Manohar

Joseph S. Nye [2012], *The Future of Power*, Publicaffairs.

Kabir, Humayun [2011], "Bangladesh-India relations", *Daily Sun*, Sept. 10.

Kaplan, Robert D. [2011], *Monsoon: The Indian Ocean and the Future of Power*, Random House Trade Paperbacks.

Mohan, C. Raja [2012], *Samudra Manthan Sino–Indian Rivalry in the Indo–Pacific*, Carnegie Endowment for International Peace.

Tammen, Ronald L. & Kugler, Jacek [2014], "Power Transition and China–US Conflicts," *The Chinese Journal of International Politics*, Summer 2006. http://cjip.oxfordjournals.org/content/1/1/35.fullAccessed on January 13, 2014.

Yamazaki, Toshio & Takahasi [1993], *Japan and India History of Intercourse* (in Japanese), Sanseido.

4

Extra-Regional Powers in SAARC: Japan

H.S. Prabhakar

Introduction

As it can be observed from the case of ASEAN, outside support is critical for any regional integration attempt to be successful. Japan looks at SAARC as a productive economic forum and believes that being a part of it adds to its influence in the region besides its own economic future. Unlike ASEAN which was formed way back in 1967, SAARC is a late entrant, and it was formed in 1985. By 1993 Japan had established a special bilateral fund for SAARC to finance select programs while avoiding any political involvement.

This chapter begins with a very brief introduction to SAARC membership and its objectives. It then depicts what were Japanese interests and involvement in the region before SAARC was established and goes on to show how it has been deepening its commitment by contributing US$7 million to the SAARC Japan special fund which has been established to support the various infrastructure and transportation projects. However, besides economic support which is generally the Japanese practice in the SAARC forum, it is also encouraging the process of democratization in Nepal and Bhutan.

Despite the encouraging move, the chapter attempts to show how the speed and scale of Japanese economic involvement in SAARC is negligible to what can be seen in ASEAN region. With declining growth in China and especially with territorial disputes taking centre stage in the last two years, Japanese FDI is moving greatly into ASEAN and year 2013 marked the return of Japan to the ASEAN region. Japanese PM Abe has already visited the region five times, inclusive of stops in all 10 ASEAN countries.

Notwithstanding natural disasters, Japan is increasing focus on countries like the Philippines, Vietnam and Myanmar. While fighting to revive Japanese domestic economy out of long time recession through '*Abenomics*', Abe is also pulling a reluctant Japan through a dragging negotiation process into TPP agreement and urging Japanese FDI to take risks in investing in emerging ASEAN economies.

The Asian regional political and economic environment has undergone quite a visible change in the last twenty years. After consolidating its economic power Japan has improved its regional trade and investment linkages. The advance of globalization has increased the movement of trade, technology and capital resources notably in Asia-Pacific region. Its dynamism has provided East Asian countries with many opportunities to raise their level of productive efficiency and competitiveness and to participate more effectively in global as well as regional economy. Considering its economic stagnation in the last twenty odd years, currently widening trade deficits, and faced with present energy and regional geopolitical challenges, many scholars feel, Japan is not a model worth emulating today. Still, as world's third largest economic power Japan has technological and capital prowess to partner many developing countries in Asia and elsewhere.

South Asian countries were rather late in catching up and adopting a host of economic policies in order to develop a strong industrial, infrastructural and human resource base. The SAARC is supposed to provide a corrective course at least for policies and their implementation.

South Asia is endowed with a huge market and skilled human resource, a comparatively cheap work force and diversified resource base and as such provides a great opportunity for growth and development. However, the region has low per capita income and observable scarcity of infrastructural facility that have constrained potential for growth.

Commensurate with its economic might, Japan's international role has changed in the recent past and has been a catalyst for fast growth in East Asia, taking keen interest in its security structure. The East Asian and Southeast Asian experience reveal strong representation of Japan in their economies. It is only expected that a favorably disposed Japan could help ameliorate economic and political conditions in South Asia too, provided the SAARC countries sustain and advance the tempo of economic reforms. A regular and continuous political negotiation between South Asian countries and with Japan will pave the way for improved growth in SAARC countries.

Japan's economic relations with South Asia till recently focused around ODA and trade and investment. The ADB started lending to India in 1986 and Japan became the largest bilateral donor of the ODA to Bangladesh, India, Nepal, Pakistan and Sri Lanka in 1987. Despite ODA continuing to be important to these countries, investment also attained significance as they moved to industrialize. Japanese FDI is a channel through which capital and technology, management practices are also entering the South Asian region significantly. Though India has achieved considerable economic strides in the last several years, even more is expected of it as it has a vast unfulfilled development potential. Like India, other South Asian countries are also still waiting for the 'geese' (to be led by the 'leading goose Japan') to fly in their way. At the same time there is a need for South Asian countries to redefine their economic priorities.

South Asian countries currently present a stark image of contradictions; on the one hand there is a huge population living below poverty line and unemployed. On the other, it has immense opportunities for economic growth and expansion. South Asia needs the assistance from Japan to bring it closer to the development level of the ASEAN region. Unity among the SAARC member countries, a show of combined economic strength and efforts to improve prospects can further attract Japan into the region. Japanese strength lies in infrastructure technology and India alone has scope for US$ 1 trillion investments in the sector. Though desirable and welcome, Japan is not yet ready to enter simply without any advancement of economic reforms and quality of infrastructure in SAARC countries.

Japan–SAARC: History and Objectives

SAARC was established in 1985 that currently has following members—Afghanistan, Bangladesh, Bhutan, India, Maldives, Nepal, Pakistan, and Sri Lanka. Nine Observers are China, Japan, European Union, Republic of Korea, United States, Iran, Australia, Mauritius and Myanmar.[1] Requests from Turkey and Russia are pending. The purpose of SAARC is to seek promotion of the welfare of the people of South Asia, strengthen collective self-reliance, promote active collaboration and mutual assistance in various fields, and cooperate with international and regional organizations. SAARC countries represent just 1 percent of world trade and they also account for almost 30 per cent of world's population.[2]

The decision to expand its membership and provide Observer status to some of the extra-regional powers was with the view that these measures would make SAARC stronger and serve to make the association more dynamic and vibrant. Organizations like the European Union (EU) and the Association of Southeast Asian Nations (ASEAN) also have the practice of allowing countries and international organizations to attend their summit meetings as Observers. The process initiated by SAARC to associate extra-regional powers as Observers is being perceived as an act to enlarge its vision and opening itself to the outside world.

At the 14th summit, in April 2007, the Islamic Republic of Afghanistan was admitted as a full-fledged member of SAARC. China, Japan, European Union, Republic of Korea, United States of America, and Iran were allowed as Observers. "Regional cooperation in SAARC involving Iran can help in the development and democratization of Iran," opined Mitsuo Sakaba,[3] then director-general for press and public relations in Japan's ministry of foreign affairs. Admitting countries as Observers is perceived as an act of SAARC to enlarge its vision and opening itself to the outside world. Observers might contribute to the growth of economic cooperation among the member states and the organization; it can also lead to new power games. Sakaba also mentioned, "Japan is in favor of India playing a key role in invigorating SAARC. It is time for SAARC to strengthen its vision of bilateral ties." The main consideration in inviting Japan to any regional organization is the fact that it brings in investment, capital and technology. Japan has contributed an additional US$ 7 million to the 'SAARC-Japan Special Fund' for furthering social and cultural exchanges with South Asia while pledging support for improving regional connectivity.

In 2007, Japanese Foreign Minister Taro Aso had mentioned that 'the government of Japan shall cooperate more with SAARC to achieve better regional connectivity and is keen on supporting priority projects'. Japan also works together with the Asian Development Bank to improve transportation in the region and improve disaster management services. Besides, it stated its support to the democratization process in Nepal and Bhutan. In his address, Aso said that as part of the SAARC as Observer nation, Japan was advancing a new initiative to create an arc of freedom and prosperity.

Aso had also mentioned that 'when Japan's post-war economic miracle was yet to take shape, South Asia helped its people and India and Pakistan provided Japan with crucial materials like iron ore and raw cotton.' Further, Aso said "South Asia is a 'growth region' and a central pillar of the arc of advantage and prosperity emerging in Asia. 300 years ago, South Asia alone produced one fourth of the world's output. What is now unfolding is not a new rise but a great comeback of the region and the SAARC fully deserves the drama."

Japan's assistance to the region also includes support in disaster mitigation and earthquake prevention. Japan is also concerned about growing terrorism in the region and has advocated regional cooperation on this issue. Japan's support for Pakistan's efforts to combat terrorism and commitment of US$30 million for rural electrification in Nepal are also noticeable.

Till the late 1990s, Japan focused on multilateral negotiations as a means of opening up foreign markets to Japanese corporate interests. However, Japan is increasingly suffering the loss of market shares that FTAs between other countries produce. Until recently, Japan focused its bilateral negotiating agenda on a few countries around the Pacific. Major deals have been signed with Singapore (2002), Malaysia (2004), Mexico (2004), Philippines (2006), Indonesia (2007), Chile (2007), Thailand (2007), ASEAN as a whole (2008) and Vietnam (2008).

By mid-2006, Japan had announced the start of FTA talks with Brunei and these were wrapped up in 2008. Japan's deals with both Brunei and Indonesia are unique because they guarantee Tokyo access to oil and gas supplies. In mid-2006, Japan also proposed an overarching East Asian FTA encompassing Japan, ASEAN, India, China, Korea, Australia and New Zealand. The ASEAN, among others, gave this idea a cool response. In 2007, negotiations with India and Australia began, and efforts to bring in Colombia, China, Korea, Cambodia and Laos also continued.

Other countries that were creeping into Japan's bilateral trade agenda are:

- In early 2005, Japan started exploring the possibility of talks with Switzerland, and the actual negotiations started in 2007.
- Spurred by concerns about access to energy resources, Japan moved towards talks in 2006 for an FTA with Kuwait and other oil and gas-rich Gulf Cooperation Council (GCC) countries.
- There are also growing concerns about trade disadvantages for Japanese firms on a wider international scale, leading to FTA overtures towards Brazil, South Africa, New Zealand and even some wishful talk of a US-Japan deal.
- In late 2011, Japan showed interest in negotiating an FTA with Myanmar.
- In March 2012, there were indications of upcoming FTA talks with Mongolia and Canada.

Japan prefers to call these deals "Economic Partnership Agreements" (EPAs), though these deals are to quite an extent similar to FTAs but it engages in a broader spectrum.

Domestic opposition to FTAs has crystallized around the announcement that the Japanese government intends to join the Trans-Pacific Partnership (TPP). The years 2011, 2012 and 2013 have seen major demonstrations against the agreement by Japanese farmers, targeting the undermining of food security which agricultural liberalization under the proposed deal could bring about, especially in relation to rice. National Confederation of Trade Unions (*Zenroren*) also kept opposing the deal, with concerns about job losses, the opening up of the economy to US capital, and the erosion of living standards and working conditions. Many Japanese opponents view the TPP as being essentially a bilateral FTA with the US.

The Japanese government had suspended SAARC-Japan Special Fund in 2010 due to austerity measures, citing non-utilization of the fund as also the main reason. "Japan has suspended the assistance for the current fiscal year. The country has reduced its budget for external assistance this year and the suspension is a part of it."[4] Starting from the year 1993 the Japanese government has been providing around US$ 250,000 every year. The fund consists of two key components. One finances the selected programs and activities identified and managed by member states while the other component goes to programs and activities identified by the Japanese government itself.[5] SAARC has a greater affinity in terms of culture, language and, above all, poverty, but does not represent high level of mutual trust. India's Prime Minister Manmohan Singh echoed a similar view when he mentioned, 'despite the telecommunication connectivity, intra-trade and investments flow are far less compared with East and Southeast Asia."[6]

Comparisons with other regional groupings, specially the ASEAN are made often and the contrast with them highlighted. Geographically and therefore in geopolitics too the problem with SAARC is different from other regional associations. No single nation for example, large or otherwise, dominates Southeast Asia as does India in South Asia. The region also faces critical challenges from terrorism, extremism, narcotics and organized crime.

One can notice how SAARC leaders at the Thimpu summit even admitted to many of the region's shortcomings on cooperation and pledged to work together to achieve better outcomes and pursue mutual trust that has been lacking. Seven key initiatives were addressed at the summit:

- The need for SAARC to become truly action-oriented through implementing declarations and decisions and operating instruments to fulfill the hopes and aspirations of the people of the region.
- To form a 'South Asia Forum' for generating debate and exchange of ideas on South Asia and its future. The forum, comprising eminent personalities from diverse backgrounds, must function as a public-private partnership.
- To convene a 'Conclave of SAARC Parliamentarians' in line with the SAARC Charter.
- Initiate a process to formulate a common SAARC policy position for the Mexico–United Nations Conference on Climate Change in December to be held in Mexico that year.
- Have an action plan on energy conservation prepared by SAARC Energy Centre in Islamabad.

- Welcomed Bhutan's offer of a SAARC workshop on Gross National Happiness (GNH) that year—focusing on people-centric development in the region.
- Cooperate to root out terrorism and commit to addressing illegal trafficking in drugs, firearms and people.

Besides, the summit also adopted a 37-point 'Thimpu Silver Jubilee Declaration' and the 'Thimpu Statement on Climate Change'.

Bangladesh's call for the development of a regional power grid and harnessing renewable energy sources is one idea that ought to be dealt with on a priority basis. India went a step further with this view and stated that regional cooperation should mean an opportunity for a free movement of people, goods, services and ideas. Bhutan, then the new SAARC chair, put it bluntly at the summit: 'Some 200 meetings take place every year among SAARC countries but these meetings are not matched by results.'

Since the common threats countries face are connectivity, climate-related issues, poverty and militancy looms. SAARC needs to adapt to changing circumstances.

Japan and SAARC member states have decided to make efforts to promote public awareness on the need for regional energy cooperation and energy conservation. It was recommended that Japan and SAARC member states should expedite energy cooperation in SAARC region through active participation of Japan and SAARC member states. SAARC member states may expect to make use of the technical assistance from bilateral and multilateral sources for capacity building, technology transfer, energy efficiency and specific project formulation.

It was decided that SAARC member states should mutually share information on their own progress, technical know-how, identify their needs, barriers and possible solutions. Priority areas of energy cooperation in the SAARC region may include energy infrastructure development, regional trade of energy, sharing of hydroelectric resources and demand side management including sharing and promoting efficient and cleaner energy technologies, promotion of renewable sources of energy and human resource development.

Japan ASEAN China Triangle

ASEAN countries are major FDI destinations for Japanese business corporations. They established close business partnerships with a total bilateral trade of around US$ 250 billion in 2011.

The year 2013 was the 40th anniversary of ASEAN-Japan Dialogue relations and celebration of commemorative activities was held throughout

2013. Japan and ASEAN have forged close cooperation towards peace, stability, development and prosperity in Asia.[7]

Due to domestic economic slowdown, Japan is experiencing 'industrial hollowing out' since quite some time and many Japanese enterprises are bound for ASEAN region and China as well, to intensify trade and business. For instance, Malaysia is seen as an attractive FDI destination, with a well developed infrastructure and abundant natural resources, Japan-friendly people and an important 'stepping stone' providing easy access to rest of the Asian market.

Due to bilateral political issues with China, especially in the last two years, Japan is attempting to reduce its dependence on China and diversify its economic interaction with the ASEAN regional grouping which it finds inherent to good trade and business potentials. In addition to modern infrastructure, a pro-business government and an equally pro-business work force, Japanese companies are equally impressed with the high level of positive perceptions about Japan. Most surveys indicate that 'Japan is viewed favorably by ASEAN member countries in contrast to the negative sentiments against Japan in China.[8]

Japan has returned to the ASEAN region in a significant way in 2013. By the end of 2013, Abe had already visited Southeast Asia five times including stops in all 10 ASEAN countries. No doubt Japan's renewed interest in the region is driven by its island dispute with China. Interest in the Philippines and Myanmar may be seen as Japan seeks to distance itself from China. Abe is particularly urging Japanese FDI to take risk in investing in emerging ASEAN economies.

In 2012 Japan invested US$6.4 billion into ASEAN mainly in Singapore, Thailand, Malaysia, Vietnam and the Philippines. The value of M&A pursued by Japanese companies in 2013 has hit US$8.2 billion. A weaker yen is also prompting Japanese outward investment. Japanese Bankers are buying into insurers in the region. Mitsubishi UFJ launched a bid for majority stake in Bank of Ayudhaya in Thailand. A Japanese financial consortium won a contract in May to build a metro system in Jakarta.

The presence of Japan's trading companies in ASEAN though not new, now SMEs are also becoming part of the trend. Such Japanese engagement with ASEAN now comes with solid political backing. However, even with all this it is not likely to be easy for Japan due to competition from China.

Small and medium businesses from Japan have begun to invest heavily in Southeast Asia. Previously they focused their investment on China, but after relations worsened between the two countries over islands in the East China Sea, Japanese firms are looking to ASEAN region for added opportunities.

Leaders from China and Japan have recently visited Southeast Asian nations with increasing frequency, highlighting their competing interests in the region.

Large enterprises have actively built up industrial zones and strengthened infrastructure enabling Japanese small businesses find their feet in the Southeast Asian market as well. In 2012, Japan invested US$ 6.4 billion in ASEAN, mainly in Singapore, Indonesia, Thailand, Vietnam and the Philippines. In the first half of 2013, Japanese investments in Southeast Asia jumped 55.4 per cent compared to a year earlier with a value more than doubling their investments in China. In the first eight months of 2013, Japanese mergers and acquisitions in Southeast Asia totaled US$ 7.9 billion, 13 times the figure for the same period in 2012, touching a new record.

Chinese enterprises are also actively seeking opportunities in Southeast Asia in the meantime, with some already investing in infrastructure projects. In Southeast Asia, Chinese enterprises are competing directly with Japanese firms in terms of railway construction and will face rising competition with Korean businesses in building highways.

China confidently declares that its economic ties with Southeast Asia and influence on people there will exceed Japan's. China has advantages in the region as its market share in the Asia-Pacific region and the potential of its future economic development are seen as bringing benefits for its neighboring countries.[9] However, two nations that are visibly excluded from China's focus are the Philippines and Japan. Beijing continues to have tensions with them and has rejected all overtures from the leaders of both those countries.

China continues to have tensions with the Philippines and Japan while improving relations with other countries, even those with whom it maintains territorial disputes such as Vietnam and India.[10] Deteriorating political relationship between Japan and China is reflected in redirecting of the Japanese investment. JFDI in the first half of 2013 simply quadrupled to more than US$10.29 billion. But in China it fell by 31 per cent to US$5 billion. China may be missing out on the new wave of Japanese FDI.

Japan turned to Southeast Asia for manufacturing since the 1960s but looked increasingly to China in the 1990s. But since last year Japanese FDI in China began to decline. Today, ASEAN and Japan are twin engines; ASEAN will plan an enormously important role for the Japanese economy.[11]

Japan-India

Since Japan–SAARC relations are pivoted by Japan–India relations it therefore requires a scrutiny, to enable understanding of how the future of Japan–SAARC relations will emerge.

India, Japan and the US will explore the possibility of pooling their strengths in the area of development assistance to work together in Africa, Afghanistan and Myanmar. This was decided at the third meeting among the three countries in New Delhi in November 2013. The three nations "shared their strategic overviews over the Asia-Pacific region"—a reference to the maritime tensions among countries in East and South East Asia due to overlapping claims over island chains in the area and the rise of China.

India and Japan have agreed for an early resumption of negotiations for civil nuclear cooperation and hope for an early conclusion of agreement. Japan also has expanded the bilateral currency swap arrangement to US$50 billion; talks on introducing high speed railway system in India, the progressing Delhi-Mumbai Freight Corridor, Delhi-Mumbai Industrial Corridor and Chennai-Bangalore Industrial Corridor, progress in defense and security cooperation even in maritime security and counter terrorism—all augur well in the expanding bilateral framework.

Trade, ODA and Investment

In 2012-13, India-Japan bilateral trade touched US$ 18.6 billion. Indian exports to Japan were at US$ 6 billion, and imports at US$ 12.5 billion. In effect, India's exports and deficit were nearly equal. As of March 2013, cumulative commitment of ODA was Yen 3807 billion. Comprehensive Economic Partnership Agreement (CEPA) is in force since August 2011 and covers such areas as trade in goods and services, investments, intellectual property rights, and customs procedures. The goal of the CEPA is to abolish tariffs over 94 per cent items bilaterally traded over a period of next ten years.

Tension in East Asia

India has not officially commented on the rising tensions between China and Japan, whereas China "viewed the visit of Their Majesty, the Emperor and Empress of Japan and recently warming India-Japan ties as favorable to regional stability." Tensions are on the rise in the East Asian region since China declared a new Air Defense Identification Zone last year. The brewing tensions may persist with U.S. dispatching two B-52 bombers to fly through without information to China. If Japan and China had successfully managed the territorial problems, it would have added to the economic gains accrued hitherto but when the diplomatic mechanism collapsed all of a sudden then it highlighted failure of diplomatic and crisis management instruments.

The conflict threatens to accelerate Japan's slow but sure military buildup. Japan considers that its military must be capable of countering any threat to its territorial integrity. Its navy already has one of the strongest fleets in the world, despite constitutional restrictions on military expenditure and capabilities.

ASEAN member countries together with Japan, China, South Korea, India, Australia and New Zealand are creating a partnership of 16 countries. This will represent about US $ 20 trillion GDP; i.e. 30 per cent of the global total and a population of 3.4 billion.[12] As such, activities of Japan, China and South Korea will also draw attention.

Unlike ASEAN, India is more than reasonably convinced that it need not get involved in East Asian regional tensions. In the backdrop of India's own problems with China, avoidance of identification as a member in anti-China camp is the need of the day since an insecure China is certainly not in India's future security interests.

Changing Environment: Focus on SAARC

The New Element

As Japan's power gets eclipsed by China, it needs friends and allies beyond just the US. In a way Abe is overseeing an unprecedented expansion in ties with Southeast Asia as a counterbalance. He is building Japan's economic links with the region by developing and firming up security relationships, offering coast-guard vessels to the Philippines, conducting counter terrorism exercises with Indonesia and considering a provision of ships to Vietnam. Abe is now helping the region in the defense area as well instead of just focusing on economic ties.

Japan's "Great Exodus"

The graph below reflects "The Great Exodus" of capital from Japan since 1990. When the Japanese economy burst in 1990, Japan ceased to attract investment at the rate it had historically attracted investment capital post-WWII. Japan's bubble economy came to a halt during 1990, while short-term interest rates lowered from 5 per cent to 2.5 per cent. The subsequent rise of short-term interest rates from 2.5 per cent to 6 per cent by 1991 brought an end to a great run for the Japanese economy.

As reflected above, the sun began to set on Japan's economy the day the Bank of Japan began to raise interest rates in 1990. Short-term interest rates have remained near 0 per cent since 1996. The graph below reflects what has happened with regard to the decline in investment in Japan since 1990.

When the Liberal Democratic Party resumed power in late 2012 under Abe's leadership, as one of his first policy directions, he came up with three arrows giving economic direction for fighting recession and to help induce

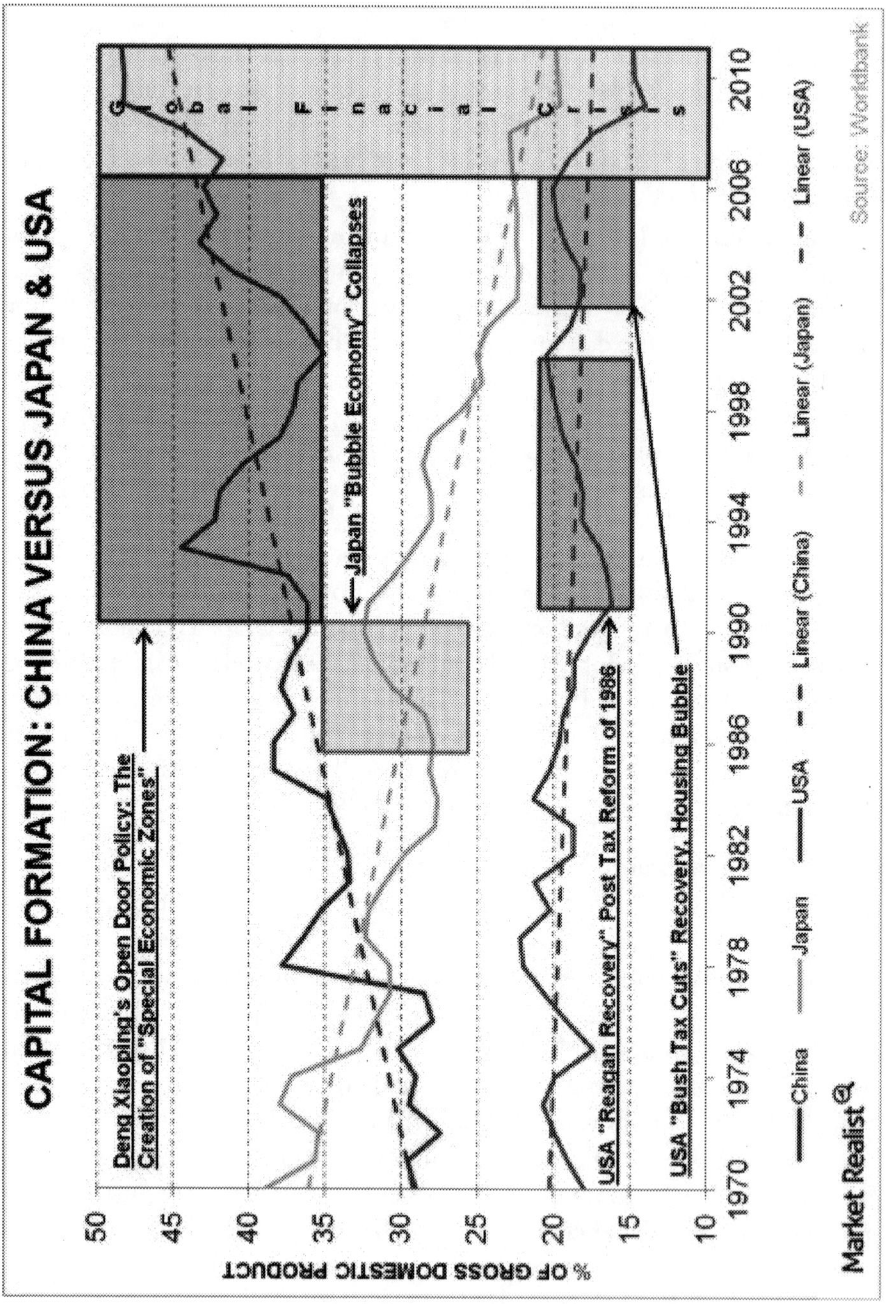
CAPITAL FORMATION: CHINA VERSUS JAPAN & USA
% OF GROSS DOMESTIC PRODUCT
Deng Xiaoping's Open Door Policy: The Creation of "Special Economic Zones"
Japan "Bubble Economy" Collapses
USA "Reagan Recovery" Post Tax Reform of 1986
USA "Bush Tax Cuts" Recovery, Housing Bubble
Global Financial Crisis
50
45
40
35
30
25
20
15
10
1970
1974
1978
1982
1986
1990
1994
1998
2002
2006
2010
China
Japan
USA
Linear (China)
Linear (Japan)
Linear (USA)
Market Realist
Source: Worldbank

recovery. These policies, known as "*Abenomics*," will attempt to encourage private investment through a more aggressive mix of monetary and fiscal policy. "*Abenomics*" aims to end deflation by targeting a 2 per cent inflation rate, as well as to increase fiscal spending by 2 per cent of gross domestic product.[13]

A growing number of Japanese companies have moved some of their headquarters or key functions to Singapore, viewing the city-state as a strategic location where they can oversee a new wave of investment in Southeast Asia. With the rise of Asia, companies have "increasingly relocated their senior decision makers to Singapore. Observers say the trend accelerated after the devastating earthquake and tsunami that hit Japan in March 2012 and awakened Japanese companies to the need to diversify their operations to reduce future risks. JETRO President Hidehiro Yokoo said at a forum in Singapore recently that Japanese foreign direct investment in Southeast Asia has exceeded Japanese investment in China in recent years."We can see the new trend of Japanese FDI to ASEAN," he said, citing increased Japanese corporate interest in countries in regional emerging countries.[14]

The advantages often cited for investing in Singapore are its strategic geographical location, an efficient infrastructure such as Internet connectivity, and one of the world's busiest seaports. Another factor is the government's pro-business policies, such as competitive taxes.

Singapore has been slashing its corporate tax rate in recent years and at 17 percent has one of the lowest tax rates in Asia. Japan's corporate tax rate is 30 percent. Singapore also has a flexible immigration policy that makes it easier for companies to recruit staff from all over the world, while a bilingual education policy has ensured a workforce that can speak not only English but also Chinese and other local languages.

Japan's small and midsize enterprises are also moving their headquarters from Japan to Singapore."While the growth of the Chinese market is slowing, on the contrary some Asian countries such as Indonesia or Myanmar are growing, and Singapore is an ideal hub to enter these neighboring markets," Yoshikawa said.

Resurgent Japan

Japan is still the third largest economy in the world with a combined GDP of France, Italy, Spain, and Portugal. Its industries have the competence to challenge the US, European and Korean manufacturers. *Abenomics* is a promising program with its 3 arrows of radical economic policy – monetary expansion, fiscal stimulus and structure reform. By late 2013, structural reforms in labor regulation, corporate governance, competition policy and pension management were slowing. Increased consumption tax from April 2014 threatens hopes of economic acceleration in 2014 and 2015.

Consumption tax rise from 5 per cent to 8 per cent from April 2014 and again in October 2015 to 10 per cent impacts a fiscal tightening worth about 2.5 per cent of GDP in 2014 with another 1 per cent in 2015 according to IMF. As per official forecasts, such squeeze will cut Japan's economic growth from 2.5 per cent in 2013 to 1.4 per cent in 2014.

Hopes relate to increase in wage, bonus and seniority payments. Additional public works spending may be in line for a 5 trillion yen increase, and further supplementary budgets are likely if growth suffers after consumption tax hike. Scope for boosting consumer confidence and domestic demand is limited. Hence, the last resort could be aggressive monetary expansion but it is still not clear that simply expanding bond purchases would have much effect on growth.

It appears that Japan lacks any convincing options and hope alone is not a strategy. Abe agrees that "deregulation is the first and foremost core of growth strategies" but moves too slowly in implementing it. The key for Abe now will be nailing down the tax incentives to boost domestic business and specifying areas of deregulation. The third arrow of *Abenomics* comprises the following: (a) Strategic special zones will be set up to promote deregulation. (b) Electricity-related investment will be raised to ¥30 trillion within 10 years. (c) The scale of infrastructure projects through public-private partnerships and private finance initiatives will be expanded to ¥12 trillion within 10 years. (d) The government will raise the per-capita gross national income by ¥1.5 million within 10 years.[15]

Japan also has accumulated a huge public debt, which at more than double the GDP, is proportionately the world's largest, and the future of the world's third-largest economy rests on tackling it.[16] Japan logged a record trade deficit of ¥8.17 trillion in fiscal 2012, the second straight year of red ink, as a territorial spat with China and the European debt crisis stifled exports, with energy imports surging due to the halt of nuclear power plants. It was the first time that the trade balance has remained in deficit for two years in a row since 1980. Some pundits blame the slowdown in the US and Chinese economies, while others warn that Abe's run of success might have come to an end. Notwithstanding these, in an era of declining ODA budget due to domestic constraints, Japan's engagement with emerging economies and regions continue but with its own ambiguous pace.[17]

Conclusion

Though India is at the centre stage of SAARC it is affected by developments occurring around it in the region. Regional cooperation among the SAARC countries must improve in all sectors. Absence of regional symmetry, trust deficit among member countries, multiple bilateral disputes, plethora of bureaucratic hurdles, no reforms or slow reforms in land acquisition and tax regime add up to negative factors. However, a rising middle class, increasing domestic demand and a huge market provide great opportunity to Japanese manufacturers and investors. It is no time to rest on the laurels of verifiable achievements so far, instead there is need to strive more to reach advanced level of reforms.

By the of 2014, Japan is likely to revise its ODA Charter (created in 1992 and revised in 2003) to further help Japanese firms to perform better business overseas and serve Japan's security. In 2013, Japan has disbursed US$ 10.60 billion ODA in all, of which Vietnam received US$ 1.64 billion, Afghanistan US$ 873 million, India US$ 740 million, and Iraq US$ 360 million.[18]

Emphasis on the centrality of ODA flow in the future development of Japan-South Asia relations should continue as well as Japan's support for revitalizing SAARC activities needs to be maintained. Besides, various connectivity, introduction of a ferry service between India, Sri Lanka, Maldives as also a container train between India, Nepal and Bangladesh and be helped by Japan technologically. Exchange and interaction in the educational sector needs to multiply immediately. As Japan's economic diplomacy is carried out at bilateral and regional as well as multilateral forums at the same time, SAARC cannot afford to ignore levels of Japan-ASEAN economic integration but work to convince Japan of its intent to improve ties in the region, achieve better quality reforms in all member countries and also meet some of their demands. Pressed with increasing energy demand in Japan post-Fukushima closure of nuclear plants and ever increasing LNG and related energy imports, declining exports, increasing trade deficits, Japan is looking for opportunities outside and it is time that SAARC countries introspect and re-launch focused relations with Japan.

Rising wages and labor shortages in China's coastal regions have caused a 'China risk' and hence Japanese investment from China is moving increasingly to ASEAN counties. Therefore, SAARC needs to address the above challenges to lure Japanese investments to its own region. As cloud hangs over Abe's East Asian diplomacy with no prospects of holding immediate meetings with Chinese and South Korean leadership, all Japanese interactions with the SAARC countries need to be encouraged.

END NOTES

1. Iran's presence in SAARC as an observer state may cause some embarrassment to EU and the United States who sit in the SAARC as observer states.
2. http://ictsd.org/i/news/bridgesweekly/94912/#sthash.Tc19LvnE.dpuf
3. Japan says SAARC link can help in democratizing Iran, Manish Chand, IANS, New Delhi, April 04, 2007
4. Japan stops SAARC aid, *Kathamandu Post*, 11 October 2010.
5. 10 years ago: Japan suspends special SAARC fund, *The Hindustan Times*, 29.09.2013.
6. Mahendra Ved, South Asian Cooperation – SAARC can do better, May 20, 2010. http://www.eastasiaforum.org/2010/05/20/south-asian-cooperation-saarc-can-do-better/
7. http://www.mofa.go.jp/region/asia-paci/asean/relation/ja40/
8. Malaysia-stands-to-benefit-from-Japans-shift-from-China-to-ASEAN http://www.thestar.com.my/Business/Business-News/2013/10/30/.aspx
9. The Battle for Influence in Southeast Asia. http://www.wantchinatimes.com/news-subclass-cnt.aspx
10. Japan China Why is China Isolating Japan and the Philippines? *The Diplomat*, Oct 27 2013
11. This can be gleaned from Abe visit to Singapore in July 2013 .Are we seeing the end of Japan's 30-year investment collapse? (Part 1) By Marc Wiersum,
12. www.jri.co.jp/file/english/periodical/asia/2013/3/12/contents.pdf
13. Are we seeing the end of Japan's 30-year investment collapse? (Part 1) http://marketrealist.com/2013/09/japan-series-1-b-investment-abenomics(Marc Wiersum, Capital investment in Japan.
14. Siti Rahl, Kyodo, More Japanese firms relocating to Singapore, *The Japan Times*, Aug. 14, 2012.
15. Jun Hongo and Reiji Yoshida, Abe's Growth Strategy Hit for Lack of Details, *Japan Times*, Jun 6, 2013.
16. http://www.google.com/hostednews/afp/article/july2013
17. Record trade deficit in 2012 Kyodo, *The Japan Times*, Apr 19, 2013 and Record trade deficit logged in fiscal 2012, *The Daily Yomiuri*, April 19, 2013.
18. *Kyodo International News*, 28 March 2014.

REFERENCES

Anatole Kaletsky, Japan as the Crisis Next Time, cnbc.com/id/101505329

David Flath, The Japanese Economy, Oxford University Press, 2005.

Robert J Barro and Xavier Sala-i-Martin, Economic Growth, McGraw-Hill, 1995.

Juro Teranishi and Yutaka Kosai, The Japanese Experience of Economic Reforms, St Martins Press, New York, 1993.

David Weinstein, "Foreign Direct Investment and Keiretsu: US and Japanese Policy" in Robert C Feenstra (ed) The Effects of Trade Protection and Promotion Policies, university of Chicago Press, Chicago, 1996.

ESCAP, Expansion of Trade and investment in ESCAP Developing Countries within a Regional Framework, Published for the United Nations, 1992.

Committee on Studies for Cooperation in South Asia; Trade Expansion in South Asia: Liberalization and Mechanisms, ed by V. Kanesalingam and A R Kemal, Macmilan, 1990.

Geoffrey Shepherd and Carlos Geraldo Langoni, Lessons from Eight Countries, International Centre for Economic Growth, San Fransacisco, 1991.

Wadhwa, Charan, Economic cooperation among countries of ASEAN and SAARC. Chapter 4 in Commodities, Complementarities and Cooperation, ed by Prem Vashishtha, ADIPA, Kaula Lumpur, 1989.

World Bank, Global Economic Prospects and Developing Countries, World Bank, Washington D.C., 1992.

Inoguchi Takashi, Japan's Role in International Affairs, Survival IISS Quarterly London Summer 1992.

Nagesh Kumar, 'Liberalization and Japanese FDI in India' in Building a Global Partenrrship: 50 years of India-Japan Relationship, ed. K V Kesavan, Lancers Book, New Delhi, 2002.

http://ictsd.org/i/news/bridgesweekly/94912/#sthash.Tc19LvnE.dpuf).

Rashid Ahmad Khan, The Role of Observers in SAARC, *IPRI Journal*, Vol. IX, no.2 (Summer 2009): 1-16.

THT 10 YEARS AGO: Japan suspends special SAARC fund 2013-09-29).

Mahendra Ved, South Asian Cooperation – SAARC can do better, May 20, 2010.

http://www.eastasiaforum.org/2010/05/20/south-asian-cooperation-saarc-can-do-better/

Japan, SAARC members agree to overcome energy crisis, June 12, 2008.

http://www.dailytimes.com.pk/default.asp?page=2008\06\12\story_12-6-2008_pg 5_9

http://www.mofa.go.jp/region/asia-paci/asean/relation/ja40/

http://www.thestar.com.my/Business/Business-News/2013/10/30/Malaysia

http://www.thestar.com.my/Business/Business-News/2013/10/30/MALAYSIA-STANDS-TO-BENEFIT-FROM-JAPANS-SHIFT-FROM-CHINA-TO-ASEAN.aspx

http://www.wantchinatimes.com/news-subclass-cnt.aspx?cid=1202&MainCatID=12&id=20131025000041

Japan China Why is China Isolating Japan and the Philippines?, *The Diplomat*, Oct 27 2013.

Abe in July 2013 during visit to Singapore.

http://ictsd.org/i/news/bridgesweekly/94912/#sthash.Tc19LvnE.dpuf

Japan shows keen interest in joining SAARC. http://dawn.com/news/109317/japan-shows-keen-interest-in-joining-saarc

Japan, SAARC members agree to overcome energy crisis, June 12, 2008.

http://www.dailytimes.com.pk/default.asp?page=2008\06\12\story_12-6-2008_pg5_9)

Jun Hongo and Reiji Yoshida Abe's growth strategy hit for lack of details, Japan Times Jun 6, 2013.

Strong yen may force further shift abroad | The Japan Times. www.japantimes.co.jp/news/.../strong-yen-may-force-further-shift-abroad/, 15 Jul 2013.

Japan Alarmed Over Strong Yen | The Moscow Times. www.themoscowtimes.com/news/...strong-yen/340837.

5

Perspectives on 'China's Engagement with SAARC' in India

Alka Acharya

Introduction

Well until the turn of the century, the official Indian position regarding China's engagement and/or involvement in South Asia, as also the regional organization SAARC, has been at best, somewhat mixed and at the other extreme, fundamentally opposed. Two decades after the SAARC came into existence, and after a fairly public division of opinion within it, the 13th SAARC Summit Declaration in 2005 approved the incorporation of countries as also regional and international Organizations as 'Observers'. The first two countries to be accorded "Observer Status" were the PRC and Japan (SAARC Website). As yet India has not taken a positive stand on the question of China's membership and its deeper role in SAARC. India's objections stem not only from the fact that it considers the PRC to be an extra-regional power, but more critically, from the history of China's engagement with the individual SAARC countries in the aftermath of the Sino-Indian border conflict of 1962. In other words, we need to make a distinction between China's long-standing bilateral engagement with all the countries that constitute the SAARC, all of which are India's immediate neighbors, and the interest evinced/attempts made on the part of the PRC to engage with SAARC as a regional organization since the last decade of the 20th century. The former, that is to say, the history of China's bilateral relationships, has played a significant role in shaping both the domestic discourse as also the official position in India, about China's engagement with SAARC. Since the beginning of the 21st century, the matter has acquired greater complexity as we witness the phenomenon of the 'rise of China' – an economic ascendancy on the world stage, as remarkable for its speed as for its structural implications for international relations and the globalizing world. Even as the world debates the ramifications, there is a clear divergence in South Asia, and within SAARC, as to the opportunities and challenges presented by this rise. While Pakistan, Bangladesh, Nepal and Sri Lanka have been extremely vocal in favor of China's membership of SAARC, India (supported by Bhutan) has made its opposition fairly evident while Maldives has in recent years also begun to argue in favor of the matter.

SAARC—Nature and Characteristics

However, there are some fundamental conceptual questions that must be first addressed and comprehended. These pertain to the region itself and the specific features of regionalism in South Asia, which is in marked contrast to the regionalism that we see elsewhere. It is instructive to bear in mind that compared to other Asian or African regions, SAARC came into being almost two decades after ASEAN and a decade after the establishment of the West African Economic Community in 1975. As a regional organization, SAARC in fact stands out in almost all the indicators—political, economic and social—as an extremely rudimentary one. In addition, we have other problematic features which characterize SAARC—it is by far the most conflict-prone, criss-crossed by separatist groupings, wracked by terrorism and has some of the worst poverty and human development indices in critical aspects such as infant and maternal mortality, education and health etc. Historical factors as well have shaped the fissures and bilateral tensions within the region.[1] Insofar as trade is concerned, in 2012, only 4.23 per cent of the total trade was intraregional—compared to nearly 25 per cent in ASEAN – and the trend since 2005 is a declining one (Asian Regional Integration Centre).As we look at China's role and objectives, we need therefore to bear in mind these complex issues regarding SAARC itself.

Secondly, the dominance of India in the subcontinent – in territorial, as well as other aspects, viz, comprising 74 per cent of the population, 76 per cent of the GNP and 64 per cent of the export trade – makes the regional scenario highly asymmetrical. All of the SAARC countries share a border with India (Maldives and Sri Lanka share maritime borders with India) but not with each other. These facts are often seen as fairly insurmountable barriers to regionalism, in that the distribution of all elements of power is completely skewed in India's favor. But even asymmetry, according to the Interdependency theorists, does not, or at any rate, should not disturb the logic of interdependence. Even if the other states are more dependent on India, the logic of interdependence is stronger for them. The larger player is then constrained to that extent. A cursory look appears to indicate that the SAARC experience does not bear out the fundamental thesis of Interdependency.

China, India and South Asia

China's engagement with South Asia has undergone two major shifts. In the immediate aftermath of the emergence of the PRC, it was India's centrality in the region and the primacy of the Sino-Indian relationship, which was the dominant feature of the regional scenario. The 1962 border conflict between the two Asian giants however, punctured the possibilities of the Sino-Indian script that "independent" India and "liberated" China's leaders had visualized. Since then, China's 'enduring entente' with Pakistan, and its transfer of military (civilian and nuclear) technology and equipment to Pakistan, transformed the regional geopolitics. China was increasingly seen by other South Asian states as a useful countervailing power. It is evident that China has been a factor in India's relationships with its neighbors as well as in its SAARC policy. Equally, not many would contest the fact that for nearly two decades after the 1962 conflict, India was a factor in China's relationships with the other countries in South Asia, with security being the chief concern. There was no coherent regional strategy of the PRC through the 1970s–studies, supported by official pronouncements have established that well into the 1980s, bilateralism was the PRC's preferred foreign policy plank (Shambaugh: 2005). China's policies appeared to primarily take advantage of the tensions between India and its immediate neighbors – indeed they were interpreted and understood as such in India. This was an important factor in shaping India's opposition to China's role in the subcontinent.

With the consolidation of power by Deng Xiaoping in late 1979, began a period of domestic economic reforms intended to promote modernization and development. The counterpart was an independent foreign policy of peace and development which comprised steering clear of any alignments or alliances, promoting a peaceful and stable external environment and establishing friendly relations with all countries, especially the neighboring states. The post-Mao ruling elite laid great emphasis on stability – both internal and external – to pursue its domestic socio-economic growth, and to construct economic bridges, both to its peripheral environment and the world beyond. It still constitutes the pivot on which China's domestic and external policies rest (Shambaugh, 2005; Sutter, 2005). The process of change and adaptation gathered momentum over the eighties as China devoted all its energies to achieve its strategic objective of "comprehensive national power". By the end of the 1990s, China had further stabilized its policy towards South Asia and India-China relations started to acquire less conflictual and less antagonistic character (For a detailed analysis see Acharya, 2008). This turnaround has been the critical factor in the gradual, but clear movement in the strategic and security perceptions within India, regarding China and its role in South Asia.

Shambaugh's study on the changing dynamics in Asia since the last decade of the twentieth century has identified "four pillars" on which China's "regional posture" is founded: "(1) participation in Regional Organizations; (2) establishment of strategic partnerships and deepening of bilateral relations; (3) expansion of regional economic ties; and (4) reduction of distrust and anxiety in the security sphere." (Shambaugh, 2005:72).China's strategy in South Asia has also seen a systematic utilization of these "pillars"—though not in that order. With the fourth pillar however, China has been unable to make similar impressive strides and it is possible to argue that the first pillar has not achieved the desired levels of engagement largely due to the problems with respect to the fourth pillar.

A quick glance at the profile of China's relationships and specific agreements with the South Asian countries will provide a better understanding of the undercurrents and dynamics at play, which have a bearing on the China-SAARC issue. As mentioned earlier, the India-China relationship has begun to re-acquire the centrality that it had in the early years when both countries had begun to engage with each other as independent nation states. An incremental, but no less significant transformation has come about from the post-1962 period, which was marked by a lot of tension and uncertainty, as also a great deal of mistrust, to a phase in which the areas of conflict and dispute are gradually being mediated through the establishment of a range of important mechanisms and landmark official agreements since 1993. Trade is at an all-time high. Both countries are now cooperating more intensively on global issues and deepening bilateral ties. The possibilities—and necessity—of a substantial India-China partnership in Asia are consistently reiterated at the highest levels of leadership in both countries.

But the scenario is more complex – there are layers of strategic competition and distrust[2] that leaven the macro-picture of the India-China tapestry—which at times tends to take on acrimonious and contentious hues. And as we bring in the discourse of a 'rising' India, the competitive dynamics tend to get underscored—most significantly in the realm of regional ambitions.

China's activities in India's neighborhood, particularly those which have a bearing on security issues and which have the potential to effect a transformation in strategic terms, have raised even more unease within the security establishment in India. China's construction of the Chittagong port (Bangladesh), which directly borders the northeast region of India;[3] the Hambantota Deep Sea port (Sri Lanka) and the Gwadar Port (Pakistan) has only added more grist to the mill, viz the much-bandied formulation of the 'String of Pearls', which evokes fears of being encircled by China (Pehrson, 2009; Bajaj, 2010). This is however a matter of perception and persuasion—

and reflects the intensity with which suspicions are nurtured in this regard. Analysts have pointed out that China's economic and commercial interests as also its drive for energy security have underpinned the construction of these ports. (Kostecka, 2010)

Similarly, China's infrastructure projects as also the investment in multiple hydropower plants in Nepal raise Indian misgivings, but which can be viewed in the context of the second and third pillars of China's regional strategy. Additionally, in the case of Nepal, the issue of Tibetan refugees and China's interest in securing a favorable Nepalese response with regard to the stance vis-à-vis these refugees is a compelling argument for deepening its ties with Nepal.[4] It is thus possible to argue that what we are witnessing here is the fusion of economic and strategic objectives. A study referred to earlier has highlighted the manner in which China has combined its investments and trade (which are high on economic returns) with the other smaller soft-power oriented projects such as stadiums, bridges, convention centres, theatres etc, which do not have any economic returns, but are designed to "curry favor" with the respective governments (Brunjes et al, 2013: 31-32) A beneficial fallout can also be the positive influence on the people at large in these countries.

China-South Asia: Economic Dimension

In less than a decade since the turn of the century, China's economic profile in South Asia changed dramatically – from a total of around US $20 billion in 2004, trade figures doubled to nearly US $90 billion by 2010-11 (Asian Regional Integration Centre). There was an even sharper rise in investment, from approximately US $500 million in 2005 to nearly $3billion by 2010-11. In addition, China has begun to invest in these countries and had taken up infrastructure projects in the countries of South Asia – all of which has certainly contributed to employment and growth. While it may be conceded that China took up these massive infrastructure projects as part of larger diplomatic and strategic objectives, there is no gainsaying that these are economically extremely profitable ventures as well. Recent studies show that "economic profit" as also China's "goal to rise in prominence in international affairs", more than any specific attempt to counter-balance India's influence in South Asia, appears to be China's primary motive for increasing involvement in South Asia (Brunjes et al, 2013: ix). The study highlights the six-fold increase in China-South Asia trade between 2003 and 2011, whereas there was only a four-fold increase of China world trade volume in the same time period. (Ibid) The pie-charts below illustrate this impressive trajectory.

Graph 1: China-South Asia Trade Growth % from Previous Year (2004)

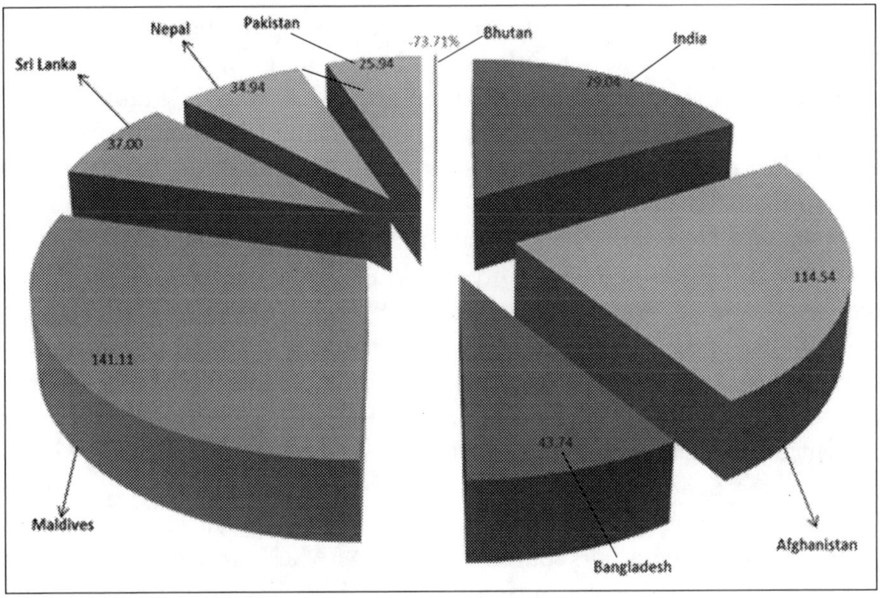

Graph 2: China-South Asia Trade Growth % from Previous Year (2011)

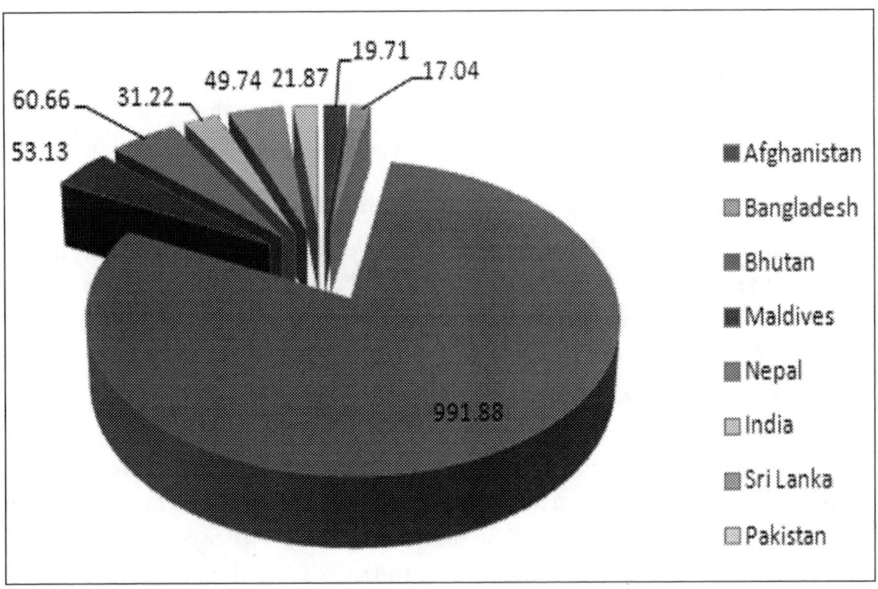

Source: *Asian Regional Integration Centre: Tracking Asian Integration*, Asian Development Bank. Source: IMF Directions of Trade Statistics. Available at http://aric.adb.org/integrationindicators/result?sort=country&filter=all

China's Bid for SAARC Membership

Since the mid-1990s, the PRC had been expressing its interest in SAARC. During his official visit to South Asia in November 1996, the then President Jiang Zemin in a speech to the Pakistani Senate had voiced China's approval of the role of SAARC in promoting regional stability. "...(we) are pleased to see the heartening progress made by the South Asian countries in recent years in improving their relations with one another and strengthening regional cooperation. The South Asian Association for Regional Cooperation (SAARC) has played a meaningful role in promoting peace, stability and economic cooperation in the region." (Jiang Zemin, 1996). From the turn of the century, the PRC stepped up its campaign to pave the way for a deeper engagement with SAARC. Several ministerial-level joint communiqués with different South Asian countries incorporated China's interest in multilateral platforms to enhance cooperation and development in South Asia. On 27 March 2007, shortly before the departure of the Chinese foreign minister Li Zhaoxing to participate in the 14th SAARC Summit, the spokesman for the Chinese Ministry of Foreign Affairs commented that "SAARC is an important regional cooperation organization in South Asia. China has been following and supporting the cooperation process of SAARC. Not long ago, China was accepted as an Observer of SAARC in light of the principles of equality, mutual benefit, and win-win cooperation with a view to making positive contributions to the cooperation, development and prosperity of South Asia." (Ministry of Foreign Affairs, 2007). Li Zhaoxing, in his address to the leaders of the South Asian countries at that summit, underscored China's interest in SAARC in terms of "...the fundamental objective of China's policy towards South Asia (as being) stability, development and good neighborly relations." (As cited in Su, 2007). Subsequently, in his inaugural speech at the 2008 Beijing Olympics, President Hu Jintao declared that, "China is ready to conduct equal dialogue and pragmatic cooperation with SAARC based on the spirit of equality, mutual trust and win-win cooperation and play a constructive role in pushing forward the SAARC cooperation process." (As cited in Saez, 2011: 39)

Even as China was making systematic overtures in its bid to achieve membership, the larger Asian dynamics after 2005 were being altered by some changes in China's regional posture, in terms of a more assertive foreign policy stance, especially with regard to the territorial and maritime disputes in the South China Seas (Johnson, 2013; Suettinger, 2004; Keller & Rawski, 2007). After the successful South Asian tour in 2005 of the then Chinese Premier Wen Jiabao, due to a variety of factors, the Sino-Indian relationship also ran into some difficulties, which became more prominent shortly thereafter

(Acharya, 2010). Clearly, these developments colored the perceptions within India regarding China's role in South Asia and/or SAARC.

During 2008-10 in fact, there had been repeated episodes of "intrusions" into Indian territory which had considerably damaged the positive ambience of India-China bilateral ties that had been underway since 2003 (Acharya, 2013). Thus when China attempted to push its bid for membership in SAARC, India took a rather hard stand. During the 16th SAARC Summit in Thimpu in April 2010, China and Iran formally sought to have the matter of their membership included in the agenda. Reportedly, the Secretary-General subsequently had agreed to do so. This was categorically rejected by New Delhi. The rationale for not taking up the matter given by the Secretary-General was that since the SAARC had failed to develop sufficient momentum, the membership "would not be extended." (As cited in Saez, 2011: 40). Shortly after this, the then Indian Foreign Secretary Nirupama Rao, when asked by the media whether another country (although China was not mentioned specifically) would be allowed to join SAARC as a full member in the near future, responded: "A fresh entry into SAARC? I'm afraid not. We have eight members and that is the way it is going to stay." (Foreign Secretary's Briefing).

Recent Perspectives on the China-SAARC Engagement

Three dominant lines of argument have emerged since the last five years in the Indian discourse regarding China's engagement with SAARC. The first of these perspectives, which emerges largely from the strategic and security community and which tends to dominate current thinking, is the realist or power politics perspective. (Abdi, 2010; Hariharan, 2009; Mohan, 2009; Roy, 2009; Khurana, 2008; Chellaney, 2006; Malik, 2006). This perspective—essentially geostrategic and geo-political in nature—takes China's rise as its starting point and then brings on the factor of India's rising as well. The security dimension is overriding, as China's policy towards South Asia is seen as intrinsically tied to China's military and security concerns and its engagement with SAARC countries, as part of its efforts to put pressure on India. In fact even with the improvement in the Sino-Indian relationship, this perspective does not change much, since the argument is that as Sino-Indian relations improve, China tends to reassure its other South Asian partners that it will not abandon them but will continue to have stakes in their development. Thus, this is another way of putting pressure on and encircling India, with the objective of keeping it boxed within the region, by continuing to engage with its neighbors with whom India has ongoing problems. The economic engagement, in this perspective, also has security implications. The most significant argument that realists put forward is that even though China is investing in infrastructure, arms sales constitutes a very important part of China's trade with the South Asian countries, which has a direct impact on the power balance. China continues to be the most reliable supplier of weapons to most of these smaller South Asian states (*SIPRI Yearbook 2005).* Bangladesh has in fact emerged as the largest buyer of Chinese arms (*Dhaka Tribune*, 18 March 2014 citing SIPRI). Sino-Indian competition (and possibly rivalry) will, according to this perspective, be the key factor in shaping China's role in SAARC. Unresolved issues and bitter conflicts continue to plague the region; South Asia is not a cohesive entity at present, which provides sufficient scope and potential for this competition to take a negative turn.

In contrast to the realist perspective we have liberal perspectives, which are beginning to carve a niche within the larger Indian discourse (Brunjes et al, 2013; Palit, 2010; Palit, 2009; Bhuimali & Mukhopadhyay, 2008; Ghosh, 2007; Srinivasan, 2005). This comes from the scholarly, academic community and those sections of people who are engaged in trade and commerce in China or other neighbors. And this perspective is located in the changes that have taken place in the post-cold war era, which opens the possibility for countries across the board to engage with each other in a vastly transformed manner. The cold war no longer ought to shape our mindsets. This discourse highlights the fact that China is a major neighbor of all the SAARC countries—it shares borders with 4 of them, there are historical, civilizational connections, common mountains, rivers, culture, religion, the socio-ethnic diversity cuts across boundaries in this part of the world and several parts of China are geopolitically closer to South Asia, than to other parts of the country. They also argue that China's experience in eradicating poverty and low standards of living and its transformation of the country's economy can be invaluable for South Asian countries which are also facing endemic poverty, rife with violence and underdevelopment. The post-cold war Chinese policy of good neighborliness and stress on stability has in fact provided the opportunity to respond to the changing winds in international relations and we should take advantage of China's position and role to also benefit South Asia. The liberals also point out that in addition to the flexibility and a greater freedom of choice that the post-cold war environment offers, new imperatives are now coming down to bear upon us, which are literally going to push countries in the direction of greater cooperation. The new threats to security, which emanate from environmental concerns, water resources management and from energy concerns, are eventually going to bring countries together. We should take advantage of the positive features that exist in the current period to push for greater engagement to benefit each other's development.

There is a third strand in this discourse—which originates from the Constructivist theoretical frameworks. The arguments made here share many of the premises of the liberal thinking, but go on to refer—and this where this line of reasoning differs somewhat from the liberal—to the example of China's engagement with ASEAN, and the potentially rewarding and promising role China can play, if given the opportunity. As yet there are not many writings in India in this genre – there are more non-Indian proponents of this argument (Mukherji, 2006 and 2004; Kalegama, 2012; Dosch:, 2008,; Ripsman, 2005; Lake & Morgan, 1997). This discourse highlights the Chinese acceptance of the 'ASEAN way' in its engagement with ASEAN—which testifies to China's ability to socialize itself in multilateral settings. They point to the increased technological and economic independence in the wake of economic globalization; to the growing trend of dialogue and even increasing intra-regional trade and therefore the need to move in an institutionalized manner towards engaging with China.

However it is necessary to bear in mind that there are enormous differences in the ASEAN and SAARC regional integration process. Therefore it is necessary to examine what SAARC needs to do before it can take truly take advantage of China engagement. We need to first see how to evolve mechanisms to deal with the endemic conflict in South Asia, which fundamentally would involve bilateral agreements between the SAARC countries to bring peace to the region. In a situation where there is a glaring lack of adequate stability, the role of a controversial extra-regional player would likely exaggerate the situation. A critical prerequisite is therefore a decline in the conflict levels and the forging of a consensus—if not unanimity—regarding the question of expanding SAARC membership.

Issues for Consideration

Most of the prescriptions provided within the constructivist framework are important lessons from the successful and flourishing Regional Organizations around the world: The South Asian region needs to have steady economic growth of sufficiently high levels which can deepen industrialization and lead to expansion of trade and specialization in division of labor, good institutional and physical connectivity within the SAARC region and greater inclusiveness. These are the irreducible minimum core requirements for a burgeoning regional organization. In this context, India as the dominant power in the region, would be required to play the key role. The SAARC Charter does not have a clear definition about the precise role of Observers; it merely says that the guiding principle is common pursuit of partnership for growth (SAARC Website). China's position has been that it would like to expand substantial cooperation with SAARC in the "spirit of equality, mutual benefit and win-win cooperation" (As cited in Saez, 2011: 38-39).

As mentioned earlier, there had been a shift since 2007-08 in the Indian perception, which sees a preponderance of the realist stance. The oft-raised question has been whether, in the light of the uncertainties regarding China's "rise", to see China as a 'threat' or 'opportunity'. The argument appeared to be that China and SAARC is a possible opportunity; but China in SAARC is a threat. In other words, till the two large Asian powers have addressed their outstanding issues, it would be highly unrealistic to expect India to discard its objections to China's full membership of SAARC. The other side of the coin is the lack of a substantial and firm intra-regional understanding on the matter of extra-regional cooperation. It could be argued that this does not take us very far, given the level of development of countries in South Asia and the fact that so far India has not emerged as the economic driver of the region, nor has it so far been able to successfully control/stem the ongoing disputes in the region. We are also looking at the South Asian region, which is dotted with substantial Chinese contributions to the infrastructure development and growth. Therefore the question arises of how India should address the issue of playing a leading role in taking the South Asian region towards prosperity. India is also now acknowledged as rising power—hence much depends on its ability to be the catalyst in the formation of an active and dynamic SAARC.

India too requires a stable region if it wishes to play a bigger role on the world stage. A divisive or fractured region would pull India down. The world has vastly transformed since late 1980's and early 1990's. There are certain legacies of the cold war years of the bilateral relationships—but to assume that China will continue to play the role of troublemaker in the region if it is given even a toe-hold, would be disregarding the massive changes that have come about in Asia as also the potentially ground-transforming trends. Undoubtedly, there are problematic legacies of the post-1962 period and China's relation with the South Asian countries, and there is a critical need to address—not shirk—the sensitive outstanding issues. One can go further and state that China would not do well in the longer run, without India playing an active and positive role. China could significantly contribute towards bringing about development, growth and modernization opportunities to SAARC, but this would have to be done not just strategically, but also pragmatically.

END NOTES

1. For a survey of different perspectives see Dipankar Banerjee ed. (2002) *SAARC in the Twenty-First Century: Towards a Cooperative Future*, New Delhi, India Research Press.

2. These largely stem from an unresolved boundary dispute, the differences with regard to the Dalai Lama and the Tibetan Government-in-exile in India and the Sino-Pak nexus.
3. It may be recalled that India had suspected China of "exporting revolution" to its northeast and fomenting anti-state activities during the 1960s.
4. A $3billion renovation project of the Buddha's birthplace in Lumbini has been undertaken to possibly keep the Dalai Lama out of the picture.

REFERENCES

Abdi, S.N.M. (2010) "India Foils Attempt to Bring China into South Asian Group", *South China Morning Post,* April 26.

Acharya, Alka (2013) 'The Strategic Stasis in India-China Relationship,' *Economic and Political Weekly,* June 29, pp. 25-29.

Acharya, Alka (2010) 'One Step Forward, Three Steps Backward: The Danger of Drift in India-China Relations,' *Economic and Political Weekly*, September 7-13.

Acharya, Alka (2008) *China-India: Politics of Incremental Engagement*, New Delhi, Har-Anand Publications Pvt. Ltd.

Asian Regional Integration Centre: Tracking Asian Integration, Asian Development Bank. Source: IMF Directions of Trade Statistics. Available at http://aric.adb.org/integrationindicators/result?sort=country&filter=all

Bajaj, Vikas (2010) "India Worries as China Builds Ports in South Asia", *New York Times,* February 15.

Basrur, Rajesh (1996) 'South Asia's Persistent Cold war', *ACDIS Occasional Paper*, November, available at http://www.ideals.illinois.edu/bitstream/handle/2142/15/Basrur%2520OP.pdf?sequence=1 (Accessed 4July 2011).

Bhuimali, Anil & Chandan K. Mukhopadhyay (2008) *Economic Issues in SAARC Context*, Delhi, Abhijeet Publications.

Brunjes et al (2013) 'China's Increased Trade and Investment in South Asia (Spoiler Alert: It's the Economy)' Workshop in International Public Affairs, Spring, Robert M. La Follette, School of Public Affairs, University of Wisconsin-Madison.

Chellaney, Brahma (2006) *Asian Juggernaut: The Rise of China, India and Japan*, New Delhi, HarperCollins Publishers.

Dhaka Tribune, 18 March 2014. http://www.dhakatribune.com/foreign-affairs/2014/mar/18/china-biggest-arms-supplier-bangladesh Accessed 18 March 2014. The source cited was SIPRI.

Dosch, Joern (2008) 'Who's Leading Who in ASEAN-China Relations? Community-building versus *Pax Sinica* in the Management of Security', in Christopher M. Dent ed, *China, Japan and Regional Leadership in East Asia*, Cheltenham, UK, Edward Elgar Publishing Ltd.

Dutta, Sujit (1998) 'China's Emerging Power and Military Role: Implications for South Asia' in Jonathan D. Pollack and Richard H. Yang eds. *In China's Shadow: Regional Perspectives on China's Foreign Policy and Military Development*, Rand Corporation Report, Washington, pp. 91-114.

Foreign Secretary's Briefing http://mea.gov.in/outoging-visit-detail.htm?2876/Briefing+by+Foreign+Secretary+on+Prime+Ministers+visit+to+Thimphu+for+SAARC+Summit

Ganguly, Sumit (2002) 'Assessing India's Responses to the Rise of China: Fears and Misgivings', in Carolyn W. Pumphrey (ed.) *The Rise of China in Asia: Security Implications*, Carlisle Barracks: The Strategic Studies Institute, available at http://www.strategicstudiesinstitute.army.mil/pdffiles/PUB61.pdf

Gautam, Upendra ed. (2003) *South Asia and China: Towards Inter-regional Cooperation*, Kathmandu, China Study Centre.

Ghosh, D.K. (2004) *New Frontiers: Pathways for SAARC*, New Delhi, Sunrise Publications.

Hariharan, R. (2009) 'China's Influence in India's Neighbourhood', Paper no. 2084, *South Asia Analysis Group,* available at www.southasiaanalysis.org (Accessed 4July 2011).

'India-China Relations in the New Era' (2006) *ORF Discourse*, vol.1, no.4, December. Available at http://www.orfonline.org

Jiang, Zemin (1996) Speech at Islamabad, Pakistan. Available at www.fmprc.gov.cn/eng/wjdt/zyjh/t24909.htm

Johnston, Alastair Iain (2013) 'How New and Assertive is China's New Assertiveness', *International Security*, Vol.37, No.4 Spring, pp. 7-48.

Kadirgamar, Lakhsman (2009) 'The Peaceful Ascendance of China: A South Asian Perspective', *Daily News* (Colombo) 15 January. Available at http://www.dailynews.lk/2005/01/15/fea01.html Accessed 5 March 2009.

Kalegama, Saman (2012) 'China involvement in SAARC beneficial for all'http://www.ips.lk/staff/ed/publications_ed/international/china_saarc/economic_cooperation.pdf Accessed 18 March 2014

Kapila, Subhash (2005) 'China-India Strategic Alliance – Should Not be Unthinkable: An Analysis', *South Asia Analysis Group*, May. Available at http://www.saag.org (Accessed 1 February 2006).

Keller, William W. & Thomas G. Rawski (2007) 'China's Peaceful Rise: Road Map or Fantsay', in Keller and Rawskieds, *China's Rise and the Balance of Influence in Asia* Pittsburg, Pittsburg University Press, pp. 1913-209.

Khurana, Gurpreet S. (2008) 'China's "String of Pearls" in the Indian Ocean and Its Security Implications', *Strategic Analysis*, vol. 32, no.1, pp. 1-39.

Kostecka, Daniel (2010) "Hambantota, Chittagong, and the Maldives – Unlikely Pearls for the Chinese Navy." *China Brief* 10 (23): 8-11.

Kumar, Vikas (2012) 'Understanding China's North-East and South Asia Policies', Associate Paper, *Future Directions International*, 21 June.

Lake, D. & P.M. Morgan eds. (1997) *Regional Orders: Building Security in A New World*, University Park, PA, Pennsylvania University Press.

Malik, J. Mohan (2006) "China's Strategy of Containing India", *PINR*, 6 February .http://www.pinr.com/report.php?ac=view_report&report_id=434

Malik, J. Mohan (1995) "China-India Relations in the Post-Soviet Era: The Continuing Rivalry", *The China Quarterly* (London), No. 142, June.

Ministry of Foreign Affairs (2007) Press Conference of the Foreign Ministry Spokesman on March 27. Available at www.mfa.gov.cn/eng/xwfw/s2510/2511/t306984.html

Mohan, C. Raja (2009) 'Maritime Power: India and China Turn to Mahan', *ISAS Working Paper*, No.71, 7 July. *A Resurgent China: South Asian Perspectives*, Routledge, London.

Mukherji, I.N. (2006) 'Asian Economic Integration', Keynote Address delivered at the 89th Annual Conference of the Indian Economic Association, Kurukshetra University, 27-29 December 2006.

Mukherji, I.N. (2004) 'Towards a Free Trade Area in South Asia: With Special Reference to the Role of India', *Discussion Paper 86*, Research and Information Systems for the Non-aligned and Other Developing Countries, New Delhi. Available at http://www.ris.org.in/images/RIS_images/pdf/dp86_pap.pdf

Muni, S.D. & Tan Tai Yong eds. (2012) *A Resurgent China: South Asian Perspectives* New Delhi, Routledge.

Niazi, Tarique (2009) 'China's Foot in India's Door', *Asia Times*, 24 August. Available at www.asiatimes.com (Accessed 7 July 2011)

Palit, ParamaSinha (2010) 'China's Soft Power in South Asia', *RSIS Working Paper* No 200.

Pehrson, Christopher J. (2009) *String of Pearls: Meeting the Challenge of China's Rising Power*

Across the Asian Littoral, Strategic Studies Institute, United States Army War College. Available at http://www.strategicstudiesinstitute.army.mil/pubs?display.cfm?Pubid=721. Accessed 10 July 2010.

Ramakant, ed (1988) *China and South Asia* South Asia Studies Series 18, South Asia Publishers Pvt. Lt, New Delhi.

Roy, Bhaskar (2009) 'China: Back to Containing India', *South Asia Analysis Group*, Paper No. 3296, 7 July, available at http://www.southasiaanalysis.org/%5Cpapers33%3296.html (Accessed 7 July 2011)

SAARC Website: www.saarc-sec.org/Cooperation-with-Observers/13)

Saez, Lawrence (2011) *The South Asian Association for Regional Cooperation (SAARC): An Emerging Collaboration Architecture,* New York, Routledge.

Shambaugh, David (2004-05) 'China Engages Asia: Reshaping the Regional Order', *International Security*, vol. 29, no. 3, Winter, pp. 64-99.

Shambaugh, David (2005) *Power Shift: China and Asia's New Dynamics*, University of California Press, Berkeley.

Sharma, Rajeev (2013) "Unfolding China-Bhutan-India Triangle No Threat to New Delhi", *Global Times,* February 27. http://www.globaltimes.cn/content/764651.shtml.

Srinivasan, T.N (2005) 'Productivity and Economic Growth in South Asia and China', *The Pakistan Development Review*, vol. 44, no. 4, Winter, pp. 479-503.

Su Qiang (2007) 'China Makes First Visit to SAARC', *China Daily*, 3 April.

Sutter, Robert (2005) *China's Rise in Asia: Promises and Perils*, New York, Rowman & Littlefield Publishers Inc.

Suettinger, Robert L. (2004) 'The Rise and Descent of China's Peaceful Rise', *China Leadership Monitor*, No.12 Hoover Institution, Stanford University. Available at http://www.hoover.org/publications/china-leadership-monitor

Yuan, Jing-dong, 'Sizing up the Elephant: Beijing's Perspectives on a Rising India', *East Asian Policy*, vol.1, no. 4, October-December, pp. 25-33.

Zhang, Guihong (2006) 'The Rise of China: India's Perceptions and Responses', *South Asian Survey*, vol. 13, no.1, pp. 93-102.

Zhang, Guihong (2005) 'China's Peaceful Rise and Sino-Indian Relations', *China Report*, vol. 41, no. 2, pp. 159-71.

6

Japan's Security Cooperation with SAARC Countries

Tomoko Kiyota

Introduction

Although quite a few scholars have tried to define a causal relationship between regional integration and peace,[1] it is still a chicken-and-egg debate. Does economic interdependence promote peace? Does trade promote confidence-building among the nations? Is it possible to promote regional integration without enough trust? Those questions are more difficult to answer when we consider the relationships between the nations in North-East Asia and South Asia. Whereas nations in North-East Asia are yet to succeed in integrating their economies because of the diplomatic problems, the volume of trade between them are massive. On the other hand, South Asian nations established South Asian Association for Regional Cooperation (SAARC) in 1985, but they are criticized as being "less-effective"[2] in ensuring peace and development. This paper will examine this paradox and suggest a new framework for regional security.

Does Trade Promote Peace?

The question whether economic integration promotes peace has been discussed among scholars as well as economists who study international security. According to Bela Balassa, economic integration can take several forms that represent varying degrees of integration. The first one is a free-trade area, in which tariffs (and quantitative restrictions) between the participating countries are abolished, but each country retains its own tariffs against nonmembers. At another level, a customs union involves the equalization of tariffs in trade with nonmember countries, as well as the suppression of discrimination in the field commodity movements within the union. A higher form of economic integration is attained in a common market, where not only trade restrictions, but also restrictions on factor movements are abolished. Another form is an economic union which combines the suppression of restrictions on commodity and factor movements with some degree of harmonization of national economic policies, in order to remove discrimination that was caused by disparities in these policies. Finally, complete economic integration presupposes the unification of monetary, fiscal, social, and countercyclical policies and requires the setting-up of a supra-national authority whose decisions are binding for the member states.[3]

This well explains the case of the European Union (EU). The EU was formed as a customs union and developed a common market, and today it reached the level of economic union.[4] Although the EU type of economic integration is rare even today, regional trade agreement (RTA) has been increasing all over the world since 1990. According to the WTO, 233 RTA are active as of November 2011.[5] This trend is expected to further increase in the future.

According to the classical liberals, economic integration promotes peace because military conflict reduces trade that policy-makers value. Indeed, it is highly unlikely that the member states of EU will use military force against the other European countries. On the contrary, within the SAARC, India and Pakistan fought the Kargil War in 1999, even after South Asian countries started aiming toward economic integration. Beijing has been using military force to expand China's territory against her neighboring states, even though these neighboring states are trying to strengthen their economic integration with China. Therefore, classical realists argue that trade has no systematic effect on military conflict. Neo-mercantilists also envision trade as a tool of influence and exploitation, which can lead to conflict if countries resent it, or to peace if they comply.[6]

Although this debate has not yet settled, policy-makers often tend to expect too much of the effect of economic integration. People tend to think that actual military conflicts can be avoided because it is irrational to fight each other in this era of interdependency. However, even though trade could reduce the tension, it is not necessary that any minor conflict can be avoided. The historical and territorial issues of North-East and South Asia show us clearly that such expectation is too optimistic.

Economic Integration and Security Dilemmas in North-East Asia

The long historical relationship among the nations in North-East Asia has been impacting the security environment of the region since the end of World War II. This is especially true in the case of the Japanese invasion of Korean Peninsula and China, the Korean War and the "Two-China" problem which were main causes for preventing regional integration in North-East Asia. The North Korean missile and nuclear weapons development program might also be one of the factors.

The First Sino-Japanese War occurred in 1894 and resulted in Japanese victory in 1895. Japan had then trampled Chinese land underfoot till she lost the World War II in 1945. After the war, the Japanese government sought to resume trade with mainland China, but it was forced by Washington to enter diplomatic relations with the Republic of China (ROC, Taiwan) in 1952 due to the Cold War politics. At this time, the Taipei government agreed to forego war reparations from Japan to aid speedy negotiations. This fact positively impacted the diplomatic normalization negotiation between Beijing and Tokyo during the 1970s. The leaders of the People's Republic of China (PRC) also renounced their demands for war reparations from Japan as done by the ROC. This surprising proposal by Mao Zedong and Zhou Enlai aroused a feeling of gratitude among the Japanese people toward China, but aggravated the Chinese peoples grievances later. The Chinese people were never satisfied with the Japanese official development assistance and criticized any justification of historical matters by Japan.[7]

Furthermore, South Korea also never forgot the humiliating colonization by Japan. Like Beijing, Seoul also keeps a close watch on every move of the Japanese regarding historical issues. For example Prime Minister Abe's visit to the Yasukuni Shrine in December 2013 caused much angst both in Seoul as well as in Beijing. It is also seen that successive South Korean Presidents as well as Chinese leaders use Japan bashing to attain popularity and to be seen as patriotic.

Both PRC and South Korea have ongoing territorial disputes with Japan. China has been claiming the Japanese controlled Senkaku Islands as Diaoyu Islands after the potential oil reserves in the East China Sea was found during the 1970s. After 2008, China gradually increased her assertiveness on the Senkaku/Diaoyu territorial issue. In particular, when the Japanese authorities arrested the captain of a Chinese fishing vessel near the islands in 2010, Beijing openly threatened Tokyo with imposing an embargo on rare earths, one of China's natural resources, against Japan to demand release of the captain.[8]

The territorial dispute over the sovereignty of the Takeshima/Dokto Islands has been an important issue between Japan and South Korea since January 1952 when the then ROK President Syngman Rhee unilaterally drew the so-called "Syngman Rhee Line" and started controlling the islands. During the negotiation of the San Francisco Peace Treaty after the WWII, Washington rejected a Korean request to include Takeshima/Dokdo Islands in ROK territory. According to the Japanese government, the islands had never been treated as Korean territory before the war. Although Japan has repeatedly lodged protests against the ROK's 'illegal occupation' of the islands, the South Korean government has never agreed to put this issue on the negotiating table.[9]

Although China and South Korea seem to have a common cause against Japan on territorial issues, they often fail to keep the peace with each other. For long Seoul has been worried of a possible Chinese invasion, and is cautious about its military buildup. In fact, Beijing's declaration of a new air defence identification zone (ADIZ) in December 2013 surprised not only Seoul but also Tokyo and Washington, because the ADIZ includes a maritime rock named Ieodo which ROK controls, as well as the Senkaku/Diaoyu Islands. Two weeks after the Chinese declaration, the South Korean government also extended its air defence zone to overlap with China's ADIZ.[10]

In addition, North Korea has further complicated an already complicated situation in this region. The Korean Peninsula was divided into two after WWII, and North Korea installed a dictatorship since its formation in 1948. North Korea, led by the Kim family has been developing various missiles which is said to be capable of even reaching American territories. The country officially acknowledged its nuclear program and also that it conducted the third nuclear test in 2013. The neighboring countries, including South Korea, China, and Japan have to deal with this issue along with the United States.

Besides this, the relations between PRC and ROC has been marked by tensions for a long time. Since the end of the Chinese Civil War, both Beijing and Taipei have tried to legitimize themselves as the formal Chinese government. Taipei faced a predicament when the PRC prevailed over the ROC and succeeded in becoming a member of the United Nations and established diplomatic ties with the United States during the 1970s. Chinese military officials do not hesitate to threaten Taiwan openly that China would prevent Taiwan's attempt at independence by the use of force.[11]

Despite the delicate relations between them, the volume of regional trade in North-East Asia exceeds the volume of trade among SAARC nations. During the 2000s, China surpassed the US as the leading trade partner of Japan and South Korea. For China, the US became the largest, but even so, Japan and South Korea maintain a higher position on the list of Chinese important trading partners during the same period.[12]

However, those strong economic relations do not resolve the above mentioned historical problems. Rather, those problems gradually began to negatively impact the economy. Nikkei Shimbun quoted an announcement by Chinese authorities that the total volume of trade between Japan and China in 2013 decreased 9 percent as compared to the figure of its peak (2011).[13] Trade between South Korea and Japan also decreased more than 10 percent in 2013 as compared to 2012.[14]

Although the idea of economic integration among Japan, China and South Korea has been discussed for a long time, it hasn't been actually sustainable because of long exisiting historical and political matters. Instead of the limited North-East regional integration, these countries have joined the wider regional economic cooperation such as APEC and ASEAN Plus Three (APT).[15] The first informal APT summit was convened in Kuala Lumpur in December 1997, against the backdrop of the Asian Financial Crisis. In the beginning, the APT's main task was to overcome the financial crisis, but later the area of cooperation has broadened and deepened to include food and energy security, trade facilitation, disaster management, people-to-people contact, and so on.[16] Although this framework of APT triggered seeking of added economic cooperation among Japan, China and South Korea, it is still under negotiation. The Trans-Pacific Strategic Economic Partnership Agreement (TPP) is also seen as a new approach to economic cooperation among the nations of the Asia-Pacific. However, the TPP has also struggled to sustain. Diplomatic issues between North-East Asian nations is one of the reasons for this.

The case of the North-East Asian region shows us that economic relations neither promote peace automatically nor resolve any historical and security problems. Lack of trust could be one of the reasons. People can expand trade without trust, but trade itself is not enough to increase trust among the nations. Even though the volume of trade between Japan and China is massive, there is no guarantee that no minor conflict will occur in the region.

Economic Integration and Security Dilemmas in South Asia

On the other hand, SAARC was established between India, Pakistan, Bangladesh, Sri Lanka, Bhutan, Nepal, and Maldives in 1985. Afghanistan joined it as an official member in April 2007. As of December 2013, nine countries including Japan, China and the United States also joined SAARC as Observers.[17]

The main goal of SAARC is to promote economic and development cooperation, and discussions about security concerns are limited to terrorism or drug issues. In 2004, South Asian Free Trade Area (SAFTA) Agreement was signed during the Twelfth SAARC Summit in Pakistan and the Agreement came into effect on 1 January 2006. The South Asia region has one fourth of the world's population and the potential market size is quite huge. Nevertheless, intra regional trade amongst SAARC countries is a mere 6 percent.[18]

One of the obstacles for the trade growth amongst SAARC countries is the business visa. Even though SAARC countries agreed to the SAFTA and to increase intra trade, businessmen have to still struggle to obtain a business visa for their entry to other SAARC countries. This is mainly because of lack of trust between those nations. Indian Commerce and Industry Minister Anand Sharma said there is a need to work toward creating a more trusting environment which would enable easier movement of professionals across borders during the SAARC Business Leaders Conclave in January 2014.[19]

The South Asia region also has various historical issues among the nations, especially between India and Pakistan. The problems between those two nations are rooted in the partition after their independence in 1947 from British rule. They were engaged in military conflicts with each other in 1947-48, 1965, 1971 and 1999. Both countries disagree on their borders which remains undefined with both claiming greater territory. Both India and Pakistan are now nuclear-capable states after they demonstrated their nuclear strength with tests at the end of the 1990s. Moreover, New Delhi has accused the Pakistani government of sponsoring terrorists who attacked and continue attack India openly.

The idea of SAARC's foundation came from the former Bangladesh President, Ziaur Rahman. He had emphasized that regional cooperation was essential for peace and progress of South Asia and called for other nations in the region to establish SAARC. His vision was accepted by the most of the South Asian nations except India and Pakistan. Islamabad was sceptical of ZiaurRahman's vision as they suspected that he might be an Indian puppet. New Delhi was concerned at first that the founding of a regional organization would provide an opportunity for smaller neighbors to gang up against India. Indian policy-makers were also afraid that the bilateral issues between India and other SAARC nations would be discussed in this multilateral forum, which India considered un-necessary.[20]

India shares a common border with most nations in South Asia. Due to the asymmetrical national power in terms of geographical size, population, and military capability, India's neighbors tend to worry about India's excessive influence. For example, Nepal has been trying its utmost to maintain an independent posture on matters such as the declaration of an international security zone, acquisition of Chinese weaponry, and the refusal of a transit treaty with India. However, due to the economical dependency, Nepal could not avoid facing the economic blockade from India.

India also showed her hegemonic attitude towards other South Asian nations, especially during the 1970-80s.When Sri Lanka came under the massive ethnic conflict between the majority Sinhalese and minority Tamil separatists seeking independence, India finally sent troops—the Indian Peace-Keeping Force (IPKF)—to Sri Lanka in 1987. This operation ended in failure, and impacted diplomatic relations and caused an imbroglio in the Indo-Sri Lanka relations, the consequences of which are felt even today.

Indo-Bangladesh relations also deteriorated over a dispute concerning the Farakka Barrage. While India has built a feeder canal to divert water to its side of the river, Bangladesh claimed that the Farakka Barrage cuts off the country's water supply. This led a minor border confrontation between the two countries in 2001. India and Bangladesh also have other diplomatic issues regarding border security.[21]

The problems between SAARC nations also impacted the trade and economic cooperation negatively, as already mentioned above. The case of SAARC could be another example that economic integration without enough trust does not work properly and does not necessarily promote peace. What is needed is a more concrete framework which concentrates on security cooperation including Confidence Building Measures (CBMs) in North-East and South Asia for stabilization of the region.

Confidence Building Measures (CBMs) for Regional Security

Confidence Building Measures (CBMs) have the objective of preventing, managing and resolving crisis that are likely to escalate into violent conflict between states. They include any set of unilateral or multilateral actions or procedures that act to reduce not only military actions but also tensions perhaps caused by cultural, political and diplomatic misunderstandings. For military actions, the basic tools of CBMs are communication, transparency, constraint and verification measures. Communication measures include setting up hotlines, communication centers, and holding regularly scheduled consultations to defuse tensions. Constraint measures are developed to keep the military forces of the involved states at distance from one another, such as time-out zones and pre-notification requirements on military exercise. Transparency measures are important to foster greater "openness" of their military capabilities and activities, such as pre-notification requirements on military exercises, voluntary observations of another state's military exercise, and data exchanges including defense budgets, and planned weapons procurements. Verification measures include aerial inspections, on-site inspections carried out by third parties or even opposing parties to confirm that the information is true.[22]

These concepts and tools of CBMs were developed in Europe during the Cold War. The Conference on Security and Co-operation in Europe, known as CSCE was set up in August 1975. After the Cold War, in 1995, the

Conference became the Organization for Security and Co-operation in Europe (OSCE). In 1975, the participating countries signed the Helsinki Final Act. This act established various rules for CBM but the most important part in this is a guideline for transparency. It required the participants to notify their major military manoeuvres at least 21 days in advance to all other participating states, if exceeding a total of 25,000 troops, independently or combined with any possible air or naval components.[23]

During the 1980s, the Stockholm Document came into effect, which strengthened the transparency measures and added more conditions of constraint and verification. The document also set a guideline to exchange the observers. In principal, this is a politically binding agreement, so that participants cannot refuse the verification.[24] This was further strengthened after the end of Cold War with the 1992 Vienna Document.[25] In this document, the participating countries agreed on even stricter restriction of military activities. For example, it decided that no participating state will carry out within two calendar years only one military activity subject to prior notification involving more than 40,000 troops or 900 battle tanks.

After the end of Cold War, several mechanisms of CBM have been developed in Asia. The biggest framework among them is the ASEAN Regional Forum (ARF).[26] The first session of the ARF was held in Bangkok in July 1994 with 18 members. The ARF was founded to enhance the trust and confidence amongst participants for maintaining the peace and prosperity of the region. The ARF's first step was to promote CBM and gradually shifted to the second stage—development of preventive mechanisms—and the third stage—development of conflict resolution mechanisms. The most significant point is that the ARF today has expanded to 27 countries which include the US, China, Russia, Japan, India, EU and other major countries in the Asia-Pacific. Foreign ministers and other governmental officials meet regularly to discuss the CBMs, peacekeeping operations, and disaster relief.

Besides the ARF, ASEAN Defence Ministers Meeting Plus (ADMM-Plus) was also established in 2010, based on ADMM which was set up only for ASEAN members in 2004. ADMM-Plus includes Australia, China, India, Japan, New Zealand, Republic of Korea, Russia, the US and ASEAN countries. This is the highest forum in Asia for defence ministers to discuss and exchange views on current defence and security issues in the region.[27]

These frameworks provide valuable opportunities for leaders of Asian countries to create an impression that they are at least discussing the security issues in the region. However, when compared to CSCE, the CBM has not been a very effective tool for both ARF and ADMM-Plus. There are certain negative perspectives on those frameworks, as they seem to be more of a 'Talk

Fest'. Ministers of member states participate in the several meetings to talk about the issues, but these meetings rarely produce concrete results.[28] As a matter of fact, ARF and even ADMM-Plus are too large to discuss the problems in detail. Moreover, member states do not always share their security concerns. In the case of Europe, due to the iron curtain, the main problem among the members was clear. However, due to various issues of its numerous members, ARF cannot concentrate enough to deal with the several crucial issues.

The CBMs between India and Pakistan started after the war of 1971 but are also struggling to arrive at a concrete solution due to an unfavorable political environment on both sides. For example, although the two countries have established a hotline to communicate more often with each other, important information has not been shared over the hot line during the times of tension. The agreement on non-violation of air space which was agreed in 1991 has also not been very effective to create trust between India and Pakistan. According to this agreement, fighter aircrafts are not allowed to enter within 10 kilometers of foreign space, while logistic and unarmed aircraft including unarmed helicopters are allowed up to 1,000 metres from the international border. However, the conflict zone, Siachen Glacier is not covered under this rule so there are many incidents that happened there.[29]

It should be noted that the author is not of the opinion that CBMs bring eternal peace automatically. CBMs do not change the hostile relations immediately. Nevertheless it is still important for countries concerned to realize that other parties would also like to avoid unnecessary conflicts. In Europe, the participating countries also agreed to sign several treaties and agreements to decide arms reduction between the west and the east during the Cold War. The negotiations on arms reduction were promoted in Europe because they could successfully implement CBMs. In Asia, CBMs are still at the communication stage. Particularly between China and other countries, even transparency measures have not yet been accepted.

Need for a New Framework for Regional Security in North, East and South Asia

Here the author would like to suggest a new framework for regional security which includes North-East Asian countries, Russia, the US and SAARC countries. North-East Asian countries include China, South and North Korea, Japan and Taiwan.

Promoting regional security involves including all major countries concerned. Even the SAARC involves only China to discuss regional security, but this does not work well because China also has other security concerns, which could be with Japan, the US and Russia. North-East Asian countries plus India are also not enough because India has concerns about Pakistan.

On the other hand, the ARF countries have been promoting CBM among the Asian nations, but it is not yet very effective, as mentioned above. Although they also agreed on many measures for CBM, a look at the relations between China and Japan, and India and China would indicate that the ARF framework needs a drastic change. One of the reasons why ARF is not effective is because it is too large. ARF has also expanded to Europe and North America. It is now similar to the UN.

The new framework must be compact enough to discuss delicate issues, and still need to involve most of those countries. One of the problems of SAARC is unequal military forces within the participants. India dwarfs the other SAARC nations both in terms of geography and military might. In the new security framework, this problem could be offset. Pakistan and other small nations do not have to be afraid of India's control. India also can promote CBM with China and Pakistan at the same time, as well as deter united challenges from small countries of SAARC, if she cooperates with the other bigger countries. China also can talk about its security concern with India, Japan, Russia and the US together. Japan will also find advantage because a Chinese and South Korean team up can be thwarted because Indian people are supportive of Japan's position. The US too can cooperate with India and Japan to promote CBM with China and Russia at the same time.

Theoretically, or as seen from the experience of the US-USSR relations, countries only agree to control the arms race after establishing a military power balance. This could be a catch. Which means, China will agree to arms control only when it catches up with American military power. However, in this case, America has lots of allies so the military balance is more complicated. Japan and India will not stop building up their forces. If no measures are taken, the turning point will never come. Waiting until SAARC's economic relations become more effective or for North-East Asia's economic ties to improve will not serve the purpose. ... Revisions to the existing framework are needed at the earliest. Japan and India and other SAARC nations should cooperate to develop such a framework for regional security.

END NOTES

1. For example, Havard Hegre, John R. Oneal and Bruce Russett, "Trade Does Promote Peace: New Simultaneous Estimates of the Reciprocal Effects of Trade and Conflict," *Journal of Peace Research*, Vol. 47, No. 6, November 2010, pp. 763-774; Shaheen Rafi Khan, Faisal Haq Shaheen, Moeed Yusuf and Aska Tanveer, *Regional Integration, Trade and Conflict in South Asia,* Sustainable Development Policy Institute, January 2007, available at http://www.iisd.org/pdf/2007/tas_rta_south_asia.pdf.

2. Noor Mohammad Sarker, "Why SAARC is Less-effective? : A Neo-realist Explanation of India's Role in SAARC,"*BILIA Working Paper*, No. 1, 2013, available at http://www.biliabd.org/docfolder/BILIA%20WPaper%2001,%202013.pdf.
3. Bela Balassa, *The Theory of Economic Integration*, Allen and Unwin, 1962, p. 2.
4. Satoko Tanabe, "Higashi Asia Keizai Togo wo Meguru Ronten [Issues over East Asia Economic Integration]," *Chosa to Jyoho [National Diet Library Issue Brief]*, No. 489, July 28, 2005, pp. 1-2.
5. Takako Kanemaru-Ohnish, "Minami Asia Chiki Kyoryoku Rengo (SAARC) no Hatten, Boeki, Seido [Development, Trade, and Institutions of South Asia Association for Regional Cooperation (SAARC)]," *Jyosai Kokusai Daigaku Kiyo, Keiei Joho Gakubu* [*Josai International University bulletin. Faculty of Management and Information Sciences*], Vol. 21, No. 2, March 2013, p. 54.
6. Quan Li and Rafael Reuveny, "Trading for Peace? Disaggregated Bilateral Trade and Interstate Military Conflict Initiation," Conference on Theories of International Politics Economy and China," December 2008, available at http://www.princeton.edu/~pcglobal/conferences/beijing08/papers/Li-Reuveny.pdf.
7. Kazuko Mori, *Nicchu Kankei: Sengokara Shinjidai he [Sino-Japanese Relations: The Post-war towards New Era]*, Iwanami Shinsho, 2006, p. 68-87.
8. For the detail, see Reinhard Drifte, "The Senkaku/Diaoyu Islands Territorial Dispute between Japan and China: Between the Materialization of the 'China Threat' and Japan 'Reversing the Outcome of World War II'?"*UNISCI Discussion Papers*, No. 32, May 2013, available at http://pendientedemigracion.ucm.es/info/unisci/revistas/UNISCIDP32-1DRIFTE.pdf.
9. For example, Ministry of Foreign Affairs of Japan, "Takeshima: Seeking a Solution based on Law and Dialogue," available at http://www.mofa.go.jp/files/000018520.pdf.
10. "South Korea Extends Its Air Defence Zone to Overlap with China's," The Guardian, 8 December, 2013, available at http://www.theguardian.com/world/2013/dec/08/south-korea-air-defence-zone-overlap-chinas.
11. For example, see Joseph Kahn, "Chinese Officers Warn That Taiwan Referendum Could Lead to War," *The New York Times*, 3 December, 2003, http://www.nytimes.com/2003/12/03/international/asia/03CND-CHIN.html.
12. Gu Gyeongmo, "Hokuto Asia Nicchukan no Ikinai Butsuryu Mondainikansuru Kosatsu [Study of Intra-regional Distribution of Goods in North East Asia]," *Higashi Asia heno Shiten [Perspective for East Asia]*, December 2012, pp. 15-29.
13. "Nicchu Boeki Ninen Renzoku Shukusho [The Sino-Japan Trade Shrink for the Second Consecutive Year]," *Nikkei Shimbun*, January 10, 2014.
14. "Chu-kan Boeki, Higashi Asia de Taito, Shukusho Tsuzuku Nicchu Gyakuten Mo [Trade between China and South Korea, Increase in East Asia, Catching up the Decreasing Sino-Japan Trade]," *Nikkei Shimbun*, January 4, 2014.
15. Satoko Tanabe, "Higashi Asia Keizai Togo wo Meguru Ronten [Issues over East Asia Economic Integration]," pp. 5-8.
16. "Overview ASEAN Plus Three Cooperation," ASEAN Official Website, http://www.asean.org/news/item/asean-plus-three-cooperation.
17. South Asian Association for Regional Cooperation Official Website, http://www.saarc-sec.org.
18. "Anand Sharma Urges SAARC Nations to Recognize Opportunities for Economic Growth," *Asian News International*, January 16, 2014.
19. "India Pitches for Visa Liberalisation in SAARC Region," *The Economic Times*, January 16, 2014.
20. Muhammad Jamshed Iqbal, "SAARC: Origin, Growth, Potential and Achievements," *Pakistan Journal of History and Culture*, Vol. XXVII/2, 2006, p. 131.
21. Khan, Shaheen, Yusuf and Tanveer, *Regional Integration, Trade and Conflict in South Asia*, pp. 12-14.

22. "Confidence-Building and Nuclear Risk-Reduction Measures in South Asia," Stimson Center, http://www.stimson.org/research-pages/confidence-building-measures-in-south-asia-/; Noriko Sado, "OSCE niokeru Shinrai Anzen Jyosei Sochi: Mechanism no Hatten to Hyoka [Confidence- and Security-Building Measures in the OSCE: the Mechanism and an Assessment]," *Kokusai Kokyo Seisaku Kenkyu*, Vol. 2, No. 1, pp. 219-236; Jun Tsubouchi, "OSCE Process to ASEAN: Asia-Taiheiyo no Anzen Hosho Bunseki Wakugumiheno Jyosetsu [The OSCE Process and ASEAN: Searching for Framework on Analysis in Asia-Pacific Security]," *Kokusai Seiji*, Vol. 116, October 1997, pp. 64-79.
23. "Conference on Security and Co-operation in Europe Final Act, Helsinki 1975, http://www.osce.org/mc/39501?download=true.
24. "Document of the Stochkolm Conference on Confidence- and Security-Building Measures and Disarmament in Europe Convened in Accordance with the Relevant Provisions of the Concluding Document of the Madrid Meeting of the Conference on Security and Co-operation in Europe, Stockholm, 19 September 1986, http://www.osce.org/fsc/41238.
25. "Vienna Document 1992 of the Negotiations on Confidence- and Security-Building Measures Convened in Accordance with the Relevant Provisions of the Concluding Document of the Vienna Meeting of the Conference on Security and Co-Operation in Europe," Vienna 1992, http://www.osce.org/fsc/41253.
26. See, for example, ASEAN Official Website, http://www.asean.org/; Ministry of Foreign Affairs of Japan, Official Website, http://www.mofa.go.jp/mofaj/area/asean/arf/gaiyo.html; Georgeina Whelan, "Does the ARF Have a Role in ASEAN's Pursuit of Regional Security in the Next Decade," October 2012, available at http://www.defence.gov.au/adc/docs/Publications2012/10_CDSS%20SAP.pdf.
27. ASEAN Defence Ministers' Meeting (ADMM) Official Website, https://admm.asean.org/
28. Whelan, "Does the ARF Have a Role in ASEAN's Pursuit of Regional Security in the Next Decade."
29. See, for example, T. Najmudheen and Farhana Kausar, "Importance of Confidence Building Measures in India-Pakistan Relations: A South Asian Perspective," *Asia Pacific Journal of Social Sciences*, Vol. V. (1), Jan-June 2013, pp. 61-91.

7

Japan–SAARC Security Relations: A Maritime Perspective

Joshy M. Paul

Japan is considered as one of the leading powers of Asia, along with India and China. All the three countries pursue military modernization without antagonizing the other. At the same time, they are developing strategic relationship with other regional countries. Japan-SAARC security relationship has not evolved in such a manner as that of Japan-Southeast Asia relations. Even within the SAARC, it is India which drives the security relations with Japan.

Overview of Japan-SAARC Security Cooperation

Unlike in the economic aspects, Japan's involvement in the security aspects of South Asia is a new development and very minimal. Japan for a long period considered South Asia as an extended region of its security calculation and the region was affected by various kinds of instability viz, terrorism, religious extremism, internal ethnic conflicts, territorial disputes and nuclear impasse. The nuclear standoff between India and Pakistan has been reflected as the main source of concern for regional cooperation, and so Japan's policy towards South Asia was largely dependent on its own position about nuclear weapons. With the changing strategic dynamics of East Asia as well the growing importance of the Indian Ocean Region (IOR), especially the concern about Sea Lines of Communication (SLOC), has driven Japan and South Asia to come closer. In fact, much before the term Indo-Pacific was coined, the importance of the two oceans—the Pacific and the Indian—had got prominence in Japan's strategic thinking. Japan's concern about the SLOC security in the Indian Ocean and its strategic relationship with India generated academic thinking about considering the two oceans as a single entity. The volatility in different parts of the trade route such as the disputed South China Sea, an embroiled Middle East and the piracy prone area from Gulf of Eden to the Strait of Malacca can severely affect Japan's security calculation. In this regard, security relations with South Asian countries will help in protecting Japan's SLOC in the region.

Japan and Sri Lanka

Japan-Sri Lanka security cooperation is a recent development which is in consonance with Tokyo's maritime security concerns in the Indian Ocean region. During the visit of Sri Lankan President Mahinda Rajapaksa to Japan in March 2013, both countries decided to strengthen the security cooperation, especially in the maritime front. Japanese Prime Minster Shinzo Abe expressed his intention to promote cooperation and dialogues concerning shared maritime challenges.[1] Both leaders have expressed mutual gratification for port calls by Japanese Maritime Self-Defense Force vessels in Sri Lankan territory and the intention to expand exchanges between defense authorities as well as capacity building and cooperation between the coast guards. The Japan-Sri Lanka joint statement titled "Strengthening Japan-Sri Lanka Partnership beyond the 60th Anniversary of Diplomatic Relations" emphasizes the need for maritime security cooperation between the two in the IOR.

In April 2011, a fleet of ships of the Japan Maritime Self-Defense Force (JMSDF) engaging in a counter piracy mission visited the Colombo Port after a long interval. Since then, there have been 14 port calls by the JMSDF fleet.[2] Japan considers Sri Lanka a major destination to anchor its ships and get logistical support for its naval ships deployed in anti-piracy operations in the Gulf of Aden and west coast of Africa.

Japan and Pakistan

As far as Pakistan is concerned, Japan's engagement is very minimal perhaps because of greater Chinese involvement in Pakistan's security establishment. Both countries instituted the Pakistan-Japan Security Dialogue in 2002, when Japanese Prime Minister Junichiro Koizumi visited Pakistan in May 2002and five rounds of talks have been held so far.[3] The first round of Security Dialogue was held at Islamabad on January 24, 2004, and the second round of the Dialogue was held in Tokyo on September 14, 2006. In the first round of dialogues both countries have agreed to cooperate on (1) to deal with counter-terrorism issues and (2) disarmament, non-proliferation, dual use of technology, the peaceful uses of nuclear energy, nuclear safety, and space technology.[4]

Pakistan expected a greater role from Japan in the aftermath of 9/11 to weed out terrorism from the region, both with money and material. The 2002 visit of Koizumi and the following Security Dialogue generated enthusiasm in Islamabad about Japan-Pakistan security relations, particularly because of the equal treatment Tokyo meted out to New Delhi and Islamabad when both conducted nuclear explosions in 1998. Pakistan believed that Tokyo would follow the Washington line with money and material assistance to improve the security situation in and around Pakistan's region. The participation of Japan in the first Pakistan initiated Aman Naval Exercise in March 2007 was an indication of the need for closer cooperation between the two.

However, the expectation turned into dismay when Japanese Prime Minister Shinzo Abe (in his first term) restricted his visit only to India in September 2007, instead of visiting Pakistan also. Islamabad felt that Abe's 'India fever',[5] which includes Japan's tilt towards the Indo-US nuclear deal, Japanese willingness to initiate negotiation to sell nuclear material to India, and the concept of "broader Asia", which takes shape at the "confluence of the two seas" of the Indian and Pacific Oceans, was not in consonance with Pakistan's interests. Along with Abe's plan, the Arc of Democracy and Freedom mooted by the then foreign minister, Taro Aso to forge a group of countries comprising Japan, United States, Australia, India, and other Western democracies, to push democratic values in Asia, created anxiety and confusion about Japan's future policy toward Pakistan and South Asia in general.

However, Pakistan, as a frontline state against terrorism, expects that Japan would play a higher role in its effort to combat terrorism; especially in the context of Japan being an important financial provider of the Operation Enduring Freedom-Maritime Interdiction Operation (OEF-MIO) mission designed for anti-terrorism in the Indian Ocean. Although Japan cannot facilitate boots on the ground of its personnel, Tokyo is one of the frontline states which support US's counter terrorism mechanism in the region. In this regard, Pakistan hopes for greater financial support from Tokyo in its effort to counter terrorism within and outside Pakistan.

A major reason why Japan is not a major player in the security aspect of South Asia is because its contribution to capacity building on security issues has been low key. Arms sales are perceived as a factor to stabilize security cooperation between the buyer and supplier, Japan's domestic policy doesn't allow export of weapons for offensive purposes. Some of the regional countries now look at China for arms and other materials for their security purposes which has provided China a foothold in the South Asian region. China is the leading supplier of arms to Pakistan, Bangladesh and Sri Lanka. Pakistan-China security cooperation is publicized as all-weather relations, and Islamabad is getting various kinds military aid from Beijing which include 'PLA Package' instituted in 1981, the NORINCO package which began in 1999 with military aid of $60 million that increased to $300 million in 2003. Apart from that Pakistan gets 100 million Yuan (RMB) every year since 2004 as grant from the Chinese government for defense related procurement. Both countries are mulling joint military equipment development projects, such as the JF-17 thunder aircraft, which the Pakistani Air Force has already ordered a large number.[6] During the period of 2000-2009, China was the leading supplier of arms and ammunition to Sri Lanka and Bangladesh with exports worth $150 million and $270 million respectively.[7]

Top Arms Suppliers to Sri Lanka during 2000-2009 (USD Million)

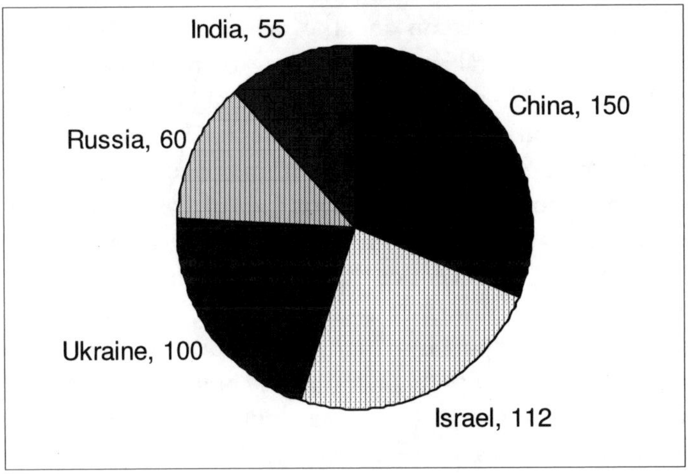

Top Arms Suppliers to Bangladesh during 2000-2009 (USD Million)

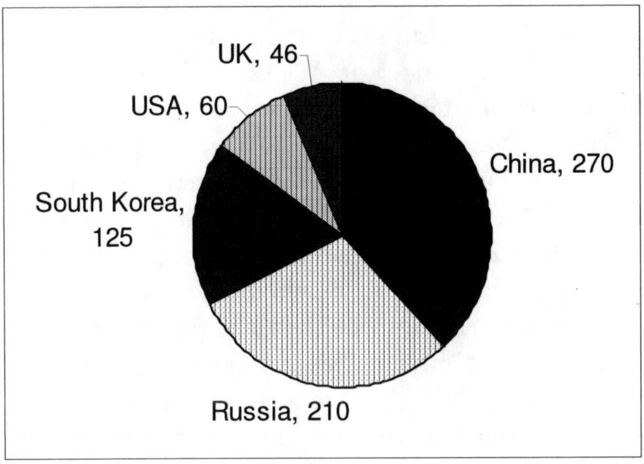

In many ways, Japan's security partnership with South Asia has been largely concentrated to its SLOC security concern in the Indian Ocean region and to counter Beijing's "string of pearls" strategy, designed to enhance its military presence in the Indian Ocean, and for that matter India attained an important role in the region. It is described that India is an important nation to Japan because of its geopolitical position and economic potential.[8] Japan seeks logistical support from the littoral countries for ships deployed in the Indian Ocean in anti-piracy operations.

Japan and the SLOC Security in the Indian Ocean

Maritime security has become one of the major aspects of Japan's defence policy in the post-cold war period. Threats to sea-lane security cannot be restricted to one area or region and the ramification is also wider. More cooperation between littoral countries is vital to counter such menace. The *Diplomatic Bluebook 2013* says, "it is important that Japan strives to strengthen relations with the countries with which it shares interests in maritime security including freedom of navigation."[9] SLOC from the Persian Gulf has assumed greater importance to almost all the countries of East Asia in the light of growing energy demand across the region. Japan is a major shipping nation and controls around 15 per cent of the global shipping fleet,[10] and Japanese ships have frequently faced pirate attacks, including in Somali waters. Japan's dependence on energy import is so high, as 99.6 per cent of oil, 100 per cent of its coal and 96. 4 per cent of its natural gas comes from overseas.[11] Japan's primary interest in the Indian Ocean has long been the safe passage of its energy supplies from the Middle East. As a result, SLOC security has become a 'top foreign policy issue in Tokyo' and 'a potential turning point' for Article 9 of the Japanese Constitution.[12]

According to the International Maritime Organization (IMO), Somalia-based piracy attacks dropped from 286 incidents in 2011 to 99 incidents in 2012. However, the success rate (of attacks) has increased.[13] In the South China Sea the number of attacks declined from 113 incidents in 2011 to 90 incidents in 2012, in West Africa it increased from 61 incidents in 2011 to 64 in 2012, while those in the Indian Ocean decreased from 63 to 33 within the same period.[14] The attacks in the Malacca Strait rose from 22 incidents in 2011 to 24 incidents in 2012.[15] In financial terms, maritime piracy off Somali coast alone cost the global economy between $5.7 and $6.1 billion in 2012, a reduction of 12.6 per cent from 2011.[16] The piracy prone areas of South China Sea, Malacca Strait, Indian Ocean, Western Africa and the Gulf of Aden are all linked to Japan's SLOCs so any disruption in any of these areas can affect Japan's economic and security interest. Since Japan does not have direct access to protect its interests in this region, it requires cooperation with friendly countries to ensure safety of the shipping route.

As early as the 1990s Japan identified maritime security challenges as one of the main aspects of its future security concerns. In 1994, Prime Minster Hosokawa Morihiro appointed a committee under Higuchi Hirotaro to identify Japan's security concerns in the post-cold war period. In his report, also known as 'Higuchi Report of 1994',[17] Higuchi clearly identified maritime security as a major challenge for Japan in the coming century. The report says 'interference in the safety of maritime traffic' together with the violation of territorial airspace, limited missile attack, illegal occupation of part of the country, terrorism and an influx of armed refugees are among the potential military dangers confronting Japan in the post-cold war period.[18] Due to extremely high degree of overseas dependence for energy supplies and trade in manufactured goods, Higuchi's nine member team stressed that the safety of maritime traffic was 'a matter of life and death to Japan'.

In the aftermath of the East Asian financial crisis of 1997, a tendency of organised crime on the maritime front in Southeast Asia became very evident. Various terrorist groups, some of which were affiliated to Al-Qaeda such as Jemaah Islamiya and Abu Sayyaf, engaged in maritime terrorism in the waters. The incidents of *Superferry 14* bombing in Manila Bay in February 2004, and the purported hijack training on a ship in the Indonesian waters by an unidentified group in 2003,[19] have spread the fear that maritime terrorism is genuine and a real threat to the region. After the 9/11 attacks, soft targets such as tourist sites and commercial establishments by home grown terrorist groups, have also raised concerns about maritime terrorism. Piracy became common phenomena in Southeast Asia during this period as the region experienced 35 per cent of global piracy incidents in 2003, even though it decreased from 47 per cent in 2000. An overwhelming percentage of the incidents involving Japanese ships occurred in Southeast Asian waters during these period; 27 out of 39 incidents took place in 1999 and 11 out of 12 of them in 2003.[20] A total of 138 out of 194 incidents, or 71 per cent of the total of the number of incidents involving Japanese ships, reported in the 14-year period from 1989 to 2003, have occurred in Southeast Asian waters,[21] and most of it was in Indonesian waters.

Acts of piracy and armed robbery, although reduced now, is a frequent phenomenon in the Indian Ocean region from Malacca Strait to the Gulf of Aden. The September 1998 hijacking of *Tenyu*, a Japanese owned cargo vessel chartered to carry aluminium ingots from the Sumatran port of Kuala Tanjung, and the October 1999 hijacking of Panama flagged *Alondra Rainbow* from the Malacca Strait, which was carrying aluminium to Japan, have proved that piracy is a major security issue. In July 2010, a Japanese tanker *M. Star*, approaching the Hormuz Strait, was attacked by a shadowy Islamist terrorist organisation Abdullah Azzam Brigades, which basically operated in Egyptian Sinai and Lebanon and had Al-Qaeda trained members. This served to highlight the vulnerability of Japanese energy in the region.[22] In June 2013, the Joint War Committee of Lloyds of London lists extensive areas of the Indo-Pacific as 'war risk' areas due to the risk of pirate attacks, including Eritrea, Gulf of Guinea, Libya, Nigeria, Somalia, Togo, north-west of Red Sea, west of the Gulf of Oman, Gulf of Aden, Yemen, the ports of Balikpapan and Jakarta in Indonesia, the Sulu archipelago, and northeast coast of Sumatra.[23]

Various government and semi-government documents published in Japan in the early 2000s show concern about Japan's vulnerability at sea. The 2000 edition of the *East Asian Strategic Review*, a quasi-official statement of the Ministry of Defence's analysis on regional security published annually by the National Institute for Defence Studies (NIDS), argued that "ensuring unhindered use of sea-lanes and the maintenance of peace and order on the high seas have become one of the major challenges for the security of East Asia."[24] The *Diplomatic Blue Book 2003* of the Ministry of Foreign Affairs stated that piracy "has become a major threat to Japan's maritime transport of its oil and other energy supplies via Southeast Asian sea on which it is largely dependent and also an adverse factor on the region's stability and economic development as a whole."[25] Further, the 2005 issue of the East Asian Strategic Review also highlighted the importance of threat of piracy and maritime terrorism in the region and the need for cooperation among the littoral countries to counter such threat.[26] The *Diplomatic Blue Book 2012* says, "Securing maritime security is not only crucial for Japan's existence and prosperity as a maritime and trading nation but also extremely important for regional economic development."[27]

Much before piracy attracted increased global attention, first in the Malacca Strait and then off Somalia from 2008 onwards, Japan was active in promoting cooperation to improve the safety and security of shipping. In 2000, the Japan Coast Guard took the lead in establishing the annual North Pacific Coast Guard Forum (NPCGF), which now includes as members the coast guards (or equivalent forces) of Canada, Japan, Russia, South Korea, and the United States. Indeed, Japan's anti-piracy maritime security cooperation is not just restricted to the Pacific, but increased largely to the Indo-Pacific region. By the middle of the 2000s, Southeast Asia, especially the Malacca Strait became the hotspot of piracy incidents as it is the one the busiest shipping routes in the world, as approximately 90 per cent of the oil imported to Japan goes through this strait, which therefore, is an extremely important sea lane for

Japan. In 2004, Tokyo initiated to convene Heads of the Asian Coast Guard Agencies Meeting (HACGM), which drew up various measures to address maritime security concerns, including piracy and terrorism affecting the region, and the 8th meeting was held in New Delhi in October 2012 in which 17 coast guard agencies participated.[28] Japan was instrumental in setting up of Regional Cooperation Agreement on Combating Piracy and Armed Robbery against Ships in Asia (***ReCAAP***) in November 2004, a regional governmental organisation to promote and enhance cooperation against piracy and armed robbery in Asia.[29]

In fact, Japan's financial and technical support to Southeast Asian countries has helped to reduce piracy, including the successful operation of MALSINDO. Japan extended grants up to a total of ¥1,921 million to Indonesia under the project for the construction of three patrol vessels for the "prevention of piracy, maritime terrorism and proliferation of weapons." Concretely, these sophisticated high speed patrol boats actually helped in countering piracy and other crimes in the Malacca Strait, apart from the coordinated MALSINDO naval operations. In 2012, Japan offered 10 brand new patrol ships to the Philippines "to boost the country's territorial defense in the West Philippine Sea".[30] Incidentally, the emergence of China and its actions in the maritime arena in the region has also seen by the Japanese leaders as a long-term threat to Japan's maritime security.

By playing a supportive role to ensure maritime security in the Southeast Asian region, Japan plays an active role in the in the Indian Ocean region, especially in the Somali waters. Since Tokyo's vulnerability in the region is more explicit, Japan decided in January 2009 to deploy JMSDF ships to protect Japanese commercial vessels off the coast of Somalia.[31] Following that, two destroyers were sent to Somalia in March 2009 to join the multinational naval forces operating in the area.[32] In May 2011, Japan sent two P-3C long range maritime patrol aircraft to Djibouti to strengthen its anti-piracy operation in the area.[33] With the aim of increased presence of JMSDF in the non-traditional security front such as anti-piracy operations, Japan set up a military base in Djibouti, for the first time after the World War II, where there will be an airfield and for maritime patrol aircraft and a permanent port facility for JMSDF warships.[34] Until then Japan was using American bases for logistical support for its warships ships in the region.

The deployment of Japanese warships for military operations beyond the territorial waters could not be done under the provision of Japanese constitution. In order to overcome this constitutional obstacle Japan passed Law on the Penalization of Acts of Piracy and Measures against Acts of Piracy in June 2009.[35] Initially the JMSDF ships were only meant to guard Japanese vessels, but the new law allows it to take more effective and appropriate measures against acts of piracy in cooperation with all countries concerned, and to escort vessels of other countries also.[36] However, weapons may still only be used for self-defence.

Against this backdrop, Japan has pursued various mechanisms to counter piracy and maritime terrorism which include strengthening MSDF and Coast Guard; enhancing cooperation with the littoral states; combating piracy through participating in multilateral mechanisms; and non-governmental responses. It must also be looked at in the context of China's increasing naval expedition in the Indian Ocean region in the name of anti-piracy operations. Beijing is looking for a legitimate presence in the Indian Ocean region by providing logistical support to various regional countries and actively participating in the antipiracy operations. Japan's security cooperation with India, a dominant power in the Indian Ocean region, mitigates Tokyo's maritime security concern in the Indian Ocean region. Importantly, piracy has become a strategic point for some Japanese policy makers and commentators in that it offers an uncontroversial pretext for exploring new security alignments with maritime states in the Indo-Pacific region. Prime Minster Koizumi exercised maritime security as a suitable platform to enhance Japan's role in the region and potentially a coalitional containment strategy directed at China.

Japan-India Security Cooperation

The security cooperation between India and Japan is part of extending their sphere of influence to other areas, as well as to counter China's perceived threat. For Japan, it necessarily needs India's support to ensure Japan's SLOC security. The strategic cooperation has begun with the Koizumi administration's process of "normalization". Prior to that, there was no common security interest for both the countries, while the relationship was hampered by nuclear squabbles.[37] Apart from the SLOC security, China's pursuit of pre-eminence in Asia and the emergence of India as a prominent economic and political power in Asia, especially in the Indian Ocean, have accelerated the need to bridge the gap between the two.[38] Japan believes that closer cooperation with India can counter China's possible hegemony in Asia as well as ensure its maritime security in the Indian Ocean region. It was during Prime Minister Koizumi's visit to New Delhi in 2005 that the relationship received the much needed momentum. He signed the "Japan-India Partnership in a New Asian Era: Strategic Orientation of Japan-India Global Partnership," and put in place an action plan called the "Eight-fold Initiative for Strengthening Japan-India Global Partnership" with his Indian counterpart Dr. Manmohan Singh.[39] Since then Indian and Japanese Prime Ministers make reciprocal visits to other's country every alternate year.

The relationship moved forward in 2007 when Japanese Prime Minister Shinzo Abe and his Foreign Minister Taro Aso visited New Delhi. Abe, in particular, had a strong belief in the key role of India in Japan's future, claiming that the India-Japan relationship 'will be the most important bilateral relationship (for Japan) in the world'.[40] He emphasized the importance of coming together of the two maritime nations in his concept of "broader Asia", which takes shape at the "confluence of the two seas" of the Indian and Pacific Oceans. Similarly, during Prime Minister Manmohan Singh's second visit to Japan in October 2008, he and Prime Minister Taro Aso issued a landmark "Japan-India Joint Declaration on Security Cooperation", the third such document on defense cooperation Tokyo has signed with a foreign partner, apart from its alliance treaty with the US and the 2007 agreement with Australia.[41]

Considering the importance of India for Japan, it has begun to particularly include South Asia, in its Defence White Paper from 2007 onwards. In the 2008 issue of the *Defence of Japan,* it says that historically India and Japan have been on good terms and need to "deepen dialogue and cooperation in the field of defence". The 2008 issue of the *East Asian Strategic Review* published by The National Institute for Defense Studies of Japan also portrayed India as "a major power in the region that plays a key rôle in the security of the Indian Ocean". It further says, "in any effort by Japan to enhance the security of those sea lanes, it is important to promote capacity building and the formation of multilateral cooperative frameworks among nations in Southeast Asia, a region that is not populated with any big powers. However, the key to improving security in the Indian Ocean is for Japan to strengthen its ties with India, the sole dominant power in that region". The 2011 issue of the *Defence of Japan* says that because of its location, India is an "extremely important country in a geopolitical sense for Japan".[42] Even the 2013 *Defence White Paper* says that India "has achieved steady economic growth in recent years, and has significant influence in the South Asian region", and also its location is "of strategic and geographical importance in terms of maritime traffic, connecting the Asia-Pacific region with the Middle East and Europe".[43]

India-Japan Maritime Security Cooperation

In fact, cooperation on the maritime front generated the necessity for close cooperation between India and Japan strategically in the current century. The cooperation was initiated mainly to protect the SLOCs and provide security for Japan-bound ships in the Indian Ocean, but lately it has become genuine bilateral defense cooperation with the aim of preserving Asian security per se. Since 80 per cent of oil meant for Japan passes through the Indian Ocean and 20 per cent of the ships bound for Japan that pass through the Indian Ocean are Japanese owned, their protection is a matter of concern for Japan. In 1999, a Japanese merchant ship *MV Alondra Rainbow* was hijacked in the Malacca Straits which was later recovered off the coast of Goa in a joint operation by the Indian Navy and the Coast Guard.[44] This rescue operation was appreciated by the Japanese government, which stated that the Indian initiative in this regard underscored the importance of international cooperation to challenge piracy.

During the visit of the then Indian Defence Minister George Fernandes to Tokyo in 2000, both countries initiated a security dialogue involving joint naval exercises, search and rescue missions and anti-piracy operations on the high seas. As a major power with considerable naval prowess, Japan understandably realised that India could assume a high-profile role in patrolling and safeguarding the busiest sea lane in the Indian Ocean. Close cooperation with India would therefore guarantee safe passage of Japan-bound oil and merchandise ships. As a gesture to enhance the maritime cooperation, Japan participated in the International Fleet Review held in Mumbai in February 2001. This was followed by the visit of a Maritime Self Defence Force (MSDF) squadron to Chennai in May 2001 and these kinds of friendly visits have been going on a continuing basis since then. This was followed by the first Japan-India Security Dialogue and the Japan-India Military-to-Military Consultation held in the same year. Both India and Japan have also hosted each other's naval chiefs. The Coast Guards of the two countries now conduct joint exercises, alternately in Indian and Japanese waters.[45] During the visit of the then Japanese Foreign Minister Kawaguchi Yoriko to Delhi in 2003, she stated that "cooperative maintenance of the security of maritime traffic in the sea lanes that stretch across the Indian Ocean and the Strait of Malacca (is) among the security and defence issues that deserve our increased attention. Both countries share common interest and concerns regarding the issues."[46] When Indian Defence Minister Pranab Muhkerjee visited Tokyo in May 2006 both countries agreed to enhance maritime cooperation which include service-to-service exchanges, including capacity building, which could lead to cooperation in disaster relief, maritime security, or other areas of mutual interest, exchange of ship visits between the Indian Navy and the Japan Maritime Self Defence Force, holding of goodwill exercises between the Indian Navy and the Japan Maritime Self Defence Force, and exchange of information and experiences in tackling regional and global issues, including international terrorism, proliferation of WMDs and their means of delivery, disaster relief and peace keeping operations.[47]

The prompt humanitarian relief operation after the tsunami in December 2004 has effectively demonstrated the capabilities of the Indian Navy in the Indian Ocean. In recent times, India has increased its manoeuvrability across the Indian Ocean with an advanced naval fleet that can deter any impending conventional challenge as well as 'new' threats like terrorism and fissile material proliferation. With increased military prowess in the Indian Ocean Region, combined with its economic growth, it is but natural for other countries to consider New Delhi as a 'net security provider in the Indian Ocean'. India provides technical and personnel assistance to small littoral countries such as Mauritius, Mozambique, Madagascar, Maldives and Sri Lanka to safeguard its shores as well as territorial waters, apart from transferring naval ships to them. At the same time India advocates that oceans are part of the global commons and maritime commons should remain open for the use of all. India is enhancing cooperation with other navies for the protection of SLOCs and other common maritime interests. In this regard, a stronger partnership with India will protect Japan's maritime interest in the Indian Ocean Region.

When Shinzo Abe took over the Prime Ministership from Koizumi in 2006, he sought to enlarge Japan's strategic profile in Asia and identified maritime domain as a conducive platform to push its case. He envisaged the coming together of the two maritime nations, India and Japan which will ensure Japan's maritime security in the Indian Ocean region. Abe's talk of "confluence of the two seas"[48] in the Indian parliament highlighted the necessity of cooperation between the two countries for the stability of the region. His idea of 'Quadrilateral Initiative' for the stability of 'broader Asia', from the Pacific to the India Ocean comprising of the US and Australia, Japan and India was to enhance maritime cooperation between them so that Japan's vulnerability of SLOC security in the Indian Ocean would be minimal. Tokyo wanted to enlarge its presence in the Indian Ocean following the US and in conjunction with Australia and India which made them participate in the Malabar-07 naval exercises held in the Bay of Bengal.

In April 2007, for the first time Japan participated in a naval exercise with India when the Indo-US Malabar exercises were held in the western Pacific. Following that the first ever PASSEX naval exercises conducted between India and Japan near the Boso Peninsula in central Japan in April 16, 2007 saw the participation of four destroyers from Japan's Maritime Self-Defence Force, and three warships from the Indian Navy. It was the first-ever trilateral naval exercise among the United States, Japan, and India. Taking the defence cooperation a step further, Japanese Maritime Self Defence Force (MSDF) participated along with the US, Australia and Singapore navies in a multilateral maritime exercise "Malabar 07-2" hosted by India in the Bay of Bengal from

September 4-9, 2007. Subsequently, PASSEX exercise was conducted in Mumbai from August 23-26, 2008, in which MSDF Kashima Training Ship and *Asagiri* and *Umagiri*, two frontline guided missile destroyers, and one Delhi class and one Corvette class ship from Indian side also participated.[49] Apart from this, the Coast Guard of India and the JMSDF conduct joint exercises, alternately in Indian and Japanese waters every year. To boost the defence cooperation between the two, Indian Naval Chief Admiral Sureesh Mehta visited Japan in August 2008, and held discussions with various defence officials of Japan. During the visit of Indian Defence Minster A. K Antony to Tokyo in November 2011, both countries decided to conduct first official bilateral naval exercise in 2012.[50] The first-ever bilateral naval exercise *JIMEX 12* was conducted off Sagami Bay in Japan in June 2012, in which two Japanese destroyers, one maritime patrol aircraft and a helicopter participated, while the Indian Navy was represented by INS Rana, INS Shivalik, INS Karmukh and INS Shakti.[51] Also, JMSDF and the Indian Navy have enhanced their cooperation in the anti-piracy operation in the Gulf of Aden and exchange schedules for escorts of civilian vessels.[52] Japan considers India as an important partner in the maritime security aspects in the Indo-Pacific region.

Taking the defense cooperation forward, India and Japan have started defense technology cooperation in recent times, albeit modestly. During the visit of Indian PM Dr. Manmohan Singh in May 2013 to Tokyo, a Joint Working Group (JWG) has been set up to explore the modalities for the cooperation on the US-2 (Shin Maywa) amphibian aircraft. This aircraft, capable of being used for air-sea rescue missions, will soon be provided to the Indian Coast Guard. The Shin Maywa agreement could be a harbinger of greater cooperation in the defense technology and hardware sector which will help cement the relationship between the two countries.

The other critical area of cooperation is maritime security and stability in the Indo-Pacific. The joint statement emphasized the mutual commitment towards "the freedom of navigation and unimpeded commerce based on the principles of international law, including the 1982 United Nations Convention on the Law of the Sea (UNCLOS)"—an indirect reference to the territorial dispute in the East and South China Sea. In a way both countries are expanding their interest to each other's areas and both are facilitating it.

Conclusion

The strategic relationship between India and Japan has become one of the most significant developments in the international relations of Asia-Pacific in the 21st century. It can address some of the pertinent security concerns of the region. Both India and Japan do not harbor any kind of ambition to dominate the region or for that matter, to be a threat to any other power. At the same time both are concerned by the domination of any single power in Asia. So a robust India-Japan defense cooperation can become an effective counter mechanism to China's possible hegemonistic ambitions in Asia.

Japan's overtures to the littoral countries in Southeast Asia and the Indian Ocean proved to establish Japan's increasing strategic presence in key areas where Japan has a vital stake. The provision in the Japanese constitution necessitates increased cooperation with littoral countries for the protection of the SLOC. It also allows Japan to overcome China's "feel-good" diplomacy that helped Beijing in winning the hearts of many of the Southeast Asian countries, which had pushed Japan to the back-seat of the Asian strategic scenario. At the same time it also provides the catalyst for widening the scope of the Japanese constitution to permit overseas deployment of the JMSDF. However, with the lack of auxiliary capacity to deploy JMSDF for long durations in the Indian Ocean and prohibition of using arms pre-emptively against pirates, Japan seeks cooperation with littoral countries, especially India.

END NOTES

1. Ministry of Foreign Affairs, "The Japan-Sri Lanka Summit Meeting", Government of Japan Tokyo, 14 March 2013. http://www.mofa.go.jp/region/page3e_000002.html
2. Nobuhito Hobo, "Message of Mr. Nobuhito Hobo Ambassador of Japan to the Democratic Socialist Republic of Sri Lanka", Ambassador of Japan to Sri Lanka, 29 October, 2013. http://www.lk.emb-japan.go.jp/eg/contents/ambmessageslenng.html
3. "Pak-Japan dialogue: Defence cooperation discussed", *The Express Tribune,* 25 October 2012. http://tribune.com.pk/story/456606/pak-japan-dialogue-defence-cooperation-discussed/
4. Ahmad Rashid Malik, "Pakistan-Japan Security Cooperation", *The Nation*, 24 February 2009. http://www.nation.com.pk/pakistan-news-newspaper-daily-english-online/columns/24-Feb-2009/PakistanJapan-Security-Cooperation
5. Ibid.
6. "Pakistan, China to step up security cooperation", China.org.cn, 4September 2013. http://www.china.org.cn/world/2013-09/04/content_29920324.htm
7. *SIPRI Yearbook*, Stockholm International Peace Research Institute (Oxford University Press), various years.
8. Japan's future path with India", The *Japan Times*, 13 December 2013.
9. Ministry of Foreign Affairs, Japan, *Diplomatic Blue Book, 2012*, Government of Japan, Tokyo, 2013, p. 22. http://www.mofa.go.jp/files/000019042.pdf
10. Tetsuo Kotani, Japan's maritime Challenges and Priorities", in Sam Bateman and Joshua Ho (eds.), *Maritime Challenges and Priorities in Asia: Implication for Regional Security*, Routledge, Abingdon, 2012, p. 204.
11. Ibid, p. 209.
12. Michael Penn, "Somali pirates and Political Winds Drive Japan to the Gate of Tears", *Japan Focus: The Asia Pacific Journal*, Vol. 4-2-09, 20 January 2009.
13. International Maritime Organization, "Reports on Acts of Piracy and Armed Robbery against Ships, Annual Report–2012" 2 April 2013. http://www.imo.org/OurWork/Security/SecDocs/Documents/PiracyReports/193_Annual2012.pdf

14. Ibid.
15. Ibid.
16. Economic Cost of Somali Piracy 2012.http://oceansbeyondpiracy.org/cost-of-piracy/economic
17. Advisory Group on Defence Issues, *The Modality of the Security and Defense Capability of Japan: The Outlook for the 21st Century*, Japanese government translation, GM" 3338, 12 August 1994.
18. Ibid, p. 18.
19. In March 2003, a group of 10 pirates took the helm of an oil tanker and steered it, altering the speed for about an hour off the coast of Sumatra, only to take custody of the vessel by the security forces. This incident touched off speculation that the terrorists might have used the tanker for training purposes in order to learn how to steer a ship. (National Institute for Defense Studies (NIDS), "Maritime Security in East Asia and the Nonproliferation of Weapons of mass Destruction", *East Asian Strategic Review-2005*, NIDS, Tokyo, 2005. P. 19).
20. National Institute for Defense Studies (NIDS), "Maritime Security in East Asia and the Nonproliferation of Weapons of mass Destruction", *East Asian Strategic Review-2005*, NIDS, Tokyo, 2005, p. 14.
21. Ibid.
22. William Maclean and Jonathan Saul, "Analysis: Militant raid on tanker shows Gulf security gap", *Reuters*, 22 November 2010. http://ru.reuters.com/article/idUKTRE6AL3VD 20101122
23. The war risk areas of 12 June 2013 can be found at http://www.lmalloyds.com/Web/market_places/marine/JWC/JW_Bulletins/JWLA021.aspx
24. National Institute for Defense Studies (NIDS), "Maritime Security Environment in East Asia", *East Asian Strategic Review-2000*, NIDS, Tokyo, 2000, p. 95.
25. Ministry of Foreign Affairs, Japan, *Diplomatic Blue Book, 2003*, Government of Japan, Tokyo, 2003, p. 176. http://www.mofa.go.jp/policy/other/bluebook/2003/
26. *East Asian Strategic Review-2000*, op cit.
27. Ministry of Foreign Affairs, Japan, *Diplomatic Blue Book, 2012*, Government of Japan, Tokyo, 2012, p. 31. http://www.mofa.go.jp/policy/other/bluebook/2012/pdfs/chapter3_p30_42.pdf
28. Press Information Bureau, "8th Heads of Asian Coast Guard Agencies Meeting (HACGAM):, Government of India, http://pib.nic.in/newsite/erelease.aspx?relid=88102
29. ReCAAP. http://www.recaap.org/AboutReCAAPISC.aspx
30. Frances Mangosing, "Philippines to receive 10 new patrol ships from Japan", http://globalnation.inquirer.net/37265/philippines-to-receive-10-new-patrol-ships-from-japan
31. Norimitsu Onishi and Mark McDonald, "Japan to deploy anti-piracy naval mission to Somalia waters" *New York Times*, 8 February 2009.http://www.nytimes.com/2009/01/28/world/asia/28iht-piracy.2.19743655.html?_r=0
32. "Japanese Navy Hits Somali Seas", 09 Apr 2009. http://www.isn.ethz.ch/Digital-Library/Articles/Detail/?lng=en&id=98783
33. "Japan to send P-3C aircraft on antipiracy mission off Somalia", *cctv*. http://english.cctv.com/20090515/110620.shtml
34. Alex Martin, "First overseas military base since WWII to open in Djibouti, *Japan Times*, 2 July 2011. http://www.japantimes.co.jp/news/2011/07/02/national/first-overseas-military-base-since-wwii-to-open-in-djibouti/#.UkVc_dKnqxU
35. "Anti-piracy law", *Japan Times*, 23 June 2009.http://www.japantimes.co.jp/opinion/2009/06/23/editorials/anti-piracy-law/#.UkVjuNKnqxU
36. "Statement by Prime Minister Taro Aso on the Enactment of the Law on the Penalization of Acts of Piracy and Measures against Acts of Piracy" Cabinet office of the Japanese Prime

Minster, 19 June 2009. http://www.kantei.go.jp/foreign/asospeech/2009/06/19danwa_e.html

37. In fact, India and Japan pursued identical view on nuclear disarmament and non-proliferation in the initial period of their relationship, but similarities began to blur after 1960 when Japan and US renewed their security pact. Since then Japan became an integral part of Cold War security set for East Asia. The main discord was about the nature of elimination of nuclear weapons. India stood for a comprehensive ban of all nuclear fissile materials while Japan's stand was ambiguous since the US nuclear umbrella protected it from a possible Soviet security threat. The situation was further aggravated when India conducted a peaceful nuclear test in 1974, to which Japan reacted severely, suspended aid loans to India, and passed a unanimous resolution in the Japanese *Diet* condemning India's action. Wasting no time, Japan ratified the Nuclear Non Proliferation Treaty (NPT) in 1976. Since then, Japan has been cooperating with the US and other nuclear countries in preventing further expansion of the nuclear club. Japan reacted harshly to India's nuclear tests in 1998 by suspending all grant aid and subsequent new yen loans. Japan took on the role of the chief global advocate of punishing' India for its defiance of the NPT regime in the UN, at the G-8 summit, at the ASEAN Regional Forum (ARF) meeting and other international forums. Japan also played a leading role in drafting and proposing a UN resolution that was unanimously adopted by the UN General Assembly on 6 June 1998. At the bilateral level, Japan had always demanded India to sign the NPT until recently. When the Indian Foreign Minister Madhav Singh Solanki visited Tokyo in 1992, Japan threw a broad hint that Japan may cut off its developmental aid to India unless New Delhi signed NPT, otherwise, India has to accept International Atomic Energy Agency (IAEA) inspectors to India's nuclear facilities to confirm that it is indeed not developing nuclear weapons.
38. Joshy M. Paul, "India and Japan: Reluctant Idealism to Practical realism", *South Asian Survey*, Vol. 15, No.1, 2008, p. 110
39. Ministry of Foreign Affairs, "Japan-India Partnership in a New Asian Era: Strategic Orientation of Japan-India Global Partnership", Government of Japan, Tokyo, http://www.mofa.go.jp/region/asia-paci/india/partner0504.html
40. David Brewster, "The India-Japan Security Relationship: An Enduring Security Partnership?"*Asian Security*, Vol. 6, No.2, (2010), p. 97.
41. 'The New Security Architecture: Binding Japan And Australia, Containing China', *Nautilus Institute*, 15 March 2007.http://www.nautilus.org/~rmit/forum-reports/0707a-tanter.html
42. Ministry of Defence, *Defence of Japan 2011*, Government of Japan, Tokyo, 2011, p . 335.
43. Ministry of Defence, *Defence of Japan 2013*, Government of Japan, Tokyo, 2013, p.92.
44. Vijay Sakhuja, 'Indo-Japanese Maritime Security Cooperation', *Strategic Analysis, Vol.* XXIV, No. 1, 2000, p. 187.
45. Arunkumar Bhatt, 'India, Japan Hold Joint Coast Guard Exercise', *The Hindu,* 26 November 2006.
46. Madhuchanda Ghose, "India and Japan's Growing Synergy", *Asian Survey*, Vol. 48, No. 2, 9 April 2008, pp. 287-88.
47. Ministry of External Affairs, "Joint Statement, Visit of Mr. Pranab Mukherjee, Minister of Defence to Japan", Government of India, New Delhi, May 25, 2006. http://mea.gov.in/bilateral-documents.htm?dtl/6159/Joint+Statement+Visit+of+Mr+Pranab+Mukherjee+Minister+of+Defence+to+Japan
48. *Confluence of the Two Seas,* Speech by H.E. Mr. Shinzo Abe, Prime Minister of Japan at the Parliament of the Republic of India, Ministry of Foreign Affairs, Government of Japan, Tokyo, August 22, 2007, http://www.mofa.go.jp/region/asia-paci/pmv0708/speech-2.html
49. "PASSEX 2008: Japanese naval ships to visit India from Aug. 23-26", *India Defence,* August 2008, http://www.india-defence.com/reports-3981

50. "Japan-India Defence Ministers Meeting", Embassy of Japan in India, New Delhi, 2 November 2011, http://www.mod.go.jp/j/press/youjin/2011/11/02_pr_e.pdf
51. "First Indo-Japan bilateral Naval Exercise 'JIMEX12 underway", Indian Navy. http://indiannavy.nic.in/press-release/first-indo-japan-bilateral-naval-exercise-jimex12-underwayhttp://indiannavy.nic.in/press-release/first-indo-japan-bilateral-naval-exercise-jimex12-underway
52. National Institute for Defence Studies (NIDS), *East Asian Strategic Review 2013*, NIDS, Tokyo, 2013, Japan, p. 57.

8

Knocking at the Himalayan Gates: China's Perspectives on SAARC

Srikanth Kondapalli

Introduction

China is geographically contiguous to South Asia. After the successive dynasties of yore expanded their territorial limits to far-flung western regions, China today borders five of the eight SAARC countries, viz., Afghanistan, Pakistan, India, Nepal and Bhutan; although with the latter it does not have formal diplomatic relations. With Maldives, China had upgraded its diplomatic ties by opening an embassy in Male only recently. Apart from China, the other eight Observers (*guanchayuan guo*) include Australia, Iran, Japan, Mauritius, Myanmar, the European Union, South Korea and the United States who were admitted in phases. As an Observer, China has little to do in the decision-making process of the SAARC, although through like-minded parties it had sought to influence the course of the SAARC process. An Observer of the SAARC gets only a few minutes to make a formal address at the summit meetings. Hence, being an Observer, all the basic aspects of multilateralism, viz., equality, reciprocity, non-discrimination, common security, peaceful resolution of conflicts, mutual trust, confidence building measures, non-specificity of enemy, etc. are technically not applicable to China even though it had shown increasing interest in these issues. This article traces the main triggers for China to associate with the SAARC, outlines issues related to membership, delves into the main contours of China's political and economic interactions in the SAARC process, identifies broad perceptions, issues and dynamics of such Chinese participation—mainly in the economic field—and offers concluding comments. A cross-section of official, semi-official/think-tank and scholarly perspectives in China are consulted below.

Triggers

As a geographically contiguous entity, China has several core interests vis-à-vis the SAARC region. Recent geo-political changes in the region also have added this urgency for Beijing to get connected to the region. Foremost, China is concerned with the stability of its western regions that border South Asia and Central Asia. The disintegration of the then Soviet Union in the late 1980s, formation of independent states in Central Asia in the early 1990s, gradual spread of religious extremism in the last decade have all brought new challenges to the peripheries of China. Starting from its Mongolian borders, through Altai Mountains and Central Asian and the Himalayan borders up to Southeast Asia, several Chinese analysts view these peripheries as potentially destabilising to the peaceful rise of China.[1] Developments related to political disturbances in Mongolia, "coloured revolutions" in Central Asia, the resurgence of the Taliban and Al Qaeda forces in Afghanistan and Pakistan, "saffron revolution" in Myanmar, political turmoil in Thailand and insurgency in the Philippines—are all part of the so-called "arc of destabilisation" for China. According to Chen Xiangyang, an Associate Researcher of Institute of World Political Studies of China Academy of Contemporary International Relations:

> "The political disturbances in China's peripheral countries have brought a series of severe challenges to the peaceful development of China. First, the "spillover" effect has jeopardized China's frontier stability and security. In particular, instability in central Asia, South Asia, and West Asia likely will have an impact on China's geo-west front and the "three forces" [viz., extremism, separatism and splittism] again will stupidly try to take action, and thus China's "great development of the West" program and security on the west side will face a new and complicated trial. Second, major Western countries and others will take advantage of the opportunity to fish in troubled waters and invade and erode the geo-supportive areas for China's peaceful development. Third, the disturbances have affected China's strategy to encourage the economy to expand to the peripheral regions, and the pressure on protecting our overseas interests has increased. Fourth, the disturbances have brought new challenges to China's peripheral diplomacy, and ensuring our sovereignty and stability has become more difficult and China's diplomatic principle of "not interfering in other countries' internal affairs" is facing the impact of the "Chinese responsibility theory". Fifth, the disturbances have affected the regional cooperation processes around China and held back the economic integration in Asia."[2]

Specifically on Afghanistan and Pakistan, Chinese analysts view the recent periodic violence in these countries as a manifestation of the long-term instability. In order to overcome these problems that pose destabilizing effects on its western frontiers, a series of measures are proposed by China, including proactive relations with regional states, multilateral interactions, political communications with emerging actors (including with the Taliban), bilateral/multilateral counter-terrorism exercises, military cooperation, nuclear stability, economic inroads aimed at creating dependencies and coping with the possible withdrawal of the US forces from the region and seizing strategic initiatives.

Secondly, for creating conditions of domestic stability and building a "well-off society" by 2020 (as the 16th, 17th and 18th Party Congresses resolved in 2002, 2007 and 2012 respectively) it is essential for China to follow, in its periphery, a policy of good neighbourliness in the early part of the 21st century.[3] China revised its 1954 formulations of good neighbourliness recently in view of its increasing dependence on the neighbourhood and the US's entry into the Central and Southwest Asian region as part of its counter-terrorism efforts. Along with the good neighbourliness policy is the Chinese emphasis on Five Principles of Peaceful Co-existence (*Panch Sheel*) formulated in the 1950s and revived recently. These provide a cushioning effect to the Chinese state's sovereignty and territorial integrity and wards off critical challenges emanating from outside. These emphasise minimalist positions of China on issues related to Tibet, Xinjiang, Inner Mongolia and Taiwan. By proposing these policies to other countries, China binds them in politico-legal framework conducive for China's national interests.

Thirdly, and related to the above, are the counter-terrorism imperatives. China is attracted to the main agenda of the SAARC, viz., counter-terrorism, in this context. At the 12th SAARC summit in Islamabad, an Additional Protocol to the 1987 SAARC Convention on Terrorism was signed. Two major developments in the last decade have led to the furthering of counter-terrorism cooperation and measures towards protecting law and order in Pakistan. One, according to the Chinese view, there exist links between the separatist groups among Uighurs of Xinjiang region and the Al Qaeda units in Pakistan/Afghanistan training camps. Second, several Chinese nationals living in Pakistan and Afghanistan were targeted by militants in these countries. To overcome these issues, China had initiated a qualitatively higher form of cooperation with Pakistan, specifically with its armed and law enforcement forces.[4]

Fourthly, as a comprehensive package to address its domestic regional inequalities and to shift the focus away from security and usher in development and seize the initiative, China is making all efforts for the success of its Western Development Campaign. A corrective measure has been launched by the Chinese leadership is to expand economic growth from eastern regions to the backward western areas of the country. This is also meant to secure the peripheries by further integrating these regions economically and politically as well as shifting Han nationals into these peripheries and demographically changing the region. Han nationalism in these peripheries could also serve the Chinese state in subjugating the restive minorities in the longer term.

Current efforts are in terms of developing infrastructure projects in the western regions which are relatively inaccessible. Mention should be made of the 1,118 kilometre long Tibetan railway from Golmud to Lhasa completed by 2006 and extension to Xigaze to be completed in 2014, expanding the road, airfield and fibre optic network, apart from the East-West energy pipelines from Xinjiang to Shanghai. Adjoining India, China had expanded its infrastructure rapidly. China built a highway through Aksai Chin in 1954-57. Four such highways exist today in Tibet. In 2007, Pakistan announced plans to connect Havellian with the Karakoram highway with a railway line.[5] Gwadhar naval port in the western Makran coast of Pakistan was built with Chinese assistance by the China Harbour Engineering Company, a subsidiary of China Communications Construction. The first phase of the project, conceived in 1964 but started in 2002, was completed in 2006 with China spending $198 million as against the Pakistani share of about $50 million in a project estimated at over $1 billion. In 2013, a Chinese company took over its operations following an invitation by the Pakistan Defence Ministry to do so.

Fifthly, as a maximalist policy, China has of late, been striving for big power status and attempting to balance the United States at the global and regional levels and India at the regional levels. China is striving for this position primarily through economic, trade and infrastructure development as the South Asian region had been traditionally cut-off owing to the Himalayan barriers. As elaborated below, China had made concerted efforts in becoming a full-fledged member of the SAARC even as it tried to deny the same to the United States and India in other multilateral institutions. For instance, Indian efforts to enter into the East Asian Summit (EAS) around the same time as China joined the SAARC as Observer, is a case in point. While on paper and official rhetoric, China maintained a cooperative position on this issue, Malaysia and China were reluctant to admit India as a member of the EAS initially.[6] China was keen to retain lead by the ASEAN+3 rather than ASEAN+6 and was initially averse to the expansion of the grouping to include India, Australia and New Zealand. It was also reported that due to pressures from Japan and Singapore, Indian candidature in the EAS was finally accepted. Diplomatic parleys between India and China from the time of Premier Wen Jiabao's visit to New Delhi in April 2005 and President Hu Jintao's visit in November 2006 reportedly also contributed to the relative "accommodation" of India in the EAS. It needs to be noted that Japan and Singapore played a crucial role in the Indian candidature in the EAS process.[7]

Another case is that of the membership in the Shanghai Cooperation Organization (SCO). Membership of the SCO is based on Article 13 of the SCO Charter adopted in June 2002. Apart from respecting "the objectives and principles" of the SCO Charter, the aspirants have to "comply with the provisions of other international treaties and instruments adopted in the framework of SCO".[8] In April 2004, the SCO adopted regulations on admitting Observer states and/or institutions. These regulations suggest that aspirant states should show "respect for the sovereignty, territorial integrity and equal rights of the member states".[9] The above provisions—positive and negative demands on the aspirant states/organizations—imply that the potential entrants should have a clean record with the United Nations system (in terms of no sanctions, violations, etc. as the SCO charter suggests that it abides by the UN Charter); secondly, that the potential candidates should not have any territorial disputes with the SCO states; and thirdly that they should not have any conflicting interests with that of the SCO states.[10] While these implications may or may not be enforced by the SCO in admitting new members, these restrictions do suggest to a lot of diplomatic bargaining, specifically as consensus of the SCO members is invoked here. In 2010, "Regulations on Accepting New Members" were formally signed although no progress was achieved in this regard so far in admitting new members. In June and October 2002 and again in February 2003, India had indicated that it subscribes to the principles of the SCO and that it intends to apply for membership.[11] In April 2004, India applied for membership in the SCO. However, so far there is no progress on this issue.

Membership Issue

While China has become an Observer in the SAARC since 2005 in principle, it has ambitions to become a full-fledged member of this multilateral organization. Several Chinese have cited geographical contiguity, trade and political interactions, historical links to the region as the basis for desiring membership in the SAARC. Overall, the role of an Observer—as against a full-fledged member—is limited in nature in any organisation.[12] At the twice-postponed 13th SAARC summit in Dhaka, China's candidature for Observer position was accepted reportedly under the pressure of Bangladesh, Pakistan and Nepal, while India wanted China first to sign bilateral MoUs with respective South Asian countries. Before the 2008 summit meeting in Sri Lanka, China's assistant foreign minister He Yafei stated: "We are hoping for a bigger role at this year's summit in Sri Lanka".[13] At the 16th summit meeting of the SAARC in Thimpu in 2010, Nepal reportedly supported China's candidature as a member, with backing from Pakistan and Bangladesh,[14] although opposed by India, Bhutan, Afghanistan and Maldives.[15]

While the Addu Summit of the SAARC in November 2011 had stated that it should "undertake a comprehensive review of all matters relating to SAARC's engagement with Observers, including the question of dialogue partnership before the next Session of the Council of Ministers in 2012", it is nullified by the provision that "institutionalisation process" and firming up of the SAARC identity should first take place before the membership is opened further. To recall, by 2008 a moratorium on admitting new Observers in the organisation was made.[16] Later, India's External Affairs minister stated in Male in February 2014 that

> "SAARC needs to clarify its thinking on the nature and the direction of its relationships with partner States who have Observer status...Some of the Observer States have done commendable work with our Association, but it is important that we define a clear set of policies and objectives for these relationships and their future direction, before we move further."[17]

As the membership drive of China in the SAARC had taken twists and turns, China had suggested other alternatives. Given its recent status as the 2nd largest economy in the world and having substantial trade relations with the SAARC constituents, China had proposed the SAARC+1 (China) initiative much in the format of the ASEAN+3 (China, Japan and South Korea). This proposal however, did not gain much support in the SAARC, although it was an indication of China's ambitions.[18]

China's Interactions

China's interactions with the SAARC as a multilateral institution have been modest so far with very few high-level political or diplomatic leaders willing to engage with the organization. [See Annexure 1 & 2] Its agenda also has been modest. China joined the SAARC in principle at the November 2005 meeting at Dhaka as an Observer. Foreign minister Li Zhaoxing became the first high-level official to attend the SAARC meeting at its 14th summit in New Delhi in 2007.[19] On this occasion, China's Foreign Ministry's annual report for 2008 outlined the following policies towards the SAARC, thus:

> "As the biggest neighboring country of South Asia, China hoped to see harmony and common development of South Asian countries and a growing SAARC with greater role in international and regional affairs. China welcomed and appreciated SAARC's decision to accept China as an Observer and supported the goal and priority areas of development of SAARC, respecting the will of its member countries in the spirit of equality,

mutual trust, cooperation and win-win outcome. China also proposed ideas for future cooperation with SAARC on specific projects."[20]

Li, in his address to the SARC summit meeting, underlined the rising status of the South Asian region in economic terms. He suggested China's inputs in five areas, viz., poverty alleviation, disaster relief, training programs in human resources development, infrastructure and energy, and hosting seminars.[21]

Next year, China sent vice foreign minister Wu Dawei to the summit meeting in Sri Lanka. Here China suggested that apart from project-based proposals, it will "enhance cooperation in economy, trade, agriculture, transport, human resources training, disaster prevention and reduction..."[22]

In April 2010, attending the 16th Summit meeting in Bhutan, Deputy Foreign Minister Wang Guangya stated that China intends to expand relations with SAARC on the basis of the Five Principles of Peaceful Co-existence.[23] Wang announced a donation of $300,000 to the SAARC Development Fund.[24] The SAARC Development Fund was formed at the 16th summit meeting of the SAARC in 2010. On the eve of the Maldives meeting in 2011, China's foreign ministry spokesman stated that China is looking forward for "more pragmatic and effective cooperation" with the SAARC.[25] At the 17th summit meeting in November 2011 at Addu in Maldives, Vice Foreign Minister Zhang Zhijun of China announced another $300,000 to the SAARC Development Fund and suggested "pragmatic and more effective cooperation mechanisms".[26] In June 2012, China named its Ambassador to Nepal as the Ambassador to SAARC concurrently – indicating an institutional approach in the making, much like its Middle East Envoy (who also looks after Africa). In November 2012, Yang donated $300,000 for the 2012 Development Fund during his visit to Bhutan.[27]

Economic Interactions

China's interactions with the SAARC member states in the economic field have been more intensive than in other areas.[28] SAARC's huge geography expanses, diversity, huge resources—human, financial and raw materials—all are gainful to China. So far China's main initiatives in this field include expansion of trade, bringing the SAARC constituents under the fold of Business Forum and Commodity Fairs at Kunming and forming free trade agreements. By these, it had emerged as the largest trading partner for many a South Asian state, and of late, often displacing even India in this field. It had signed a Free Trade Agreement (FTA) with Pakistan in 2006 and is poised to do the same with Sri Lanka in 2014. In April 1993, the SAARC countries had agreed to form an FTA, although ever since then they have been sorting out various issues related to trade liberalization and other aspects. This agreement, the South Asian Free Trade Agreement (SAFTA), came into force in January 2006.

China's trade with South Asia has increased substantially—by almost 26 percent in the last decade from $5.7 billion in 2000 to $26.7 billion in 2005 to $30 billion in 2007 and to $93 billion in 2012, with China's imports from the region increasing from $ 1.9 billion in 2000 to $ 22.6 billion in 2012.[29] More than half of China's trade with South Asia, however, is with India. This economic dimension—trade figures in terms of importing raw materials from these SAARC countries, and export of consumer products to these countries – is beneficial to China [See Annexure III]. However, despite trade surpluses with the region, we have not seen major capital exports or tourism outflows from China to this region. According to Li Jinzao, China's Vice Minister of Commerce, by 2012, China's non-financial direct investment in South Asia amounted to about $4 billion—which represents a miniscule of China's investments in other parts of the world.[30] However, to what extent this economic clout will influence Beijing's political overtures in the region are not clear yet. According to a study conducted at the University of Wisconsin-Madison, the findings suggested as follows:

> "It is difficult to discern whether China has geopolitical reasons for strengthening economic ties with South Asia. On the one hand, Chinese objectives could be strictly a function of export-led growth strategies and a desire to expand trade routes. On the other hand, ties to the region could be equally important for China to exercise diplomatic pressure and extend the reach of its military. This potential development is the particular fear of India, China's prime rival in South Asia."[31]

Another initiative of China is to invite the SAARC chambers of commerce and industry to China. To promote trade, the China-South Asia Business Forum was established in December 2004 in Kunming with the initial meeting focusing on "Communication, Cooperation, Development and Mutual Benefits".[32] China's nodal agency in this effort is the China Council for the Promotion of International Trade. Two years later, the China-South Asia Business Council was established as a link between nearly 40 Chinese companies and SAARC chambers of commerce and industry.[33] At the third such meeting of this business council in June 2008, it was suggested that Kunming, where the three annual meetings were held so far, should be made the venue for the subsequent meetings, indeed for all business, commodity fairs etc., between China and the SAARC countries.[34]

Although Xinjiang is contiguous to Afghanistan, Pakistan and India, apart from Central Asia, and even though China had identified Kashgar as one of the Special Economic Zones, there has been much emphasis on Kunming which borders Myanmar. Since the 1990s Yunnan and Sichuan provinces are at the forefront of economic reforms and growth in the south-western regions of China. Chinese capitalism is more robust in Yunnan than in the far-flung Xinjiang which is only witnessing marketization recently with capital influx from coastal regions of China. Yunnan had expressed the desire to connect to the Indian Ocean through Myanmar. The Bangladesh-China-India-Myanmar (Kunming) Initiative was triggered with this idea of connectivity to the Indian Ocean.[35] Yunnan could also be a bridge between Southeast Asian regionalism and South Asian regionalism.[36] For the Chinese leaders Yunnan is more secure than the restive Xinjiang. However, it was not until the 4th such business council meeting at Kunming in 2009 that all SAARC member states' chambers of commerce and industry were represented.[37] In June 2013, another initiative—China-South Asia Exposition began at Kunming with Bangladesh as the theme country for that year.[38]

The third initiative of China is to access the South Asian market through FTA proposals. China has an FTA with Pakistan. This is the first FTA with the South Asian region.[39] In November 2003, both signed a preferential trade agreement, which became operational from January 2004. After the visit of premier Wen Jiabao to Islamabad in 2005, both sides agreed to implement the Early Harvest Programme (which became operational from January 2006). By this, China agreed to reduce tariffs on 767 items to zero. By 2008, the FTA was implemented covering nearly 90 percent of commodities.[40] In all, about 2,500 tariff lines are allowed under this FTA. However, to the chagrin of the Pakistani Directorate-General of Intelligence and Investigation, a department of its Federal Board of Revenue, massive misuse of this facility had been reported, including sudden jump in the import of mobile phone sets, wrong "certificates of origin", false declaration of imports (from Hong Kong), resulting in loss of revenue for Pakistan.[41] China plans to have a similar FTA with Sri Lanka and the negotiations are expected to be completed in 2014.[42] While China had proposed an FTA with India, the latter had not cleared the idea yet, instead suggesting a toned-down version of a regional trade agreement.[43]

However, China does not have robust economic cooperation agreements with all countries in South Asia. China had signed trade agreements and protocols, economic cooperation agreements and taxation agreements with five countries, viz., Nepal, Bangladesh, Sri Lanka, India and Pakistan and bilateral investment protection with four countries, viz., Bangladesh, Sri Lanka, India and Pakistan.[44] Also, China's investments in the SAARC region (although it has picked up recently) have only been marginal so far.

China's Perceptions

China's official and diplomatic views on SAARC, as mentioned above, are positive, forthcoming but cautious. These indicate the eagerness of China to enter into the SAARC in a systematic manner without possibly ruffling feathers in the region. However, the research output from China in the universities and think-tanks, are either prescriptive or ne-realist in orientation. A cross section of views from China is outlined below briefly.

Chen Jidong of Sichuan University—major base where South Asian Studies program had been uninterrupted in comparison to other centers of study in China—argued that the SAARC region is crucial for China from economic, strategic and national security point of view. In order to gain membership in the SAARC, Chen suggested that China should push for thrust in four areas, viz., further training programs for the SAARC officials, interact with the SAARC Secretariat, initiate "cooperation funds" with the organization, and enhance exchanges.[45] Moreover, China's approach should not be a "high profile" but "active and natural" in approaching the SAARC members. Another incremental approach was suggested by Shen Dingli in the backdrop of the Indian reservations on China's membership in the SAARC, thus:

> "..., China ought not to be in a hurry to seek the full membership of SAARC. It should do so when it feels it to be necessary, and when it can make a contribution to South Asia without India feeling its legitimate interests undermined. There is still some distance to go in this direction before attaining an all-win outcome."[46]

There were other suggestions as well from the Chinese side, including learning from the other multilateral institutions like the ASEAN. Ma Ying of the Shanghai Institute of International Studies suggested that although huge differences exist between the SAARC and the ASEAN in terms of territory, productivity, political issues, integration process, working mechanism in the institutions etc, the SAARC needs to accommodate views of smaller countries and not be confined to the India-Pakistan rivalry.[47] Another, Jiang Yaping suggested that the SAARC countries should further liberalize trade and conclude an FTA quickly.[48] In the economic field, He Zhijuan argued that China will be able to bring in more resources to the SAARC in future if it is given the membership.[49] Tian Yun suggested that unlike the ASEAN, the SAARC has greater market potential for China and hence Beijing needs to further economic cooperation with the SAARC countries.[50]

On December 14, 2006, China Institutes of Contemporary International Relations organized an international conference on China-SAARC with scholars and diplomats from different countries. Hu Shisheng suggested in his presentation here that China has four objectives in the SAARC, viz., to enhance the international influence of the SAARC, prioritize economic issues, promote SAARC economic integration process and evolve an equal negotiation mechanism [*pingdeng xieshang jizhi*] in the organization. Hu also suggested that in order to usher in a win-win situation [*shuangying jumian*] efforts should be made to avoid formation of camps in the SAARC.[51]

A paper presenter at the China Institute of International Studies-Sichuan University-Bhandaranayake International Affairs Research Centre held at Chengdu in August 25-26, 2009 argued that the SAARC region is not conducive for China to enter as the whole region exhibits turbulence [*dongdang*], chaos [*hunluan*] or is poverty-ridden [*pinqiong*]. While China had prioritised bilateral relations with the South Asian countries, there is however, a need look at the multilateral processes as well.[52] For enhancing ties between China and the SAARC, four suggestions were made, viz., free flow of goods and services through transportation corridors and infrastructure projects; economic cooperation through business councils and fora, expanding cultural and educational contacts and promoting tourism. Further, it was suggested that institutionalisation of relations between the members and Observers in the SAARC should be made. A year before, similar suggestions were made at an international conference at Beijing from April 19-20, 2008 on the subject. The ten points made were:

1. Establish consultative mechanisms, including practical and efficient regular meetings to discuss proposals and plans
2. Project work as the basis for economic cooperation and integration in South Asia
3. Consultations in the United Nations and other fora
4. Strengthen infrastructure construction and various forms of transportation through the SAARC Development Fund
5. Eradication of poverty, and cooperation in other areas of rural development
6. Strengthen exchanges in human resources development, technical cooperation, training facilities and academic fields
7. Counter-terrorism and countering arms, human and drug trafficking
8. Strengthen bilateral technical exchanges in non-traditional security issues such as the environment, climate change and food security
9. Promote balanced development of both trade and economic cooperation and other forms of cooperation in the South Asia Economic Forum Annual Meeting—SAARC trade fairs and others, with China

10. Through tourism, exchange student exchanges, sports and culture, to strengthen mutual understanding and contact[53]

According to Ye Hailin of the Chinese Academy of Social Sciences, China had a one-dimensional focus on the SAARC countries with its security as the main concern. However, now it is adjusting its policy in a multidimensional multilateral diplomatic framework. Ye suggested that China faces two main problems in integrating with the SAARC, viz.,

> "As a main regional cooperative organization, SAARC is too weak to play a connecting tie and dialogue stage between China and South Asian countries. SAARC hasn't been an entity with an unanimous voice and failed to play a crucial role in the interaction between China and South Asia. In the near future, the traditional bilateral diplomacy would remain as the pillars of Chinese South Asian policy. [Secondly,] India, the core member of SAARC and engine of the regional integration, is suspicious of the Chinese intention and function in this process, not willing to live comfortably under more significant influence of China. And India is not the only one murmured against Chinese participation in the region. Some external elements also wish to "balance" China in South Asia, such as Japan, a very zealot advocator of "Democracy Community"."[54]

In a post-graduate (MA) dissertation submitted to Hebei Normal University in 2012, Fan Yibing recognised the central and leading position of India in the SAARC process given its size, resources, development and influence. However, as "counter-measures" to such dominance, and almost echoing Hu Shisheng's prescription as cited above, Fan suggested the following as policy options for China:

- Promoting and continuing the integration of each member states of the SAARC;
- Efforts to reduce Indian domination in South Asia and "properly handling" relations with other South Asian countries;
- Reducing tensions between India and Pakistan
- Strengthening cooperation between SAARC countries and other countries/international organisations.[55]

Liu Zhujun in the MA dissertation submitted to the Foreign Affairs College in 2010 suggested that China should strive for improving relations with India and economic diplomacy with the other SAARC members.[56] Han Bing of Yunnan University Development Research Institute argued that mere Observer position of China in the SAARC and lack of institutional procedures for China's participation in this grouping hampers such relations and that China should strive to become a full member by primarily emphasising on functional cooperation with member states.[57]

Conclusions

China's interactions with the SAARC have been only recent and that too as an Observer. As an Observer it has participated only in four summits so far and was represented by mid-level officials with the exception of foreign minister Li Zhaoxing in 2007. No President or Premier of China had ever addressed such summits and possibly indicates to the low-level of symbolic importance attached by China to this process. Yet, many an official or scholar had suggested that China is keen on joining the organisation. On the main issues that have been generally identified as the core aspects of the SAARC, viz., social sector, counter-terrorism, climate change and economic integration, China had shown much interest and is reflected in its "pragmatic and effective cooperation" approach and "five-point" initiative.

As a new entrant to multilateral institutions—internationally isolated as it were till about the 1980s—China had shown tremendous interest in such processes recently. China had either joined, along with others, or had made efforts to form/shape multilateral institutions in the last two decades. Aiming for regional security, cooperation, prosperity and stability of its border areas, China had been a major beneficiary of such institutions. These have also contributed to the profile of China in the international and regional systems. Mention should be made of the SCO, EAS, ASEAN Regional Forum and others—apart from the United Nations – where China had been increasingly exerting itself and contributing to its big power status. In the case of both the SCO and ARF, China made net gains as Central Asia and Southeast Asia were spaces previously of the Soviet Union and the United States. China has similar objectives in the SAARC, although check-mated to an extent by India or other Observers.[58] A dominant Indian position in the SAARC is not conducive for the global and regional ambitions of China. Hence this needs to be addressed by Beijing even if it has to invoke its ancient realist strategy of "*hexiao kongda*" [cooperate with the small to counter the big] in South Asia. Such Cold War mentality is still prevalent in China's actions and words in South Asia, although some moderate voices are also heard once in a while. Also, being an Observer in the SAARC, all the basic principles of multilateralism, viz., equality, reciprocity, non-discrimination, common security, peaceful resolution of conflicts, mutual trust, confidence building measures, non-specificity of enemy, etc. are technically not applicable to China even though it had shown increasing interest in these issues. Hence, China's efforts in the SAARC appear to be either muted or pragmatic, even though it had been making active efforts to enter this process systematically through transportation corridors or emerging as largest trader or in hosting business groups and others from the SAARC countries. Clearly then, a balance of power approach is visible in some of the

Chinese perceptions as with a "wait and watch" approach. What is also clear from the above analyses is that China has been making active preparations – reflected in the infrastructure projects (even in disputed territories), selective investments, geo-strategic positioning, influencing the chambers of commerce and industry and the like. It is then for India and other SAARC constituents to respond appropriately to these knocks at the Himalayan gates.

END NOTES

1. See concerns of China as well as for the good neighbourliness policy and efforts to stabilise its peripheries, Srikanth Kondapalli and Emi Mifune, Eds., *China and its Neighbours* (New Delhi: Pentagon Press, 2010).
2. Chen Xiangyang, "Properly Deal with Peripheral Chaotic Political Situations," *Liaowang*, April 28, 2010, *NEWSEDGE Document Number*: 201004281477.1_383202e6aeaef982, *World News Connection*, File Number 985 Accession Number 298100225
3. See Liu Qingcai, "*Xin shiqi Zhongguo de mulin waijiao zhengsi*" [Good neighbourliness foreign policy of China in the new period] *Guoji Guancha* [International Survey] May 2005.
4. See Liu Hongliang, "*Lun nanya diqu de fankong hezuo jizhi*" [Counter-terror cooperation mechanism in the South Asia region], *Journal of Southwest Petroleum University*, Vol. 15, No. 3 (May 2013), pp. 74-79.
5. Chen Jidong argued that while the railway line will be costly—from the security, technical and finance point of view—the long-term benefits for China outweigh the short-term problems. See "*Guanyu jianshe Zhongguo-Bajisitan tielu lianjie xian de ji dian sikao*" [Reflections on the construction of China-Pakistan Railway line], *Nanya Yanjiu Qikan*, Issue 150, No. 3, March 2012, pp. 58-61 & 80.
6. See "East Asia Summit: in the shadow of sharp divisions," *People's Daily*, December 7, 2005 accessed at http://english.people.com.cn/200512/07/eng20051207_226350.html and Zhang Meihong, "*Dongya hezuo jincheng zhong de ZhongYin guanxi*" [China-India relations in the course of East Asian Cooperation], *Fazhi yu Shehui* [Legal System & Society], February 2007.
7. See Mohan Malik, "The East Asia Summit: More Discord than Accord," *YaleGlobal*, December 20, 2005 at http://yaleglobal.yale.edu/display.article?id=6645; Barry Desker, "Why the East Asian summit matters," December 14, 2005 at http://www.csis.org/media/csis/pubs/pac0555b.pdf and Chietigj Bajpaee, "India rediscovers East Asia," *Asia Times*, October 31, 2007 at http://www.atimes.com/atimes/South_Asia/IJ31Df01.html
8. "Charter of the SCO" accessed at http://www.sectsco.org/EN/show.asp?id=69
9. These observer states, however, do not have voting rights at the summit meetings. See "The Regulations on Observer Status at the SCO" accessed at http://www.sectsco.org/EN/show.asp?id=65
10. Hypothetically, for instance, China could point out to the unresolved territorial disputes of India with China, Pakistan, Nepal, Myanmar, Bangladesh or Sri Lanka. Also, it could cite the UNSC resolution 1172 (which it crafted with the US in the lead in 1998) on rolling back of the South Asian nuclear capability, although India (or Pakistan) had not violated any treaty that it had signed. This could also be applied to Iran which is facing sanctions from the international bodies on the nuclear issue. Again, the UN panel discussions on the issue of handling Tamils in Sri Lanka could be invoked as Colombo is now associated with the SCO.
11. See the statement of the Indian ambassador K Raghunath in this regard, Valery Agarkov,

"Indian diplomat says country ready to join Shanghai Cooperation Organization," *ITAR-TASS*, February 28, 2003 *NEWSEDGE Document Number:* 200303271477.1_a9a70004a 92bef26 File Number 985 Accession Number 167300623

12. See Hu Shisheng, "Role of SAARC Observers: A Chinese Perspective" in S.D. Muni (ed), *The Emerging Dimensions of SAARC* (New Delhi: Cambridge University Press, 2010) and Rashid Ahmad Khan, "The Role of Observers in SAARC" accessed at http://ipripak.org/journal/summer2009/Article1.pdf
13. He Yafei, however, said that this is done with consensus of all member states in the SAARC. See Rahul Karmakar, "China seeks bigger role in SAARC," *The Hindustan Times*, May 23, 2008 accessed at http://www.hindustantimes.com/world-news/china-seeks-bigger-role-in-saarc/article1-312557.aspx
14. Bangladesh leader Khaleda Zia met with secretary to the Communist Party of China's Beijing committee, Liu Xi in Dhaka along with the Chinese Ambassador to Bangladesh Zhang Xianyi in November 2011. At this meeting Liu sought Bangladesh support for the SAARC membership bidding of China. Zia in her turn assured the Chinese delegation that her party will support China's request. See "SAARC Membership: BNP backs China's bid," *The Daily Star*, November 11, 2011 accessed at http://wikileaks.org/gifiles/docs/18/183008_-os-china-bangladesh-bangladesh-party-backs-china-s-bid-for.html
15. SNM Abdi, "India foils attempt to bring China into South Asian group," *South China Morning Post*, April 26, 2010 accessed at http://www.scmp.com/article/712578/india-foils-attempt-bring-china-south-asian-group
16. Manish Chand, "China unleashes charm for SAARC-plus one summit," *IANS*, November 14, 2011 accessed at http://twocircles.net/2011nov14/china_unleashes_charm_saarcplus_one_summit.html
17. Salman Khurshid cited by Shastri Ramachandran, "China in SAARC: Time to weigh the pros and cons," *DNA*, February 24, 2014 accessed at http://www.dnaindia.com/analysis/column-china-in-saarc-time-to-weigh-the-pros-and-cons-1964516
18. Chen Jidong, "Dui Zhongguo canyu Nanya quyu hezuo xiangguan wenti de sikao" [Reflections on China's participation in South Asian regional cooperation] "Nanya Yanjiu Qikan," *South Asia Quarterly*, No. 1 Issue 148, 2012, pp. 52-55 (p.53).
19. Su Qiang, "China makes first visit to SAARC" *China Daily*, April 3, 2007 accessed at http://www.chinadaily.com.cn/china/2007-04/03/content_842112.htm; Li cited stability, development and good neighbourly relations as the fundamental objectives of China in the SAARC.
20. Department of Policy Planning, Ministry of Foreign Affairs, PRC, *China's Foreign Affairs 2008* (Beijing: World Affairs Press, 2008) p. 375.
21. Li Zhaoxing, "An Observer Country: China Extends Cooperation to SAARC," *Beyond Borders*, Vol. 3, No. 2, pp. 65-66 accessed at http://www.foundationsaarcwriters.com/beyondborderpdf/Vol.%203-No.%202/65-66.pdf
22. Department of Policy Planning, Ministry of Foreign Affairs, PRC, *China's Foreign Affairs 2009* (Beijing: World Affairs Press, 2009) p. 399.
23. "China to boost cooperation with SAARC," *Xinhua*, May 5, 2010 accessed at http://www.china.org.cn/world/2010-05/05/content_19976731.htm
24. Department of Policy Planning, Ministry of Foreign Affairs, PRC, *China's Foreign Affairs*, (Beijing: World Affairs Press, 2011) p. 402.
25. "China wants more pragmatic, effective cooperation with SAARC," *PTI*, November 16, 2011 accessed at http://articles.economictimes.indiatimes.com/2011-11-16/news/30405830_1_saarc-summit-saarc-member-states-dialogue-partner
26. Department of Policy Planning, Ministry of Foreign Affairs, PRC, *China's Foreign Affairs* (Beijing: World Affairs Press, 2012), p. 355.

27. Department of Policy Planning, Ministry of Foreign Affairs, PRC, *China's Foreign Affairs* (Beijing: World Affairs Press, 2013) p. 366.
28. See Saman Kelegama, "Economic Cooperation: The Emerging Scenario," *Policy Perspectives*, May 23, 2008 accessed at http://www.ips.lk/staff/ed/publications_ed/international/china_saarc/economic_cooperation.pdf
29. See "China looks to deepen trade with South Asia at upcoming expo," *PTI*, May 7, 2013 accessed at http://articles.economictimes.indiatimes.com/2013-05-07/news/39091343_1_over-usd-countries-balanced-trade and "8th China-South Asia Business Forum" accessed at http://www.saarcchamber.org/index.php?option=com_content& view=article&id=423:8th-china-south-asia-business-forum-csabf&catid=3:main-news-articles&Itemid=911
30. Li cited at "China looks to deepen trade with South Asia at upcoming expo," *PTI*, May 7, 2013 accessed at http://articles.economictimes.indiatimes.com/2013-05-07/news/39091343_1_over-usd-countries-balanced-trade
31. Emily Brunjes et.al, "China's Increased Trade and Investment in South Asia," Workshop in International Public Affairs Spring 2013 accessed at http://www.lafollette.wisc.edu/publications/workshops/2013/China.pdf
32. "The 1st China-South Asia Business Forum" accessed at http://csabf.ccpit.org/ccpit/website/201303001/en/content.jsp?id=DA7282E1209A2873E040A8C048013AE4&flag=1&mid=DA7282E120932873E040A8C048013AE4&curpager=null
33. "Establishment of China-South Asia Business Council" accessed at http://csabf.ccpit.org/ccpit/website/201303001/en/content.jsp?id=DAF088FAB580FC2EE040A8C048017E58&flag=1&mid=DA7282E120942873E040A8C048013AE4&curpager=null
34. "Success of the 3rd China-South Asia Business Forum" accessed at http://csabf.ccpit.org/ccpit/website/201303001/en/content.jsp?id=DAF088FAB581FC2EE040A8C048017E58&flag=1&mid=DA7282E120952873E040A8C048013AE4&curpager=null
35. See Chen Jidong, "*Zhong Yin Mian Meng qucheng jingji hezuo chutan*" [Preliminary explorations of China-India-Myanmar-Bangladesh regional Economic Cooperation] *Nanya Yanqiu Qikan* [*South Asia Quarterly*], April 1999 pp. 24-27.
36. See Chen Hongyan, "*Dongnanya, nanya guojia quyuhua taishji dui Yunnan de yingxiang*" [Southeast Asian, South Asian regionalization trend and its influence on Yunnan] *Yunnan Minzu daxue xuebao (Zhexue shehukexue ban)* Yunnan Nationalities University Journal (Philosophy social sciences edition) February2004.
37. "The 4th "China-South Asia Business Forum" Successfully Held in Kunming" accessed at http://csabf.ccpit.org/ccpit/website/201303001/en/content.jsp?id=DAF088FAB582FC2EE040A8C048017E58&flag=1&mid=DA7282E120962873E040A8C048013AE4&curpager=null
38. "China-South Asia Exposition Will Create New Opportunities for China-Bangladesh Economic and Trade Cooperation" accessed at http://bd.china-embassy.org/eng/sghd/t1045297.htm
39. See Sajjad Malik "China advises Pak to retailer market strategy," *Pakistan Observer Online*, April 28, 2010, *NewsEdge Document Number:* 201004281477.1_6898007602b41a92, *World News Connection*, File Number 985 Accession Number 298100508
40. See Samina Shabir and Reema Kazmi, "Economic Effects of the Recently Signed Pak-China Free Trade Agreement," *The Lahore Journal of Economics*, Special Edition (September 2007) pp. 173-202.
41. See Sohail Sarfraz, "Massive misuse of Pak-China FTA detected" *Business Recorder Online*, (Karachi) April 15, 2010, *NewsEdge Document Number:* 201004151477.1_21340163442cf073, *World News Connection*, File Number 985 Accession Number 297450439
42. "Sri Lanka, China FTA expected to conclude this year: Foreign Minister," *Xinhua*, February 13, 2014 accessed at http://news.xinhuanet.com/english/business/2014-02/13/

c_126124207.htm

43. Ministry of Commerce, PRC, "China-India Regional Trade Arrangement Joint Feasibility Study" accessed at http://fta.mofcom.gov.cn/topic/enindia.shtml
44. See Ministry of Commerce, PRC, *China Commerce Yearbook*, accessed at http://www.yearbook.org.cn/english/yearbook_view/2013/jb.htm
45. Chen Jidong, "*Dui Zhongguo canyu nanya quyu hezuo xiangguan wenti de sikao*" [Reflections on China's participation in South Asian regional cooperation] *Nanya Yanjiu Qikan* [*South Asia Quarterly*], No. 1, Issue 148 (2012), pp. 52-55 (p.54).
46. Shen Dingli, "China in SAARC? Too Early to Worry," *Strategic Analysis*, Vol. 35, No.3, (2011), pp. 502-504 (p.504).
47. Ma Ying, "*Dongmeng yu Nanmeng zhi bijiao*" [Comparing ASEAN and SAARC] *Daiping Yang Xuebao* [*Pacific Journal*], No. 5 (2005) pp. 22-27.
48. Jiang Yaping, "*Dongmeng dui Nanmeng de qishi*" [ASEAN inspires the SAARC] Liaowang Xinwen Zhoukan (*Outlook*), December 12, 2005.
49. He Zhijuan, "*Zhongguo yu Nanmeng kaizhan quyu jingji hezuo de SWOT fenxi*" [SWOT analysis of China-SAARC economic cooperation] Nanya Yanjiu Qikan, No. 2, Issue 145 (2011), pp. 80-83.
50. Tian Yun, "*Yunnan shijiao de Dongmeng, Nanmeng Kaifeng huanjing fenxi*" [Analysis of Yunnan's perspective on ASEAN, SAARC open environment], *Journal of Yunnan Provincial Committee School of the CPC*, Vol. 9, No. 3 (June 2008), pp. 117-119.
51. See Hu Shiheng and Lou Chunhua, "'*Nanmeng zai Zhongguo—Nanya guanxi zhongde zuoyong' yantao hui jiyao*" [Symposium on 'SAARC in China—Role in South Asian relations'] *Xiandai Guoji Wenti* [Contemporary International Relations], No. 1 (2007) p.60.
52. See for the report of the conference, Li Tao and Wang Yongzheng, "*Zhongguo-Nanmeng: Jiali gongtong fanrong de huoban guanxi guoji yantao hui zongshu*" [International symposium on "China-SAARC: Partnership for the establishment of prosperity"] *Nanya Yanjiu Qikan* [*South Asia Quarterly*], Issue 138, No. 3 (2009), pp. 107-08.
53. See Li Tao, "*Zhongguo he Nanmeng: Jianli mianxiang gongtong fanrong de huoban guanxi*" [China and the SAARC: Building Partnerships for shared prosperity], *Nanya Yanjiu Qikan*, No. 2, Issue 133 (2008), pp. 88-89.
54. See Ye Hailin, "China and South Asian relations in a new perspective" October 23, 2008 accessed at http://yataisuo.cass.cn/English/Articles/showcontent.asp?id=1118
55. Fan Yibing, "*Yindu zai nanya quyu hezuo lianmeng zhongde zhudao diwei ji qi yingxiang*" [The leading position and influence of India in the SAARC], *MA Dissertation, Hebei Normal University*, May 2012, pp. 31-35.
56. Liu Zhujun, "*Nanya quyu hezuo yiji Zhongguo de canyu*" [Regional Cooperation in South Asia and China's participation], *Foreign Affairs College*, June 2010 p. 42.
57. Han Bing, "*Zhongguo canyu Nanya quyu hezuo lianmeng de biyao xing yu jizhi xuanze*" [The necessity and choice of China's participation in the SAARC], *Quanguo Shangqing* (National Business) May 2011.
58. Significant multilateral cooperation and coordination mechanisms exist between India and China though. See Huang Zhengduo and Yan Xiangfeng, "*Duobian zhuyi shijiao xia de ZhongYin guoji hezuo*" [Multilateralism and international cooperation between China and India] *Nanya Yanjiu Qikan*, No. 2, Issue 149 (2012), pp. 20-25.

9

SAARC Nations' Markets: Opportunities for Japanese Business

Srabani Roy Choudhury

Introduction

SAARC as a regional entity came into existence in 1985 in which seven nations Bhutan, Bangladesh, India, Nepal, Maldives, Pakistan and Sri Lanka, adopted the charter, proclaiming to promote the welfare of its people through acceleration of economic growth, social progress and cultural development. It also aimed to strengthen cooperation with other developing nations, international and regional organizations with comparable aims and purpose. Visualized on the lines of ASEAN, it has since grown in its commitments to improve economic and social conditions of its member nations. Asia as a continent houses advanced nations like Japan, South Korea and Singapore; emerging nations like China and India and large number of fast advancing nations like Philippines, Thailand and Malaysia. China, Japan, United States of America, Republic of Korea (ROK) and European Union were granted Observer status in 2007. Enlargement of SAARC came about when Afghanistan formally requested to join this regional entity and after great deliberation[1] was granted entry on 4 April 2007. Thus as of 2014, there are eight member nations that comprise SAARC with nine Observer states namely, Australia, China, European Union, Japan, Iran, Mauritius, Myanmar,[2] ROK and the United States. China and Myanmar are seeking to be full members of SAARC, and Russia and Turkey are seeking Observer status.

SAARC as a forum did not have much attention of the world in the 1980's and 1990's, and due to political discontent in many of the member nations and distrust among each other, SAARC suffered a stunted growth and had become a mere platform for annual talks among its members. It had put together SAPTA (SAARC Preferential Trading Agreement) in 1995 to negotiate tariff reforms, and help recognize special needs of least developed contracting member nations. In 2006, SAFTA (South Asian Free Trade Agreement) was made operational as an extension of SAPTA towards free trade to achieve economic benefits among its members. In the era of globalization, and a growing interest among nations to seek more platforms for interactions; and with positive development among SAARC nations, most of the advanced nations joined in as Observers. While politically this was considered as a way to gain understanding of the intentions of the SAARC nations; as the contest of gaining control over the Indian Ocean region become apparent, SAARC nations – India, Sri Lanka and Maldives became the focus of interest to United States of America, Japan and China. The geo-strategic importance gained mainly due to some of the member states' control over Sea Lines of Communication was therefore a considerable basis for these states to seek Observer status. However with a growing market in the Middle East and with economic focus slowly shifting to Africa, East Asian nations—Japan, South Korea and China began to look for an industrial base closer to these regions. SAARC as a region with its cheap labor and large amount of resources has the possibility to emerge as a geo-economic strategic region, providing an abode for manufacturing cheaply and then exporting to the closer destination of Middle East and Africa. Further, it is undeniable that SAARC as a region comprising of three strata of developing nations has immense market potential for a large spectrum of industry. While India leads the pack as the significant economically emerging nation, Bangladesh, Pakistan and Sri Lanka are not far behind and are considered frontier economies.[3] In 2011 Maldives also moved up in rank as a developing nation. Nepal, Bhutan and Afghanistan are still bracketed under less developed nations. While Afghanistan and Nepal are fraught with political unrest, uncertainty and insecurity, and would find itself difficult to push forward a more affirmative economic development program, Bhutan with its strong political will of following a path of 'gross national happiness' has been carefully progressing in its economic development keeping a strong assessment on its character of 'sustainable' development. Thus the nations in this forum, positioned at various levels of economic development, provide industries with a variety of opportunities. While the levels of development among the member nations creates the complexity of addressing the region as one entity by the industry (as done for ASEAN), it also gives the industry the chance to undertake diverse types of activities. These activities could commence in one member nation where there is comparative advantage and then moved up the value chain to another member nation where it is more profitable due to advanced technology, infrastructure or skill-set. This would ensue a hub like activity within the region and ultimately lead to exporting from this region to other regions of the world.

This paper would thus delve into understanding the SAARC market by throwing light on the region's demographics, its strength as an emerging market and its potential to develop into an industrial hub. While defining the SAARC market, this paper will restrict itself to the emerging economy India and frontier economies of Bangladesh, Maldives, Pakistan and Sri Lanka. However, while addressing the opportunities available for Japanese companies, a section will be devoted to the less developed member states of Bhutan, Nepal and Afghanistan.

Demographics

To understand opportunities that Japanese business can harness in the consumer sector, it is important to understand the changing consumer dynamics of the SAARC region. The demographics of the member nations who have reached a level of economic development, and have a growing consumer market are therefore the focus of this section. Thus this section will exclusively deal with India, Bangladesh, Pakistan, Maldives and Sri Lanka. In the demographic profiling of the nations under consideration, the most important factor is the population. This region is inhabited by almost 30 per cent of the world population and these five nations make up 22 per cent. The break-up of this 22 per cent in various age bracket gives us an insightful understanding of the changing dynamics of consumerism and also enables one to focus on the desired group deemed fit for the product under consideration.

Age Distribution

Fig. 1: Age-wise Population Distribution in Percent (%)

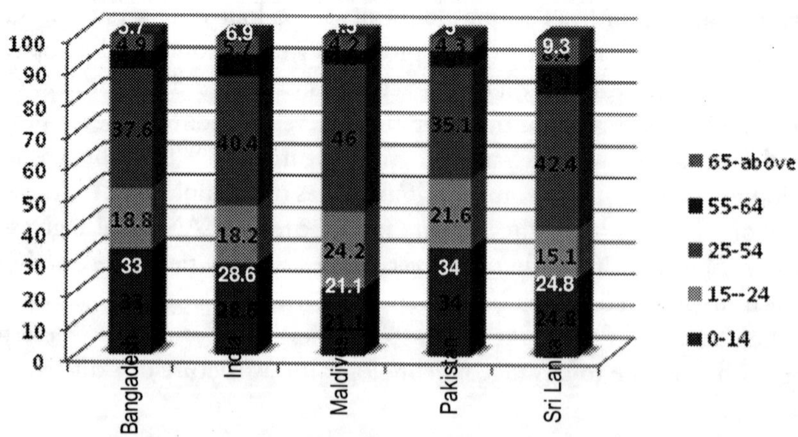

Source: Complied from www.indexmundi.com and ADB indicators for Asia and Pacific 2012

The most salient feature of these nations is that they are young population nations and if one considers the most active consumer age group that is from 15 years of age to 54 years of age one can see that for Bangladesh it is 56.4 per cent, India 62.6 per cent, Maldives 67.8 per cent, Pakistan 48.6 per cent, and Sri Lanka 69.7 per cent, thus on the average it is about 60 per cent of the population which translates to 95,795,280 million people. This is a huge market and identifying the major decision makers of this market could help target and reap benefits for players in the consumer market.

Purchasing Power

According to the International Monetary Fund's ranking of the nations on Gross domestic Product on Purchasing Power Parity in 2012, India stood third with \$4.716, followed by Pakistan at twenty seven with \$515, Bangladesh at forty two with \$306, Sri Lanka was ranked sixty fifth with \$126.20, followed by Nepal at \$40.5 (Rank 96), Afghanistan at \$31.8 (Rank 104), Bhutan at \$4.8 (Rank 156) and Maldives at 2.89 (Rank 163). Further, with the latest World Economic Outlook update, it is visibly clear that the world growth has been better than that anticipated in October 2013 and is projected to increase from 3 per cent to 3.7 per cent. Further, growth in India has picked up after a favorable monsoon season and higher export growth and is expected to strengthen further on stronger structural policies supporting investment. Other nations like Pakistan and Sri Lanka too are being projected as nations that will be growing due to corrective measures that are being introduced, especially in Sri Lanka as the nation is working constructively to put its period of political uncertainty behind and shift to the process of economic development that had in 1980's often linked it to the then "Emerging New Tigers" of the ASEAN. Given this background, it is expected that a large base of consumers will emerge who would be demanding a variety of consumer products.

Urbanization

Fig. 2: Urban Population (%)

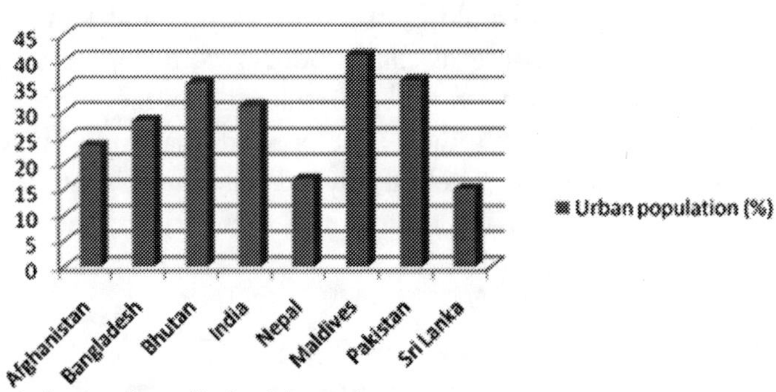

Source: www.indexmundi.com/factbook/countries

Fig. 3: Rate of Urbanization (%)

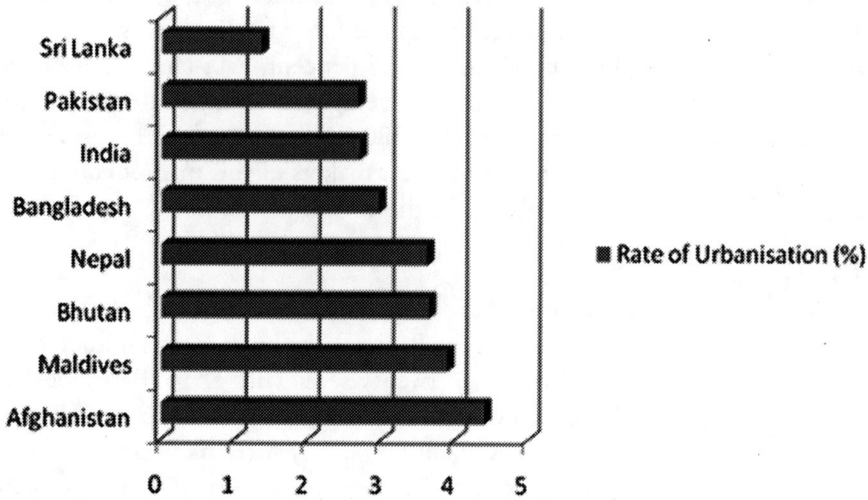

Source: www.indexmundi.com/factbook/countries

The urbanization process is a good indicator for increasing income as well as growing needs of differentiated products. Figure 2 shows the urban population as percentage of the total population and it is interesting to see that Bhutan and Afghanistan have the largest population living in urban centres, which essentially translates into the fact that work opportunities are greater in urban localities. Though it does not augur well from an economic development point of view; to the consumer market, it translates to a large population which can be reached easily as it is urban centric and not dispersed in a larger region. If one gleans the rate of urbanization, few important highlights can be perceived. Urbanization is highest among nations that are less developed, which means that purchasing power is likely to grow in the urban centres of these countries. Further, in a country like India the rate of urbanization has slowed down which translates to job opportunities being created in rural areas. This would be true for Pakistan and Bangladesh also. To the market observers, it means that products would be differentiated in line of urban vs rural and thus would penetrate the market more effectively. Urbanization and its rate also indicate the pressure that would be created in urban centres like housing, water, electricity etc. This means that the respective government would be deploying money into these activities and thus open doors for business opportunities.

The Consumer Market

These figures also have a strong implication for the consumer market. With the economies of India, Bangladesh, Maldives, Pakistan and Sri Lanka on the growth path and a larger population participating in the growth process, it follows that disposable income of the households will increase over a period of time. The new wave of consumerism that has set in, in the metropolitan cities is projected to spread and reach the rural areas. All this necessarily means that there is a great opportunity for any business, provided they are able to identify the decision makers of this new trend and target their product accordingly.

Today, every city has its premium consumers and its middle class consumers (fig 4). The market can be broadly classified into three segments (as the bottom of the pyramid is not included in the net). The first consists of the top end with the mind-set: "I pay more to get more", where the purchase is driven by the emotional surplus that the consumer experiences. The second is the mid-level which thinks: "I get good value at a reasonable price". More important however, is the large block at the bottom which says: "I pay less and I get less" and is totally satisfied with that. This is probably the segment that many marketers tend to overlook since they feel that there is no existing demand there. Nothing could be further from the truth. Furthermore, the factors behind purchasing decisions are merging in urban and rural areas.

Fig. 4: The New Urban Consumer Pyramid

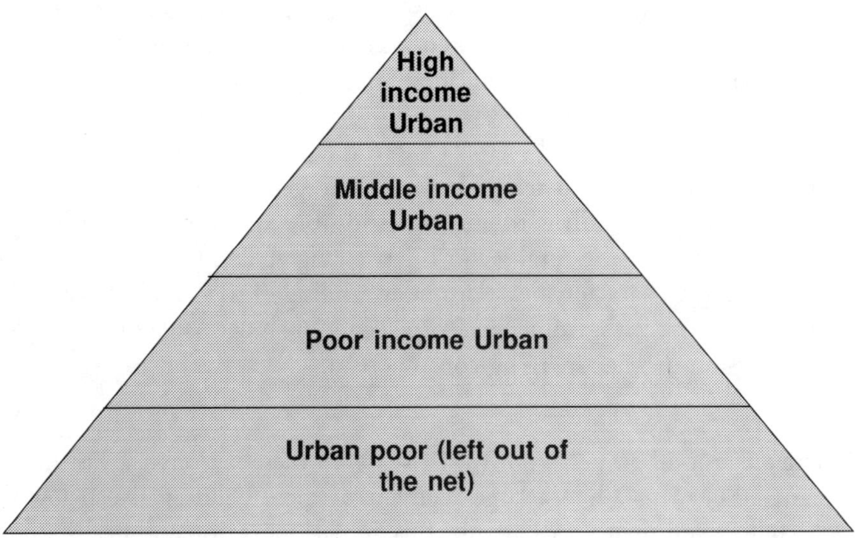

Today, the reasons behind a purchase are the same, differing only in order. In urban markets, aspiration is the key—it is all about brands, lifestyles and show-off value. This is followed by quality and finally price. In the rural economy it is primarily by price, followed by aspiration and then quality. However, what is important to understand is that the consumer, in-spite of showing tendency towards some homogeneity is yet individually different and this can be seen in the metro versus the non-metro consumer, whether it is regarding their philosophy, their thoughts or their approach to life. Thus, marketers today also need to think about creating brands that address these differences. Added to this has been the shift of attitude towards buying on loan, which was abhorred by the previous generations. The age group of 35-40 years of age have high propensity to indulge in consumerism through loans and have thus been a very attractive segment for consumer durables.

The middle income consumer is also maturing fast and is upgrading within the product segments at a pace that consumer companies are struggling to keep up with. The mobile phone category is a classic example. Companies therefore have to straddle the whole consumer pyramid rather than being focused on one part of it.

A study done by Spencer Stuart identified three major emerging segments – kids, the youth (including working singles) and the urban women, with an addition of the rural sector as the fourth (and has been seconded by many other such studies) in India, which has found acceptance among the marketing community for the fast emerging SAARC nations especially with reference to Sri Lanka, Bangladesh and Pakistan. These segments have shown as increasingly influencing and driving purchase decisions and hence changing the profile of the consumer market. A high-potential emerging market is also the rural hinterland. For nations like Bangladesh and Maldives, rapid urbanization is blurring the divide. But in Pakistan and India there is still a sizeable number who still reside in the rural sector. Due to the intervention of Governments of respective nations and technology, income generation in rural sector is gaining strength leading to more disposable income. Therefore, the composition within the rural sector is fast changing and it has emerged with its own unique characteristics. An understanding of the four new emerging segment—kids, youth, women and rural economy is necessitated to complete the discussion on the emerging consumerism.

Kids

There are around 30 per cent[4] (0–14 years) in these nations—a vast market by any standards. While a large segment of these children live below the poverty line and their needs are more to do with nutrition and health care, a small 0.7 per cent of this group belongs to the higher middle and high income group. These children are no different from children of the advanced nations. They are educated in the best of the schools; lead a life style of wealth and affluence; and have the acumen to source and sieve information. The role that these children play in purchase decisions has changed dramatically in the past 4–5 years. At the same time double income has boosted economic power and parents have become more indulgent towards their children. Often the parents are willing to spend a sizable amount of their income in meeting demands of these children which can include products in the range of Rs 50,000 ($833[5]) or expensive vacations. While this consumer segment is in itself huge for their own needs, they are today influencing purchase of products like mobiles, cars and air conditioners, which were earlier decided by their parents. Moreover, the age bracket of 10-14 years are often playing the role of consultants as they are tech savvy and are able to access comparative data and give a justification to the product choice.

Youth

With the vast majority of its population below the age of 30 years young consumers of the SAARC nations identified above are the primary targets of every consumer goods company. This group has high disposable incomes, is internet savvy and has a great love for brands and gadgets. They are well informed about global fashion and aspire to be trendy and in sync with the youth of the world. This has bought about significant change in the cosmetic market, mobile phones and apparels. Interestingly, this segment is also very visible in Afghanistan, Nepal and Bhutan. Though they comprise a small segment as rate of employment is low, but they too show similar buying patterns and aspiration begins with a high-end mobile phone, branded clothing and with rising income, a small car. High on consumerism and ever looking for new features in consumer durable products, they are high on replacement and thus a "darling" for the consumer goods industry.

Women

Women, essentially in the urban areas have been silently influencing the family purchases and expenditures. However, in the last five years a dramatic change has been seen. Anjali Bansal, Managing Director of Spencer Stuart's India business explained this as follows: "The urban woman wants to break out from her traditional sacrificing image, but does not want to go all the way. She wants to conform to the values she believes in and yet wants to do her own thing." In Sri Lanka they are called the "mod-trad". Typically, they would go about the daily chores like any of the advanced nations' women, often contributing equally to the household income but also showing strong commitment to child rearing and often being a "single parent" in a double income household, thus taking on the responsibility of running the household. Further, they also consciously try to imbibe the culture and values of the family and thus continue to enforce celebration of festivals, rituals and customs. And in the midst of this soul-searching process, the marketer is bewildered. It is a challenge to identify the boundaries correctly and to touch the right chord with this new consumer. Apart from the behavioral change another major structural change has been the big retail outlets with a very secure environment. When women feel more secure it allows them to go into a store and actually get the product themselves. However, unlike the youth which is moving towards homogeneity; women are perhaps the least homogeneous in their buying pattern and continue to be an enigma. Even so, there is no denial that in urban societies the woman is not only deciding about family purchase but is also getting into pampering herself, especially, if she is an earner.

Rural Sector

There is agreement across the board on the fact that the rural market can no longer be ignored by consumer companies. There are regions of India and Sri Lanka that are growing at 15–30 per cent in terms of spending power; in Bangladesh and Pakistan too they have broken the barrier of 10 per cent. The aspirations of the populations in the semi-urban and rural areas are also much greater than their urban counterparts, especially because they are being exposed through electronic media to a range of products and services that they have never seen before. This translates into a larger marketing opportunity for companies.

Technology has given rural sector of Sri Lanka and India a new identity. An area with potential is the 'smart card', which can be used for multiple purposes—whether it is to draw cash or make payments for seeds and fertilizers. The biggest benefit is that a smart card can be used by individuals who may be illiterate as well, since it stores cardholder information and is linked to the purchase centres. In 5–10 years, it is certain that a very different rural India will emerge. In terms of sheer economics, there will be 30 per cent more expenditure in the next 20 years compared with the past 20 years—this is a significant shift and will impact India very differently. A similar story is unfolding in Sri Lanka and Bangladesh too. With a lot of policies driving literacy, health and community development in the rural sector, and a strong move to integrate the two worlds, future for marketers in the rural sector of these countries is remarkable. Further, as this sector is at the nascent stage, the late entrants into these economies who may have found it difficult in the urban sector would have an opportunity in making their presence felt in the rural sector.

So what does the consumer market look like? In a nutshell, it means a huge opportunity for the marketer who studies the market, invests in finding a niche for the product and uses the right media to advertise and target its potential customers.

Opportunities in the Consumer Sector

Having identified the changing demographics in the five selected SAARC nations, it is important to look at the opportunities that it can throw open to Japanese companies.

Among the fast moving consumer goods (FMCG), it has been reported that in Bangladesh, Pakistan and India[6] there has been a dramatic growth in both quantitative and qualitative terms. In low involvement products like salt, sugar, pens, chocolates etc, there has been growing movement from buying these products "loose" to buying them not only packaged but also of various brands. This is distinctively applicable to the urban middle class. Further, there has been growing palate change towards packaged foods and ready to eat foods, sauces etc, and high growth has been witnessed in purchase of noodles and its various varieties, and flavoured tea including green tea. In confectionary there has been a move to buy packaged, branded products especially in biscuits, breakfast bars/ cereals and cakes. The Japanese companies are leaders in this segment in most of the South East Asian region and thus can seek this growing market of SAARC nations. In Sri Lanka, Nielsen data[7] has repeatedly thrown to light that the rural sector in Sri Lanka has emerged as the driving force of FMCG products and their buying pattern is strongly influenced by the income generated by harvesting. Thus a differentiated marketing strategy is desirable, especially with regard to longer shelf life products like stationery, cosmetics etc. An example of the cosmetic sector (personal care, oral hygiene and beauty products) and consumer durables are discussed below to highlight the marketing opportunities.

Cosmetic Sector

Major impact of rising incomes has been seen in the cosmetic industry. The cosmetic industry consists of not only the personal care and beauty products but also oral hygiene as classified by the RNCOS report. In Bangladesh alone, which is considered a very resilient sector, this sector has grown at 4.5 per cent every year since 2008. According to the Associated Chambers of Commerce and Industry of India (ASSOCHAM) the projected market size of the cosmetics industry which is currently estimated at Rs.1000 million will double to be worth Rs. 2000 million by 2014 due to emergence of a young urban elite population with rising disposable incomes and increase in working women looking for lifestyle-oriented and luxury products. According to Umesh Modi[8] of Revlon, Lanka "Sri Lanka offers untapped potential in the cosmetic market not only in terms of potential consumers but also low cost". In Pakistan while a specific trend is not seen, there is a sizeable increase in income of middle urban families; a factor that contributes to cosmetic buying pattern, and it can be concluded that Pakistan can also be a growing market. As Emami's CEO[9] claims, "With its large population, very similar consumer habits and social mores and overflow of Indian advertising, Pakistan is a very attractive market".

Three factors play a significant role in making this sector a profitable one. Firstly, more women are in the job market and are also becoming independent financial decision makers. This has resulted in women spending more on themselves. Further, women in the age group of 30 and above are getting very selective about the type of products they choose. As older women have more cash and are more conscious of their appearance, especially skin, they are willing to spend more on separate sets of creams and lotions that target problem areas. These women also are more open to buying higher-priced products. Secondly, various surveys in India and Sri Lanka in 2010 and 2011 have also came out with an interesting fact, highlighting that males have developed a special craze for cosmetic application, comparable to their females counterparts and their monthly expenses on cosmetics rose by about 60-80 per cent during the period. Thirdly, as mentioned earlier, the rural sector has been introduced to and is getting more and more influenced by the urban sector in terms of fashion and the companies are playing this up, by way of creating more awareness, thus, resulting in a strong demand pull for this sector. This industry is expected to grow at the rate of 7-8 per cent overall with spa and color cosmetics estimated to grow at 20-30 per cent.

Some products which are going to find themselves increasingly in a consumer basket are, one: the skin cream promoted as "fairness cream". The obsession for light skin among Indian and Bangladesh and indeed all South Asian women was well documented but in the recent past, surveys have revealed that Indian and Sri Lankan men are also obsessed by the "fair-ness" of skin and this has been addressed by the companies. Thus one expects a notable growth and this will be furthered by deeper penetration in the rural market than has been in the recent past. Two, hair colorant as a substitute of hair dye has today found great following as "looking young" becomes the mantra for the middle class of these nations. Three, the spa is a promising market for beauty services in India with a projected growth of 20 per cent or more. With increasing income, people are also becoming increasingly stressed at work and at home. Spa centres are popular as mental and physical de-stress destinations.

As the upper middle class and the elite class with an increasing disposable income adopt this new concept, the growth would be phenomenal.

The Oral Care Market is a distinct sub group in this sector. With a ratio of one dentist for every 10,000 people in urban areas in India and the number grows substantially in Bangladesh and Pakistan, and even more dispersed in the rural sector, the lack in dental care is effectively utilized by major market players, as products are positioned as precautionary cure and in the form of a substitute to dental treatment. Given this background, this market which has three products in the form of tooth powder, tooth paste and tooth brush is going to see a growth of 2 per cent to 3 per cent. As more consumers move to toothpaste from tooth powder, a change in consumption pattern is apparent and thus the forecasted 3 per cent may actually be around 5 per cent as deeper penetration and shifting consumers add to its growth.

In the above identified products, Japanese companies have a sizeable presence in the international market. The attempt should be to enter one of these nations either through an export arrangement with a well-established distribution network or to tie up with a retail company. Looking at a subsidiary arrangement would also be a good strategy as production in one of these nations can be cost effective in terms of distribution to other nations.

Consumer Durables

The consumer durables industry in the identified SAARC countries has witnessed a considerable change in the past couple of years. Changing lifestyles, higher disposable incomes coupled with greater affordability and a surge in advertising has been instrumental in bringing about a sea change in the consumer behavior pattern. Apart from steady income gains, consumer financing and hire-purchase schemes have become a major driver in the consumer durables industry.

In the case of more expensive consumer goods, such as refrigerators, washing machines, colour televisions and personal computers, retailers are joining forces with banks and finance companies to market their goods more aggressively.

A key trend in this sector that is encouraging for companies intending to set foot in these nations are the projection of 23 per cent growth of this sector in the next five years in India, 16 per cent projected growth in Bangladesh, around 18 per cent growth in Sri Lanka. This sector has come of age with improved and affordable technology at low cost which has helped in progressively creating demand of two kinds. One is pure demand and the other is replacement demand. The pure demand is created because of large disposable incomes which has often moved these goods from luxury to need.

Fig. 5: Types of Consumer Durables

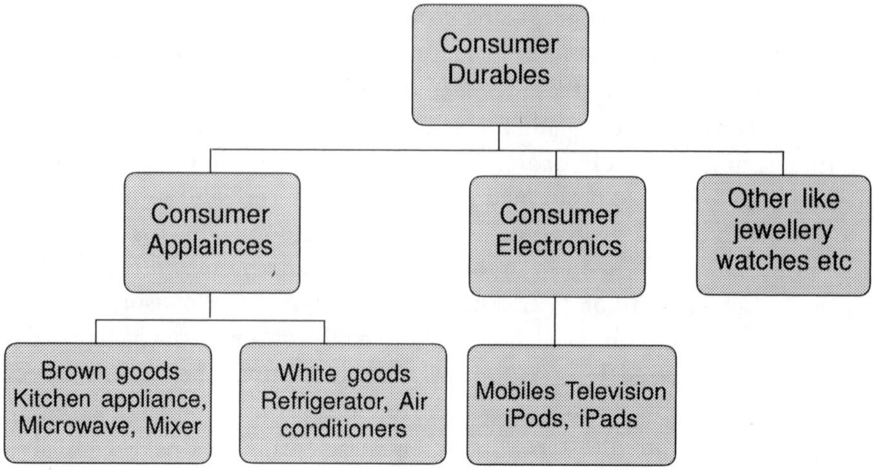

Case in point is mobile phones and air conditioners. With customised high-end products with aesthetic designs being made available, a significant portion of this demand has come from the replacement segment of the household. Large retail players allowing for different brands all under one roof, has also created a healthy competition in this sector.

The rural sector is emerging as the new market for this sector. Here the aspiration is slowly and surely being turned into demand not only because of higher disposable incomes but also because of increased electrification of smaller towns and villages. Thus market penetration which not only reaches more locales but also goes deep can ensure a huge market.

Overall, the industry's future remains robust, and interested applicants will benefit from a holistic learning experience. Many of the research, sales, marketing and advertising related roles will necessitate a good on-the-job learning of target audiences, who may well be a totally new segment, based in never-before visited Class II and III towns. In addition, those with technical backgrounds will be able to leverage their knowledge and experience to constantly develop and innovate on product variants. All this will require a good distribution system and it is suggested that in this sector the Japanese business houses should look for a good distributor who has a well-established distribution network, ideally in consumer electronics or in consumer durables.

Mobile Phone Sector

The telecom sector has been revolutionized by the mobile telephone network and the ever changing technology of the handset has made this sector a lucrative business proposition. Vast populations in SAARC nations live in rural areas. Mobile phones, by virtue of their role as carriers and conduits of information are making rural and undeveloped markets more efficient. Whether it is farmers seeking information about weather, seed procurement or fertilizer, the fishing community using mobile phones at sea, allowing for fishermen to respond quickly to market demand and prevent unnecessary wastage of catch—fish being a highly perishable commodity—a common occurrence before the adoption of phones. At the marketing end, mobile phones help coordinate supply and demand, and merchants and transporters are able to take advantage of the free flow of price information by catering to demand in undersupplied markets. There is also far less wastage of time and resources in all segments of the economy. In the SAARC region it has led to closing the gap between urban and rural areas. In a country like India, it has for the first time linked the entire nation across various previously unreachable terrains. A similar story has also been repeated in other countries especially in Pakistan, Bhutan and Nepal. Through this integration, it has enabled harnessing economic development by market integration and also in providing much needed help during emergencies. Accessing information in remote areas has empowered the marginal community to venture into business beyond farming and fishing. Afghanistan, which has been the latest entrant in the economic development process, has over 18 million mobile users. India and Sri Lanka are at the top as far as penetration of mobiles phones is concerned. India has 89.2 per cent per thousand citizens and Sri Lanka boasts of 80.95 per cent. The rest of the SAARC nations range between 67-70 per cent with respect to mobile penetration.

This opens up two kinds of opportunities for Japanese companies. One is the mobile handset which have many Japanese companies in the market. There are two interesting features in this market. In the large populous states of SAARC nations there is a growing demand of mobile handsets. Further, due to fast changing technology there is a large segment of consumers who are upgrading their handsets. A dynamic market with a very small window of shelf life of the products; as newer options emerge sometimes in even a two month period; and significant number of consumers looking at superior products, this market is straddled between the low priced products to the very high priced product and thus allows for a company to seek and service a segment that it so desires.

The other is the establishing of the network towers and the accessories required for operations. In this too Japan has been fore runner. In India NTT DoCoMo has a venture with Tata in providing service network system which has a strong presence. With changing government policies towards a more liberalized telecom sector and with growing income, the mobile telephony segment within the telecom sector provides a vibrant market to its players.

Opportunities in Infrastructure Development

So far, the discussion of markets was limited to the consumer driven market. However, all eight SAARC nations have a strong demand for both hard and soft infrastructure in which Japanese businesses can find and reap large benefits. The areas of concerns are the infrastructures of road, railways, water supply and energy. While much of it is addressed by the ODA given by Japan, there is a scope for private partnership with the respective governments in this large underutilized sector. The current notions of public-private partnership promoted in these nations have opened doors to foreign investment in most of the sectors. The Japanese companies that have developed many innovative technologies and are fore runners in areas like railway tracks and system[10] have a big opportunity awaiting them. The following section will thus give an understanding of the immense prospects available for exploration.

Railways

Among the SAARC nations Afghanistan, Nepal and Bhutan are less developed and have little or no rail network. Afghanistan has no passenger service or stations. There is a rail service between Mazar-i-Sharif in Afghanistan and Uzbekistan in the north. A 10-kilometer long line extends from Serhetabat in Turkmenistan to the town of Towraghondi. The Afghan Government expects to have the line extended to Kabul and then to the eastern border town of Torkham, connecting with Pakistan Railways in Afghanistan. Bhutan does not have a railway network. Bhutan and India have signed an MOU to connect Bhutan with the Indian Railways network. In December 2009, the King of Bhutan approved the final plan to build a 11-mile (18 km) long 1,676 mm (5 ft 6 in) broad gauge rail link between Hashimara in West Bengal and Toribari in Bhutan. Nepal has a total physical railway line of 53 km. Nepal Railways Company (NRC), a government agency, owns the 53-kilometer narrow-gauge rail line, which is composed of two sections—32-kilometer section between Jaynagar in India to Janakpur in Nepal, and a 21-kilometer portion from Janakpur to Bijalpura. Janakpur to Bijalpura network is not operational at present. The remaining lines are operated by the Indian Railways. Linking the nations with rail network is a priority for Afghanistan and Nepal. The Japanese companies thus have a huge investment opportunity in these countries. In countries like India and Pakistan it is the subway system in urban localities that has gained importance due to congestion on the roads. Japan has showcased its technology and its capability in partnering the Delhi-Metro project, which has successfully concluded two phases.

Roadways

Priority to roadways has gained momentum in the SAARC region because of the growing need in each of these countries to increase connectivity within their nation. The development process was triggered off in India and Sri Lanka and developing highways for movement of goods has become a priority. Sri Lanka is a forerunner in this sector. Road density per 2 km is one of the highest in the region. Most of the national and provincial roads and majority of urban roads are paved roads. Nearly 30 per cent of these roads have been rehabilitated or are in the process of being rehabilitated. However, the remaining 70 per cent have poor navigation conditions and efforts are on by the Government of Sri Lanka to build them to international standards as majority of goods in Sri Lanka move by roadways. India's road network, spanning across 4.69 million km, is the third-largest road network in the world. However, qualitatively India's roads are a mix of modern highways and narrow, unpaved roads, and are undergoing drastic improvement. Goldman Sachs claimed that India will need to invest US$ 1.7 trillion on infrastructure projects before 2020 to meet its economic needs, a part of which would be in upgrading India's road network. The Government of India is attempting to promote foreign investment in road projects by offering financial incentives. Japan is participating in Delhi Mumbai Industrial corridor Project and the Chennai Bangalore Industrial Corridor project under the scheme of public private partnership.

In Afghanistan, new national highways, roads, and bridges have been rebuilt in the last decade to help increase travel as well as trade with neighboring countries. The network includes 12,350 kilometers of paved roads and 29,800 kilometers of unpaved roads, totaling a road system of 42,150 kilometers. The highway system is currently going through a total reconstruction phase. The reconstruction process is being conducted by private participation and there is a scope for construction and road machinery equipment industries.

During the 1990s, Pakistan began an ongoing project to rebuild all national highways throughout the country; specifically to important financial, cargo and textile centers. The construction of motorways began in the early 1990s with the idea of building a world class road network and to reduce the load from the heavily used national highways throughout the country. The M2 was the first motorway completed in 1998, linking the cities of Islamabad and Lahore. This initiative has continued and the in the past 5 years, many new motorways have opened up, including the M1and M3. Today it stands at a total of 257,683 km (Paved: 152,033 km (including 339 km of expressways; Unpaved: 105,650 km). There is a considerable part that is unpaved places in the northern terrain that are inaccessible, which gives a late entrant equal opportunity.

Bhutan's primary road is the East-West highway, known locally as the Lateral Road, the construction of which was started in 1962. Because much of the geology is unstable, there are frequent slips and landslides. However, it has become a strong priority as road connectivity could enhance goods movement throughout Bhutan. Bhutan, a late developer is keen to use the latest technology and Japan already supports some activities through Official Development Assistance, thus paving way for private investment and partnership.

Nepal's total road network and density are low and only 43 percent of the population has access to all-weather roads. More than 60 percent of the network is concentrated in the lowland (Terai) areas of the country. The network consists of 17,282 km of roads. Though the development of roadways has slowed down since 2003/2004, with constant pressure from international agencies like World Bank, the Government of Nepal's (GoN) Interim Three Year Plan (2007-10) has emphasized the role of roads, civil aviation, and tourism in achieving the country's overarching objective of reducing poverty in the country. The Plan aimed to connect 5 unconnected district head quarters through roads; establish an enabling environment for public private partnerships; operate a Roads Board for financing road maintenance and efficient road management in a sustainable manner; and an institutional reform of the Department of Roads (DoR) based on the Government's reform policy. While this drive led to focus and commitment and a Road Board was established, implementation has been slow. However, the pro-poor policy in which improved modes of transportation increased access to shops, markets, schools and hospitals necessitates network of roadways; and improvements in rural connectivity would help raise non-agricultural employment and incomes. Thus the immense scope for partnering various ventures is tremendous.

Ports

Ports are fundamental to development and constitute an important link for movement of goods. The location of certain countries has helped them to use ports as a means of revenue and income generation for its people. SAARC nations Bangladesh, India, Maldives, Pakistan and Sri Lanka have large coastal area. Traditionally, most ports in the world are owned by the public sectors. In the recent years privatization of ports facilities and services are gaining momentum and it is this which can provide a lucrative business proposition for Japan under the scheme of public private partnership. Further, Sri Lanka because of its geo strategic location and larger traffic in the Indian Ocean is today a strong contender for providing state of the art facilities at its ports for parking, loading of goods for ships passing through the sea lanes of Sri Lanka.

Rising to the need and opportunity, Sri Lanka opened a $500 million container terminal at Colombo Port in August 2013, the biggest investment among the island's harbors, as the nation seeks to upgrade its infrastructure with Chinese help. The terminal, built and operated by China Merchants Holdings International Co. (144:HKG), will handle 2.4 million containers a year and boost Colombo's capacity by almost half, according to the Sri Lanka Ports Authority. This successful partnership has made the Sri Lankan authority more committed to upgrading and building ports.

India has 13 major ports and 176 non-major ones. The major ports carry about $3/4^{th}$ of the total traffic. In spite of sufficient capacity and handling facilities, the average turnaround time of major Indian ports is less than 4 days which is very high compared to the average turnaround time of about 10 hrs in Hong Kong. This affects the competitiveness of Indian ports. Since the ports are not adequately linked to the hinterland, the evacuation of cargo is slow leading to congestion. To put an end to all this, ports trust have set up groups with representatives from the National Highway Authority of India (NHAI), Railways and State Governments to prepare comprehensive plans aimed at improving road-rail connectivity of ports. The NHAI has taken up port connectivity as major component of the National Highways Development Project (NHDP). All this would result in more infrastructure development in port areas. Japan is already looking at port development of Vishakhapatnam, Andhra Pradesh located at the east coast of India off the Bay of Bengal and close to Gulf of Thailand.

Pakistan too has large tracts of coastal land and has also considered development of ports both dry and sea port. For many countries, mainly China, access to sea through Pakistan has strong implication. The port of Gwadar located in Baluchistan was officially handed over to the control of the China state owned company. Though of strategic importance,[11] it also has a strong economic component as it can help Pakistan develop a conduit for movement of goods to China and Afghanistan. Surely, Pakistan is posed to look at other ports and Japan can work towards greater involvement.

Bangladesh is a land of networked rivers and has the need to develop all types of ports ranging from low and high-tech ports. Inland ports handle about 40 percent of Bangladesh's foreign trade, with some 700 rivers and tributaries crisscrossing the country. There are 5,150–8,046 km (3,200–5,000 mi) of navigable waterways (which includes 2,575–3,058 km or 1,600–1,900 mi of main cargo routes). Because of Bangladesh's many rivers, ferries are a major form of transportation. These ferries are notoriously dangerous and cause many calamities. Chittagong port is the gateway to Bangladesh's growing exports of the garment industry, leather industry and frozen food industry. Mongla port is the second port that has been developed. Today Nepal and Bhutan too are seeking right of access through these ports. Modernizations of both ports is a prerequisite if Bangladesh wants to step up its developmental process. Given that construction and operating of ports require of large capital and involvement of large number of industries, Japanese companies have the necessary technology, competence and capability to seek out this opportunities.

Conclusions

The attempt of this paper has been to draw attention to the distinctive features of the consumer market and thus the need to understand the market segmentation that is emerging in this region due to fast development of the economies and the changing pattern of consumerism. Given the vastness of this subject, the paper has thus highlighted two industries for Japanese companies—the cosmetic sector including oral hygiene which caters to both men and women and the mobile telecom sector. Given the growing penetration of the markets in both the sectors, even latecomers have little to lose and thus ideal for Japanese companies that are looking at greener pastures. Further, both the sectors show strong upward movement of the consumers who are upgrading their brands as they earn more and reflects a very vibrant market and gives scope to high priced products, unlike the usual impression of these nations being "price conscious". Scope of participation of Japan is immense in infrastructure development; especially in SAARC nations as each of the respective governments are putting together effective plans for furthering development. While Japanese companies with their capability in both technology and capacity building can venture into this sector, the capital that rests in Japan in form of postal savings and other such low interest yielding instruments can be diverted to projects in this sector which though long term in nature, is safe because of government involvement and will earn better returns. In sum, The Japanese government has favorable bilateral relationship with all the SAARC nations and has finally started taking interest in this region. A plethora of opportunities exists in this region because the nations are poised at various levels of economic development. Since all of them are low cost economies, Japanese companies can easily develop clusters in association with their factories in South East Asian region and ensure more competitive products in the market.

END NOTES

1. Debates about Afghanistan joining SAARC ensued on two fronts. One, Afghanistan is a nation geographically positioned in Central Asia, two its political set up. SAARC member states stipulated Afghanistan to hold a general election (non-partisan election held in late 2005) and thus Dr. Manmohan Singh announced inclusion of Afghanistan in 2007.
2. Myanmar has requested to upgrade its status to member state.
3. This has been classified by MSCI.
4. Refer figure 1 which shows in this age group.
5. US$ 1=Rs.60.
6. Shafayet, Prince Rozario p. 7.
7. Since 2009 Nielsen data has shown that rural Sri Lankans are driving FMCG growth.
8. Chairman, President and CEO of Revlon Lanka and UMGI.
9. 'Indian FMCG firms eye slice of Pakistan Market' Rediff.com, September 4, 2012.
10. Railway computer systems, signaling, subway.
11. Just 180 nautical miles from Strait of Homuz from which third of the oil supply passes, it becomes a prime location to keep vigil on the ships movement. India has shown concern on this development.

REFERENCES

Association for Regional Cooperation [SAARC] and Japan', June 2009, http://www.mofa.go.jp/regional/asia-paci/saarc/overview.html. Accessed on 8 February 2014, 2013.

Bala Komaraiah .J. (2003), " India-Japan Business Relations in the 21st Century", in *Japan's Role in South East Asia* (ed.) M.D Dharamdasini, Lancer Books, New Delhi.

Daily F.T., "Sri Lanka Japan celebrates 60 years of diplomatic ties," 9 October 2012.

Moni, M.H., Japan-Bangladesh Economic Partnership Focus on Aid, Trade and Investment, Journal of International Studies 2014.

Gupta S.L. and Pal, S., Consumer Behavior Pattern in India Text and Cases, Himalaya Publishing, 2013.

Solmon, M.R., Buying, Having and Being, Prentice Hall, tenth edition 2013.

South Asian Association for Regional Cooperation/Areas of Cooperation, http;//saarc-sec.org/areaof cooperation/detail.php?activity_id==39. Last Accessed on 1 February 2014.

www.indexmundi.com/factbook/countries last accessed on 15 February 2014.

www.wsws.org

www.eastasiaforum.org

10

New Dimensions of Japan–India Economic Partnership

Makoto Kojima

Introduction

India and Japan are highly complementary economies that have yet to be fully exploited. Japan has abundant capital and is highly advanced in technological skills and product development whereas India is endowed with a huge market and abundant human resources. Japan is outstanding in terms of its manufacturing abilities, whereas India presents advantages in IT services and bioinformatics. Given a huge domestic market, a promising destination for production and export bases, and also abundant talented human resources, India is gaining much importance for Japan. Correspondingly, Japan is expected to play an indispensable role in upgrading Indian manufacturing skills[1] and infrastructure development. Japan is also expected to be a potential market for India's IT services exports.

India has conspicuously expanded its trade with East Asian countries under the 'Look East' policy since the early 1990s, yet Japan–India trade had apparently been left behind and remained far below the potential level. However, a new tide has been observed in Japan–India relations since the mid-2000s; bilateral trade began to show a rising trend, followed by a vigorous expansion of Japanese investment into India, and Japan–India Comprehensive Economic Partnership Agreement (CEPA) coming into effect in August 2011. Particularly, the following two events require much attention in terms of providing new dimensions to Japan-India relations. First, the Delhi–Mumbai Industrial Corridor (DCIM) project was launched, to which Japan has been deeply committed. Second, both countries entered into the Strategic and Global Partnership in 2006, which provides an indispensable framework for consolidating comprehensive Japan–India bilateral relations. The expansion of bilateral relations based on mutual complementarities is beneficial for both countries. It might contribute considerably to strengthen the Indian manufacturing and infrastructure base.

The visit of Japanese Emperor Akihito and Empress Michiko to India from November 30 to December 5 in 2013, followed by the invitation of Prime Minister Shinzo Abe as the chief-guest for the Republic Day celebrations in January 2014 is no less than an affirmation that both Japan and India are indispensable partners each other. It can be seen as a herald of new dimensions of Japan-India partnership. The visit of Japanese Emperor to foreign countries is well-calibrated and it is rare to be made. It was in 1992 when the Japanese Emperor paid a visit to China at the earnest invitation of the Chinese government. At that time, Western as well as Japanese foreign direct investment (FDI) into China had been reduced to low level in the aftermath of the Tiananmen Square incident. It is recalled that Japanese FDI into China has remarkably increased after the visit of Japanese Emperor to China.

In this chapter, new dimensions of Japan–India bilateral relations are indicated, addressing the recent developments in the fields of trade and FDI, the DMIC project, IT offshoring, and human exchanges, and Strategic and Global Partnerships, with special reference to the DMIC project.

Recent Trends in Japan–India Trade on a Modest Growth

Trends in Japan–India Trade

India is characterized by diversity in all respects. This diversity can also be seen in the make-up of exported goods and the make-up of its trade partners. The top 10 trade partners are not biased to a particular region, but are instead scattered across East Asia, North America, ASEAN, and Europe. Conventionally, India's largest trade partner has been the US, but in recent years, the United Arab Emirates (UAE) and China have grown rapidly in importance, and the current top three trade partners are China, the UAE and the US. The US is still the largest trade partner when looking at trade in goods and services overall; India's service exports are extremely large, and its IT-BPO exports to the US easily exceeded US$ 40 billion in 2011-12.

Along with the introduction of economic reforms in 1991, India adopted an outward-oriented policy to develop its own economy by making use of the tide of globalization. More specifically, India intended to strengthen economic ties with East Asian countries, an emerging global growth centre, under the Look East policy. Despite pursuit of the "Look East" policy, Indian trade with Japan has long remained stagnant.

Although total Japan–India bilateral trade amounted to US$ 4.19 billion in 1996-97, it had shrunk to US$ 3.64 billion in 2000-01 and US$ 3.66 billion in 2001-02 (Figure 1). It was only in 2003-04 that bilateral trade started to show an upward trend: US$ 5.36 billion in 2004-05, and US$ 18.51 billion in 2012-13. Improved bilateral trade, however, has been largely overshadowed in comparison to other bilateral trading relations such as those of India–ASEAN, India–China and India–Korea. India–Japan bilateral trade was surpassed by India–China trade in 2002-03, and even by India–Korea trade in 2005-06. In this connection, as of 2011-12, India–China and India–ASEAN trade have increased 4.1 times and 4.3 times, respectively more than that with Japan. Japan's share in all Indian trade has decreased from 5.9 per cent in 1997-98 to 2.3 per cent in 2012-13, along with a significant decline of Japan's rank in terms of total amount of trade from third to twelfth. India's share in Japan's total amount of trade, in contrast, remained less than 1 per cent during 2012-13.

Fig. 1: Trends in India's Trade with East Asia

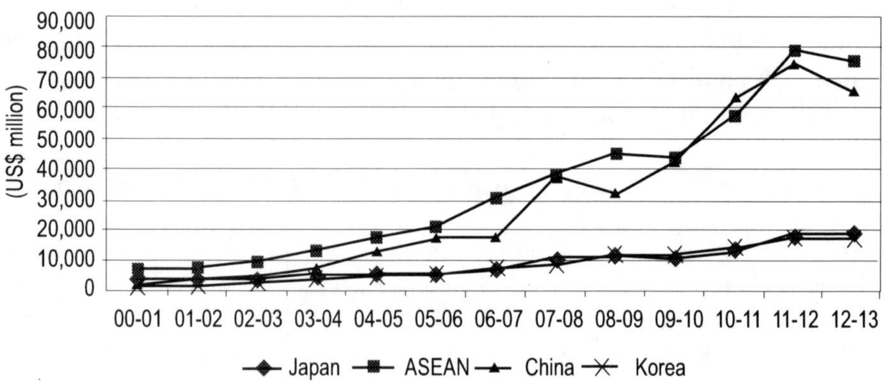

Source: Ministry of Commece and Industry.

Japan–India trade has almost constantly shown Japan's surplus, and sluggish bilateral trade was possibly a reflection of major commodities traded on both sides: imports from Japan were composed of, first and foremost, machinery and components, followed by iron and steel products, consumer electronics, auto and components, precision instruments, and so forth, and India's exports to Japan exclusively concentrated on lower-value added marine products and jewels and ornaments, of which commodities did not reflect current India's competitive and dynamic industrial structure. Recently however, because of increased petroleum products from India, which has become the most important Indian export to Japan since 2008-09, Japan–India bilateral trade has shown signs of increasing with an average annual growth rate of

21.6 per cent between 2005-06 and 2011-12. It must be noted that quite recently the annual bilateral trade showed a vigorous expansion of 33.3 per cent for two consecutive years in 2010-11 and 2011-12, although declining slightly in 2012-13.

Japan–India CEPA Coming into Effect

Under its omni-directional diplomacy, India is widely involved in FTA/EPA negotiations with many countries and regions, but those which have been concluded and implemented to date are with countries/regions including Sri Lanka, Singapore, ASEAN, SAARC, Korea, Japan and Malaysia. The Japan–India CEPA/EPA came into effect in August 2011. It is still too early to appraise the effects of the CEPA on the movement of Japan–India trade, but it is quite likely that the CEPA provided certain favourable announcement effects on the subsequent expansion of the bilateral economic relations.

Tariffs were scheduled for elimination on 90 per cent of Indian and 97 per cent Japanese goods over ten years, compared with around 75 per cent of Indian goods in the case of India–Korea CEPA over eight years. Japan is expected to export more auto parts and steel products to India, and to import more agricultural and marine products from India.

Auto components, iron and steel products, electric and electronics parts, and general machinery are included in concessionary import items on the Indian side. For example, iron and steel products (cold and hot rolling steel plates, alloy steel, and galvanized sheet iron) are currently subject to 5 per cent tariff rates, which are scheduled to be eliminated within five years so that favourable effects on bilateral trade are expected in the near future. Regarding automobile components, the tariff rates for gearboxes and diesel engines, currently 12.5 per cent, will be reduced by half within six to eight years, and muffler, currently 10 per cent, will be eliminated within 10 years, while for electric and general machinery, the tariff will be eliminated completely within 10 years. In the case of India–Korea CEPA, Korea is not permitted zero-access into India's market for auto parts and steel. Regarding concessionary import items on the Japanese side, the tariff rate for almost all goods in industrial and mining industries imported from India will be eliminated immediately, together with the rates for durian, asparagus, shrimp, and lumber, while the tariff rate for other agricultural and marine products will be diminished to zero within 7–10 years.

The treatment of generic medicine imported from India deserves special attention. Previously, it was actually quite difficult for India to export generic medicines to Japan, where many restrictive measures were instituted for the import of generic medicines. However, increased imports of generic medicines from India can be expected because of the national treatment, on the side of Japan, is accorded for applications for registration and other approvals required for the release of generic medicine. Furthermore, some improvement has been made for the mobility of human resources, including yoga instructors, English teachers, and Indian cuisine masters. It is expected that India–Japan bilateral trade will more than double to $25 billion by 2014 under the CEPA/EPA.

Before the Japan–India CEPA, India–ASEAN FTA had already come into effect in January 2010. India has increased its import machinery from ASEAN, with imports of parts or components showing a remarkable increase. Actually, in 2010, seven out of the top ten imported machinery products comprised various machine-related parts, including semiconductors and thermionic tubes, office equipment parts, auto parts and components, internal combustion engines, and superheating/cooling equipment (Ushiyama 2012). This trend indicates that India has apparently incorporated itself increasingly into the East Asian regional production network where large quantities of machine-parts are imported and exported within the region. Actually, according to a survey of the Japanese companies' activities in Asia–Oceania conducted by Japan External Trade Organization (JETRO), many Japanese companies located in Singapore and Thailand selected India as the most important country for their operations and export destination in the coming three years.[2]

It is noteworthy that while intermediate exports from East Asian countries to India have expanded, finished products exported from India destined to EU and the US have also shown a marked increase,[3] which indicates that India, while implementing omni-directional diplomacy, has also been incorporated into the East Asian production network as an important production and exporting hub. It can be reasonably inferred that such a tendency will be accelerated when the Japan–India EPA comes to fruition.

New Horizons for Japanese Investment into India

Trends in Japanese Investment into India

Throughout the 1990s, when India embarked on liberalization of foreign capital, the inflow of foreign capital was not particularly active, and India played second fiddle to the East Asian countries. However, with India's sustained high level of growth and the expansion of each industrial sector, its importance as an enormous market and as a production base has suddenly come to draw attention. FDI, which had been trending at a scale of an annual average of US$ 4.0 billion in the first half of the 2000s, jumped to US$ 15.7 billion in 2006-07. Portfolio investments also reached US$ 11.4 billion in 2003-04, and with some fluctuation, have continued an expansion trend.

It is in the field of investment rather than trade where we can witness a more dynamic trend in recent Japan–India economic relations. Japanese FDI into India reached a peak of US$ 434 million in 1997, but it decreased after that in the wake of India's nuclear experiments in 1998. Japan ranked fourth, accounting for 8 per cent of the total accumulated volume of FDI inflows into India from April 2000 to March 2013. It was as recently as 2007 that Japan's FDI into India began to show conspicuous expansion. Japan's FDI into India increased from US$ 1,562 million in 2010-11 to US$ 2,972 million in 2011-12, but declined slightly to US$ 2,111 in 2012-13, ranking third after Mauritius and Singapore (Table 1). The Japanese government aims to double Japan's FDI into India within five years. To promote Japanese investment and technology transfer into India, both Japanese and Indian governments have an intention to set up a joint investment fund in 2014.

Table 1: Share of Top Investing Countries into India: FDI Inflows

(*US $ million*)

Ranks	Country	2006-07	2007-08	2008-09	2009-10	2010-11	2011-12	2012-13	Share of Total Inflows April 2000 to March 2013
1	Mauritius	6,363	11,096	11,208	10,376	6,987	9,942	8,950	38%
2	Singapore	578	3,083	3,454	2,379	1,705	5,257	1,984	10%
3	UK	1,878	1,176	864	657	755	9,257	1,069	9%
4	Japan	85	815	405	1,183	1,562	2,972	2,111	8%
5	USA	856	1,089	1,802	1,943	1,170	1,115	537	6%
	Total Inflows	15,726	24,579	27,309	25,834	19,427	36,504	20,999	

Source: Ministry of Commerce and Industry.

Faced with stagnant markets in economically advanced countries and aggravated investment environments in China where wages are rising and industrial policies are becoming more restrictive and unpredictable for foreign companies, India has become more attractive in Japanese business circles. Until recently, Japanese companies had a negative image of India's investment environments that constituted a sense of 'psychological distance' from India. However, Korean companies' successes in gaining a large share of consumer electronics markets indicate that what Japanese companies identify as areas of concern, i.e. adverse investment environments, are not necessarily critical factors that would deter Korean or Singaporean companies.

Convinced, at long last, that India offers a huge domestic market and that it will grow to be a leading economic power, Japanese companies have committed to India increasingly. The number of Japanese companies in India has increased from 248 in January 2006 to 438 in January 2008, from 550 in October 2008 to 627 in October 2009, from 725 in October 2010 to 812 in October 2011, and further from 926 in October 2012 to 1072 in October 2013 (Figure 2). A new trend is arising in Japanese investments into India, not only in the field of FDI, but also in the field of portfolio investment. Japanese investors have increasingly turned to weigh Indian stocks in their financial portfolios via brokerage firms, thanks to a favourable expansion of the Indian economy. Given that domestic interest rates remain at low levels, Japanese investors are increasingly turning to foreign markets for their investment. Actually, Indian stocks are no less popular than Chinese stocks. Consequently, Japanese portfolio investment into India has increased conspicuously since 2005, although some reversal of trends has occurred under the global financial turmoil.

Fig. 2: Number of Japanese Companies in India

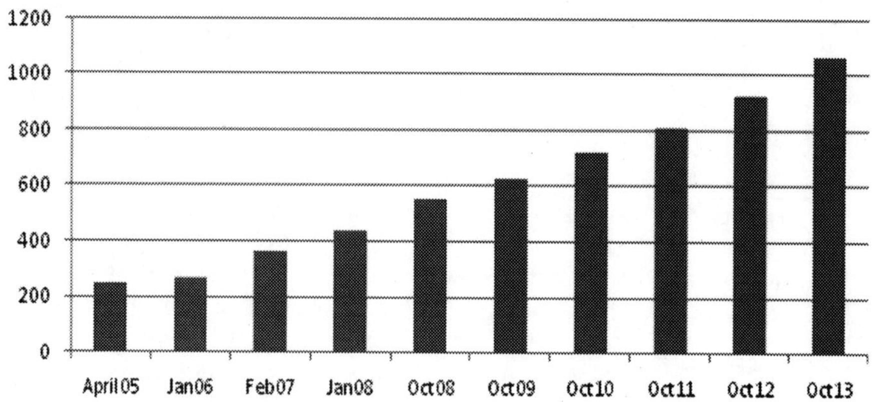

Source: Japanese Embassy in India.

In fact, since the dawn of the twenty-first century, outward FDI by Indian corporations also exhibited a marked expansion as if to keep pace with the expansion in inward FDI. Indian outward FDI have kept recording more than US$ 10 billion since 2006-07. The destination of Indian outward FDI is not limited to developing countries, but extends to advanced countries also, including the result of mergers and acquisitions to a large extent.[4] Regarding Indian FDI into Japan, it has remained quite limited, with a few exceptions among which Lupin's acquisition of Kyowa Pharmaceutical Industry in 2007 is included. However, it is expected to expand gradually under India–Japan CEPA especially in the fields of pharmaceutical and IT industries.

Deepening and Widening of Japan's FDI into India

In the past, Japan's FDI into India had been lopsided in the automobile sector. According to the FDI inflow data released by the Government of India, the top sector receiving FDI from Japan during 1991 through 2005 was the transportation industry (60.4 per cent) followed by electrical equipment (7.2 per cent), service sectors—financial and non-financial—(3.7 per cent), ceramics (2.2 per cent), and textiles (2.0 per cent).[5] In recent years, however, not only automobile assemblers and auto-parts suppliers, but also other companies in various fields including steelmakers, pharmaceutical companies, and construction machinery producers have begun to make their presence known in India. Regarding the automobile sector, following Suzuki, all major Japanese assemblers including Nissan, Toyota and Honda have positioned India as the strongpoint for production of small cars and recently, sport utility vehicles (SUVs) in their global strategy, newly releasing remarkably low-priced cars designed for emerging countries.

A firm presence of Japanese automobile assemblers and auto parts manufacturers strongly induces other companies engaged in steel production and logistics to come to India. All major Japanese steel producers have tied-up with their Indian counterparts to produce sheet iron for automobiles or to set up blast furnaces in India, with Nippon Steel & Sumitomo Metal Corp. forming an alliance with Tata Steel, JFE with JSW Steel, and Kobe Steel with SAIL. Logistics companies, including Nippon Express, Hitachi Transport System and Itochu Corporation, have already begun operations in India, and shipping companies, including Mitsui O.S.K. Lines Ltd., are ready to engage with marine transportation of automobiles exported from India to Europe. In the construction machinery sector also, both Komatsu Industries Corp. and Hitachi Construction Machinery Co. Ltd. are now increasing their production in India.

Regarding the electronics appliances sector, where Japanese companies have lagged far behind Korean companies, Panasonic Corp. and Sony Corp. have become determined to make strenuous efforts to catch up with LG and Samsung with a firm commitment from top management. Panasonic Electrical Works, currently merged with Panasonic, succeeded in expanding its sales network by acquiring Anchor Electric in 2007. Panasonic has steadily expanded its share in the Indian electronic appliances market from less than 2 per cent in 2010 to 5–6 per cent in 2010, further aiming to expand its share from 10 per cent in 2012 to 25 per cent in 2018 to be the largest electrics appliances company in the Indian market. Sony, using its own production base in Malaysia, not only outstripped the Korean companies of LG and Samsung in the sale of premium flat panel displays TVs in 2010, it became a market leader in the compact camera market, and has also been steadily increasing its share in the smart -phone market. Sony has no factory in India, but it has set up its R&D centre in Bangalore. Daikin Industries Ltd., a global leader of in the manufacturing of air conditioning systems for residential and commercial use, is also successful in expanding its share in the air-conditioning market since it entered into India in 2010.

Other promising and newly expanding areas for Japanese FDI into India include pharmaceuticals and products necessary for daily life. Currently, Japanese pharmaceutical companies are keen to establish strongholds in India, aiming to either strengthen their cost competitiveness or to enter the Indian market. Daiichi Sankyo Co. Ltd. acquired Ranbaxy Laboratories, the largest pharmaceutical company in India, in 2008. Eisai Co. Ltd. set up its manufacturing and research base in Andhra Pradesh. It is also noteworthy that many leading Japanese companies have newly started to enter into India in various fields of goods that are used daily, including foods, stationery, cosmetics, sanitary goods, and other products. For example, Kokuyo Co. Ltd. acquired the Indian third largest stationery company of Camlin in 2011 to accelerate its business expansion in the rapidly growing stationary market. Unicharm Corp. has set up its factory in Delhi in 2010 for expanding the sale of its care products in the Indian market. Pigeon Corp. is set to produce baby goods at its Delhi factory in 2015.

Japanese financial institutions such as commercial banks, insurance and security companies, have also come to approach the Indian market aggressively. This has never occurred before. Until recently, the Indian subsidiaries of Japanese commercial banks were so conservative and cautious that they used to furnish funds only to Japanese companies operating in India. However, given that infrastructural development projects require a huge capital demand and knowing that Indian companies are active in their fund-raising in global capital markets, Japanese financial institutions have come to recognize the Indian market as an important target, furnishing funds to Indian companies. Last but not least, we can witness a surge of Japanese FDI into the field of infrastructure development in India. Poor conditions in infrastructure used to constitute the most formidable barrier deterring Japanese companies from investing in India, but currently the Japanese companies have come to find major business opportunities there. Deficient infrastructure translates into a huge demand for improvement in infrastructure. India intends to invest as much as $1 trillion into infrastructural development during its Twelfth Five Year Plan. Some Japanese companies are keen to be suppliers of mechanical equipment, including power plants for Ultra Mega Power Projects and rolling stock for the Dedicated Freight Corridor (DFC).

Mitsubishi Heavy Industries set up two joint venture companies with Larsen & Toubro to produce supercritical pressure boilers and turbines in 2007, with Toshiba subsequently tying-up with Jindal South West (JSW) in 2008, and Hitachi with BGR Systems in 2010. As an episode showing its determination to be firmly committed to infrastructure business in India, Hitachi held its board meeting in Delhi in December 2012, which was the first overseas board meeting in its 102 year history. Hitachi plans 70 billion yen (Rs.4500 crore) in investments in India by fiscal 2015. Hitachi aims to increase its revenue in India from 100 billion yen in fiscal 2011 to 300 billion yen in fiscal 2015, and double its India workforce from current 6,800 to 13,000 in fiscal 2015. Power plants, railway-related items and desalinization plants are among the Hitachi's production list in India.

The DMIC Project: New Frontier for Japan–India Collaboration

The Contour of DMIC Project

Currently, the Delhi–Mumbai Industrial Corridor (DMIC), with DFC as its core backbone, is among the priority areas of Japanese government-sponsored investment into India, along with the newly mooted Chennai–Bangalore Industrial Corridor (CBIC) in southern India. These government-sponsored schemes provide a strong impetus to Japanese FDI in the field of infrastructure. The DMIC is a State-Sponsored Industrial Development Project, aimed at developing industrial zones spanning across six states along Western India. The idea of promoting the DMIC was endorsed at the Japan–India summit meeting when Prime Minister Manmohan Singh visited Japan in December 2006. It is an ambitious infrastructure project of US$ 90 billion, with financial and technical assistance from Japan. The Concept Paper was presented to both the Prime Ministers when Prime Minister Shinzo Abe visited India in August 2007. The vision of the DMIC is to develop the region as a 'Global Manufacturing and Trading Hub'. It envisages doubling employment potential in seven years, trebling industrial output in nine years, and quadrupling exports from the region in eight to nine years (DMICDC, 2011). The Dedicated Freight Corridor (DFC) between Dadri in NCR of Delhi and Jawaharlal Nehru Port (JNPT) in Mumbai, stretching an overall length of 1483 km, constitutes the backbone of the DMIC. A band of 150 km to 200 km on both sides of the alignment of the DFC is designated as the Project Influence Area (PIA) for DMIC. The PIA accounts for 13.8 per cent of total geographical area and 17 per cent of the total population of India. Under the PIA, the idea is to create 24 special industrial nodes: 11 Investment Regions with a minimum area of 200 square km and 13 Industrial Areas with a minimum area of 100 square km, along with a 4000-MW power plant, three greenfield ports, and six airports. The special industrial nodes will incorporate Special Economic Zones (SEZs), logistics bases, power plants, well-developed roads, housing and commercial centres along the DFC.

DMIC Development Corporation (DMICDC) was established under the Indian government in January 2008. The mission of DMICDC is to make a selection of projects, taking charge of the master plan and detailed feasibility studies of each project and monitoring them. It is obligated to work in partnership with the state government housing the projects. During his visit to India in December 2009, Prime Minister Yukio Hatoyama made a contract that Japan Bank for International Cooperation (JBIC) provide US$ 75 million for establishing the Project Development Fund (PDF) under DMICDC and signed a MOU that both JETRO and DMICDC cooperate to promote the constructing of smart communities. Furthermore, during his visit to India in December 2011, Prime Minster Yoshihiko Noda expressed the Japanese government's intention to provide a 450 billion yen credit and JBIC finance for the DMIC project in the next five years, and also to depute Japanese experts to DMICDC.[6]

As of January 2011, as many as 30 early bird projects had been presented: nine from Japan and 21 from India. Finally, in October 2012 the Ministry of Economy, Trade and Industry of Japan presented 19 prospective projects for Japan's US$ 4.5 billion loan facility as a final proposal. Among them, the project of water desalination and water supply to Dahej SEZ in Gujarat by the consortium (Hitachi, Hyflux and Itochu) was the first to be finalized in January 2013. The 19 projects mentioned above include seven projects for power supply, five projects for railway (metro), five projects for water supply, one project for IT (logistics data bank business plan), of which six projects are intended for constructing environmental-friendly smart communities/eco-cities covering water supply and efficient energy management system. These 19 projects are expected to be completed within five years.

The DFC Project

As for the DFC project, as early as April 2005, Prime Ministers of Japan and India made a joint declaration for feasibility and possible funding of the dedicated rail freight corridors, with a view to provide a safe and efficient transportation system, running at the speed of 100 km/h. The Indian Railway's quadrilateral linking of the four metros, viz. Delhi, Mumbai, Chennai and Kolkata (Howrah) and their respective diagonals, viz. Delhi–Chennai and Mumbai–Howrah carry over 55 per cent of freight traffic. These routes are already overstretched under the situation that the rail borne traffic is growing

16 per cent per annum. There is no other viable option for transporting bulk/heavy materials such as coal and steel than through railways. However the existing trunk routes of Howrah–Delhi on the East and Mumbai–Delhi on the West are highly saturated with line capacity more than 100 per cent (Gupta et al. 2010).

The feasibility report for both Eastern and Western Corridors was submitted by RITES Ltd. in January 2006. Dedicated Freight Corridor Corporation of India Limited (DFCCIL) was established as a 'special purpose vehicle' in October 2006, to construct and operate the two freight corridors: the Western DFC connecting the states between Haryana and Maharashtra, and the Eastern DFC connecting the states between Punjab and West Bengal. According to a revised deadline set out in 2009, the project is expected to be completed by 2016-17. The project is to be financed in a maximum 2:1 debt–equity ratio. The Western DFC will be financed using a soft loan provided by JICA, whereas the Eastern DFC will be constructed through funds provided by the World Bank and Public Private Partnership (PPP). The Western DFC is designed for double-stack container operations, and containers will be driven by electric locomotives, although single-stack containers will be introduced into the Eastern DFC.

The Western DFC comprises three segments: (a) Dadri–Rewari, 140 km; (b) Rewari–Vadodara, 920 km; and (c) Vadodara–JNPT, 430 km. The construction work has been divided into Phase I (Rewari–Vadodara, 950 km) and Phase II (Dadri–Rewari and Vadodara–JNPT, 584 km). At the summit meeting in April 2005, Prime Ministers of Japan and India agreed that the funding offered by Japan would be made under Special Terms of Economic Partnership (STEP).[7] The conditions of STEP loan require that at least 30 per cent of Japanese funding be used for the import of equipment and goods from Japan, and that all package contracts for the Western DFC must have a Japanese company as the prime contractor. At the subsequent summit meeting in 2008, it was confirmed that a 450 billion yen loan would be provided to the Phase I and that it was recommended that Phase II be commenced as early as possible.

The criticism arises that the DMIC, especially the Western DFC project, has taken too much time to take off. Indeed, many years have passed since the idea of the DMIC project was floated at the Japan–India summit meeting in 2005, but no major construction work had yet started until recently. Many factors are responsible for the delay of the DMIC project: some of them are traced to the Indian side, such as red tape, land acquisition problems, difficulties of coordinating the interests between six states, and so on. On the Japanese side, the most severe problem is a risk-averse behaviour among Japanese companies, especially in the field of civil engineering. The participation of Japanese major construction companies in the bidding is presumed to be indispensable to the Western DFC. Otherwise, it might be difficult to meet the requirements of sourcing 30 per cent of the contract from Japan as stipulated by STEP loan. Discouraged by bitter experiences in the Middle-East and faced with unprecedentedly long distance track works at the DFC project, no major Japanese construction company dared to participate in the DFC project. It is surprising that STEP loans—tied loans in favour of Japanese companies—have contributed to the delay of the Western DFC against the background of a risk-averse behaviour among Japanese major construction companies.

Meanwhile, after a prolonged period spent in feasibility studies and pre-qualification procedures, DFCCIL started to invite tenders for seven packages regarding the Phase I on design–build contract basis in late 2012. As of November 2013, Japanese companies had almost made a bid for each of all packages as the prime contractor. Japanese construction companies as well showed their interest in taking charge of the construction of bridges, although in certain packages competitive bidding did not take place because no plural Japanese companies made a bid there as the prime contractor in those packages. As far as Phase I is concerned, preparatory operations for civil, building and track works have finally started over 626 km section between Rewari (Haryana) and Ikbalgargh (Gujarat), following the MOUs which were signed between DFCCIL and Sojitz Corporation in August 2013. The Phase I aimed to be completed by March 2017, followed soon by that of the Phase II. As for the share of the work, the Japanese contractors will provide electric locomotives, head hardened rail for the entire stretch of main line, points and crossings, and signalling system, whereas the Indian partners will take charge of most of other areas including civil, building and track works. As far as Phase II is concerned, remaining land acquisition problems loom largest, and it will get started after a two-year or three-year lag.

Opening-up of Additional Japanese Investment into India

Aside from the 450 billion yen loan to the Phase I of DFC, Japan has already pledged to provide a US$4.5 billion loan to the DMIC project. It is noted that the above loans are in addition to annual 200-250 billion yen Japan's ODA to India, which is the largest recipient of Japan's ODA since 2003-04. Along with the DMIC, there is some movement among the Japanese side to place much expectation on the Chennai–Bangalore Industrial Corridor (CBIC). Indeed, Japan has a plan to construct another DFC between Chennai and Bangalore, where many Japanese companies including Toyota and Nissan are already concentrated. Both Japanese and Indian governments have shown strong interest in the CBIC projects. The master plan of CBIC prepared by JICA was approved by Mr. Sharma, Minister of Commerce and Industry in May 2013. It is highly probable that STEP loan will also be applied to the CBIC project.

Taking railway for example, there is much room left for Japan to be committed to modernization in India, including the Metro railway and the high-speed passenger corridor. The Metro connectivity railway between Ahmedabad and Dhorera is among the 19 DMIC projects of Japanese proposal. Japan has already left its footprint in Delhi Metro, which has credit of operating punctually and contributing to alleviate severe traffic congestion in Delhi. Japan's collaboration in Delhi Metro contributed to plant a new construction work culture in India: the concept of 'safety' and 'the appointed time of delivery'. Japan has already been committed to metro railway projects on ODA basis not only in Delhi, but also in Kolkata, Bangalore, and Chennai. Further, an increasing number of large cities will introduce Metro rail system, in which possibilities of Japan–India collaboration can be highly expected.

High-speed passenger corridor is another promising area for Japan–India collaboration. According the Ministry of Railways' white-paper Vision 2020, India has a plan to introduce high-speed trains to provide services at 250–350 km/h corridors in six corridors: Delhi–Amritsar, Pune–Mumbai–Ahmedabad, Hyderabad–Chennai, Howrah–Haldia, Chennai–Trivandrum, and Delhi–Patna. Of the six corridors above, the Ahmedabad–Mumbai route within the DMIC is most likely to be India's first high-speed line from the standpoint of marketability reflecting its high population density across high-income region. Japan faces severe competition with other countries in gaining an order, which is shown in the fact that the feasibility study was already conducted by French consulting company. Nevertheless, the Indian government places a high confidence on safe and punctual services of the Japanese Shinkansen (bullet train). Following the agreement made at the summit meeting in May 2013 by Prime Ministers Singh and Abe, the MOU was later signed in October between Indian Railway and JICA to conduct joint feasibility study on the Ahmedabad–Mumbai route.

IT Offshoring and Human Exchanges

New Trends of Japan's IT Offshoring to India

The Indian IT-BPO sector maintains its status as a leading industry even under global recession. The year 2011-12 was a landmark year for the Indian IT-BPO sector as its aggregate revenue crossed US$ 100 billion, with an annual growth rate of 14 per cent. As a proportion of India's GDP, the aggregate revenue increased from 1.2 per cent in 1997-98 to 7.5 per cent in 2011-12. Exports (excluding hardware) continue to be the mainstay of the sector, accounting for over 78 per cent of aggregate revenue at US$ 69 billion. Its share in the total Indian exports (merchandise and services) increased from less than 4 per cent in 1997-98 to almost 25 per cent in 2011-12 (NASSCOM, 2012). USA continues to be a dominant market, accounting for 62 per cent of the total for the Indian IT-BPO sector exports with UK subsequently at 16.9 per cent in 2011-12 (NASSCOM, 2012).

Japan is globally ranked as the second largest IT services market with an estimated annual turnover of $100 billion. However, IT collaboration between Japan and India remains far below the potential level. For India, Japan accounts for less than 2 per cent of its total software and IT services exports and it was quite natural for Indian IT companies to target Japan as a potentially important market. Major Indian IT companies, including Tata Consultancy Services (TCS), Infosys, and Wipro have come to Japan since the early 1990s, but they are still struggling to penetrate the Japanese market.[8]

Japan is renowned for its manufacturing industries and hardware production. Today, however, hardware and software are merging, and the importance of software in the manufacturing industry has increased especially in leading-edge sectors, which signifies that Japan's strength in hardware manufacturing might decline without software development capabilities. As a matter of fact, Japan now faces an acute shortage of the qualitative IT engineers to meet these demands.[9] Such a phenomenon has become accentuated since 2007, when many IT engineers belonging to the baby boomer generation began to retire. Nevertheless, Japanese companies overall have failed to tap Indian IT capabilities sufficiently.

When looking offshore, Japanese people prefer to turn to China, although numerous advantages apply to using Indian IT capabilities. India enjoys good esteem in high-quality control/management capability, wide scope of IT skills covering open to mainframe environments and rich global experience, and its intellectual property regulations are more reliable than those of China. According to the estimates conducted by PricewaterhouseCoopers (PwC) for the Japanese IT services market in 2008, in-house or in-land sourcing was decisively dominant, while offshoring accounted for only 3 per cent of the total IT services market. As for the destination of Japan's IT offshore investment, still 60 per cent of Japanese companies have outsourced to China and only 19 per cent to India (NASSCOM and PricewaterhouseCoopers 2008). Main reasons for Japan not using India fully include language barriers and cultural misunderstandings, scarcity of Indian residents in Japan, scarcity in globalized human resources on the side of Japan, and different software development styles—characterized as an *integral approach* rather than a modular one—including ambiguity in requirement specifications among Japanese companies.

While Indian IT companies are struggling to expand their activities for customers in Japan, we should not lose sight of new trends emerging in Japan–India IT relations. Faced with a stagnant domestic market attributable to declining birth rates, Japanese companies are under pressure to globalize their respective businesses. Because they must function globally to an increasing degree, it is increasingly becoming a natural choice for them to tie up with Indian IT companies or tap Indian IT capabilities directly by setting their captive centres in India rather than offshoring to China.

For example, both IBM Japan and Accenture Japan are now increasingly offshoring to their Indian counterparts, responding to the expansion of global activities of Japanese customers. Mitsubishi Corporation, Japan's largest trading company, set up a joint venture with TCS Japan in 2012. As the first case for Indian IT companies to make a big deal with Japanese companies, TCS bagged a US$ 100 million BPO project from Hitachi in 2013 to support its operation in Europe. It is no secret that Nissan, Japan's second largest automobile assembler, is already highly committed to tapping Indian IT capabilities. Nissan employs 2000 engineers at its Technology Centre in India, which would soon boost its ranking up to that of three other R&D centres in the USA, UK, and Japan in terms of its capacity to develop a whole new car. Nissan also deepened its relationship with TCS as a co-development partner. TCS provides IT support to Nissan's main development centres in the world by taking advantage of its Global Network Delivery Model.[10] Sony has already set up an R&D hub in Bangalore, which increased its employees by three times to 1000 in the past three years. With a view to consolidate its global IT system, Sony decided to reallocate its IT operation services from Japanese IT vendors to Indian IT vendors in 2012.

As for Japanese IT giants, they have been following the closed keiretsu model, resting on the top of a multi-layered subcontracting system. However, under the necessity of either reducing their operating costs or responding to the needs of their clients by expanding their focus globally beyond Japan, Japanese IT giants, including NTT Data, NTT communications, Fujitsu and NEC, have also come to set up their IT centres in India. For example, both NTT Data and Fujitsu have come to hold 4000–5000 IT engineers in their IT centres through the acquisition of American IT companies.

Challenges for Human Exchanges

The promotion of human exchange is vital for the improvement of mutual understanding and thereby consolidating further expansion of Japan–India relations. It is noteworthy that there are as many as 3 million Indian–Americans, most of whom are professionals, playing an indispensable role in deepening and cementing ties between India and the USA. Regrettably, the level of people-to-people exchange between India and Japan is far from satisfactory when viewed from any perspective, which presents a remarkable contrast with that between Japan and China (Table 2). Regarding the level of student exchange, it must be noted that the number of Chinese students studying in Japan amounted to almost 87,573 in 2011, while Indian students were only 573: they are even outnumbered not only by Bangladeshi and Sri Lankan students staying in Japan, but also by Indian students staying in China.[11] Improving scholarship and Japanese language training schemes for Indian students, increasing the number of lectures given in English at Japanese universities, and providing attractive career paths for Indian graduates to apply for expanded employment opportunities in Japanese companies are urgently necessary to attract more Indian students to Japan.

Table 2: Human Exchanges among Japan, India and China

Categories	Japan-India	Japan-China	Ratio
(A)	(B)	(C)	(D)
Number of Japanese Visitors (2010)	170,000	3,710,000	1/23
Number of Foreign Visitors to Japan (2010)	70,000	1,410,000	1/20
Number of Foreign Students in Japan (2011)	573	87,533	1/153
Number of Japanese Residents (2009)	4,000	127,000	1/32
Number of Foreign Residents in Japan (2010)	22,497	687,165	1/30
Number of People Learning Japanese Language (2009)	18,000	827,000	1/46
Sister/Friendship Cities (2010)	5 pairs	337 pairs	1/67
Number of Direct Flights (Summer 2010)	17 per week	556 per week	1/33

Source: Japanese Embassy in India.

We must also devote attention to the fact that current human exchanges between Japan and India are lagging behind even those of India and Korea. The number of Indian visitors to Korea and vice versa amounted to around 70,000 in 2009, and the number of Korean residents in India amounted to 8,518 in 2010, almost two times the number of Japanese residents in India in that year (Kabe, 2012). Currently, Japanese companies are desperately in need of young people who are qualified in promoting businesses in emerging economies. Some Japanese MNCs, including JFE, IHI, and Toshiba, which fully recognize the necessity of globalized personnel to brush up their English communications skills and enhance multicultural understanding, have started to send a certain number of their employees to India for training.

Strategic and Global Partnership

What is noteworthy in recent Japan–India relations is that bilateral strategic dialogues covering security issues are steadily advancing *pari passu* with the expansion of bilateral economic relations. Japan froze grant aids for new projects (except for emergency, humanitarian and grassroots assistance) and suspended yen loans for new projects when India conducted nuclear tests in 1998. It was the visit to India by Prime Minister Yoshiro Mori in May 2000 that marked a starting point for subsequent improvement of bilateral relations. The 'Global Partnership between Japan and India' was launched, which confirmed that the two countries would work together by pooling their strengths and expertise not only to benefit their mutual national interest but also the rest of the world.

Later, at the time when Prime Minister Junichiro Koizumi visited India in April 2005, the 'Japan–India Partnership in a New Asian Era' was launched, keeping an eye on reinforcing the strategic focus of the global partnership between the two countries. The Eight-fold Initiative was confirmed in the Partnership for realizing the full potential of their partnership.[12] The Eight-fold Initiative is quite important in terms of providing far-reaching and detailed directions for the subsequent expansion of Japan–India relations. Japan, wishing to take more weight on the 'ASEAN+6' framework for an Asian Economic Community rather than the 'ASEAN+3 (Japan, China and Korea)' framework as promulgated by China, succeeded in inviting India along with Australia and New Zealand as the founding members of the East Asian Summit when it was formed in Kuala Lumpur in December 2005.

At the summit meeting between Prime Ministers Singh and Minister Shinzo Abe held in Tokyo in December 2006, the 'Joint Statement Towards Japan–India Strategic and Global Partnership' was announced. The joint statement reaffirmed the importance of political, defence and security along with comprehensive economic partnership, science and technology initiative, people-to-people exchanges, and regional and multilateral cooperation. It was confirmed that both prime ministers would visit each other every other year. India is the first case for Japan to make an official promise of mutual visitation, while for India it is the second case after Russia. Since then, along with the prime ministers' mutual visitation, strategic dialogue by foreign ministers, national security dialogue by defence ministers, and other various ministerial levels of exchange including economic policy dialogue between Japan's Minister for Economic Trade and Industry and India's Minister for Industry and Commerce have been held annually. Current governmental exchanges might represent the most active period ever in the history of Japan–India relations. Based on a strategic partnership, both governments have come to forge close cooperation in economic and national security spheres.

The Japan–India Strategic and Global Partnership have gained much importance against the background of geopolitical change in Asia triggered by China. India had frosty relations with China after the 1962 border war, but since the beginning of the twenty-first century, thanks to its pragmatic diplomacy, India's economic relations with China have been showing a remarkable expansion. At the same time, China's advancement into the Indian Ocean under so-called 'string of pearls' strategy caused some concern in India. Japan–China relations have become strained over the rightful possession of the Senkaku Islands under Japanese administration.

The 'Joint Declaration on Security Cooperation between Japan-India' is noteworthy for providing a comprehensive framework for the enhancement of security cooperation between the two countries, which was signed at the summit meeting between Prime Ministers Singh and Taro Aso held in Tokyo in October 2008. It was followed up by the 'Action Plan to Advance Security Cooperation', which was concluded when Prime Minister Yukio Hatoyama visited India in December 2009. The Action Plan outlined strategic and defence cooperation, including annual strategic dialogue at Foreign Minister-level, annual sub-cabinet/senior official 2+2 dialogue and annual bilateral naval exercises.

Prime Minister Noda's visit to India in December 2011 strengthened bilateral relations in the fields of both economy and national security. The joint statement announced then underscored the growing importance of India–Japan Strategic and Global Partnership. In the field of security issues, primarily to preserve sea lanes in the Indian Ocean, both governments agreed to conduct joint military exercises between the Indian Navy and the Japanese Maritime Self-Defence Forces, with the intention of coping with troublesome piracy off the coast of Somalia and the growing Chinese influence in the Indian Ocean. In fact, maritime joint exercises started in 2012. Regarding rare earth minerals, which are critical resources especially for high-tech industries, the Japanese government has reached an agreement with India, the second largest producer after China, to launch a collaborative development project which will help Japan alleviate negative effects of overdependence on China. In the economic sphere, both leaders signed an agreement to increase the maximum dollar currency swap arrangement five times up to $15 billion from previous limits, which is expected to mitigate negative effects of the weakening Indian rupee. Both governments also agreed to make every possible effort to restart negotiations for the Japan–India Nuclear Agreement that was suspended following the unexpectedly severe accident at the Fukushima No. 1 nuclear plant caused by the Great East Japan Earthquake in March 2011. India places high expectations on Japanese nuclear technologies because it has the intention of expanding nuclear generation with a view to diversification of its energy sources. Prime Minister Singh welcomed the desire expressed by Noda that Japanese technology be used for future high-speed railways in India. It is important to note that such a gigantic scheme can be realized only amid steadily progressing formation of the Japan–India strategic partnership.

At the summit meeting held in Tokyo in May 2013, Prime Ministers Singh and Abe made the joint statement, expressing their resolve to further consolidate and strengthen the Strategic and Global Partnership between the two countries beyond the 60th anniversary of diplomatic relations. As was confirmed in the joint statement, much progress is being made for deepening Japan-India relations a wide range of areas covering economic and security spheres. Thus, the bilateral exercise between the Japan Maritime Self-Defence Force and the Indian Navy has started in 2012 in annual basis. Discussions are on for making it possible for Japan to export US-2 amphibian aircrafts to India. Pending negotiations for the Japan–India Nuclear Agreement were restarted in September 2013.

The latest summit meeting was held in Delhi in January 2014 when Prime Minister Abe was invited to India as the chief guest at India's Republic Day. The summit meeting marked a deepening and widening of Japan-India strategic partnership, although the Japan-India Nuclear Agreement was not concluded. Both Prime Ministers issued the joint statement with a rich content covering a wide range of areas including security, economy, investment, energy, science and technology, ICT, healthcare, nuclear, people-to-people exchanges and other global issues. Regarding security issues, Japan and India confirmed to strengthen maritime security cooperation, agreeing to launch the consultations at level of national security advisers and to have the trilateral dialogue between India, Japan and the US on a regular basis. To further strengthen bilateral financial cooperation, the two Prime Ministers welcomed the expansion of bilateral currency swap arrangement from $15 billion to $50 billion coming into effect in January 2014. The two Prime Ministers welcomed the progress of the DMIC/DFC project and encouraged the preparations for the CBIC project and the High Speed Railway (shinkansen) system on Mumbai-Ahmedabad route.

Concluding Remarks

Before World War II, India had been Japan's major trade partner, accounting for 10–15 per cent of Japan's foreign trade at least until 1937. Major imported products from India were cotton and pig iron. Japan found remarkable success in its modernization, overcoming competition with India in textiles and steel. Even after the World War II, India remained an important trade partner of Japan, accounting for 2–4 per cent of trade until 1965. In the post-war era, iron ore replaced pig iron as a major imported product from India, and Indian iron ore played a critical role in the remarkable post-war development of the Japanese steel industry at least until Japan started to import iron ore on a large-scale from Australia and Brazil. Thereafter, under the closed inward-looking regime, India had been long struggling with stagnated industrial development and was largely left behind by the global tide. Japan, however, joined OECD members in 1964, and has ridden on the track of high economic growth, becoming an economic superpower. It was since these times that Japan and India became economically estranged from each other.

Along with the introduction of economic reforms in 1991, India adopted an outward-oriented policy, but India–Japan trade showed no favourable expansion and came to lag behind India's trade with ASEAN, China, or Korea. It was only after 2003-04 that bilateral trade started to show an upward trend. It is expected that the Japan–India CEPA coming into effect in August 2011 can give further momentum to its expansion. It is in the field of FDI where a more dynamic trend is taking place in recent Japan–India economic relations. Japanese FDI into India is widening and deepening. In the past, it was lopsided in certain manufacturing sectors including automobiles and electric appliances, but it has recently expanded widely into other areas, including financial services and infrastructure. The expansion of Japanese FDI into India is highly anticipated to bolster the Indian manufacturing sector by bringing a high-quality production base and upgrading the skill-level of labourers. With investment risk in China rising under wage hikes and precarious bilateral Japan–China relations, India is increasingly finding favour as an investment destination.

Japan and India entered into a Strategic and Global Partnership in 2006, which marked a new era in the bilateral security as well as economic relations. Both security and economic relations exerts a marked synergy effect on consolidating bilateral Japan-India relations as a whole. For example, the construction works of the DMIC/DFC project have finally started in 2013. It is no exaggeration to say that such a gigantic project could not have taken shape had it not been for the framework of Japan–India Strategic and Global Partnership. The summit meeting taking place every year under the above framework has been instrumental in confirming and enforcing the Japanese commitment for the DMIC/DFC project. Needless to say, many challenges lie ahead in the areas of land acquisition, coordinating projects among six states, and streamlining permits and clearances. The greatest efforts possible should be taken on both sides to fructify an unprecedentedly large-scale DMIC/ DFC project along the right lines.

As for Japan–India IT collaboration, Indian IT companies have not so far been successful in penetrating the Japanese market. However, under the pressure to globalize their business, there is a growing tendency among Japanese companies to reach out to India not only to tap Indian IT capabilities but also to enhance their intercultural skills. However, Japan–India people-to-people exchanges are still extremely limited, which constitutes a missing link for additional expansion of bilateral relations. To consolidate Japan–India collaboration further and bring huge benefits for both countries, people-to-people exchanges should be promoted using every possible channel.

Japanese has long been influenced by the Buddhist way of thinking which originated in India, and both countries share their values in democracy, freedom of speech and rule of law. Furthermore, their relations are free from any negative problem in connection with historical perceptions. Indeed, Japan-India bilateral relations have been bolstered by cordial feelings. Japanese people appreciate Indian people for their fair and warm friendship shown to Japan after the World War?. The recent visit of Japanese Emperor and Empress to India has a symbolic meaning in addressing the importance of Japan-India relations. Deepening and expansion of Japan-India relations are important not only for enhancing their mutual benefits but also for establishing the peace and prosperity in Asian regions.

END NOTES

1. Ardent India's interest in upgrading its manufacturing skills can be shown in the fact that of the total 46 companies that were awarded prestigious Deming prize during the period from 2001 to 2012, as many as 21 companies were Indian companies.
2. To put it more precisely, in the case of Japanese companies located in Thailand (644 companies replied), India ranked first (21.8 per cent), followed by Japan (14.4 per cent), and Indonesia (14.3 per cent); in the case of Japanese companies in Singapore (141 companies replied), India ranked first (28.4 per cent), followed by Indonesia (19.9 per cent), and China (12.8 per cent). See JETRO 2010.
3. Intermediate products exported from East Asia to India had been expanding from US$ 5.89 billion to US$ 41.89 billion during 1999–2009, while finished goods exported from India to EU and the USA increased from US$ 5.89 billion to US$ 19.67 billion, and US$ 5.47 billion to US$ 11.88 billion, respectively. See Ministry of Economy and Industry 2011, p.101.
4. During the period of 2004–2009, FDI in the US by Indian corporations included 127 cases of Greenfield investment totaling US$ 5.5 billion and leading to 16,586 jobs. See Jain and Jain 2010.

5. STEP loan offers more favourable terms of 0.1 per cent interest with 40 year repayment period including 10 year grace period, compared with 1.4 per cent interest of general terms. Sectors and fields eligible for STEP include infrastructure and environmental projects, medical equipment and /disaster prevention system/equipment. STEP loan is expected to raise the visibility of Japanese ODA in both recipient countries and Japan through best use of advanced technologies and know-how of Japanese firms.
6. See Governments of Japan and India, 2006, Chapter 4.
7. JBIC was alloted a 26 per cent stake in DMICDC in August 2012.
8. Even though the major India IT companies set up their subsidiaries in China later than in Japan, they have a much larger presence than in Japan. For example employees of TCS Japan still amount to fewer than 500, while its employees in Chinese subsidiaries exceeded 1500 in 2011.
9. According to a survey made by the Information-Technology Promotion Agency of more than five hundred IT companies in Japan, the percentage of those IT companies which felt a quantitative shortage of IT engineers declined from 75.6 per cent in 2007 to 48.8 per cent in 2008 attributable to the recession triggered by the Lehman shock, but as many as 87.0 per cent and 84.5 per cent of them acknowledged a qualitative shortage of IT engineers in 2007 and 2008, respectively. See Information-Technology Promotion Agency 2010.
10. The Global Delivery Model is TCS's industry benchmark that allows the Company to deliver services seamlessly and uniformly to global customers from multiple global locations in India, China, Europe, North America and Latin America.
11. Indian students accepted in China were already as numerous as 5694 in 2006. Currently it is estimated to increase to around 9,000, including numerous students studying in medical courses. Indian medical candidates chose to study in China, attracted by lower education fees and wider entrance acceptance.
12. The Eight-fold Initiative includes the following items: (1) enhanced dialogue and exchange, (2) comprehensive economic engagement, (3) enhanced security dialogue and cooperation, (4) science and technology initiative, (5) cultural and academic initiative and strengthening of people-to-people contacts, (6) cooperation in ushering a new Asian age, (7) cooperation in UN and other international organization, and (8) responding to international challenges.

REFERENCES

Delhi Mumbai Industrial Corridor Development Corporation (DMICDC), 2012, 'Result Framework Document (2012–13)'.

Governments of Japan and India, 2006, *Report of the India–Japan Joint Study Group.*

Gupta, J., A. Jha and R. Ray, 2010, 'Dedicated Freight Corridor on Indian Railways: A catalyst for Industrial Growth', *RITES Journal,* vol. 12, issue?, pp. 21.1-21.16

Information-Technology Promotion Agency, Japan, 2010, *White Paper on IT Human Resources 2010* (in Japanese)

Jain, Vinod K. and Kamlesh Jain, 2010, *How America Benefits from Economic Engagement with India,* Washington, D.C.: India–US World Affairs Institute.

Japan External Trade Organization (JETRO), 2010, *Survey of Actual Activities of Japanese Companies in Asia and Oceania* (in Japanese).

Kabe. Shigesaburo, 2012, 'India's Relations with Northeast Asia (South Korea and Taiwan) – South Korean Take the Lead, Taiwanese Corporations also Start Active Deployment', in Japan Center for Economic Research, ed., *India and the World,* JCER.

Kojima, Sakura and Makoto Kojima, 2007, 'Making IT Offshoring Work for the Japanese Industries', in Meyer, Bertrand and Mathai Joseph, eds., *Software Engineering Approaches for Offshore and Outsourced Development,* Springer.

Ministry of Economy and Industry, Government of Japan, 2011, *White Paper on International Economy and Trade* (in Japanese).

National Association of Software and Services Companies (NASSCOM), 2013, *The IT-BPM Sector in India: Strategic Review 2013*, NASSCOM.

NASSCOM and PricewaterhouseCoopers, 2008, *Emerging Market Series: Opportunities for Indian IT Industry in Japan*, NASSCOM.

Ushiyama, Ryuichi, 2012, 'India–ASEAN Relations – The Formation of a Production Network', in Japan Center for Economic Research, ed., *India and the World*, JCER.

11

An Overview of Japan's Support for SAARC Member States: With Reference to Nepal

Ram Chandra Dhakal and Ram Kumar Phuyal

I. Introduction

The South Asian Association for Regional Cooperation (SAARC) is a relatively broad regional cooperation framework in South Asia. Based on a proposal from President ZiaurRahman of Bangladesh in 1980, SAARC was formally established at a summit held in 1985, with its Secretariat located in Kathmandu (Nepal) since 1987. The members are eight South Asian countries such as Afghanistan, Bangladesh, Bhutan, India, Maldives, Nepal, Pakistan, and Sri Lanka. Participating as Observers are Japan, China, United States, European Union, Republic of Korea, Iran, Mauritius, Australia, and Myanmar. In this regard, Japan places importance on South Asia, with which it shares the basic values of continued economic development, democracy, freedom, and the rule of law, and supports cooperation within the region based on a history of good relations with each country. Viewing SAARC as an association significant for its ability to provide a platform for the stability and development of the South Asia region, Japan established the Japan-SAARC Special Fund in 1993 to reinforce the Association's activities and foundation, and has implemented a variety of support and exchange programs. Since then it has been continuously supporting the eight member countries in various sectors.

During the recent visit of Japanese Prime minister H.E. Mr. Shinzo Abe to India on 25-27 January, 2014, Japan and India addressed the possibility of working together to further advance regional economic cooperation in order to reinforce growth and accelerate development across the region. Japan

The earlier version of this paper was presented in JNU-SPF International Conference of Japan-SAARC Partnership: Way Ahead, on November 14-15, 2013, New Delhi, India. Authors are grateful to the anonymous referees for their invaluable comments to enrich this paper in the present shape and would like to acknowledge financial support from Jawaharlal Neharu University, India .

supports Bangladesh for the acceleration of sustainable economic growth towards the realization of becoming a middle income country by 2021. Similarly, the Government of Japan handed over two Japanese fire trucks to the Fire Service Division of the Royal Bhutan Police, through the Project for Supply of the Fire Trucks in Lhuntse and Pemagatshel, under the Japanese Grant Assistance for Grassroots Projects on 4th November, 2013. It hopes that this grant/assistance will further strengthen the friendship between Bhutan and Japan. The Government of Japan has provided a bulk grant aid for humanitarian demining in Northern Sri Lanka under its Grant Assistance for Grassroots Human Security Project on 27th January, 2014. It has also invited a delegation of 11 Pakistani University Students who were chosen by their respective universities in Rawalpindi and Islamabad to visit Japan, under the 'JENESYS 2.0' Programme, from 9th February to 18th February 2014.

Japan's basic policy for assistance to Afghanistan is to support Afghanistan's self-reliance and prevent the country from stepping back to a hotbed of terrorism. The Afghan-Japan Communicable Disease Hospital in the Darul Aman area was officially inaugurated on January 18, 2014 with the participation of H.E. Dr. Suraya Dalil, Minister of Public Health and H.E. Mr. Takao Makino, Parliamentary Vice-Minister for Foreign Affairs of Japan. H.E. Mr. Nobuhito Hobo, Ambassador of Japan to the Republic of Maldives visited Male in December 2013. As part of his visit he paid courtesy calls on H.E. Mr. Abdulla Yameen Abdul Gayoom and other cabinet ministers. The discussions with the newly formed government focussed on possible ways to further promote friendly ties between Japan and the Maldives. Among the eight member countries' relations with Japan, Nepal's history of economic and cultural relation with Japan is unique and quite different than others. His Excellency Mr. Masashi Ogawa, Ambassador of Japan to Nepal visited Ramechhap and Sindhuli Districts to inaugurate the Sukhjor Bridge and Khurkot Health Post, on January 23 and 24, 2014, respectively. Both these projects come under the Japanese ODA to Nepal.

Looking back in history, Japan Official Development Assistance (ODA) has grown through the past half century after economic relations between Japan and Nepal were established in 1956. This process accelerated after the Japanese Embassy was opened in 1968 in Kathmandu. During the period of 1959 to 1969, Japan provided services of a team of technicians to conduct a hydroelectric survey of Kali River in western part of Nepal and sent an expert to assist in the design and manufacture of simple agricultural implements.

Many scholars such as Sigdel (1996 and 2003), Gyawali (1995), Pandey (2006), Mohri (2001), Kondo (1998), Satoh (2004), and others have written papers on the Japanese assistance to Nepal. Similarly, on historical relations, Pandey (2006) tried to cover the different dimensions of friendship as well as the mode of relations between the two countries. Nishigaki and Shimomura's work entitled "The Economics of Development Assistance, Japan's ODA in a Symbiotic World", present the overview of the history, philosophy, organisation and working of Japan's ODA, bringing to bear their first hand experiences of focusing on situations that tend to be overlooked. A book by David Arase titled "Japan's Foreign Aid (2005): Old continues and new directions" examines Japanese ODA Policy and Practice at the start of the new millennium.

However, most of these works related to Japanese assistance to SAARC member states including Nepal are not purely inferential in nature. This paper offers a descriptive method to study the Japanese official development assistance to SAARC with special reference to Nepal in the process of economic development over the last four decades, and analyzes in what aspect the country has emerged as the major donor. The present work also attempts to analyze the fact that the causes of failures of the development process is not only due to the donor's policy but also due to the overall socio-economic environment of the recipient country. In fact, this paper is based on secondary published sources such as books, journal articles, reports and documents available with the government ministries, embassies, agencies and donors etc., along with newspapers, magazines, unpublished reports collected from the Japanese and Nepalese libraries, diplomatic record office of the ministry of foreign affairs of Japan and Nepal.

The paper is organised as follows: the second section deals in brief Japan's support to SAARC countries followed by a third section which is devoted to overview of Japan's ODA to Nepal, section four presents Japan's grant assistance disbursement in Nepal and section five provides the concluding remarks.

II. Japan's Support to SAARC Member Countries

Japan's gradually increasing interest in South Asia, since 1991, is reflected in the visits of several high profile investment missions. As the newly industrialized Asian countries have funds to invest overseas, South Asian countries now have alternatives in Asia to consider beyond Japan. South Korea and Singapore, for example, have become economically active in the region, and although South Asian leaders have not given up on Japan, they now actively seek greater cooperation with ASEAN. Besides many other contributing projects, Japan supports SAARC member states on issues such as climate change, regional connectivity, sustainable development, disaster prevention, people to people to exchange, democracy and peace-building.

Japan undertakes various initiatives of SAARC member states in implementing efforts to address climate change and to protect the environment as urgent issues in South Asia. Japan announced the Fast-Start Finance package under the 'Hatoyama Initiative', which amounts to about 150 million US dollars of assistance for about 3 years from 2012. Based on the Copenhagen Accord, Japan seeks to expeditiously adopt a comprehensive new legal document that establishes a fair and effective international framework in which all major economies participate. Japan supported to introduce low-carbon energy generation such as solar power and continues to assist the region's concerted efforts to address climate change.[1] The contribution of Japan in different headings is as follows.

Assistance for the Development and Facilitation of Regional Connectivity

Japan has contributed total $4.73 million to the SAARC-Japan Special Fund to provide venues to discuss issues on shared concerns and to implement a variety of programmes, namely, symposia and expert meetings on social-economic issues, especially energy and disaster reduction, which effectively promote regional connectivity of SAARC and the SAARC-Japan relationship.[2] Similarly, Japan supports building the infrastructure, such as roads, railways, energy and irrigation, in order to foster-regional connectivity in the South Asia region for its sustainable growth and development. The details about Japan's support to SAARC countries other than Nepal are:

Bangladesh: Eastern Bangladesh rural development project (ODA Loan: $78.24 million, FY08), Chittagong city outer ring road project (ODA Loan: $90.96 million, FY09), South-Western Bangladesh rural development project (ODA Loan: $142.46 million, FY08).

Bhutan: Reconstruction of bridges phase III (Grant Aid: $24.94 million, FY09), Improvement of machinery and equipment for construction of rural agriculture road, phase II (Grant Aid: $5.97million, FY09).

India: Chennai metro project (ODA Loan: $217.51 million, FY08), Hyderabad outer ring road project (Phase 2) (ODA Loan: $420.27 million, FY08), Delhi mass rapid transport system project (Phase 2) (IV) (ODA Loan: $777.53 million, FY08), Guwahati water supply project (ODA Loan: $294.53 million, FY08), Hogenakkal water supply and Fluorosis mitigation project (Phase 2) (ODA Loan: $170.95 million, FY08), Kerala water supply system project (III) (ODA Loan: $127.27 million, FY08), Dedicated Freight Corridor Project (Phase 1) (ODA Loan: $26.06 million, FY09), Delhi mass rapid transport system project (Phase 2) (V) (ODA Loan: $336.4 million, FY09), Kolkata East-West metro project (II) (ODA Loan: $234.02 million, FY09), Chennai metro project (II) (ODA Loan: $598.51 million, FY09), Dedicated

Freight Corridor Project (Phase 1) (II) (ODA Loan: $902.62 million, FY09), Rengali irrigation project (III) (ODA Loan: $30.72 million, FY09).

Sri Lanka: Southern highway construction project (II) (ODA Loan: $174.99 million, FY08), Energy diversification enhancement project (Engineering Service) (ODA Loan: $8.20 million, FY08), Greater Colombo urban transport development project (Phase2) (I) (ODA Loan: $57.18 million, FY08).

Japan supports regional disaster prevention and disaster reduction system. Recommendations of the Japan-SAARC Symposium on disaster reduction held at Kobe, Japan, Jan. 2010, about "Earthquake Risk Reduction and Recovery Preparedness Program for South Asia Region" has been implemented in Bangladesh, Bhutan, India, Nepal and Pakistan (Mar. 2007–Dec. 2009). The program assists construction of multipurpose cyclone shelters in the area affected by cyclones. For detail, refer recommendations of the 3rd SAARC-Japan symposium on "Promoting Energy Cooperation in South Asia" in Appendix IV.

Assistance for People-to-People Exchange

Japan has implemented extensive people-to-people exchange programs to cultivate young people as the future bridge between SAARC and Japan by promoting mutual understandings among SAARC member states and between SAARC and Japan. Through the Japan-East Asia Network of Exchange for Students and Youths (JENESYS) program, Japan contributed approximately $7million to SAARC-Japan special fund (103 persons for FY07, 246 persons FY08, 107 persons for FY09, Total 456 persons). The project for human resource development scholarship (Grant Aid: $2.94 million, FY08) worked to provide assistance for about 20 young administrative officials and others from Bangladesh who study abroad in Japan to get a master's degree in Japanese graduate schools.

Support for Democracy and Peace-Building

Japan continues to support the SAARC Member States that have made progressive efforts for democracy and democratization in order to promote further efforts. Other than Nepal, some of the other SAARC member states that receive support from Japan for peace building are Afghanistan, Pakistan, and Sri Lanka. Japan has provisioned for the assistance of approximately 80billion yen urgently needed in Afghanistan. Shifting up from the existing pledge of a total of approximately two billion US dollars, Japan agreed to provide assistance of about five billion US dollars for five years from 2009, based on the future situation of Afghanistan. It will provide support to Afghans for the following purposes:

(1) Support in enhancing Afghanistan's capability to maintain security: Japan will pave the way for the Afghans to upscale their security responsibilities by supporting the National Police.
(2) Assistance for reintegration of grass root level soldiers: Japan will provide financial assistance to programs such as vocational training and rural development programs for job creation.
(3) Assistance for Afghanistan's sustainable and self-reliant development: Japan will provide assistance in areas such as agriculture and rural development, infrastructure development (including energy), education, health and other basic human needs based on Afghanistan's needs.

Pakistan was being supported for the sustainable development through peace building and economic recovery in North-West Frontier Province (Grant Aid: $12.1 million, FY09).

Sri Lanka: Rural road development project (ODA Loan: $131.21 million, FY09), Eastern province water supply development project (ODA Loan : $49.04 million, FY09), project for improvement of Anuradhapura teaching hospital (Grant Aid: $3.9 million, FY08), project for the improvement of central functions of Jaffna teaching hospital (Grant Aid: $22.98 million, FY09), Project for reconstruction of 5 bridges in eastern province (Grant Aid: $0.29 million, FY09), Emergency Grant Aid $4.1 million, FY09), Non-food relief item assistance ($0.47 million, FY09), Emergency Humanitarian Grant Aid through Japan plat form (JPF) ($2.5 million, FY09), Project for demining in Northern Sri Lanka (Grant assistance for grassroots human security projects for total about $2.2 million since Jan. 2009) were rigorously undertaken.

The evidence shows that the stability and development in South Asia directly affects the peace and stability of the international society. Japan attaches great importance to the role of SAARC and actively supports it through promoting regional connectivity and enhancing SAARC-Japan relationship. Efforts to stimulate Japanese business interest in South Asia continue, including new measures to improve the region's business environment and attract Japanese investors as well.

In addition, the Japanese are yet to fully fathom the abundant stock of engineers, scientists, economists, and other professionals of South Asia who are some of the best in the world in their fields. But, the recent wave of migrant workers to Japan from Bangladesh, Pakistan, Nepal, Sri Lanka and India, who do menial and other "dirty, difficult, and dangerous" jobs, have not helped to correct the image of South Asia among ordinary Japanese. Thus, a wall of stereotypes distorts perspective on both sides. One way of breaching this wall could be through tourism, even if Japan is too expensive a country for ordinary South Asians to visit and South Asia is not a popular overseas destination for Japanese tourists and sojourners. However, further cooperation and growth will depend upon improvement in essential infrastructure such as domestic air travel service, safety, availability of quality hotel accommodation hygiene etc.

III. An Overview of Japan's ODA to Nepal

Nepal is one of the Least Developed Countries of South Asia with the lowest per capita income. Striving for socio-economic development, Nepal needs the assistance due to its harsh location. The stable development in the country, which is the buffer state between China and India, contributes to the regional stability. Japan has participated in the economic development programs of Nepal since 1954. On the basis of Nepal's national development plan and other initiatives, it has extended ODA loan policy as well.[3] The following sections deal about the ODA during the Panchayat system and post Panchayat system in Nepal.

ODA During Panchayat System in Nepal

After the establishment of diplomatic relations, friendly and cooperative relations between Japan and Nepal have existed for many decades. Japan started its economic cooperation with a commodity ODA loan to Nepal in 1969 after the opening of the Embassy in Kathmandu in 1968. The distribution of Japanese ODA to Nepal during Panchayat system is mentioned in Tables 1 and 2 respectively.

Table 1: ODA during Panchayat System from 1969 to 1979 (US$ Million)

Years	GA($)	LA($)	TA($)	Total($)
1969	0	1.0	0	1
1970	0.2	0	0	0.2
1971	0.21	0	0.36	0.57
1972	0.3	0.06	0.42	0.78
1973	0.28	0.07	0.9	1.25
1974	0	0.13	1.36	1.49
1975	0.38	0.76	1.56	2.7
1976	0.73	0.12	2.1	2.95
1977	2.11	0.13	2.73	4.97
1978	4.69	0.51	4.33	9.53
1979	10.95	5.41	3.3	19.66
Total	**19.85**	**8.19**	**17.06**	**45.1**
Mean	1.804	0.744	1.550	4.1
%	**44.013**	**18.159**	**37.827**	**100**

Source[4]: MITI. Keizai Kyoryoku Genjo to Mondaiten and MOFA. ODA Hakusho, Japan.

Table 1 shows that the trend of the inflow of Japanese ODA to Nepal for the first eleven years (1969 to 1979) during the Panchayat system has not been very encouraging. It is interesting to note that the highest fund allocated, i.e. 44 per cent, was through Grant Assistance (GA) followed by Technical Assistance (TA) 37.8 per cent and Loan Aid (LA) 18.15 per cent. The Japan's ODA to Nepal increased rapidly from the fiscal year 1977, and the actual trend of increase of ODA disbursement across different time periods is exhibited in linear form in Figure 1.

Fig. 1: Trends Line of Japan's ODA (1969-1989)

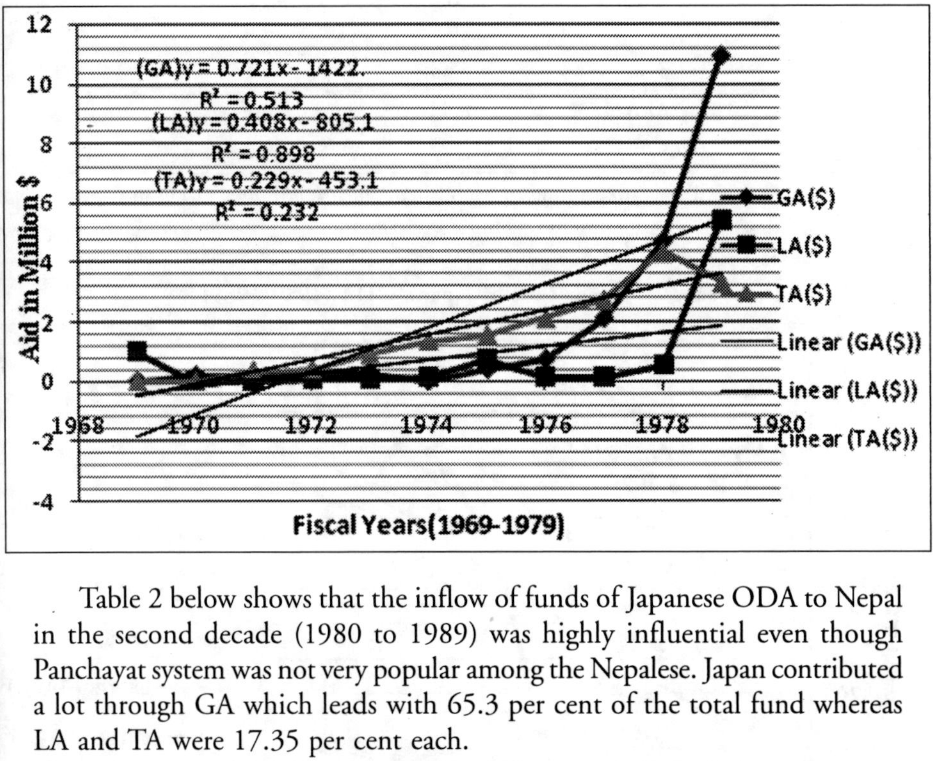

Table 2 below shows that the inflow of funds of Japanese ODA to Nepal in the second decade (1980 to 1989) was highly influential even though Panchayat system was not very popular among the Nepalese. Japan contributed a lot through GA which leads with 65.3 per cent of the total fund whereas LA and TA were 17.35 per cent each.

As compared to the first eleven years funding support, the Japanese ODA to Nepal in the years from 1980 to 1989 had been increasing significantly and it increased nearly 11 times more as compared to the figures in table 1. The extracted ODA disbursement across different time periods in simple linear form is presented as follows in Fig. 2.

While comparing $_R^2$ of GA, LA and TA of Fig. 2 with that of Fig. 1, the situation in Fig. 2 seems significantly increased. This explains that the overall inflow of the ODA during the period of 1980 to 1989 is very much commendable.

Table 2: ODA during Panchyat System from 1980 to 1989 (US$ Million)

Years	GA($)	LA($)	TA($)	Total($)
1980	16.7	4	3.6	24.3
1981	24.3	3.7	5.1	33.1
1982	26.6	2.9	5.8	35.3
1983	19.3	3.6	5.4	28.3
1984	15.2	7	6.4	28.6
1985	36.3	9.6	4.8	50.7
1986	44.7	14.4	9.1	68.2
1987	50	12.1	14.7	76.8
1988	41.4	6.4	14.6	62.4
1989	42.2	20.6	14.6	77.4
Total	316.7	84.3	84.1	485.1
Mean	31.67	8.43	8.41	48.51
%	65.285	17.377	17.336	100

Source[5]: MITI. Keizai Kyoryoku Genjo to Mondaiten and MOFA.ODA Hakusho, Japan.

Fig. 2: Trends Line of Japan's ODA (1980-1989)

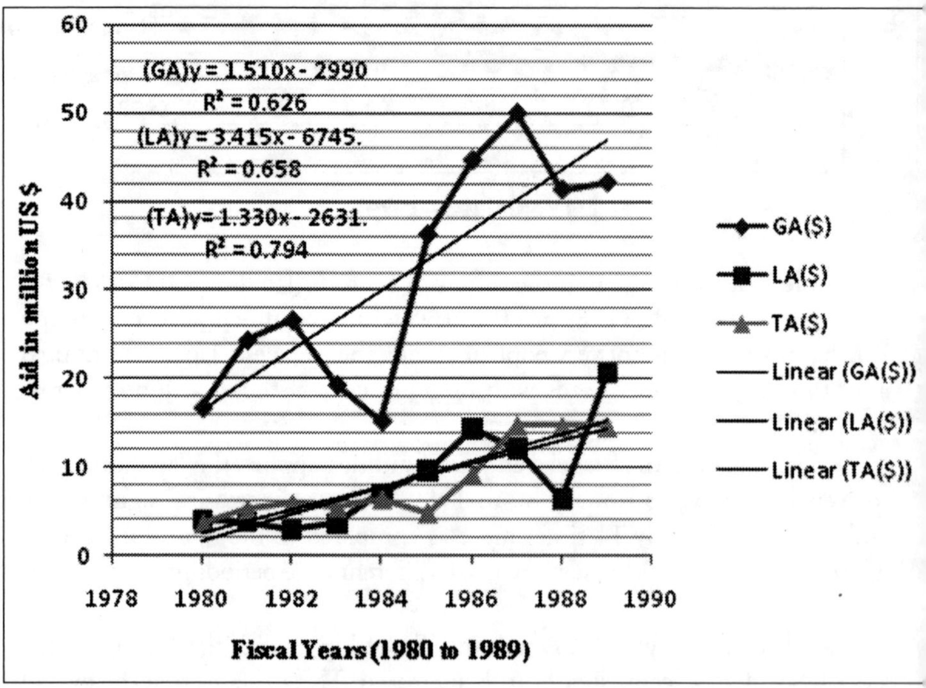

ODA After Restoration of Democratic System in Nepal

After the restoration of democracy in1990, Nepal has been striving for socio-economic development as well as a stable democratic process and economic liberalization. Nepal adopted a multi-party democratic system which might have been the cause to attract Japanese donors. That could explain the proportionate increase in GA and TA for the fiscal years from 1993 to 95.

ODA disbursements under different headings from 1990 to 1995 (US dollar million) is mentioned in Table 3.

Table 3: ODA After Restoration of Democratic System (US$ Million)

Years	GA($)	LA($)	TA($)	Total($)
1990	34.27	8.04	12.86	55.17
1991	44.33	67.69	15.52	127.54
1992	52.32	29.51	24.79	106.62
1993	68.11	7.5	35.28	110.89
1994	83.96	3.61	31.18	118.75
1995	95.38	2.8	29.42	127.6
Total	378.37	119.15	149.05	646.57
Mean	63.06167	19.85833	24.84167	107.7617
%	58.5195725	18.4280124	23.0524151	100

Source[6]: MITI. Keizai Kyoryoku Genjo to Mondaiten and MOFA.ODA Hakusho, Japan.

Approximately 59 percent of these total resources were disbursed to GA, while 23 percent to TA and over 19.8 percent was to LA. The trend of the disbursement of Japanese ODA to Nepal in the period of 1990 1995 is presented in Figure 3.

Fig. 3: ODA after Restoration of Democracy (1990-1995)

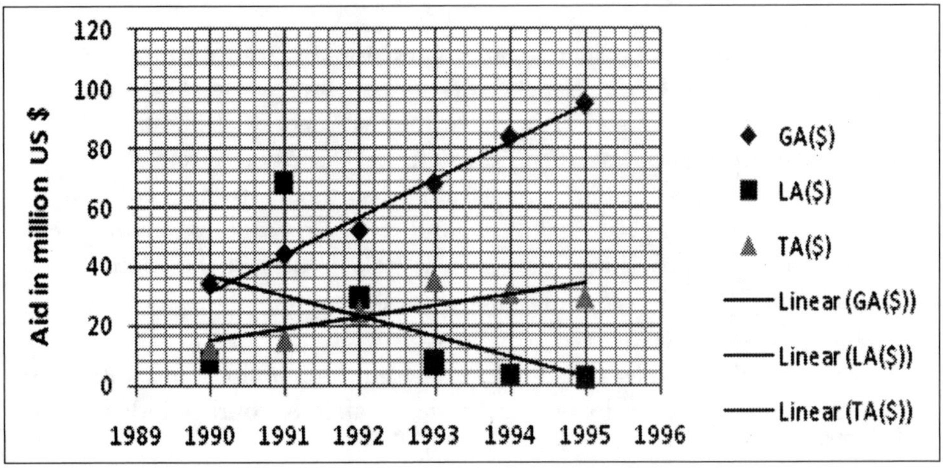

It seems that the inflow of the fund under GA, and TA headings are found quite consistent whereas the fund allocation of LA is getting lower, and there is a high degree of in discrepancy.

During Ten Years Long Conflict

The armed struggle began soon afterward with simultaneous attacks on remote police stations and district headquarters by Communist Party of Nepal-Maoists in 1996, and struggle went for ten long years. It might be one of the causes that Japan reduced its GA to Nepal from 59.11 million US dollar to 35.7 US dollar million in the fiscal year 1998 and at the end of the fiscal year 2005 it came down into 23.96 million US dollars as explained in Table 4.

Table 4: ODA for the First Seven Years of Conflict from 1996-2005 (US$ Million)

Years	GA($)	LA($)	TA($)	Total($)
1996	64.36	5.78	30.21	100.35
1997	59.11	4.05	23	86.16
1998	35.79	0.4	21.49	57.68
1999	41.63	1.08	22.88	65.59
2000	46.69	27.74	25.5	99.93
2001	49.72	15.1	19.57	84.39
2002	72.69	7.11	17.65	97.45
2003	34.87	3.47	29.49	67.83
2004	41.29	Debt Relief (211.16)	17.7	58.99
2005	23.96	Debt Relief (18.81)	14.18	38.14
Total	**404.86**	**64.73**	**189.79**	**659.38**
Mean	47.011	8.09125	22.167	75.651
%	61.400	9.816	28.783	100

Source[7]: MITI. Keizai Kyoryoku Genjo to Mondaiten and MOFA.ODA Hakusho, Japan.

The graph of Figure 4 clearly exhibits the fluctuation between disbursements of ODA in Nepal during the conflict period. The increase in difference between GA and TA with the fluctuation of total amount of ODA can be analyzed in two ways; First aid absorption capacity of a recipient country determines the level of commitments and a disbursement which is directly or indirectly affected by political unrest, conflicts, socio-economic environment, transparent and accountable government stakeholders of the country. The second depends on the economic and political condition of the donor country and its financial strength and crisis management.

In consequence, Nepal had to face a decade long political instability, lose out on a great source of foreign exchange, an affected tourism industry, and

Fig. 4: Trends of Japan's ODA to Nepal during Conflict

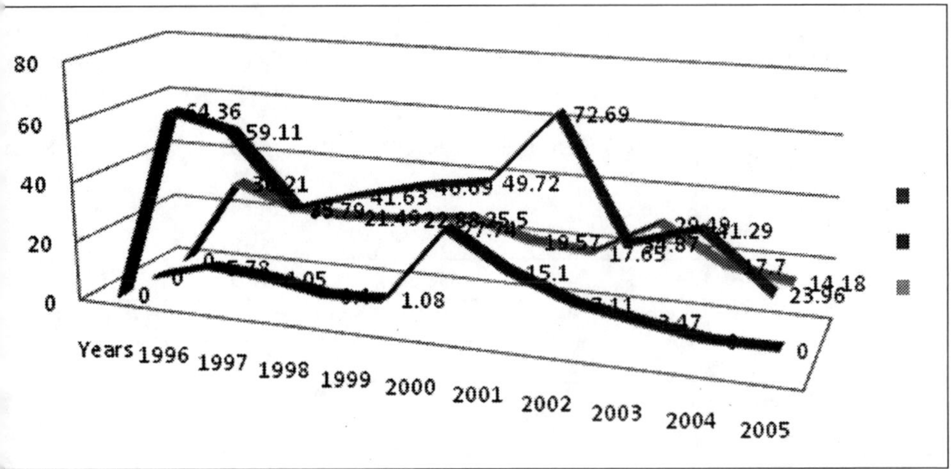

suffered in many the other sectors as well. Finally, the conflict ended on 22 November 2005 by joint CPN(M)-United People's Front issuing a 12-point resolution at a conference held in Delhi.

Comprehensive Peace Agreement

After conducting the Twelve-point Comprehensive Peace Agreement between Government of Nepal and the Communist Party of Nepal (CPN)-Maoist in 2006, the first Constitutional Assembly election was conducted in April 2008, and then the newly constituted Government took office under the leadership of CPN, Maoist in August 2008. Nepal also became a 'cool earth' partner of Japan in March 2009.Japan mainly focuses on poverty reduction in rural areas, democratization and peace building, socio-economic development and infrastructure being considering as priorities. At present Japan is established as one of the top donors to Nepal and involved in every important sector of the economy of the country.

The following Table 5 provides a clear picture about the amount funded by government of Japan after signing the peace agreement between the Government of Nepal and the CPN(M).

Table 5 shows that until the beginning of fiscal year 2012, the Government of Japan had provided a total assistance of 3,162.00 million US Dollars that constitutes grants (US$ 1,905.32 Million), loans (US$ 638.8 Million) and technical assistance (US$ 617.7 Million). The grant assistant is 66.42 per cent followed by the technical assistant which is 33.58 percentages whereas loan aid is zero.

Table 5: ODA by Fiscal Year during 2006-2011 (US$ Million)

Fiscal Year	GA($)	LA($)	TA($)	Total($)
Total until 2005	1679.96	638.89	503.89	2822.74
2006	44.36	Debt Relief (16.49)	13.69	58.05
2007	24.09	Debt Relief (16.31)	15.35	39.44
2008	25.69	Debt Relief (116.91)	18.69	44.38
2009	54.22	-	21.16	75.38
2010	39.65	-	24.61	64.26
2011	37.35	-	20.4	57.75
Total	**1,905.32**	**638.89**	**617.79**	**3,162.00**
Mean	64.38857	—	32.54285714	96.93142857
%	66.42693		33.5730708	100

Source[8]: Ministry of Foreign Affairs of Japan, 2012.

Fig. 5: ODA by Fiscal Year (2006-2011)

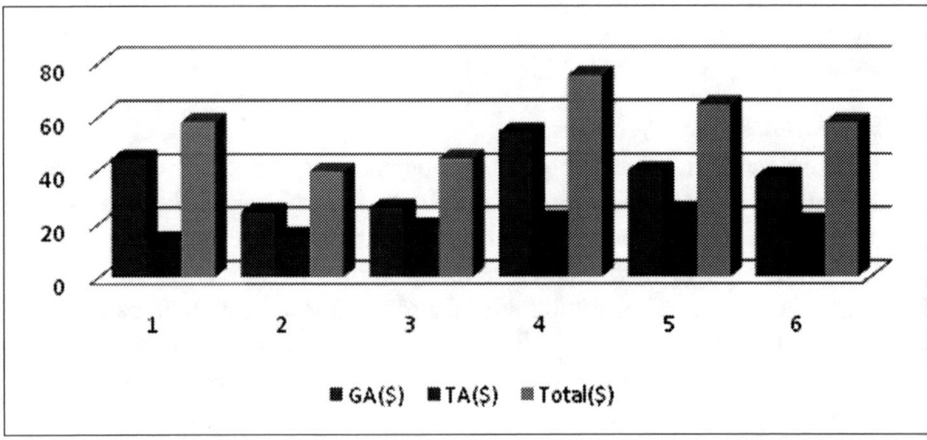

Figure 5 explains that trends of grant and technical assistances have been slightly increased but the ratio of increment is not very encouraging. From the entire analysis of disbursement of Japan's ODA to Nepal, the facts show that a big volume of the inflow of fund has been allocated to GA rather than TA and LA.

This section concludes that the Japanese ODA during conflict is found to be significantly lower than that of pre-conflict and post-conflict periods. It explains that the peace process settlement has been a major step forward in our global and strategic partnership and opens a way for new initiatives in strengthening our development cooperation goal with neighbouring countries.

IV. Japan's Grant Assistance Disbursement in Nepal

GA started with food aid in 1970 and mainly focused on the basic social sectors of health and medical services, education, as well as development of basic infrastructure in the transport and power sectors. There has been a huge assistance to Nepal in different grant aid projects that helps the country to come on the right track in the process of economic development.[9] Since the volume of GA has been great, this section analyzes the status of fund disbursements, mainly under sector-wise and project-wise headings.

There has been an extension of the grant assistance to Nepal during Japanese Fiscal Years from 1970 to 2010. The sectoral distribution of grant assistance of Japan to Nepal is explained in the following table (Table 6) for forty-two years.

Table 6: Sector-wise Distribution of Grant Assistance (1970-2010)

S.N.	Sectors	Amount in '000' Yen
1	Agriculture	35,126,900.0
2	Road/Bridge	28,432,000.0
3	DRF	19,528,678.0
4	Education	16,240,000.0
5	Energy	14,245,000.0
6	Communication	13,883,000.0
7	Drinking Water	13,173,000.0
8	Food Aid	9,948,440.0
9	Other-Infra-Public Facility	8,108,000.0
10	Disaster Mitigation	7,072,000.0
11	Civil Aviation	4,831,000.0
12	Health	4,708,000.0
13	NPGA	4,400,000.0
14	Other-Social-Sector	2,253,000.0
15	Other-Agri-Supply	1,456,000.00
16	Environment Conservation	1,260,000.0
17	Irrigation	1,202,000.0
18	Other	1,693,459.0
	Grand Total	**187,560,477.0**

Sources: Foreign Aid Development, MOF, Government of Nepal, 2012, and Ministry of Finance, Government of Japan, 2012.

Table 6 shows that the agricultural sector gets the highest allotment of the grant aid of 19 per cent. Even though the agriculture sector contributes of nearly 36 per cent of GDP in Nepal, and above 75 per cent of the population is dependent on agriculture, it has not been able to contribute greatly to the economic growth of the country. Under such circumstances, it is expected that even 19 per cent of total grant aid to this sector will definitely help

Fig. 6: Amount in '000' Yen

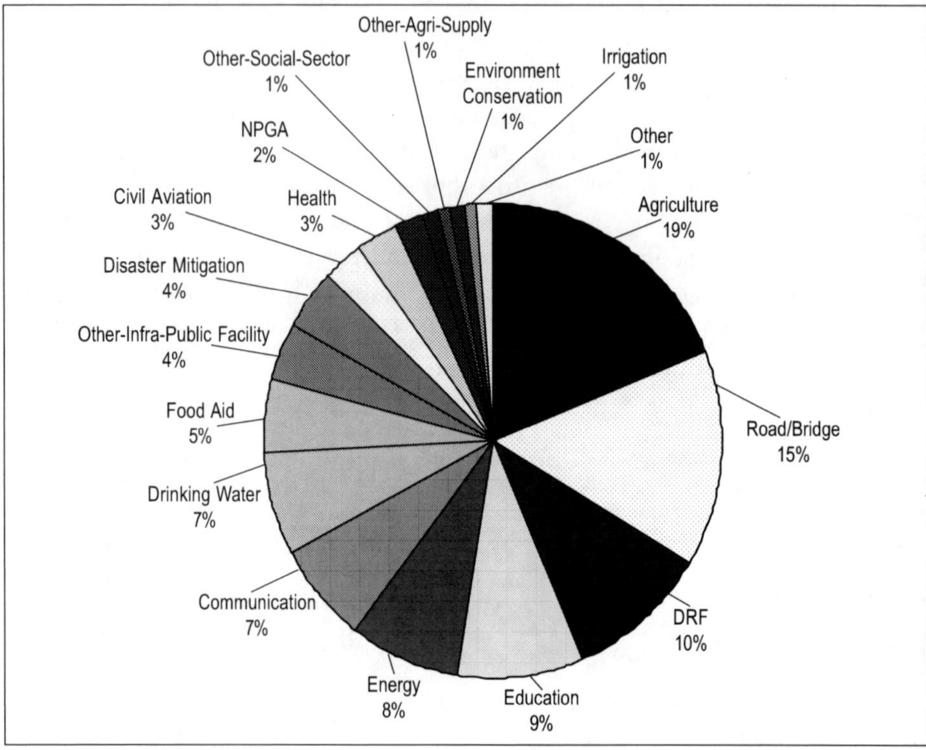

improving agricultural infrastructure, improve output of high value agriculture products as well as the development and diffusion of agricultural production technologies in order to increase employment opportunities and to raise the income level of farmers in long run.

The grant disbursement for major projects that are supported by the Japanese government through ODA for the thirteen years is mentioned as follows.

Table 7: Project-wise Disbursement of Grant Aid (1997-2011)

S.N.	Projects	Yen 100 million	%
1	Construction of Sindhuli Road	190.96	6.645
2	Kathmandu Centric Projects	141.68	4.855
3	Contribution in Education	89.04	3.051
4	Grassroots Human Security Projects	2294.48	78.641
5	Assistance for Food Security	102.6	3.515
6	Cultural Grant	1.89	0.065
7	Emergency Grant	4.86	0.167
8	Miscellaneous Projects	92.12	3.161
	Total	2917.63	100

Sources: Foreign Aid Development, MOF, Government of Nepal, 2012 and Ministry of Finance, Japan.

Table 7 shows that 78 per cent of the Japanese grant assistance to Nepal went to Grassroots Human Security Projects from 1997 to 2011. Construction of Sindhuli Road comes second with nearly 7 per cent of total grant assistant. Beside the significant investment in grass-roots projects and roads, the other major projects undertaken in the last thirteen years were; Construction of Primary Schools under Basic and Primary Education Programme, Debt Relief Fund, Improvement of Existing Air Traffic Services System under the Tribhuvan International Airport Modernization Project, Improvement of Intersections in KTM City, Supply of Microfilm and Book Binding Equipment to the Central Library of Tribhuvan University, Improvement of Kathmandu-Bhaktapur Road, Improvement of Intersections in KTM City, Construction of New Kawasoti Substation, Extention and Reinforcement of Power Transmission and Distribution System in Kathmandu Valley, Improvement of TV Programs of Nepal Television Corporation, Increase of Food Production in Nepal with special emphasis on Underprivileged Farmers etc.

Fig. 7: Trend of Disbersement of Grant Aid (1997-2011)

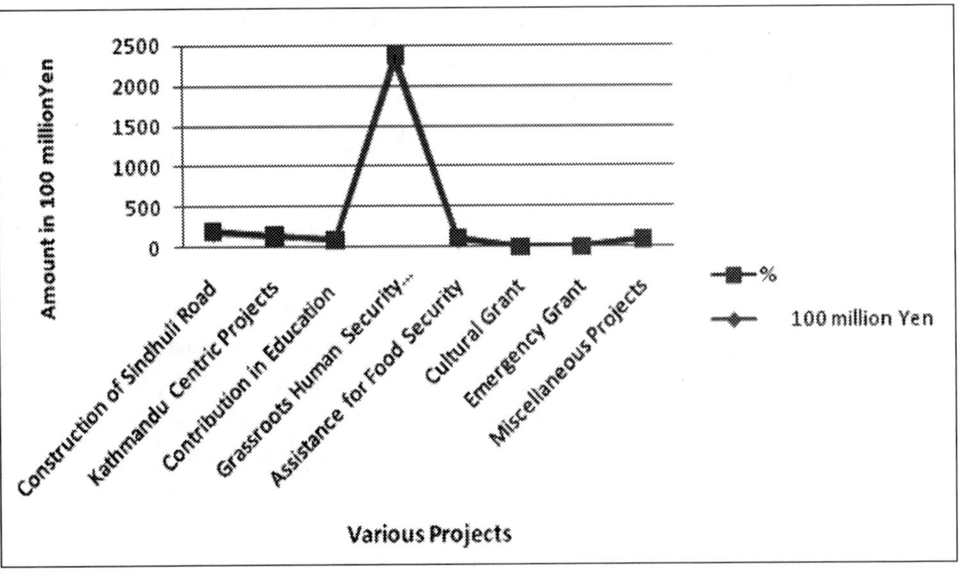

Figure 7 shows the trends of project-wise disbursement of grant aid from 1997 to 2011. The project-wise allocation of the fund has a high degree of variation from 78 per cent to 0.065 per cent (biggest to smallest projects). It would be quite practical if the government of Nepal could shift nearly 50 per cent of the proposed budget from the grassroots human security sector into other productive and potential sectors of the country which could help to achieve high economic growth and reduce poverty in the country.

V. Concluding Remarks

This paper initially discussed the share of donation of Japan to eight South Asian countries. This paper shows that Japan has become one of the major donor countries for the overall development process of the SAARC member countries. The evidence proves that South Asian nations are opening up their economies and the economic relationship is likely to strengthen with Japan. Further, the more the business environment improves in South Asia, the greater will be the chances for attracting Japanese business.

The trend of Japan's ODA to Nepal has been exhibited for the last forty-two years in four different periods on the basis of political systems of Nepal (During Panchayat system of governance, after restoration of democracy, during ten years of conflict, and after signing the Comprehensive Peace Agreement). As a close development partner and one of the major donors, Japan has been extending its ODA to Nepal in order to help promote the socio-economic development of Nepal. Japan has been extending economic and technical assistance to Nepal basically in the areas such as human resources development, education, health and medical care, agriculture development, basic economic and social infrastructure such as road and transportation, power generation, environmental conservation, communication and forth on.

It is also assumed for the corrective measure that project-wise disbursement of aid was based on a trickledown approach to development of the recipient country rather than the direct involvement in the poverty alleviation packages through the basic need approaches of the poor people in Nepal. However, it is not easy to quantify the achievements that resulted from Japanese Official Development Assistance to Nepal. So, the outcome of Japanese support to economic growth in SAARC countries, especially Nepal, cannot be explained properly without making an in-depth baseline survey of the recipient country. Hence, there is a further need to make an in-depth analysis of implemented projects to measure and evaluate quantitative contribution of Japanese aid and its major constraints from both the donor's and the recipient's sides.

END NOTES

1. **Afghanistan:** Project for Introduction of Clean Energy by Solar Electricity Generation System (Grant Aid: $7 million, FY09), **Bangladesh:** Programme for Improvement of Solid Waste Management in Dhaka City toward the Low Carbon Society (Grant Aid: $12.15 million, FY08), New Haripur Power Plant Development Project (II) (ODA Loan: $222.1 million, FY08),Central Zone Power Distribution Project (ODA Loan: $97.15 million, FY08), Bheramara Combined Cycle Power Plant Development Project (Engineering Services) (ODA Loan: $22.09 million, FY09),Rural Electrification Upgradation Project (ODA Loan: $132.41 million, FY09), **Bhutan:** Science and Technology Research Partnership for Sustainable Development SATREPS "The Study on GLOFs (Glacial Lake Outburst Floods) in the Bhutan Himalayas" (FY09-12, 3 years), **Maldives:** Project for Clean Energy Promotion in

Malé (Grant Aid: $10 million, FY09), **Pakistan:** Project for Introduction of Clean Energy by Solar Electricity Generation System (Grant Aid: $4.8 million, FY09), and **Sri Lanka:** Disaster Management Capacity Enhancement Project Applicable to Climate Change (Technical Cooperation, FY08), Project for Capacity Development of CDM Promotion in Sri Lanka (Technical Cooperation, FY09-),Project for Introduction of Clean Energy by Solar Electricity Generation System (Grant Aid: $8.6 million, FY09).

2. **Afghanistan:** Workshop on Mitigating Problems Associated with Households. Headed by Females, Seminar on Promotion of Agro technology, **Bangladesh** :SAARC Expert Group Meeting on Climate Change, Sharing of Knowledge and Technology of Vegetable Crops and Exchange of Germplasm, **Bhutan:** SAARC Expert Group Meeting to develop the SAARC Regional Strategy on Communicable Diseases, Meeting of the Technical Committee on Environmental Forestry, **India:** Meeting of the Regional Task Force to Implement the SAARC Conventions relating to Trafficking in Women and Children and Promotion of Child Welfare in South Asia, **Maldives:** SAARC Youth Camp, **Pakistan:** Workshop for Youth on Promoting Regional Harmony, and **Sri Lanka:** SAARC Film Festival.
3. ODA Loan assistance has been extended mainly for the power sector (Kaligandaki' A 'Hydroelectric Project, Kulekhani Hydro power Station), Disaster Prevention Project.
4. A Detailed Survey of Every Year's Issue of ODA's published White paper of up to 1979.
5. A Detailed Survey of Every Year's Issue of ODA's published White paper (1980 to 1989).
6. A Detailed Survey of Every Year's Issue of ODA White paper since 1990 to 1995.
7. A Detailed Survey of Every Year's Issue of Japan's ODA White paper since 1996 to 2005.
8. A Detailed Survey of Every Year's Issue of Japan's ODA White paper since 2005 to 2012.
9. Grant aid has been provided for improved traffic condition and effective transportation, for improvement of primary education environment, for stimulation of rural economy, Food Aid and Grassroots Human Security Grant Aid and so on. Project for the Improvement of Kathmandu-Baktapur Road, (Project for Construction of Primary Schools in Support of Education for All-Phase II, Project for Construction of Shindhuli Road -section 3, Total amount in FY2008: 2.389 billion Yen and Cumulative grant aid till FY 2008: 177.23 billion Yen.

REFERENCES

Embassy of Japan in Afghanistan (2013), *Japan Assistance to* Afghanistan, Kabul.

Embassy of Japan in Bangladesh (2013), *Japan Assistance to Bangladesh,* Dhaka.

Embassy of Japan in Bhutan (2013), *Japan Assistance to Bhutan,* Thimpo.

Embassy of Japan in India (2013), *Japan Assistance to India,* New Delhi.

Embassy of Japan in Republic of Maldives (2013), *Japan Assistance to Maldives.*

Embassy of Japan in Nepal (2013), *Japan Assistance to Nepal,* Kathmandu.

Embassy of Japan in Pakistan, (2013), *Japan Assistance to Pakistan,* Karachi.

Embassy of Japan in Sri Lanka (2013), *Japan Assistance to Sri Lanka,* Colombo.

Japan International Cooperation Agency (2002), JICA in Nepal since 1978, *JICA office*, Kathmandu, Nepal.

Khadka, Narayan (1997), *Foreign Aid and Foreign Policy: Major Powers and Nepal,* Vikas Publishing house, New Delhi.

Ministry of Foreign Affairs of Japan (2009), *Outline of Japan's ODA to Nepal.*

Ministry of Foreign Affairs of Japan (2012), *Japan's Official Development Assistance White Paper.*

Pandey, Ram Kumar (2006), *"Japanese Cooperation in Nepal" Economic Diplomacy in the Geographic Base,* Sakura Foundation, Kathmandu.

Sigdel, BamaDev (2003), Nepal's Relation with Japan and China, *Centre for Policy Studies*, Kathamandu.

Skar, H.O., and Cederroth (1970), Development Aid to Nepal: Issues and Options in Energy, Health, Education, Democracy, and Human Rights, *Nordic Institute of Asian Studies,* Copenhegan.

Takao, Kamibeppu (2002), History of Japanese Policies in Education Aid to Developing Countries, the Role of the sub-governmental processes, Rutledge, New York and London.

12

Japan's Contribution Towards Economic Development and Stability of Bangladesh

M. Abul Kashem Mozumder and Abdullah-Al-Mamun

Introduction

Bangladesh is constantly maintaining an exceptionally close relationship with Japan since her independence in 1971. This relationship is epitomized by mutual trust and co-operation, goodwill and respect, cordial friendship and partnership particularly in the field of economic assistance and co-operation and good governance. It is believed that a number of common factors like climate, culture, tradition, history and empathy of people have created the basis of such relationship. It is assumed that the historically well-known plane hijacking incidence had also contributed to Japan-Bangladesh relationship from a different dimension.

In 1977, a JAL flight was hijacked by the Japanese Red Army to Dhaka airport and the JAL passengers and plane were released by a successful operation of Bangladesh Air Force and airport security officials. That incident not only introduced Bangladesh to the Japanese people, but also drew the sympathy of Japanese people for Bangladesh.

Apart from this incident, Bangladesh was able to draw the attention of the Japanese people in 1970 after the devastating cyclone that took place on November 12 in the coastal areas of Bangladesh when Japanese media were contentiously reporting about the vulnerable situation of cyclone affected people. Through the contentious news in the media about the relief work, the Japanese realized how badly Yahiya Khan's government was treating Bangladeshi people. Mr. Takashi Hayakawa, an influential parliament member of the then ruling party, Liberal Democratic Party, later on known as Mr. Bangladesh, some other MPs and civil society people had taken initiative to collect relief fund for cyclone victim people of Bangladesh. On the morning of November 23, 1970 they stood in front of the Shibuya railway station of Tokyo and launched a fund raising campaign for the cyclone victims of East Pakistan. Afterwards that campaign took place in other streets of Tokyo and the money received at the office of Mr. Hayakawa, totaled a few millions. The presentation of this fact is worthwhile to mention here because Japanese people came to know about East Pakistan and also observed the negligence of West Pakistan Government to East Pakistan which eventually contributed to their positive attitude and support to the Independence War of Bangladesh. At the time of the Independence War, Japanese media had played an affirmative role in building the positive opinion of Japanese people and the Government of Japan.

Japan was among the few nations, which recognized Bangladesh as a sovereign state on 10th February, 1972 and 13th March of that year should be marked as the milestone date in the history of Japan-Bangladesh relation when a 'Special Goodwill Envoy' came to Dhaka with million-dollar worth fertilizer as gift and technical assistance for the reconstruction of Ghorasal Fertilizer Plant. Gradually, continuous support and co-operation through aid, grant and technical assistance has made Japan as the number one bilateral development partner of Bangladesh. Japan's economic relation with Bangladesh has diversified in many areas in last four decades which cover trade imbalance, investment promotion, infrastructure and human resource development, education, power generation, agriculture, technical and cultural cooperation. In fact, the success of Japan-Bangladesh relations are portrayed through a number of colossal friendship bridges including Jamuna Bridge, along with the development of power and telecommunication, construction of fertilizer factories, establishment of hospitals and technical cooperation in many fields.

Genesis of Japan's ODA to Bangladesh

Japan's aid contribution to Bangladesh started with Food Aid immediately after independence and eventually it was extended to Commodity Aid, Project Aid and Technical Aid as well. Among the 20 major international development partners providing assistance to Bangladesh, Japan stands just after IDA (International Development Association) but she is the largest development partner of Bangladesh. However, over the period of time, relationship between Japan and Bangladesh got stronger, effective and diversified to many sectors. Bangladesh was ranked as the number one recipient of Japan's Grant Aid from 1985, receiving more than 10 percent of Japan's total grant aid with a steady increase annually.

The ODA policy of Japan is institutionalized in a manner that it is always in the advantage for the recipient country. It has certain unique characteristics like flexibility in providing and disbursing assistance, priority in meeting the recipient country's needs and expectations, adaptability in maintaining bilateral relations and fostering friendship and trust based on mutual respect. It also focuses on the fulfillment of the objectives and strategies in the arena of self-reliance, poverty alleviation and development of infrastructure of the recipient country and also on non-interference in the domestic affairs of the recipient country. In the case of Bangladesh, the policy is now aimed at assisting in achieving Millennium Development Goals (MDGs) and to become a middle-income country by 2021.

In 1992 Japan introduced its ODA Charter. This was based on four fundamental principles; the incentive for facilitating market economy in anticipation to promoting private market and free trade, the protection and mitigation of environmental vulnerability, the imposition of a variety constraining conditions in military expenditures with special emphasis on stocking of mass destruction weapons and the sustenance of institutional democracy and human rights around the world. Bangladesh, due to its persistence of non-aligned foreign policy, is an ardent supporter of these principles.

In addition, through its unconditional support and allegiance to the UN and active participation in its peace keeping missions, Bangladesh is desperately trying to be a competitive contender of drawing the attention of potential donors. By encouraging free trade, demonstrating due regards to democratic process and practices, showing respect to universal human rights and pursuing for protection of environmental degradation and mitigating the effects of climate changes, it thus fulfils the desired expectation of the Japanese government in providing assistance. Bangladesh presents her as one of the competent recipients to receive Japanese assistance for economic as well as social advancement especially in certain priority sectors. These priority sectors, needless to say, include basic infrastructure including roads and bridges, energy, agriculture, rural development, human resource development (health and education), technical assistance and transfer of technology.

Apart from these, Bangladesh has also reaped the benefit of some Low Income Countries' (LICs) friendly policy measures which were introduced by the government of Japan (GOJ) in the early 2000s. For instance, in March 2006 Japan launched the Minimal Interest Rate Initiative (MIRA) for LICs with a view to facilitating the implementation of positive reform initiatives of the LICs. This was followed by two other actions namely the Debt Relief Grant Assistance (DRGA) and the Japan Debt Cancellation Fund (JDCF). With the pursuance of these policy measures, Japan re-fixed its interest rate at a very minimal rate i.e. only 0.01 percent and it was given effect from April 2006. To ensure transparency and accountability in the management of the executing agencies responsible for aid assisted projects and to enhance the quality maintenance in the assigned works of contractors and suppliers, and also to make sure the timely implementation of projects another policy measure namely the Special Term for Economic Partnership (STEP) was introduced more or less about the same time. In conformity with the STEP, a meager 0.2 percent rate has been fixed to cover the charge which is in proportion with the length of the extension of disbursement periods of the loan committed against the project(s) in question. Bangladesh is one of the largest beneficiaries of these policy measures and it started to obtain the benefit right from the 28th ODA loan package. This package, for example, consisted of twenty four thousand and nine hundred six million yen and was signed for the implementation of three priority projects—Power Generation and Transmission, Telecommunication Network and Water Supply.

Along with many other LICs, Bangladesh became eligible to earn the facility of DRGA in a meeting of 12 March 1978 of the Board of Trade and Development of UNCTAD. It is due to this eligibility that Bangladesh gets back the amount she pays to Japan in the form of debt servicing charges. On 21 March, 2004 Bangladesh has finalized a Note of Exchange under JDCF (successor of the DRGA). Through this exchange, Bangladesh has been receiving debt collection of about US $ 1 million in each and every year and this is expected to continue until 2018. This fund is being utilized by the Bangladesh for human resource development by sending government officials and students to Japan for higher education and training.

Initial Stage of ODA

Immediately after Liberation, in fact, till 1976, Japanese ODA mainly focused on Food Aid and Commodity Aid and the project assistance was increased gradually. Food Aid was a basic requirement from Bangladesh side after the devastation of Liberation War but eventually Bangladesh started gaining food sufficiency and no loan was taken from Japan as Food Aid after 1985. Later on, Japanese ODA focused on sectors like transport, power, water resources, physical infrastructure, industries, agriculture, oil and gas. Initially, Project and Non-Project loans disbursement was higher than the grant.

Japan's ODA Contribution to Different Sectors

Education is a means through which human being can be transformed to human resource. Bangladesh is very optimistic to achieve the goal of "Education for All (EFA)" by 2015. Japan had provided technical assistance for "Strengthening Primary Teacher Training on Science and Mathematics under component 2 of PEDP II". Almost 100 students went to Japan for higher education by virtue of *Monbu Kagakusho* and other programs. Government and Non Government Organizations' officials are awarded with different scholarships to go to Japan for pursuing higher education and training like JDS and others. All of them—students, officials and trainees—are bringing Japanese technology to Bangladesh.

Japan is also supporting Bangladesh to achieve PRSP (Poverty Reduction Strategy Paper) goals from 2005. This Strategy Paper includes a comprehensive medium-term strategy for the implementation of pro-poor growth, effective safety-net programs and human development, more social inclusion and empowerment of the poor and the women, promotion of good governance and service-delivery practices towards attainment of the MDGs. PRSP priority also includes employment, nutrition, quality education, maternal health, local governance, criminal justice, sanitation and safe water.

Japan is providing financial and technical support to ensure proper infrastructure which includes road, bridge and others. ODA loan and co-financing project implementation with World Bank, International Monetary Fund and Asian Development Bank has contributed to the construction of the Jamuna Bridge in 1997 (Yen 7.768 billion), the Meghna and the Meghna-Gumati Bridge in 1991 and 1996 (Yen 8.148 billion and 8.343 billion) respectively, as well as the construction of Pakshey Bridge in 2003 (Yen 18.066 billion) and the Rupsha Bridge in 2005 (Yen 8.30 billion). All these bridges provided a landmark contribution to the physical infrastructure and laid the foundation for a modern communication network of the country.

Due to its geographic location Bangladesh is naturally a disaster-prone country. Almost each year the country is witnessing the recurrence of floods, cyclones, tidal storms etc. Since the incidence of the severe cyclones of 1969 till to date, people of Japan liberally extended their cooperation to the people of Bangladesh to overcome the vulnerabilities of natural disasters. Apart from the relief assistance in the aftermath of any disaster, JICA helped Bangladesh to strengthen disaster monitoring systems, disaster forecast/warning and evacuation systems as well as the highly urgent and important area of infrastructure development projects, including Improvement of the Meteorological Radar System in Cox's Bazar and Khepupara (2005-2006) and Multi Purpose Cyclone Shelter (MCS) Project (Phase V) (2004-2005).

Bangladesh is also fortunate to receive Technical Assistance and Cooperation from JICA through funding and implementing Technical Co-operation Projects in thrust sectors like education, health, environment, disaster management, agriculture and rural development, power, transport and also in private sector over the last 43 years. A statement will help us to understand the depth of Japanese Technical assistance to Bangladesh which is mentioned in the website of Bangladesh Embassy in Japan. It says:

> '...The Government of Japan sent 743 survey teams, 308 Experts Dispatch, trained 1486 Bangladeshi participants, dispatched 257 JOCVs, a total of 20794 persons over the period of 2000-2005 for which spent a total of 13,035,995 thousand Yen including some equipment of total 643,634 thousand Yen. In FY 2004, JICA received 4722 Bangladesh trainees and dispatched 1089 experts to Bangladesh.... Agreement on technical co-operation between Japan and Bangladesh was signed in 2002 for promotion of bilateral technical cooperation. There is huge scope of strengthening technical cooperation between both the countries including transfer of advanced and appropriate technology to Bangladesh and utilization of Bangladeshi human resource in Small and Medium Enterprises as well as in ICT in Japan...' (http://www.bdembassy.jp/).

In a developing economy like Bangladesh, the role of private sector can hardly be overemphasized. After several twists and turns, the private sector of the country is growing at a reasonably appreciable pace. It is now believed that this sector has great potential and this has been reflected since 2000. During 2005-2006, for example, the rate of investment in the sector was 18.67 per cent. To keep up this pace of investment, Japan is helping the sector to develop and flourish through JICA and JBIC. Specifically, JICA is extending its cooperation in the design and implementation phases due to the shortage of technical know how in the country. It also participates in the Private Sector Development Support Project (PSDSP) which is collaboration between the GoB, and the WB, DFID, and EU.

One of the biggest challenges of Government of Bangladesh is to ensure health care services for its citizens. JICA helped Bangladesh to ensure health services to its people in many ways, especially in the area of maternal and child health and controlling infectious diseases. Some JICA projects are still going on like Safe Motherhood Promotion Projects, Expanded Program of Immunization Activities (1999-) Filariasis Control Program (2004-).

Agriculture and Rural Development is prioritized as the main area of development to achieve MDGs by 2015. JICA is very much active in this field and implementing projects like Poultry Management Technique Improvement Project and Participatory Rural Development Project. It also contributed to as high as 67 per cent of the fertilizer production capacity of Bangladesh through the setting up of a number of fertilizer plants including the Chittagong Urea Plant. In addition, the JICA extended its cooperation to the Portable Steel Bridge Construction at Upazila (sub-district) level, Rural

Roads as well as providing technical assistance, training and domestic products of inputs to the agricultural sector.

In Bangladesh, the demand for electricity is at least 7,500 MW at peak hours, but only 6,000 MW can be generated. Japan has aided 230 billion Japanese Yen of ODA so far and contributed 1,170 MW, or 22.5 per cent of total effective capacity of the country. Bangladesh has set up a target to fulfill the demands of electricity by 2020. JICA is providing strong support through financial aids, technical co-operation and Maintenance of Power Plant. It has disbursed significant amount of funding in the year 2005, 2006, 2007 and 2009. New Haripur Power Plant is now under construction in Narayanganj, under the Japanese ODA. It is a 412 MW combined cycle power plant and one of the biggest and the most efficient power plants in the country.

Realizing the growing significance of the telecommunication and the ICT, the Government of Bangladesh has recognized it as one of the thrust sectors. In June 2006, it signed a project titled 'Telecommunication Network Development Project' with JBIC. Japan provided 8040 million yen to build up Basic Infrastructure-Telecommunication Network Development Project for the growing Telecommunication and ICT sector in Bangladesh.

JICA is providing financial and technical support for the formulation and execution of the Master Plan for Solid Waste Management in Dhaka City, Dhaka Solid Waste Management Project, Construction of Water Supply and Sewerage System, Khulna Water Supply, Karnaphuli Water Supply (II) Projects and Mitigation of Arsenic problems in Jessore and other districts. JICA thus helps in redressing environmental issues.

Japan's Present ODA policy to Bangladesh

The Ministry of Foreign Affairs of the Government of Japan has outlined Japan's ODA policy to its development partners. In reference to Bangladesh, the key ingredients of this policy are as follows:

- By promoting friendly bilateral ties with Bangladesh which is seconded by a strong sense of affinity since the independence of Bangladesh, Japan will further strengthen co-operative relationship in the international arena with Bangladesh.
- Through improving investment climate in Bangladesh, Japan will promote economic relationship with Bangladesh, in particular, in the realm of trade and investment.
- By extending support to achieve the MDGs goal in Bangladesh, Japan aims at enhancing the stability not only for Bangladesh but also for the region as a whole.

Facts and Figures of Japan's ODA to Bangladesh

Table 1: Japan ODA to Bangladesh from 1972 to 2004

(*In US$ million*)

Type	Grant Aid	Loan	Total
Food Aid	245.265	163.210	408.475
Commodity Aid	2268.220	1377.468	3645.688
Project Aid	706.984	1898.821	2605.805
Total	**3220.50**	**3439.50**	**6660.00**

Source: http://www.bdembassy.jp/

The table shows that Bangladesh has received US$ 6660 million from Japan as food, commodity and project aid over the period of 1971 to 2004. Out of the total US$ 6660 million, US$ 3220 million were grant aid and 3449 was loan aid. Only US$ 408.475 million were food aid, US$ 3645.688 was commodity aid and US$ 2605 million was project aid. Bangladesh was in need of food aid in the period over 1972 to 1976 because of post war reconstruction. But food aid gradually decreased due to some positive initiatives taken by the government. In that period, Japan was in the second position after the US in regard of the disbursement of food aid. Eventually, commodity aid increased than the food and project aid.

Table 2: Japan ODA to Bangladesh from 2006 to 2011

(*100 million yen*)

FY	ODA Loan	Grant Aid	Technical Cooperation
2006	249.06	23.16	16.12
2007	429.56	25.57	16.41
2008	397.49	42.73(0.02)	21.90
2009	387.92	27.65(0.30)	25.03
2010	0	16.49	24.11
2011	599.69	12.68(1.32)	29.04
Cumulated	**7,792.73**	**4,701.73(1.64)**	**614.49**

Source: MOFA, Japan.

From the year 2006 to 2011, Bangladesh has received 13108.95 hundred million Yen from Japan as ODA loan, grant aid and technical cooperation and among which 7792.73 hundred million Yen as ODA loan, 4701.73 hundred million Yean as grant aid and 614.49 hundred million Yen as technical cooperation. Because of the world wide recession and internal democratic transition, Bangladesh has received Zero Yen of ODA loan from Japan but able to receive 16.49 hundred million yean as grant aid and 24.11 hundred million Yen as technical cooperation.

Present Focus of ODA

At present Japan is keen to assist Government of Bangladesh to achieve its goal to become a middle income country by 2021. To fulfill her commitment, Japan is contributing to infrastructure and transportation development. To solve the problem of electricity, Japan, as stated earlier, is helping to set up power generation plants and electric power cable plants. Japan believes that infrastructural development and constant power supply would improve investment climate and as a result, more foreign direct investment will turn up. Japan is also committed to help Bangladesh to achieve MDGs goals by supporting schemes in maternal and child healthcare, primary education and the distribution of safe drinking water. Japan also encourages issues of disaster mitigation and climatic change by supporting primary measures of disaster predictions and warnings, earthquake safety and river management.

Major Projects of FY 2012-13 in Priority Areas

- (ODA Loan) The Kanchpur, Meghna and Gumti Second Bridges Construction and Existing Bridges Rehabilitation Project (I): 28.945 billion Yen
- (ODA Loan) Karnaphuli Water Supply Project (phase 2): 34.847 billion Yen
- (ODA Loan) Northern Bangladesh Integrated Development Project: 20.556 billion Yen
- (ODA Loan) Renewable Energy Development Project: 11.335 billion Yen)
- (ODA Loan) Dhaka Mass Rapid Transit Development Project (I): 10.477 billion Yen
- (ODA Loan) Bheramara Combined Cycle Power Plant Development Project: 41.48 billion Yen
- National Power Transmission Network Development Project: 18.736 billion Yen
- (ODA Loan) New Haripur Power Plant Development Project

Dhaka Chittagong highway can be identified as the 'Business highway' of the country as it has connected the port city Chittagong with the capital city Dhaka. Kanchpur, Meghnan, Gumti Bridge can be treated as the most important bridge of this highway. This highway has also connected almost 20 districts with the capital. The existing Kanchpur, Meghnan, Gumti Bridge was constructed before the independence and over the years it is losing its useful life. Concerned with its deteriorating condition as well on recommendation of the engineers, Bangladesh Government has initiated maintenance work of the existing Kanchpur, Meghna and Gumti Bridge. However, considering the importance of the bridge and the traffic it takes, Bangladesh government has approved the construction of 2nd Kanchpur, Meghnan, Gumti Bridge on 23 April, 2013. JICA is providing a total of 28.948 billion Yen loan for the maintenance of 1st and 2nd Kanchpur, Meghnan, Gumti Bridge. The cooperation of Japan in these bridges is a significant contribution to the socio-economic development of Bangladesh.

Chittagong is the second largest city of the country which has around eight million inhabitants. Demand of safe water is increasing rapidly because of industrialization and increased commercial use. Realizing the need of the people, Bangladesh government has initiated second phase of the Karnaphuli Water Supply Project to minimize the supply and demand gap. This water treatment plant will be capable to supply 143 million liters of pure water every day. It will definitely improve the quality of living and will also facilitate the economic activities. Without JICA's contribution of 34.847 billion yen of ODA loan, this project could not have been initiated.

Northern region of the country is relatively underdeveloped than other regions of the country. To reduce disparity among the regions, the government has recently undertaken different initiatives for socio-economic development of the each and every region of the country. As a part of this initiative, government has initiated Northern Bangladesh Integrated Development Project with an objective to improve access of infrastructure and public services. JICA is providing a sum of 20.556 billion Yen ODA loan for this project. It is expected that this project will bring considerable change in the socio-economic sphere of the people of the northern region.

Demand of energy is increasing day by day in Bangladesh because of industrialization and urbanization. It is difficult and also expensive to meet the growing demands by conventional means. Bangladesh is exploring for alternative energy sources and accordingly trying to undertake projects through which renewable energy can be developed. Here again, JICA has extended its hands by providing 11.335 billion Yen as ODA loan to promote the use of renewable energy as well as to diversify it sources.

Recently the government of Bangladesh has launched a highly ambitious project titled Mass Rapid Transit (MRT) project to ease Dhaka city's gridlocked traffic with the help of JICA. It is providing 10.477 billion Yen ODA loan for the implementation of the project. The project is supposed to be completed by 2022. It is known that about 60,000 commuters would be able to travel every hour after completion of this project. These will not only contribute to the economic mobility that is seriously hampered by bad traffic but also reduce the cost of travel of the city dwellers.

Power crisis is quite acute in Bangladesh. 'Load Shedding' is one of the most familiar hassles regardless of the people living in the cities or in the villages, doing business or involved in production. Existing power production capability can only meet seventy percent of the demand in peak hours. Understanding the ground reality, Japanese government has extended its support to improve power sector in Bangladesh by providing loan for Bheramara Combined Cycle Power Plant Development Project, National Power Transmission Network Development Project and New Haripur Power Plant Development Project in the financial year 2012 and 2013.

Major Projects of FY 2012-13 for Reducing Social Vulnerabilities

- (Grant Assistance) The Project for Ground Water Irrigation and Development of Deep Ground Water Source in Urban and Rural Areas: 728 million Yen
- (Grant Assistance) The Food Aid Programs (through WFP): 470 million Yen
- (Grant Assistance) Grant Agreement for the Poverty Reduction Efforts: 500 million Yen
- (Grant Assistance) Improvement of the Capacity of Public Food Storage: 560 million Yen
- (Grant Assistance) the Project for Human Resource Development Scholarship: 202 million Yen
- (ODA Loan) Maternal, Neonatal and Child Health Improvement Project 1: 5 billion Yen
- (Technical Assistance) Safe Motherhood Production Project Phase: 2011-2016
- (Technical Cooperation) Project for Capacity Development on Natural Disaster-Resistant Techniques of Construction and Retrofitting for Public Buildings: 2011-2014.

Apart from the main projects in priority areas, Japanese government has also extended its support to reduce social vulnerabilities in the area of irrigation, food, human resource development, child health, maternity health and disaster management. If a second, hard look into these projects are given, it can easily understood that they are implications of these projects in the day to day socio-economic life of the people. Bangladesh's economy still relies heavily on agriculture where irrigation is a great concern. It is widely argued that if irrigation problem is properly addressed the main problem of agriculture will be substantially solved. Japan's contribution can play a significant role here.

It is already understood that the overall development of the country is not at all possible without transforming the large population of the country as human resources. Japanese help in this sector may eventually bring good results. Maternity and child health is another area of great concerns for Bangladesh. Japanese contribution may also help to improve the condition.

Inefficient Utilization of Japanese Assistance

Rahman (2004) stated that the impact of the huge aid is less than optimal and the reason is the lack of capacity of the Bangladesh government's institutions that handle or implement the aid. The implementing agencies of the concerned ministries and the External Economic Relations Division suffer from complexities and weaknesses in aid coordination-from its inception to final implementation. The less competent organizational framework and weak project implementation process to evaluate and monitor a large number of programs often lead to less optimal results. While Japan's capability in these areas has been of high quality, the capacity of Bangladesh's aid utilization needs substantial improvements in the future. In this context, the 'medium-term' project and program formulations have to be increased and efficiently implemented. Japanese aid would have made more impact on Bangladeshi society given its size if it could be channeled in critical social sector, and in areas of institutional capacity building for effective governance including local levels, human resource management and poverty reduction.

Japan's Political Contribution and its Own Interest

Immediately after independence on December 16, 1972 Japan was among the first few countries to recognize Bangladesh on 10th February 1972, and the Japanese Embassy in Dhaka was instituted on 3rd March 1972. These steps manifested Japan's strategic interests in a newly organized South-Asia in the 1970s to restrain Soviet influence and ascertain its economic and political presence in the region. A solid foundation of friendly relations' between Japan and Bangladesh was laid in 1973 by the visit of the Prime Minister of Bangladesh, Sheikh Mujibur Rahman when an agreement was signed with his counterpart Mr. Kakue Tanaka for ensuring peace and prosperity in the world, especially in South-Asia. Subsequently, visit of President Ziaur Rahman in 1978, cemented the relation between these two friendly nations. However, the contentious exchange of visits by different levels of people like head of the governments, ministers, politicians, parliament members and policy makers helped maintain warm relationship between this two nations. With the end of the Cold War in the 1990s the world has observed a new international system. In that changing environment Japan has redefined its role as a soft power in global perspective to ensure peace and prosperity of the world through economic and technological cooperation. South Asia as a poor and densely populated region of the world drew attention of Japan in that global context. Bangladesh's democratic transition in late 1990s helped Japan to think in a positive direction which resulted in the dispatch of an election observation team of Japanese Diet to observe the 1991 national election. This restated Japan's concern of democracy and stable society. Japanese commitment and patronization of democracy was also expressed when she indicated to withdraw Japanese assistance from Bangladesh at the time of the cataclysm of Ershad regime in the 1990s. Japan also expressed her concern for democracy at the time of the military backed Caretaker Government in 2007 and asked the Caretaker Government to restore democracy. In the present crisis regarding the national election, few days back government of Japan has repeated concern over the violence and said that Japan likes to see a free, fair, participatory and inclusive election. In last four decades, Japan and Bangladesh are maintaining respectful friendly relation in spite of change of regimes in both countries. Both the countries have the same foreign policy and like to see peaceful world and wish to resolve bilateral and multilateral dispute through negotiation and through the United Nations. Japanese 'Peace Constitution' and Bangladesh's geopolitical reality, poverty and technological have contributed to peaceful foreign policy. As part of the policy Japan likes to see a politically stable Bangladesh moving towards prosperity.

Japan has some political objectives to achieve through its interaction with Bangladesh. Japan is trying to be a permanent member of the United Nations Security Council and she expects Bangladesh's support. This issue was discussed extensively at the time of the visit of the Bangladesh Prime Minister Begum Khaleda Zia in 1994 when she reiterated Bangladesh support but asked for some time to decide about co-sponsorship. Japan likes to see peace and stability in Bangladesh to export its product and import some raw materials. Japan likes to develop its regional and international leadership using ODA as a means and Bangladesh as a recipient of Japanese ODA always works as supporter of that vision. Japanese diplomacy is called 'Trade Diplomacy' or 'Economic Diplomacy' and Japan intends to achieve this through cooperation i.e. helps through ODA and earn through business. Japan uses different means to accomplish political objective. Japan tried to promote political dialogue among contending political parties and stake holders in Bangladesh to ensure democracy, peace and prosperity like at the time of the visit of the Japanese Prime Minister Mr. Toshike Kaifue in 1990 when he engaged with political dialogue with President Ershad to restore democracy in Bangladesh ending his autocratic rule. Japanese political objectives are also achieved through exchange of visit by government officials and political leaders.

Future Direction and New Areas of Co-operation

In 2007, Bangladesh purchased a piece of land in the heart of the political centre of Tokyo for construction of its own mission building and it is now a permanent address for Bangladesh in Tokyo. A Shaheed Minar in the Ikebukoru park of Tokyo was constructed in 2005, funded by the Government of Bangladesh, which has not only become a cultural heart for Bangladeshis' in Japan but also a symbol of friendship between the two countries. Japan-Bangladesh Parliamentary Group was formed in 2008 which is a bipartisan caucus in the Japanese Diet (Parliament), which serves as an alternative channel to reach the key political levels. Japan's friendship towards Bangladesh was clearly demonstrated, in 2008, when the then Prime Minister Taro Aso took over as the president of the Japan-Bangladesh Parliamentary Group. These new issues very much set a strong platform to build more effective Japan-Bangladesh Relations.

During the Japanese Deputy Prime Minister Katsuya Okada's visit in the first week of May, 2012, funding for Padma Bridge, construction of metro rail and allowing more duty-free access of Bangladeshi products to Japanese market were among their prior areas of discussion. The deputy premier categorically mentioned the issue of good governance and corruption at the airport press conference.

If we ponder over the first Japanese delegate's visit and the last visit of the Deputy Prime Minister of Japan, that Japan-Bangladesh meeting could easily be observed as a donor-recipient relation and the Japanese diplomacy with Bangladesh may be considered as 'Economic Diplomacy'.

Bangladesh and Japan have maintained closed relations over the years. This relationship has strengthened their partnership not only in diplomacy but also for development in the field of economy as well as trade and commerce. The framework of co-operation between these two countries, according to one of the vernacular dailies of Bangladesh, has been under-pinned by a number of common factors, such as climate, culture, tradition and history.[1] However, the positive outcomes of these mutual relations are only seen at micro levels of people or institutions but not at the level of government services.

Time has come for Bangladesh and Japan to decide on the new areas of priority in the changing socio-political context of both the countries. Katsuya Okada asserted on governance and corruption issues and emphatically pointed out that unless proper steps are taken, future investments shall be in threat.

Japan can be considered an ideal model country in terms of political stability, good governance and effective bureaucracy supported by its glorious history of economy and social development. Bangladesh has efficient officers, but they often lack interest, and work in a bad institutional framework. In that sense, more training assistance can be imparted under the umbrella of Japan Foundation to Bangladesh in government, non-government organizations, research institutions, hospitals and local governments to improve the governance for better operation and outputs. Priorities should be given on organizational capacity building for effective governance including human resource management. Bangladesh can seek for training and technical assistance to combat corruption and joint awareness programs can be taken to learn Japanese experience in combating corruption in Japan.

Japan is considered one of the leading and most prospective electronic and technological giants in the world with an enormous export market throughout the globe. Being a pioneer in many creations of electronic items, it is a nation enriched with expertise in the field of technical and scientific education. Bangladesh can be benefited to a large extent if Japan lends its helping hand in providing scholarships for higher education and research to the highly prospective and talented Bangladeshi young students in the technical fields.

The impact of Japan's assistance is now visible in all important facets of social transformation and economic advancement in Bangladesh.[2] However, there are some concerns that Japanese aid has been earmarked mainly for infrastructural sector. The impact of such aid has been good, but less optimal because of disproportionate emphasis on this sector. From that point of view, new priorities have emerged in social sectors like health, poverty reduction, environment, disaster management, and education. These new areas should be taken into consideration by the Japan government to formulate their future policy.

Bangladesh is highly dependent on foreign remittance by its overseas workers. Lack of sufficient knowledge and expertise makes the labor market immobile and makes it difficult for the technical workers to reach their true potential. These seriously constrain the national goal and achievement. This can only be remedied by providing effective training. The Japanese government and relevant organizations can play a vital role in providing training support to the unskilled laborers' going abroad and can contribute enormously to the overall development of Bangladesh.

The present global situation brought new imperatives for Japan as well as for Bangladesh in terms of responsibilities and challenges to go ahead. The long-economic emphasis on grass-root organizations, particularly, on human resource development, and new global security environment and economic competitions are going to make a significant impact on Japan's relationship with 'South Asian' countries, including Bangladesh. Conference, dialogues, seminar and brain-storming sessions can provide guideline to form the right strategy to face the transformed challenges. Japan Foundation may work closely with the Bangladeshi Think Tanks to organize the same.

Conclusion

Japan's contribution to the economic development of Bangladesh should be considered unique in the field of bilateral cooperation. This cooperation, as stated earlier, is characterized by mutual trust and respect. Japan's cooperation has touched almost all the economic sectors of the country and is able to accelerate the pace of development. Japanese assistance in Bangladesh is very much focused on infrastructural development, education, health care, energy, ICT, disaster management, agriculture and rural development, environment and other sectors which are always prioritized as the key sectors for economic development. It means, Japan is a true development partner and is working 'heart to heart' with the Bangladesh government and facilitating those sectors which are prioritized as fundamental sectors for economic development.

From the foregoing discussion it can be further concluded that if Bangladesh intends to achieve MDGs, PRSP and above all, wants to accomplish its vision to be a middle income country by 2021, Japanese technical and financial assistance would be indispensable.

END NOTES

1. *http://*archive.*thedailystar.net.*
2. http://archive.thedailystar.net/.

REFERENCES

Bdnews24.com (2005), *Japan-Bangladesh relations strengthening: Japanese ambassador* (http://bdnews24.com/bangladesh/2005/04/01/japan-bangladesh-relations-strengthening-japanese-ambassador) [Accessed on November 5, 2013].

Chowdhury, Mahfuzul H. (2013), *Japan–Bangladesh Relations-A Review of Development Partnership* (http://isq.sagepub.com/content/45/1/1.abstract) [Accessed on November 2, 2013].

Doula, Ashraf ud (2013), Japan-Bangladesh relations: Way forward, *The Daily Star,* October 17, 2013.

Economic Relations Divisions (http://www.erd.gov.bd/index.php?Itemid=214&id=150&option=com_content&task=view) [Accessed on October 2, 2013].

Embassy of Bangladesh in Japan (http://www.bdembassy.jp/) [Accessed on October 20, 2013]

Embassy of Japan in Bangladesh (http://www.bd.emb-japan.go.jp/en/common_img/bannerTitle.gifc [Accessed on October 01, 2013].

Islam, M. Serajul (2012), Japan-Bangladesh Relations at 40: Are Relations Waning? *Daily Sun,* February 12, 2012.

Jalal, S.A. (2002), *Japan's Contribution in the Independence of Bangladesh.* Dhaka: Hakkani.

JICA (http://sv2.jice.org/e/jigyou/images/ind_tt01.gif) [Accessed on October 10, 2013].

Mamun, A.A (2012), Japanese Deputy PM's visit and New Areas of Cooperation, *Daily Sun,* 30 May, 2012.

Mazid, Muhammad Abdul, Japan Participates in the Development Process of Bangladesh (http://www.thefinancialexpress-bd.com/more.php?date=2012-02-15&news_id=120127[Accessed on October 10, 2013].

Ministry of Foreign Affairs (http://www.mofa.go.jp/) [Accessed on October 10, 2013].

Rahman, Dr. Ataur (2007) (ed.), Japan-SAARC Cooperation, Dhaka: S.N. Printers.

Rahman, Dr. Ataur (2003), Thirty Years of Japan-Bangladesh Relations: Performance, Impact and Direction (http://www.bd.emb-japan.go.jp/jp/mailMagazine/pdf/keynote-230504%28PDF%29.pdf) [Accessed on October 1, 2013].

13

Shifting Images of Bangladesh in Japan–Bangladesh Relationship

Mayumi Murayama

Three "Bangladesh Booms" in Japan

Interest towards Bangladesh in Japan is currently at the highest level in the history of the bilateral relationship between these two countries.

There have been two instances when Bangladesh gained a certain level of interest in Japan in the past. The first wave came with the Liberation War with Pakistan from March to December, 1971. Dire situations in East Pakistan, as Bangladesh was known then, were extensively covered by press reports as well as through support activities carried out by Bengali students studying in Japan.[1] The Japanese government was among the first to officially recognise the newly-independent Bangladesh on February 10, 1972. It was a notable gesture of Japan, an ally of the United States who supported Pakistan. For Bangladesh, Japan has long been acknowledged as a reliable and friendly country ever since.

The second wave of interest came with the influx of Bangladeshi migrants into Japan in the 1980's. There was a time when Bangladesh as well as Japanese nationals could stay in Japan or Bangladesh for a maximum of 90 days without a visa for tourism purposes. Taking advantage of the facility, the number of Bangladesh nationals who illegally overstay their landing permit well beyond 90 days in Japan increased drastically. This turned into a political issue and post-1989, neither country could enter the other without a visa.

From the late 1980s to the early 1990s, was perhaps the first time when Japanese people recognized Bangladeshi people who work mainly in factories, construction sites, restaurants and pubs, and those who walk past them as familiar neighbours. Nowadays, Bangladesh does not figure in the Top 10 list of illegally overstaying foreigners.[2] Figures from the Ministry of Justice show that the number of Bangladeshi residents in Japan is 8670 persons as of June 2013, making up merely 0.4 per cent of all registered foreigners.[3] However, representation of Bangladeshis among the foreign students studying in Japan is comparatively high.[4]

Migrant workers, at a state level, are Bangladesh's main source of foreign capital, whereas on a personal level, they represent opportunities to earn money which cannot be earned locally. Bangladeshi migrant workers, whose numbers increased around the late 1970's especially with the support of the government, were headed mostly to the Middle East. Saudi Arabia and United Arab Emirates account for approximately 60 per cent of the cumulative total of Bangladeshi migrant workers. The number of Bangladeshi migrant workers to Southeast Asian countries such as Malaysia and Singapore also increased in the 1990's. Of particular interest is that migrants who sought work in Japan only appear on Bangladesh's official statistics from 1999. There are an accumulated total of 1,231 migrant workers till the year 2013. On the other hand, workers began to migrate to Korea from the mid1990's; nearly 2,121 in 2012, and an accumulated total of up to approximately 29,702.[5] As far as those official figures indicate, it seems that Japan is no longer a favoured destination, but an extremely difficult alternative for Bangladeshi migrants.

At present, Japan is undergoing a third Bangladesh boom. This time, it differs from the preceding two booms in both quantity and quality. The first two booms roused the Japanese people's interest for they took notice of happenings within Bangladesh and movements of Bangladesh people. However, this time Japanese people have a definite motive for gain, whether economical or social, at the outset, in seeking Bangladesh as a partner country. Here we see two differing themes. The first one refers to interest towards Bangladesh as a source of commodity procurement via trade and a destination of investment. The other one recognizes Bangladesh as a field to make important social contributions, a popular dream among many Japanese people.

There were three instrumental events leading to the surge of interest as we see today.

One is that in 2005, Goldman Sachs included Bangladesh as one of "Next 11" countries which could potentially have global impact, next to the BRICs countries.[6] Besides Bangladesh, the group includes countries as diverse as Egypt, Indonesia, Iran, Korea, Mexico, Nigeria, Pakistan, Philippines, Turkey and Vietnam. What those countries do have in common is that all of them have a relatively large population and thereby are potentially large economies. In their analysis, Bangladesh along with Pakistan and Nigeria has broad and systematic issues across a range of areas. It is expected that these countries have potential to enjoy growth bonus of 3-4 per cent if those issues are addressed properly.

The second event was when Professor Muhammad Yunus and Grameen Bank jointly received the Nobel Peace Prize in 2006 for "for their efforts through microcredit to create economic and social development from below." Grameen Bank method is famous for giving small loans (known as microcredit) to the poor without requiring collateral. This benefitted many who used to be burdened with high interest if they had to borrow from moneylenders. This method was particularly directed towards women in the underserved population and contributed to their well-being and empowerment. Grameen Bank enabled high repayment and ensured financial soundness of lending institutions. Customers belong to groups of five to share ideas and support each other's work in order to encourage repayment. Regular meetings are held to raise awareness, and the bank sends its field officers to local areas to attend group meetings so as to monitor the loan and recover funds. Because of this well worked out method, microcredit or microfinance organizations became increasingly wide spread.

Although Professor Yunus has been invited to Japan many times, his biggest contribution that inspired the Japanese society is, in all probability, the idea of "social business". Social business, an idea that seems to attract not only CSR(Corporate Social Responsibility) conscious firms but also many young people, is carried out to attain a particular social goal and recoups its total cost simultaneously. Though Professor Yunus has already stepped down from the Managing Director post of Grameen Bank, in Japan, his name associated with Grameen still has great influence over individuals and companies that aspire to make some kind of social contributions. Grameen Yukiguni Maitake (GYM), established in 2011 as a joint venture with YukiguniMaitake, a leading Japanese agro-company renowned for its quality production of mushrooms, Grameen Krishi Foundation, and Kyushu University is one such example of companies organized to realize Yunus' social business. Yukiguni Maitake used to source almost all of its *mung* beans from China for the production of moyashi sprouts for the Japanese market; however, sourcing the *mung* beans from Bangladesh enabled the company to bring down costs in addition to securing a steady supply. This social business model is designed to create jobs in rural areas of Bangladesh with better income, based on technical know-how from Japan, and to contribute to community development by investing some of profit of GYM in the improvement of education and health.[7] This project was supported by government organizations such as Japan External Trade Organization (JETRO) and Japan International Cooperation Agency (JICA).

The third event was the adoptation of the "China Plus One" strategy of

Japanese firms. Since the 1990s, a large number of Japanese firms shifted their production bases to China in response to the appreciation of the yen and decreasing domestic price subsequent to collapse of bubble economy. The spread of SARS (severe acute respiratory syndrome) from 2002 to 2003 however, made them aware of the risk of concentration only in China. The search for alternative places for production was accelerated further by the outburst of the avian flu in 2004, the anti-Japan demonstration in 2005 as well as rising labour costs and appreciation of renminbi induced by high economic growth in China. Against such a backdrop, Bangladesh emerged as a promising site of production because of cheap labour, almost one-fourth of that in China and the large production capacity of the readymade garment industry, mainly catering to the US and the EU market.

One of the important triggers of the third boom was Fast Retailing Co. Ltd.; Japan's largest and the world's fourth largest clothing retailer which owns the shops named "UNIQLO" and others. UNIQLO shop numbered 853 in domestic market and 446 overseas as of end August 2013. Being an SPA (Specialty-store retailer of Private-label Apparel), the business model of Fast Retailing is to control the entire clothes-making process from design through manufacture and retail. The company used to procure 90 per cent of its garments from China; however, due to rising labour costs in China, they have adopted the strategy to diversify the sources of import and reduce the share dependency on China. Fast Retailing Co., Ltd. established a representative office in Bangladesh in 2008, and began toll manufacture with garment factories in the country. With this, many other Japanese readymade garments and related production and services, such as fabric manufacturers and goods inspection rapidly advanced in expanding their businesses in Bangladesh. Consequently, the surge of Japanese investment was called "UNIQLO effect". According to the information of JETRO Dhaka office, the number of Japanese-affiliated companies including overseas subsidiary, representative office, and branch office increased from 70 in 2009 to 176 as of December, 2013. In other words, in just 4 years, the number of companies increased 2.5 times. Recently, Honda Motor Co., Ltd. established a joint venture with Bangladesh's state owned Bangladesh Steel and Electric Corporation for the manufacture and sale of two-wheeled vehicles, and Ajinomoto Co., Inc. established a repacking plant in Bangladesh. As we see here, investments targeted for domestic markets catering to Bangladesh's wealthy and middle class populations have increased in recent years.

Besides procurement of garments for Japanese market, as a part of their CSR activities, UNIQLO also established a company called UNIQLO Social Business Bangladesh Ltd., in 2010. In the following year, the company tied with Grameen Healthcare Trust, a non-profit organization created by Professor Yunus and set up a joint venture named Grameen UNIQLO Ltd. with 99 per cent of shares held by UNIQLO. Initially, their business model was to sell clothes priced at 1 dollar on average to rural households through Grameen Ladies who carry out the work as their self-employed business with micro-credit from the Grameen Bank. Since April, 2012, their focus, however, has expanded or shifted to urban areas and in July, 2013, they have opened two outlets in Dhaka. By the end of 2013 the number of their outlets increased to 6 in total. According to the statement of Tadashi Yanai, CEO of First Retailing, their social business model consists of the following factors: 1) to pay attention to the specific needs of Bangladesh with respect to 'clothing', 2) to design, manufacture products attuned to their genuine wants and sell at affordable prices, 3) to employ and train people, to expand business and to reinvest all the profits back into the society.[8]

Economic and Social Transitions in Bangladesh

Japan's growing interest towards Bangladesh is clearly attributed to rising labour costs in China, as seen in the aforesaid examples of YukiguniMaitake and Fast Retailing. Nonetheless, when it comes to why Bangladesh became an alternative, it leaves us to wonder if there were other factors besides the ideals held by Professor Yunus that attracted Japanese people's interests towards Bangladesh. Bangladesh's economy, which was known as a representative example of destitute, sluggish Asian economies in the mid-1980's changed enormously to be chosen as one of "Next 11" by the mid-2000s. Let us visit the changes that occurred in Bangladesh in the past twenty years.

Toshio Watanabe, a noted development economist in Japan, in his seminal book *Seicho no Ajia Teitai no Ajia* (=Growing Asia Stagnating Asia) published in 1985,alluded to Bangladesh as "the poorest developing country that seems to have no material on the basis of which we could write a scenario for escaping from poverty."[9] Watanabe adduced the reasons for the regression of Bangladesh's economy to the acceleration of population growth, end of farmland expansion, difficulties in diffusion of agricultural technology innovations, and the dearth of job opportunities outside the farm sector. Those constraints lead to the chronic underemployment, decline in real wages and income level and the pauperization of cities through migrant labour who are pushed out from the rural area; that was the situation depicted by Watanabe about the Bangladesh economy.

In retrospect, the average annual growth rate of GDP from1970's to1980's (the years on which the above book focused) was rather low; less than 4 per cent. In addition to the underdevelopment prior to independence, reconstruction of post-war devastated economy was an extremely difficult task especially amid multiple domestic and international crises including natural disasters, oil crisis, and political instability. It was only in 1977 that the production of rice and other primary manufacturing items recovered to the pre-independence level. Moreover, per-capita income recovered back to "square one" at last in the early 1980's. There was little hope for anyone to imagine an optimistic future of Bangladesh's economic development knowing that there were issues of overpopulation, narrow territory, frequency of natural disasters, etc.

However, Bangladesh's economy took a favourable turn from the early 1990's. In the 1990's, the average annual growth rate of GDP was 5 per cent and in the first ten years of the 2000's, it marked an average of 5.9 per cent. Most recently, in 2011/12 and 2012/13 (fiscal year is between July-June) the annual growth rates recorded 6.2 and 6 per cent respectively. Therefore it can be said that Bangladesh's economy is now seen as moving on to a path of higher growth. In this period, the average population growth rate decreased from a near 3 per cent in 1980 to 2.5 per cent in 1990, 1.9 per cent in 2000, and 1.2 per cent in 2011. With this decrease, per-capita income has grown and now exceeds 5 per cent a year. The real per capita income in 2011/12 increased1.5 times compared to ten years ago, and an increase of more than double of what it was twenty years ago.

Economic development can be directly attributed to the acceleration of domestic capital accumulation. In the early 1990's, macroeconomic stabilization policies that were put into place as part of economic structural adjustment programme advocated by the World Bank and International Monetary Funds (IMF) began to yield results, which brought inflation under control, marked an increase in interest rates, and gradually increased domestic savings. Added was the large rise in remittance by migrant labourers working overseas. Consequently, investment rate as a percentage of GDP which was faltering around 10 per cent or less in the 1970's increased up to 25 per cent by the end of the first decade of the 2000's.

Industrial development can be seen as a salient feature of structural change which occurred in Bangladesh's economic development. By the mid-1970s, agriculture and forestry which dominated nearly half of GDP were falling steadily, whereas from 2005/06 onwards, manufacturing exceeded agriculture and forestry. Manufacturing used to hover at around 10 per cent up until the 1980's; however, between 1990 and 2000 it marked an average annual growth rate of more than 7 per cent. As a result, manufacturing increased its share to 18 per cent of GDP while agriculture and forestry fell to 14 per cent as of 2011/12.

Let us now see what factors confounded the "Stagnating Bangladesh" scenario. As premises for the following factors of change, production of rice, which showed relatively high growth from mid-1990s onwards due to the diffusion of high-yielding varieties, fertilizers, and irrigation systems, underpinned the economic development.

To begin with, there is the dramatic growth of the export-oriented readymade garment manufacturing industry as shall be discussed later. Secondly, expansion of microcredit, which was pioneered by Grameen Bank and later followed by many NGOs, have made lease of land possible for landless households as well as offered them chances to engage in non-farm activities. Thirdly, there is a rapid improvement of social indices in the fields of health and education as shown in the acute drop in population growth rate. Many research findings reveal that women played important roles with regard to this point. Women were primarily employed in the garment industry and being the main recipients of microcredit which led to their empowerment resulting from the rise in income levels. This also entailed a decrease in gender disparities which contributed to the improvement of social indices.

Bangladesh's improvements in such areas of social development have outweighed that of neighbouring India and Pakistan, and have been highly commended worldwide as a successful example. One of the main driving forces of this improvement is NGOs that exist in large numbers in Bangladesh. BRAC is a representative example. Not only does BRAC focus its activities on education, health, microfinance, and other social businesses but has also established universities and banks under its thought. BRAC's activities have expanded to other 10 countries such as Afghanistan, Tanzania and Haiti.

Bangladesh's NGOs began as organizations engaged in the relief and reconstruction of the post-war country. Before microcredit offered a new avenue to raise their financial solvency, their activities were dependent on aid money from abroad. In areas such as education and health where the government's function does not fully cover or falls well short off, NGOs such as BRAC made considerable achievements and were even called "second government". In that respect, the relationship between NGOs and the state differs from that in India, where the state inherited the colonial administrative capacity and funded the activities of NGOs as well. NGOs in Bangladesh have grown under a weak administrative body with the help of foreign aids. At the same time, these NGOs showed less resistance to imbibing developmental thoughts from overseas. Seen in that light, Bangladesh government is no different from these NGOs as many funds and ideas were pumped into the country by Official Development Assistance (ODA) insomuch as Bangladesh was referred to as the "experimental field of assistance". Since education, health, and employment of women are strongly linked to cultural and religious norms, it is not rare to see some section of societies that are critical of change, as apparent in Afghanistan and Pakistan. What makes Bangladesh so unique is that not only did it actively absorb these changes but also disseminated Bangladesh-made innovative ideas to the world including but not limited to microcredit, social business, and BRAC's non-formal school system.

The exertion of such entrepreneurship can also be seen in the activities of local enterprises. Another distinguishing feature of Bangladesh is that outwardly NGO's are more famous than private businesses. The possibility of industrial development was not mentioned in the scenario of a "stagnating Bangladesh". It was with the emergence of the export-oriented readymade garment industry in the late 1970's and its dramatic growth afterwards completely changed the earlier scenario. Industrialization in Bangladesh began in the 1960's, during the East Pakistan period, particularly in the textile industry (production of jute and cotton yarn and cloth). However, these factories were placed under state control immediately after independence with the aim of forming a socialist society; industrial development was state-operated, and was meant to promote import substitution. However, due to continuous poor performance of the state-run enterprises along with pressures from donors such as World Bank, policies began to shift after 1975 to the privatization of enterprises and confer central role to the private sector in economic development.

The remarkable success in the export-oriented readymade garment industry originates from Desh Garments Ltd., which had technical and marketing cooperation with Daewoo of South Korea in the late 1970s. There were many employees in the said company who were trained at Busan, South Korea, that later became entrepreneurs to establish their own businesses. Since then, the industry has expanded and made an impressive growth to become the second largest exporter of the garment in the world, following China since 2009.

The number of factories in the industry added up to 5600 in 2013, its overwhelming majority being local companies. Bangladesh's strengths are rich entrepreneurship, abundant and cheap workforce (approximately 4 million people have been employed in the sector, out of which 80 per cent are women).[10] In other words, Bangladesh's population is an asset especially since other newly emerging countries are facing the issue of rising labour costs. Never before has there been a time when Bangladesh's overpopulation and poverty were seen as its strength. Furthermore, in order to support the industry, the government undertook policy measures such as duty-free imports in order to resolve structurally constrained problems to procure many of its raw materials and intermediate commodities from abroad. In 2012/13, garment exports accounted for nearly 80 per cent total exports (Figure 1).

Fig. 1: Trend of Garment Exports (Million USD)

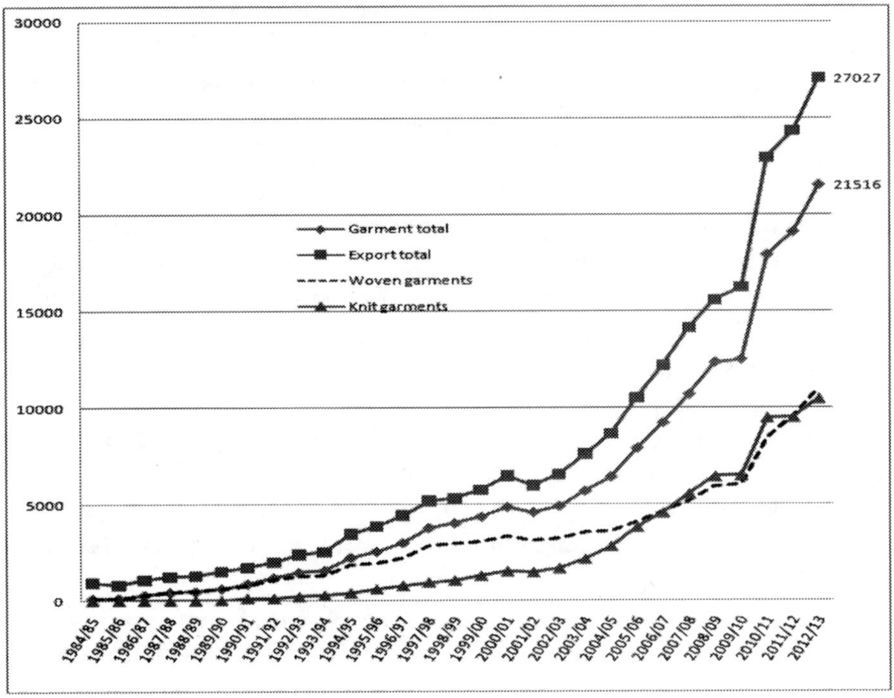

Source: Compiled from *Bangladesh Bank Quarterly and various sources.*

Recent Crises in Bangladesh Readymade Garment Industry and Japanese Response

Although it is no doubt a success story as a whole, the growth trajectory of readymade garment industry in Bangladesh has at times experienced difficulties. In retrospect, such events as imposition of export quota by the US and Canada in 1985, threat of boycott of Bangladesh garments at the US market because of child labour in 1995, and the end of the MFA (Multi-fibre Arrangement) in 2004 were considered, at least initially, to have very adverse effects on the industry. Among those, the end of the MFA was perceived with most serious concern. The MFA was implemented in 1974 by the developed countries outside the normal rules of the General Agreement on Tariffs and Trade (GATT). On the basis of bilateral negotiations, they could put quota on annual exports of textile and clothing so that the importing countries could protect the domestic industry and eventually adjust to the rising production capacity of the developing countries. By this system, the growth of large exporting countries was constrained while the smaller or newcomers to the industry could benefit from the export opportunities secured by the quota imposition on the larger exporting countries. Since the growth of the garment industry in Bangladesh has largely depended on this advantage, the termination of the MFA was considered as the end of the growth.

The industry, however, has not only overcome those negative factors but it has also shifted its growth to a higher trajectory by way of meeting the challenges successfully: the imposition of quota by the US and Canada made the industry diversify their products into non-quota items such as knitwear and also find new markets, mainly in the EU countries. Child labour was eliminated to a large extent through the programme agreed by Bangladesh Garment Manufacturers and Exporters Association (BGMEA), the line organization of the industry, UNICEF and ILO. Furthermore, some larger companies responded to the liberalization of garments trade after the end of MFA by investing in new technology and machinery, developing broader capabilities and establishing direct relationship with retailers.[11] It also worked favourably for Bangladesh that the period almost coincided with the beginning of wage increase in China as described before.[12] Moreover, the global economic crises that started in 2008 also induced consumers' shift to cheaper substitutes produced by Bangladesh.[13]

The current crises looming over the industry stems from the very period in which Bangladesh has adjusted to the changing environment in the post-MFA context; or rather, the seed of the crises were sowed in the structure of the industry from its inception. To the falling prices in the post-MFA global market, the main strategy of Bangladesh firms was to squeeze profits and wages and thereby retain their competitiveness.[14] This strategy has led many firms to neglect maintaining lawful working environment and conditions. In the post-MFA period, social compliance has become an important condition in place of export quota, by which buyers or retailers in the developed countries have not only measured the eligibility of the exporting firms but also lowered offering prices for reasons of "non-compliance."[15] Social compliance is defined as 'result of conformance to the rules of social accountability by the extended organization including not only the organization's own policies and practices but also those of its supply and distribution chains. It is a continuing process in which the involved parties keep on looking for better ways to protect the health, safety, and fundamental rights of their employees, and to protect and enhance the community and environment in which they operate'.[16] Nevertheless, except for the limited number of large firms, the issue was neglected or not well attended in the smaller and subcontracting firms. Social compliance was also addressed by NGOs and in some cases firms and NGOs have worked jointly for the sake of retaining markets and employment. Nevertheless, wages, the central concern from workers' point of view, was least addressed even in the context of social compliance, partly due to the global buyers' priority on the price. The repercussions of the situation began to show up in increasing incidents of labour unrest since May, 2006. That led to the revision of the minimum wages for garment workers after 12 years. The last wage revision was done only in 1994. In 2010, the minimum wages were raised again.

Notwithstanding some changes made for the workers' welfare, the twin disasters, one a fire in Tazreen Fashions in November, 2012 and another, the collapse of the building named Rana Plaza which housed five garment factories in April, 2013 dealt a fresh blow to the industry. More than 1,200 people lost their lives because of the owners' sheer negligence of the worker's safety and security.

In fact, similar incidents, not one but quite many, have happened in the past. Some estimate says that between 1990 and 2004, at least 231 garment workers died and more than 1,100 were injured in fire-related incidents.[17] In April 2005, a nine-story building of Spectrum Sweater Industries Ltd. collapsed leaving 64 workers dead. The building was only three years old but faulty design and construction reportedly caused the collapse. That was not the only similarity between Rana Plaza and Spectrum but just like workers in Rana Plaza, the Spectrum workers had detected the cracks in the supporting column about 16 hours before the building caved in but the owners ignored workers' warnings and continued production to meet an export deadline.[18] Data shows at least 730 workers have been killed in building-collapses, factory fires, and other incidents in several garment factories from 2002 to April 2013 before Rana Plaza collapse.[19] Through the limited inspection and inquiry that follows major incidents, the government was fully aware that most garment units lack basic safety arrangements but they did not move much beyond warning and providing some training such as disaster preparedness to the garment owners.

When the collapse of the Spectrum building happened, the buyers of the developing countries merely warned the industry owners that they would switch their sourcing to other countries if working conditions did not improve.[20] In other words, they believed that the responsibility rests only with the owners. The Tazreen Fashions and Rana Plaza incidents, however, have brought about differed responses from the stakeholders related to the industry. While workers' safety and security, excessively low wages and deprivation of workers' rights remained the issues of concern, what was different in the recent case was that now there was a focus on the lack of accountability in the supply chain, or more precisely, responsibility of the buyers or major retailers in the developed countries who prioritise low price and make social compliance as a token issue. The reasons for the different reflections of the two incidents may be firstly due to the size of tragedy. Secondly, the degree of integration between the markets in the developed countries and Bangladesh has been more deepened as garment exports from Bangladesh increased substantially since 2005. Moreover, some firms were subcontracted by the main contracting firms, which the retailers denied their direct involvement, shirking their responsibility; and this shed light on the lack of transparency in the supply chain management.[21] Consequently, two alliances of major retailers: the "Accord on Fire and Building Safety in Bangladesh" and the "Alliance for Bangladesh Worker Safety" were established to show their commitment to improving safety standards in the Bangladesh garment industry. The former includes 150 retailers of 20 countries as of February 2014[22] and the latter is comprised of 26, mainly the US firms including Wal-Mart and Gap.[23] In contrast to those positive approaches taken by the stakeholders in general, the US government suspended the Generalised System of Preference (GSP) eligibility of Bangladesh on the ground of "serious shortcomings" in safety and labour standards.

Table 1: Major Export Markets of Bangladesh Garments, 2011-12 (%)

	Country	Total	Woven	Knitwear
1	USA	23.7	36.6	10.7
2	Germany	17.8	14.2	21.5
3	UK	11.2	10.7	11.6
4	France	6.7	4.3	9.0
5	Spain	5.6	4.3	7.0
6	Canada	4.6	4.9	4.2
7	Italy	4.5	3.0	6.0
8	Netherlands	2.9	2.4	3.4
9	Denmark	2.1	0.9	3.4
10	Japan	2.0	2.5	1.4
11	Sweden	1.6	1.1	2.1
12	Australia	1.6	1.0	2.2
	Total	100.0	100.0	100.0

Source: Compiled from *Statistical Yearbook of Bangladesh*, 2012.

As Table 1 shows, the US and EU are the major markets for Bangladesh garments and Japan is ranked tenth accounting for only two percent of the total garment exports. Nevertheless, the export to the Japanese market has been picking up. From 2010/11 to 2011/12, garments exported to Japan increased 51 per cent whereas the total garment export increased 7 per cent over the same period. The increasing flow of Bangladesh garments into the Japanese market is more visible from Table 2. It shows declining dependence on China and the remarkable rise of Bangladesh's position as a source of garment products in the Japanese market. Besides Bangladesh, Cambodia is an only country that has recorded the similar rapid rise in the recent years.

Table 2: Changes in the Ranking of Major Garment Exporting Countries to Japan

Country	Country share 2013 (%)	Ranking									
		2013	2012	2011	2010	2009	2008	2007	2006	2005	2004
China	74.6	1	1	1	1	1	1	1	1	1	1
Vietnam	7.3	2	2	2	2	2	3	3	3	3	3
Italy	2.9	3	3	3	3	3	2	2	2	2	2
Indonesia	2.5	4	4	5	8	8	10	10	10	10	9
Bangladesh	1.7	5	6	6	9	12	16	21	23	22	23
Thailand	1.6	6	5	4	4	4	4	4	5	6	5
Myanmar	1.4	7	7	7	10	10	11	11	13	14	15
Malaysia	0.9	8	8	8	6	7	6	8	9	8	8
Cambodia	0.9	9	12	13	13	17	27	29	32	36	34
India	0.8	10	9	9	7	6	7	9	8	9	10
Share of China (%)		74.5	77.1	79.8	82.2	82.9	82.7	82.5	82.0	81.0	80.9

Source: Compiled from *Trade Statistics of Finance Ministry*, Japan.

In the backdrop of increasing flow of Bangladeshi garments to the Japanese market, it is interesting to know what the Japanese responses were to the fallout from the tragic incidents in the Bangladesh garment industry.

At the government level, there were two major actions: firstly after the US announced suspension of GSP on June 27, 2013, on July 5, the Japanese Ambassador in Dhaka assured that Japan would not cut trade benefits; by which Bangladesh as one of the Least Developed Countries (LDC) could continue to export garments to Japan duty-free. The second move announced on July 11, 2013 was to provide low-interest loan to small and medium sized factories for rebuilding or relocation of factories and purchase of equipment to ensure the health and safety of workers. Applications for loans are jointly assessed by the engineers of JICA and the government's public works department, which will also monitor the utilisation of funds. By diverting Tk 100 crore from the Tk 500 crore given to Bangladesh Bank's SME Refinancing Scheme, a fund was created to help upgrade working conditions in garment factories without delay. The scheme is also in conformity with the Japanese policy of small and medium enterprises promotion.

Among the private sector, the stance of First Retailing should be noted. Regarding the "Accord on Fire and Building Safety in Bangladesh", the company initially expressed their unwillingness to take the joint approach, preferring to improve disaster preparedness and bolster building inspections at its partner factories on its own.[24] Chairman of GRAMEEN UNIQLO who is also one of the top officials of First Retailing voiced the company's refusal to sign the fire and safety accord: "We have the willingness to continue doing business here for a long time, so we will implement our own safety measures in the factories that we source from".[25] As mentioned earlier in this paper, the company opened the first two outlets on July 5 in the midst of criticism against their stance regarding non-joining the Accord. However, on August 8, First Retailing changed their decision and joined the Accord. It is a sole Japanese signatory till date.

Another notable private initiative is a proposal to build a dormitory for female garment workers as a social investment project.[26] The organiser of the initiative emphasises secure returns to the investors while providing better living environment for workers and imparting skill training to them so that they can shift to better paid jobs. Their model includes some element of fair trade, too.

Conclusion

This paper has described the changing Japanese perception about Bangladesh as the result of deepening economic linkages through trade and investment since the mid-2000s. The changes have been caused chiefly by the social and economic progress of Bangladesh since the 1990s.

The Japanese people have always been attracted to Bangladeshi people because of three reasons: strong pro-Japan attitude among Bangladesh people; Bangladesh's developmental experiences, actors, ideas and struggles of ordinary people which are highly acclaimed by scholars, practitioners and students; favourable perception of Bangladeshi people who are seen as hard workers. These factors have created a solid pro-Bangladesh opinion among Japanese. This opinion is held by Japanese who came into contact with Bangladesh mainly through personal interaction. Therefore, the relationship has been deep but it had a limitation that the relationship did not expand much beyond those who have direct personal interaction.

The current phase of bilateral relationship has started to provide a somewhat different and diverse type of interaction between the two countries and people, as we have seen in the responses towards the issue of garment workers. In this overview, there remain many questions unanswered: whether the proliferation of 'social business' label used by Japanese firms and people is benefiting both countries; especially for the socially and economically weakest stakeholders; whether this approach defines the responsibility of Japanese consumers properly, to mention a few. One thing however is certain that as the stance of First Retailing has swayed regarding the Accord, the relationship between Japan and Bangladesh in the context of Bangladesh's changing position in the global economy has just begun, and people, firms and the states of both countries are in the process of learning afresh how to associate with each other.

END NOTES

1. Jalal, Sheikh Ahmed (2002) *Japan's Contribution in the Independence of Bangladesh,* Dhaka: Hakkani Publishers; Biswas, Sukumar (1998) *Japan and the Emergence of Bangladesh*, Dhaka: Agamee Prakashani.
2. As of January 2013, there were 62,009 illegally overstaying foreigners in Japan. The top 10 list of the countries are as follows: Korea, China, the Philippines, Taiwan, Thailand, Malaysia, Singapore, Peru, Vietnam and Sri Lanka (http://www.moj.go.jp/nyuukokukanri/kouhou/nyuukokukanri04_00031.html accessed on February 21, 2014)
3. The largest group is Chinese (31.6%) followed by Korean (25.7%) and Filipino (10.1%) whereas the number of resident Indians are 22, 230 accounting for 1.1% of all the foreign residents in Japan as of June 2013(http://www.moj.go.jp/housei/toukei/toukei_ichiran_touroku.html accessed on February 21, 2014.)
4. As of May 2012, the share of Bangladeshis among all the foreign students was 1.0%, which is higher than the share of Bangladeshis among the total foreign residents (http://www.jasso.go.jp/statistics/intl_student/data12.html#no3 accessed on February 21, 2014.)
5. Bureau of Manpower and Training, "Overseas Employment & Remittances from 1976 to 2013," (http://www.bmet.org.bd/BMET/stattisticalDataAction.)
6. Goldman Sachs (2007) "The N-11: More Than an Acronym," Global Economics Paper, No.153.
7. http://www.maitake.co.jp/csr/ accessed on February 25, 2014.
8. First Retailing Co., Ltd., CSR Report 2014 (http://www.fastretailing.com/jp/csr/report/pdf/csr2014.pdf)
9. Watanabe, Toshio (1985) *Seicho no Ajia Teitai no Ajia* (=Growing Asia Stagnating Asia), Tokyo: Toyo Keizai Shinposha.
10. The data regarding the number of factories and employees are from Bangladesh Garment Manufacturers and Exporters Association (BGMEA) website (http://www.bgmea.com.bd/).
11. Compared with larger firms, smaller and subcontracting firms were not well prepared and some closed in the changing environment (Acevedo, Gladys Lopez and Raymond Robertson eds, (2012) *Sewing Success? Employment and Wages Following the End of the Multi-fibre Arrangement*, Washington, D.C.: The World Bank.)
12. Against the sudden surge of Chinese garment exports in the post-MFA period, the US exercised safeguards and the EU requested China to put voluntary export cap. Subsequently they agreed to regulate the annual export increase until 2008. Besides the wage rise, these measures no doubt saved other garment exporting countries.
13. It is described as "Wal-Mart effect" in which during the recession, retail sectors suffered in general but discounters such as Wal-Mart increased their sales. Wal-Mart is the largest buyer of garments from Bangladesh (Acevedo et al. eds., op cit.)
14. Acevedo et al. eds., op cit.
15. 'Buyers lower RMG price on non-compliance ground: Orders placed at 25-60pc lower rate, says govt report,' *New Age*, August 15, 2005.
16. http://www.businessdictionary.com/ Accessed on February 26, 2014.
17. 'Garment fire kills 231 in 15 years,' *The Daily Star*, January 8, 2005.

18. 'Savar factory collapse: Workers' warnings of cracks overlooked,' *The Daily Star*, April 25, 2005.
19. '730 RMG workers killed in fires, factory collapses in 11 years,' *New Age*, April 25, 2013.
20. 'RMG buyers inquiring about bldg collapse,' *The Daily Star*, April 13, 2005: 'RMG order to shift unless work condition improves,' *The Daily Star*, June 9, 2005.
21. After the fire in Tazreen Fashions, Walt Disney Co. said none of its authorized licensees had manufactured Disney-branded products there. Later Disney pulled out of Bangladesh production altogether.
22. http://www.bangladeshaccord.org/news/ accessed on Feb 27, 2014.
23. http://www.bangladeshworkersafety.org/about accessed on Feb 27, 2014.
24. 'Fast Retailing Stays Out of Peers' Safety Pact', Wall Street Journal, May 28, 2013.
25. 'Japan's clothing retailer Uniqlo to buy more from Bangladesh: Top official speaks on future plan for garment industry,' *The Daily Star*, June 21, 2013.
26. http://bangla-business-partners.com/?page_id=594 Accessed on February 28, 2014.

REFERENCES

Acevedo, Gladys Lopez and Raymond Robertson eds, (2012) *Sewing Success? Employment and Wages Following the End of the Multi-fibre Arrangement*, Washington, D.C.: The World Bank

Biswas, Sukumar (1998) *Japan and the Emergence of Bangladesh*, Dhaka: Agamee Prakashani.

Goldman Sachs (2007) "The N-11: More Than an Acronym," Global Economics Paper, No.153.

Jalal, Sheikh Ahmed (2002) *Japan's Contribution in the Independence of Bangladesh*, Dhaka: Hakkani Publishers.

Watanabe, Toshio (1985) *Seicho no Ajia Teitai no Ajia* (=Growing Asia Stagnating Asia), Tokyo: Toyo Keizai Shinposha.

14

Japan–SAARC Relations: Addressing Challenges of Afghan Women, Post-2014

Mondira Dutta

Background

The South Asian Association of Regional Cooperation (SAARC) is the most populous regional grouping in the world. The SAARC countries together house around 23 per cent of the world population within approximately 3 per cent of the land area. The total GDP (PPP) is less than 7 per cent of the world GDP. As such, the SAARC countries are densely populated, with a low GDP in comparison to the world average. However restoring peace and development in the SAARC region, ensures that at least one fourth of the world population would live a life of peace and prosperity. The SAARC countries are bestowed with strengths such as a huge skilled manpower available at a cheap rate, a huge market, vast mines and mineral resources, accessible and environment friendly region with a great potential for travel and leisure activities. Founded in 1985, SAARC countries comprises of India, Pakistan, Sri Lanka, Nepal, Bhutan, the Maldives, Bangladesh, and now Afghanistan. Afghanistan was endorsed by SAARC as its eighth member in 2007 forming the much-needed bridge between South and Central Asia.

But unfortunately, because of its strategic location it is being ravaged by unfriendly foreign powers beginning with Alexander the Great, Genghis Khan and others. In the current times it has been ravaged by Russians followed by Americans though they went under different circumstances to destroy Osama bin Laden and the Taliban. With concerted effort by its people and with the help of its immediate neighbour Pakistan and other SAARC members, notably India, it can, over time, become the Switzerland of Asia. Afghanistan's strategic location particularly is of critical significance. The country sits at an important geostrategic location and is literally considered as heaven on earth, located in the heart of Asia, with its borders sprawling towards Pakistan in the Southeast, Iran in the West, the three countries of Central Asia—Turkmenistan, Uzbekistan and Tajikistan in the north and China in the far North-east. This has been the focal point of the ancient Silk route and the melting point of several cultures and civilization.

Unfortunately its strategic location has become its biggest drawback today, with unfriendly foreign powers, seeking to establish a firm foot in the region. One of the most resource rich countries has today been reduced to one of the poorest of the poor, with a life expectancy of 49.1 years and a Human Development Index (HDI) of 0.374 (HDI, 2012). It ranks at 175th position among 178 countries. Today the outcome of decades of foreign occupation, lack of roads, successive droughts, landmines, Russian bombing, US cluster bombs, terrorism, violence and war-related impoverishment have all contributed in forcing the peaceful and tranquil society to take an ugly turn and pull it down to its present position. The Human Poverty Index describes Afghanistan as "One of the worst in the World".

Following the "Operation on Terror", the international community pledged and took on the task of ushering in stability and sustainability into the region post Bonn in 2001. Afghanistan emerged as a major concentration centre of international aid, security and military resources, totalling to around US$ 286.4 billion which comes to about US$ 9,426 per Afghan citizen. If such an amount had actually reached the Afghan people, matters would have looked much better than what they are at present. Unfortunately the inflow of the vast international aid into the country has been a source of fuelling corruption depriving the locals for whom this inflow was meant to be (Stars and Stripes, 2013). Afghanistan was the leading global recipient of official development assistance (ODA) for the second consecutive year in 2009. Afghanistan also hosts the world's largest and most costly international peace keeping force mandated by the United Nations (UN). It is also a known fact that the foreign military operations in the country have cost in excess of what was stipulated (US$ 242.9 billion). Huge funding inflow in support of building the security sector and counter narcotics activities are not only difficult to monitor but are untraceable. The table below shows the percentage wise total aids pledged, committed and the total percentage of pledges disbursed by the end of 2009 by various countries [Refer Table 1].

The same table has been depicted through graphical interpretation (Refer Figure 1). A sum of US$ 62.1 billion aid for the reconstruction of Afghanistan was pledged by the donor agencies through several conferences and meetings during the period 2002-13 (Poole, 2011). However there is a wide gap among the donor agencies in delivering their pledges. Amongst the leading ten donors, the European Union (EU) Institutions, Germany, Sweden and the Netherlands disbursed more than they had pledged, while at the end of 2009, the United States and India had yet to deliver 60 per cent of the amounts that they pledged for the whole period up to 2013 (Poole, 2011).

Table 1: Aids, Pledges, Commitments and Disbursements

	Total Pledged 2002-2013 US $ bn	Total Committed 2002-2009 US $ bn	% of Pledges Disbursed by end 2009
United States	38.0	28.4	28.8
EU Institution	2.0	2.0	1.2.8
United Kingdom	2.9	1.8	63.3
Germany	1.2	1.0	108.0
Canada	1.7	1.2	70.3
Japan	1.9	1.4	52.5
Netherlands	0.8	0.9	102.4
Norway	0.9	0.6	71.0
India*	1.2	1.2	36.1
Sweden	0.3	0.5	147.3
Italy	0.5	0.4	79.6
Turkey	0.2	0.2	213.7
Australia	0.4	0.2	98.8
Iran*	0.9	0.3	39.5
Spain	0.5	0.1	59.8
Denmark	0.7	0.3	40.2
France	0.2	0.2	105.9
Finland	0.2	0.2	97.0
Russia*	0.1	0.1	104.1
Switzerland	0.1	0.1	102.9
Multilateral Age	5.3	4.0	50.6
Others	5.9	3.3	12.3
Total	62.0	46.1	43.1

Sources: Development Initiatives based on GIRoA, Ministry of Finance data; Afghanistan DAD; and OECD DAC data. *All Disbursements are based on OECD DAC data, excluding India and Russia, which are based on Afghanistan DAD data.

Afghanistan and Other Aid Recipients

The "Official Development Assistance (ODA) is a grant or loan from an 'official' (government) source to a developing country or multilateral agency for the promotion of economic development and welfare. ODA is a term coined by the 'Development Assistance Committee' (DAC) of the 'Organisation for Economic Co-operation and Development' (OECD) to measure aid. It is widely used as an indicator of international aid flow

Fig. 1: Total Aids Pledged, Committed and Disbursed (2002-2009)

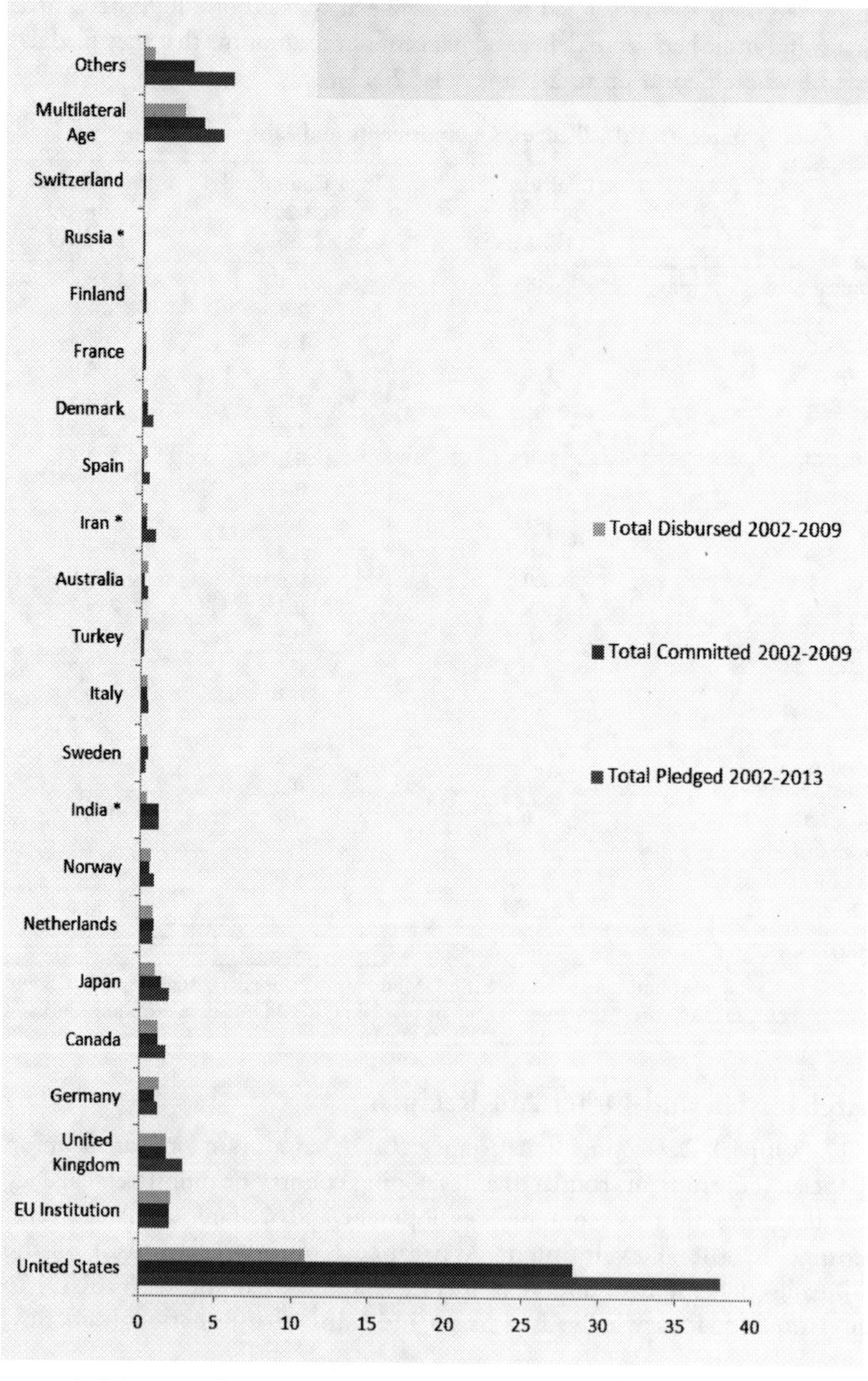

(wikipedia.org). Prior to the 'War on Terror' in 2000, Afghanistan was the 69th largest recipient of ODA worldwide, receiving 0.3 per cent of total ODA flowing to the developing countries. By 2008, it had become the world's leading aid recipient. Afghanistan's share of total ODA to developing countries increased again by a massive US$1.3 billion in 2009 to a historic high of US$6.2 billion (constant 2008 prices), the second largest amount ever received in a single year by any recipient country, behind Iraq's US$8.8 billion in 2005. In 2009, Afghanistan received 4.9 per cent of total ODA to developing countries (Refer Table 2).

Table 2: Top Five Recipients of AID, from all Donors Reporting to the OECD/DCA, 2002-09, (in US billion $)

2001	2002	2003	2004	2005	2006	2007	2008	2009
India 2.5	Pakistan 2.8	Iraq 2.8	Iraq 5.1	Iraq 8.8	Iraq 5.9	Iraq 4.5	Afghanistan 4.9	Afghanistan 6.2
Pakistan 2.5	Palestine/ OPT 2.5	Vietnam 2.2	Afghanistan 2.7	Afghanistan 3.2	Afghanistan 3.3	Afghanistan 4.1	Ethiopia 3.3	Ethiopia 3.9
Serbia 2.3	India 2.4	Tanzania 2.2	Vietnam 2.1	Indonesia 2.3	Pakistan 2.4	Vietnam 2.7	Iraq 3.3	Vietnam 3.7
China 2.2	China 2.0	Afghanistan 2.1	Ethiopia 2.0	Vietnam 2.2	Sudan 2.3	Ethiopia 2.7	Palestine/ OPT 2.6	Palestine/ OPT 3.1
Vietnam 2.1	Afghanistan 2.0	Ethiopia 2.0	Tanzania 2.0	Ethiopia 2.2	Vietnam 2.1	Pakistan 2.3	Vietnam 2.5	Tanzania 3.0

Source: Development Initiatives based on OECD DAC data.

It is interesting to note from Figure 2 how the trend analysis gradually shows a complete shift in focus from Iraq to Afghanistan. While Iraq shows a declining trend, Afghanistan and Ethiopia seem to be on the rise. While 2006 shows the lowest flow to Ethiopia and Iraq the trend for Afghanistan shows a gradual and steady increase. It will be interesting to study as to what extent of this funding has actually reached the local Afghans in the far flung areas where 'people continue to believe that they are still being governed by King Zahir Shah (Dutta, 2010).

While the US prepares itself to withdraw all its troops by the end of 2014, the atmosphere is agog with speculation. What is most baffling is that with the US withdrawal in 2014, resources are sure to dwindle. Apprehensions are that this will have a tremendous impact on the women as funds that trickled in for women specific projects will be drastically decreased. Undoubtedly, the brunt of this will be faced and borne mainly by the Afghan women. With the escalation of violence, women would once again face one of the worst disasters like their gruesome past of the Taliban days.

Fig. 2: Top Aid Recipients—A Trend Analysis

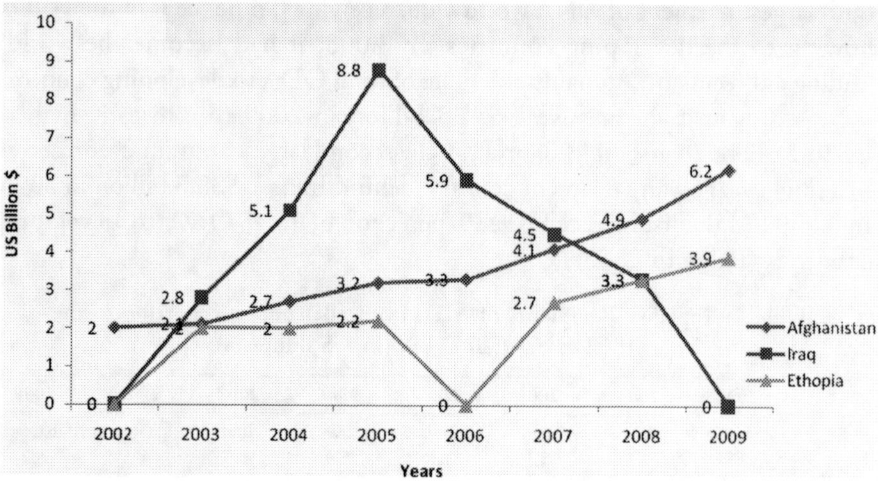

Source: Development Initiatives based on OECD/DAC data.

The "Vanished Gender" (Rashid, 2013) of Afghanistan will have to go underground once again and continue to live in "one of the most dangerous places for a woman to live in the world" (UNDP, 2010). The Human Rights Commission in March 2001 reported 1026 cases of violence against women. Today this has grown to more than 2700 cases. According to Amnesty International 'Violence Against Women' is widely tolerated by the community and widely practiced while abusers were rarely prosecuted. Women who report rape often have to face being locked up and accused of having committed crimes of 'zina'. According to the United Nations, more than 87 per cent of all women in Afghanistan suffer from domestic violence. Unfortunately the most common perpetrators happen to be family members, including intimate partners (82 per cent) (UNDP, 2006). As insecurity looms large over Afghanistan and tends to seep in, diverse security considerations starts cropping up ranging from local anti-government elements, seasonal clashes with the nomadic Kuchi over pasture terrain, tensions with other ethnicities over natural resources and disobedience of the Shariat law.

Japan-Afghanistan Relations

Japan has always shared a history of good relations with every country in South Asia. It was officially conferred the Observer status in the 13th SAARC Summit meeting, held at Bangladesh in November 2005. In 2007, Japan committed to support SAARC in the areas of democracy and peace-building, promotion of regional connectivity and promotion of person-to-person exchanges. Japan has assisted Afghanistan since 2001, even before the latter became a part of SAARC. It invested to the tune of 4.797 billion USD towards Afghanistan's assistance and was the first to address issues of human security. The Tokyo Conference attended by more than 60 countries and 20 international organizations in January 2002 and was on 'Recovery and Reconstruction of Afghanistan'. It marked the start of the reconstruction process. Subsequently a series of conferences in Berlin (2004), London (2006), Paris (2008), London (2010), Kabul (2010) and again in Tokyo (July 2012) was held to bring back Afghanistan into the mainstream. On the sidelines there were other meetings held where Japan, Germany, France and India assured President Hamid Karzai of continued support for Afghanistan.

On 8th July 2012, a decade after the first Tokyo Conference, more than 70 governments, international organisations and other stakeholders re-convened in that same city to pledge assistance to Afghanistan for the remaining transition years and beyond. At the 2012 Tokyo Conference on Afghanistan, Japan declared to provide an additional three billion USD to assist Afghanistan for the next five years. What is interesting is that while past conferences had sustained support to the Afghan National Security Forces (ANSF), the Tokyo Conference highlighted the "non-security aspects" of the on-going transition process and the volumes of development assistance that were to be provided towards socio-economic development and human security issues. The main goal of the Tokyo Conference emphasized building on existing mutual commitments by the international community and the Afghan government and "to ensure the viability of the Afghan state up to transition and throughout the Decade of Transformation" (Oskarsson, 2012). In addition the conference served to assure Afghanistan that "development aid will not dry up when the United States and its allies leave the country" (The Canadian Press, 2010). Donors from around 70 countries and organizations pledged a sum of $16 billion in development aid for Afghanistan at the one-day conference in Tokyo. In fact Canada promised to contribute an extra $227 million in development aid between 2014 and 2017, particularly to empower the women and girls in the areas of education, human rights and humanitarian assistance. Focusing on the economic development and governance pillars, the Tokyo Conference marked the culmination of two years of work that started in 2010 in Lisbon. However despite the pledges made at the Tokyo Conference, there are pertinent concerns about future funding of Afghanistan's development. It is beyond doubt that the Afghan government is going to see a reduction in the amount of money it gets from the international community. In fact countries have already started to withdraw military and diplomatic personnel.

Even though the thrust areas of Japan's assistance to Afghanistan has been mostly on human security issues such as socio-economic development, enhancement of security capacity, human resources development and humanitarian assistance, much remains to be achieved as far as the Afghan women are concerned.

Achievements, Concerns and Challenges of the Afghan Women

In the context of Afghanistan, women have faced one of the worst catastrophes with a gruesome past. They are the most under-utilized resource in Afghanistan (Afghan Women's Network (AWN), 2011). Across the country, women and girls continue to face endemic domestic violence, trafficking, so-called "honour" killings, forced into marriages and/or child marriages, and being traded to settle disputes. Attacks on schools and on female students also continue. The AIHRC documented more than 4,000 cases of violence against women from 21 March to 21 October 2012, although the true number is likely to be far higher (Amnesty International, 2013). More than 87 per cent of all women in Afghanistan suffer from domestic violence (Oxfam, 2009) and the most common perpetrators in Afghanistan happen to be family members, including intimate partners (82 per cent) (UNDP, 2006). The act of fleeing domestic abuse, forced prostitution or even being stabbed by an abusive husband, may land them in jail while their abusers walk free. The incarceration of women and girls for "moral crimes" such as running away from home—even when doing so is not prohibited by statutory law—also continues to be a major concern, with an estimated half of the approximately 700 women and girls in jail and prison facing such charges. (Human Rights Watch, 2012). 'Violence against Women' (VAW) such as beheading the women, inflicting torture and violence, rape, forced marriage, physical abuse and women being bartered still seems to be in practice. It is bizarre to learn that a woman who has been raped is imprisoned for adultery. Around 400 women and girls are believed to be imprisoned at present on grounds of 'moral crime'.

A study undertaken on Violence against Women (VAW) by UNIFEM and the Ministry of Women's Affairs, Government of Afghanistan, shows that the maximum nature of incidents was in terms of physical attack and forced marriages.

One such case in point was the gruesome treatment meted out to Biwi Aisha, an 18-year old from Uruzgan province on 9 Aug 2010, who was only trying to escape her abusive husband's family but was tracked down by the Taliban and had her nose and ears chopped off by her husband. She was later

Fig. 3: Nature of Incidents, 2006-2007

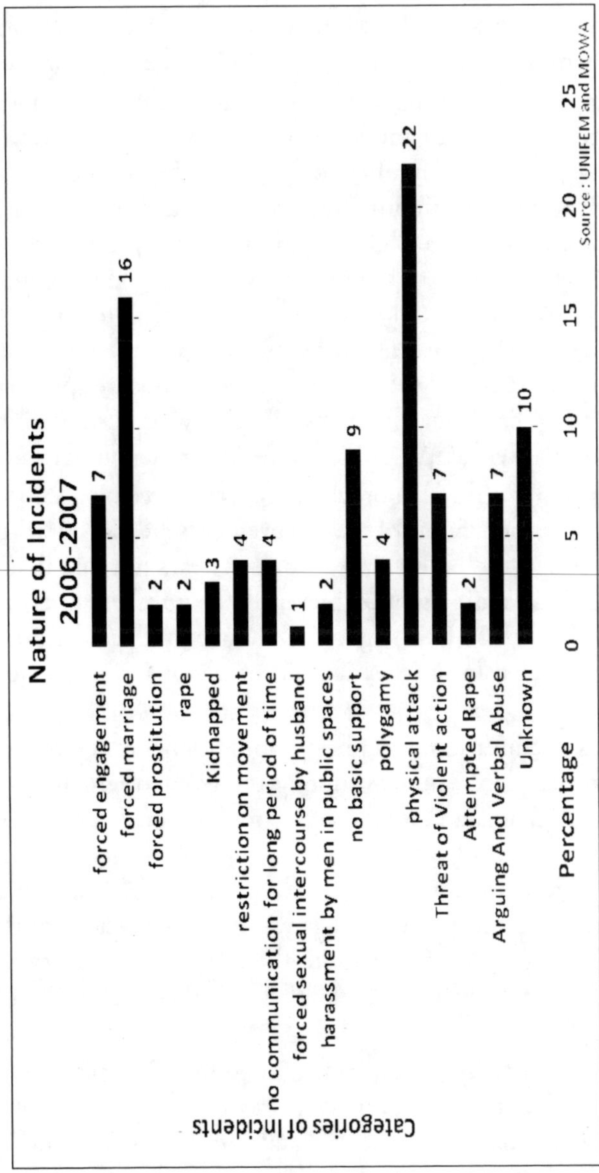

flown to the U.S. where she received reconstructive surgery. Such horrendous incidents leave an eerie and frightening atmosphere for the Afghan women. Besides physical abuse and forced marriage, violence against women includes beheading women, inflicting torture and violence, rape, and imprisonment.

It is however heartening to find activities gathering momentum towards achieving gender equality and women's empowerment. Several studies show that women contribute significantly towards the economy and society of a country, although their contribution continues to remain invisible and underestimated. In the era of globalization it is the women, who come forward to be the shock absorbers of their families by taking in the major brunt of the impact of globalization, and who protect their children and save the family from starvation. They also hold themselves solely responsible for restoring their family's honour and yet remain the most insecure species of the society. Post Bonn there has been initiatives to uplift women's conditions and usher in women's empowerment in order to meet the millennium development goals.

Afghanistan is certainly not where it was in December 2001 and has come a long way since then. Some of the achievements are indeed worth mentioning such as the longevity has increased from 44 years to more than 60 yrs. From almost no girls attending school, presently the number has crossed well above 3 million. Nearly 120,000 Afghan girls have graduated from high schools, 15,000 are enrolled in universities and nearly 500 women are on university faculties.

In terms of education, excepting Kabul (48 per cent), Herat (28 per cent) and a few other places, literacy among the women remains at a dismal 0 to 11 per cent (Afghanistan Provincial Reconstruction Team, 2011). Even today less than 50 percent of the children are enrolled in schools with Zabul and Uruzgan recording as low as <1 per cent. Access to health facilities for the women is still at a rudimentary stage where a large section of the women (50 per cent on an average) travel more than 10 kms for a health care facility. Women constitute only 9 per cent of the decision making sectors (Afghanistan [PRT], 2011).

Maternal mortality, infant mortality, under-five mortality rates have all declined significantly. However if one sees the top causes of death for the Afghan women it happens to be prenatal conditions implying that pregnancy related facilities are not easily accessible to the Afghan women. Total fertility rate in 2008 showed a woman produces around 6.3 children on an average (Refer Figure 4). What is striking is there seems to be a negative correlation between the number of births and the proportion of skilled health personnel available in the area. This implies the higher the number of births, lower is the number of skilled personnel available. Possibly the infant mortality may

Fig. 4: Top Ten Causes of Death (%)

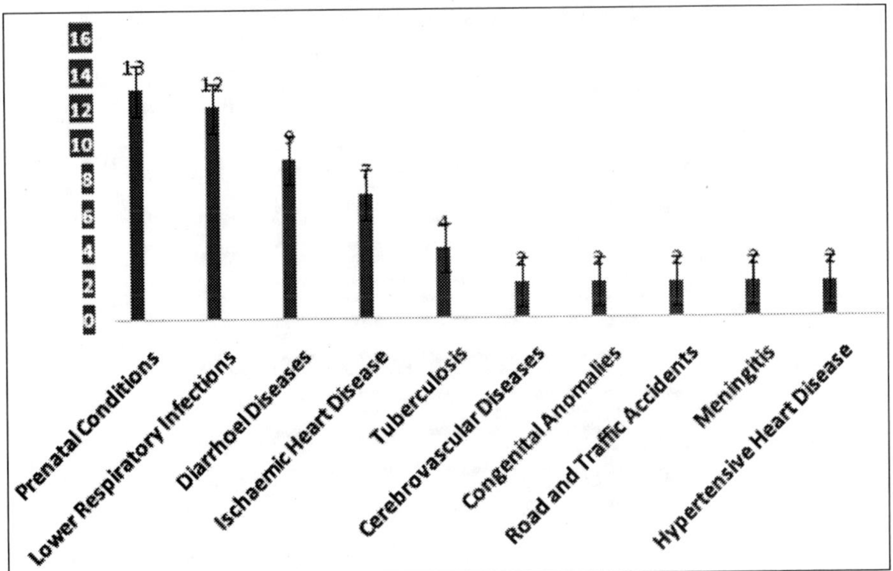

Source: http://www.who.int/whosis/mort/profiles/mort-emro_afg_afghanistan.pdf, 2010.

be higher in these provinces and hence women produce more no of children as their survival rate is low (Refer Figs. 5 and 6).

It was also found that more than 50 percent of the women have to travel more than 10 kms to access health care facility excepting for the provinces of Wardak and Kabul where the women have to travel more than 5 kms to access health facilities. Data shows there is a negative correlation between maternal mortality ratio and proportion of births attended by skilled health personnel. It has been observed that the higher the maternal mortality rate, the lesser the availability of skilled health personnel (Afghanistan PRT, 2011).

One cannot ignore the fact that Afghan women constitute 28 percent of legislators in Afghan parliament including 9 percent at the decision-making level. Women are represented among the doctors and medical workers, pilots, army, police officers, media, sports activities and constitute many active civil society groups. They make up 40 percent of voters as per the last presidential elections. A total of 69 Women Parliamentarians were elected including Frishta Amini—a doctor by profession who won her parliament seat with second highest votes in Nimroz province and Farida Hamidi, also from Nimroz. They have been instrumental in promoting girls' education after the fall of the Taliban regime. There have been other eminent women in the Afghan Government such as the Minister for Health (Dr. Soraya Dalil) who is an Uzbek from Kabul and attended the medical school in Afghanistan in the late 1980s, the

Fig. 5: Total Fertility Rate, 2008

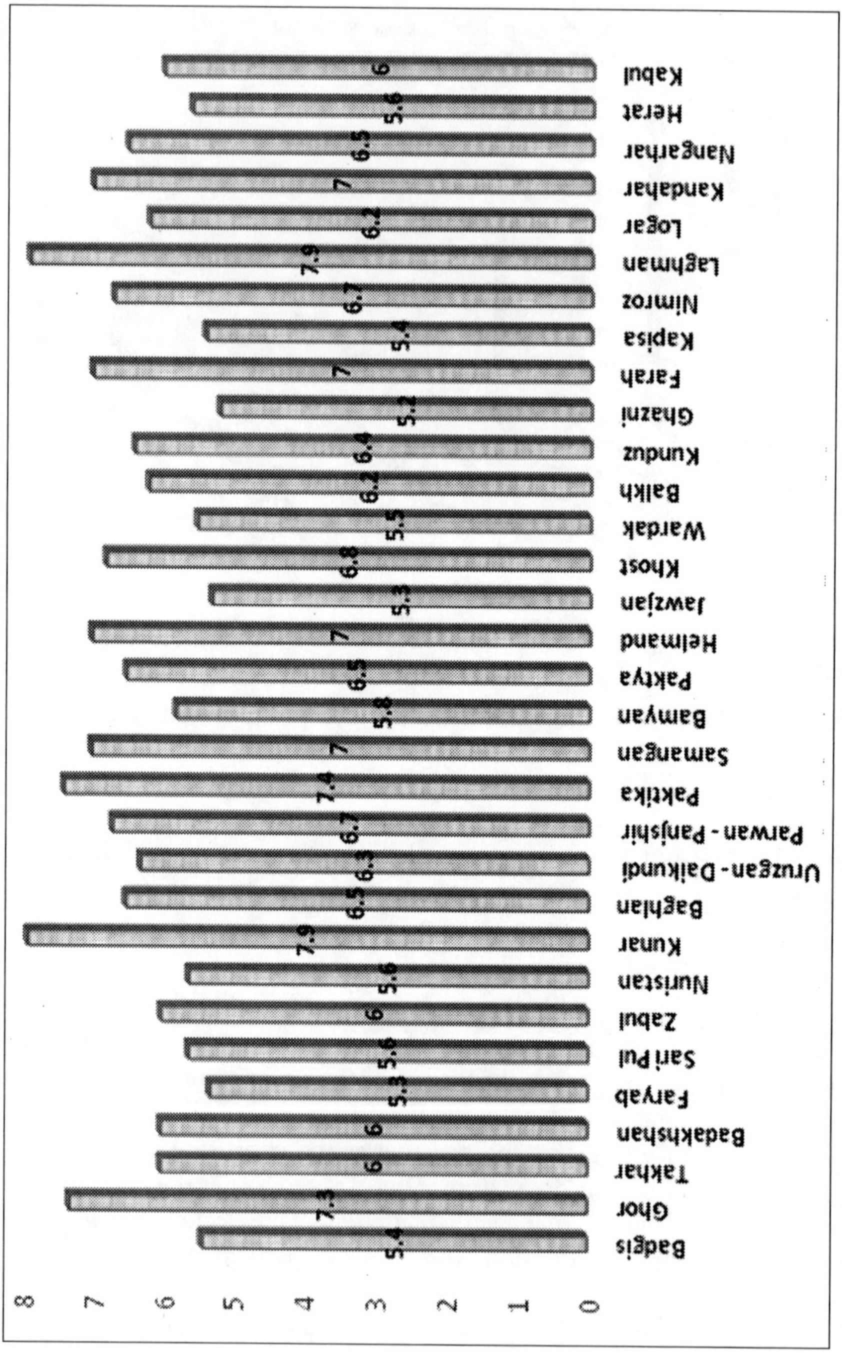

Source: Men & Women in Afghanistan: Baseline Statistics on Gender, 2008.

Fig. 6: Proportion of Births Attended by Skilled Health Personnel 2008 (%)

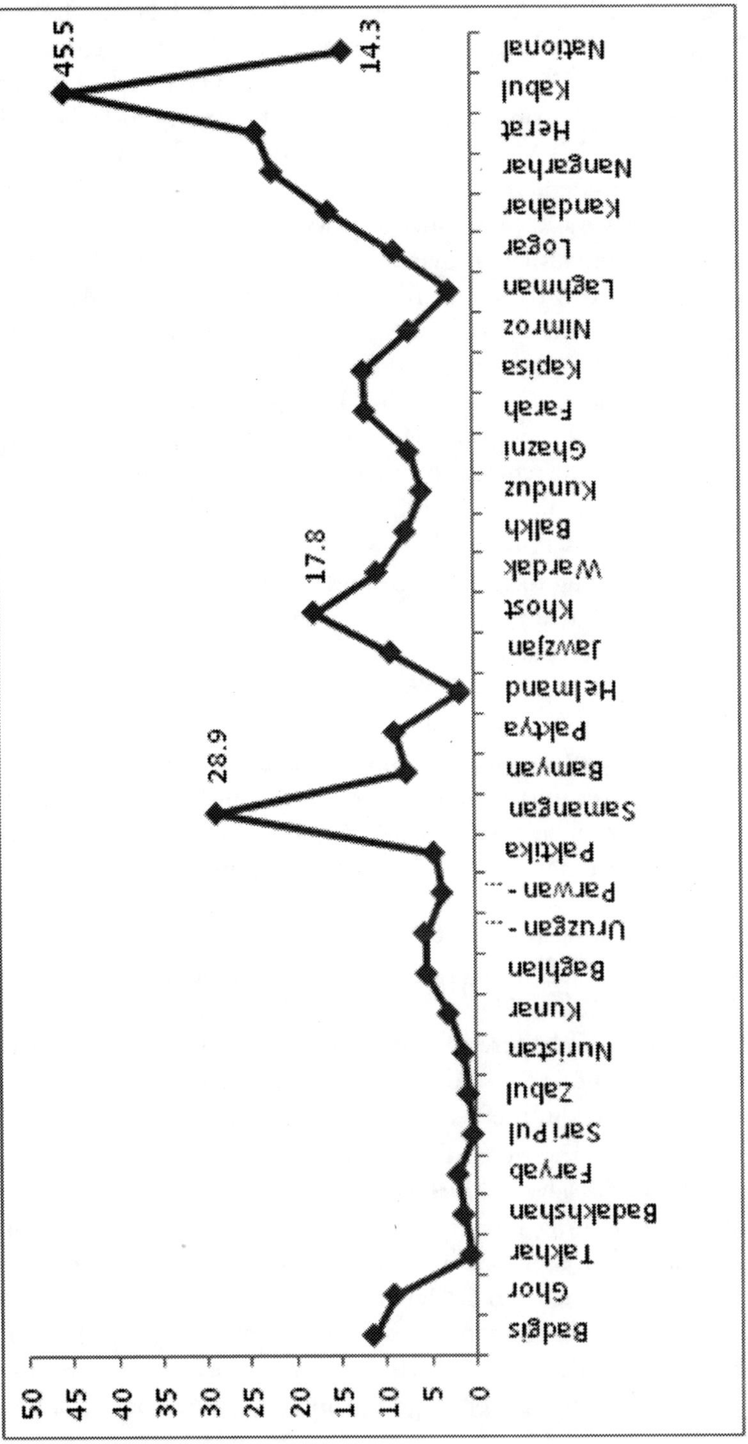

Source: Men & Women in Afghanistan: Baseline Statistics on Gender, 2008.

Minister for Labor, Social Affairs (Ms. Amina Afzaly) from Herat, the Minister of Women Affairs (Ms. Bano Ghazanfar) from Balkh Province, the Deputy Ministers for Women Affairs and Health, the General Director for Independent Human Rights Commission (Dr. Sima Samar) belonging to Jaghori district of Ghazni Province, Ms Manizha Bakhtari, Afghanistan's Ambassador to the Nordic countries in September 2009. It is heartening to note that eminent women in politics are also visible such as Fawzia Koofi, an Afghan Presidential Candidate from Badakshan Province, and Ms Shukria Barakzai who has contributed significantly in drafting the constitution of Afghanistan. Afghanistan's only woman governor, Ms Habiba Sarobi from Mazar-i-Sharief personally inspects the restoration work being conducted on the huge Bamiyan Statues that were destroyed in March 2001. Women also are active in the security forces. Brig. Gen. Khatool Mohammadzai, from Kabul is the Director for Women's Affairs, the senior-most personnel in the Afghan National Army, and is responsible for physical training of recruits. In addition some 1,000 women are currently serving in the Afghan armed forces.

It is most satisfying to come across news such as Women's boxing being represented by Afghan women in the Olympics for the first time in 2012. Seventeen year old Ms Sadaf Rahimi was bold enough to be gearing up for the event despite all odds. Ms Shakila Naderi—Kabul's only female driving instructor has helped women to obtain an approximate 312 driving licenses in 2011 in Kabul according to the traffic department. Naderi's driving school is backed by the government and has encouraged female employees to attend. Besides there are women pilots, army and police officers, and professional martial artists and women activists. Women have demonstrated and protested from all walks of life on the streets of Kabul. Most importantly, the government of Afghanistan has approved a new constitution in 2004 guaranteeing women of equal rights. In 2009, a law was declared stating that 'Violence against Women' (VAW) is a crime. Figure 7 shows the seven top sectors where women concentrate. An overall 10 percent of the women are in decision making bodies although they need not necessarily be in the creamy layer of these sectors and may hardly have a say in the decisions passed on women in the assembly.

Despite the proactive steps, there is a lingering fear that the troop pullout in 2014, will result in a lack of interest among the international community's commitment in pushing the Afghan government to promote and protect women's rights. This is especially so as a result of the endorsement of the Ulema Council statement on 6 March 2012 by President Karzai. There are apprehensions that a decrease in the foreign aid which helped in the running of schools and clinics is bound to effect the functioning of these institutes and the Afghan women may be forgotten and abandoned once again by the

Figure 7: Seven Top Sectors of Women's Concentration out of 33 Sectors in Afghanistan
(Overall Men: Women = 9:91%)

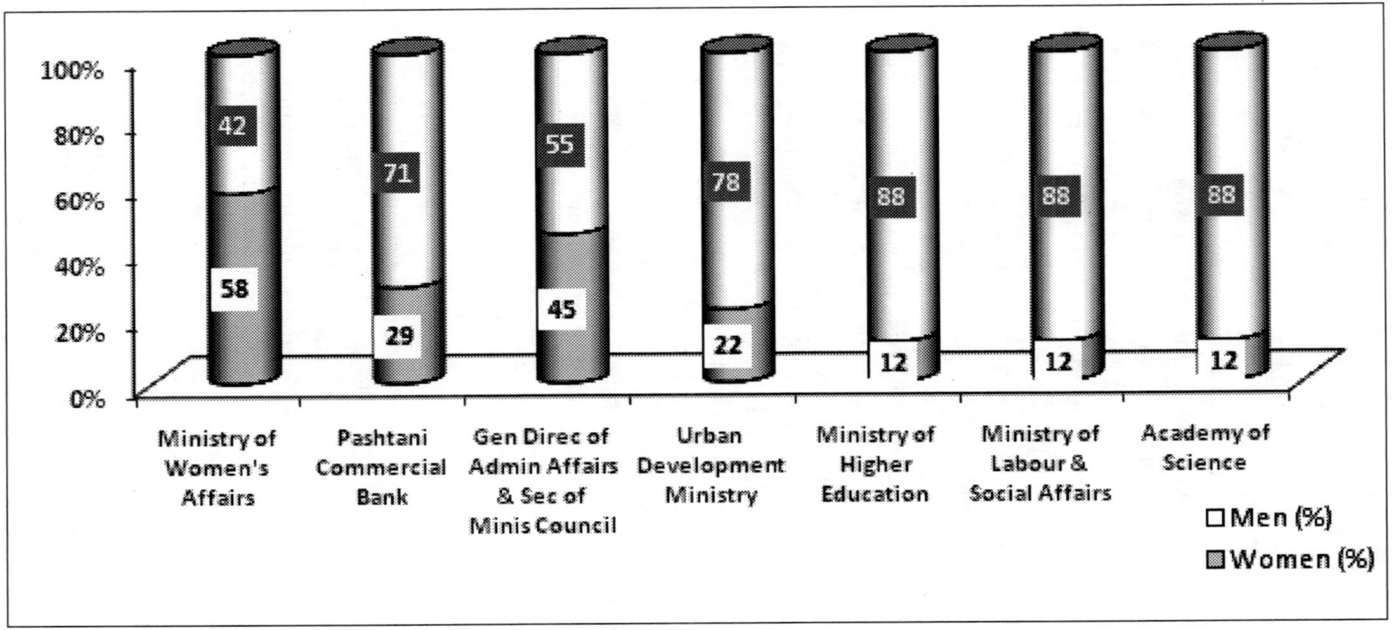

Sources: 1. *Research & Statistics Office, MOWA*; 2. *Women and Men in Afghanistan: Baseline Statistics on Gender*, 2008.

rest of the world. The women's organisations and women activists are apprehensive (Dutta, 2010) of a bleak post-2014 scenario.

Huge investments of blood and money by more than 50 nations of the world, the numerous sacrifices of Afghan National Security Forces and enormous sacrifice by the citizens of the country—women, men and children cannot be compromised with, while pushing the women and girls back into the Dark Ages. There is a lingering fear that the troop pull-out will in turn result in a lack of interest among the international community to push the Afghan government for promoting and protecting the women's rights which had been gained so painstakingly. Peace negotiations between the Taliban and the Afghan government especially in the absence of any women does raise suspicions that women's rights may get bargained away.

What is most alarming to the women's groups and other international organizations is the endorsement by President Karzai, of the Ulema Council statement on 6 March 2012, prescribing a "code of conduct" for women in Afghanistan. It is being apprehended that such an action will put women's rights in complete jeopardy. It suggests that while a Muslim woman has many rights, [she also] has duties and obligations, in complete adherence and observance with the Shariah law. This includes avoiding mingling with strange men in various social situations, such as education, shopping, the office and other affairs of life, accepting multiplicity of wives (polygamy), avoiding travel without a [Shariah-sanctioned] mahram (male companion). With the President declaring that 'men are fundamental and women are secondary' and the on-going negotiations with the Taliban, chances are that women's rights may get a raw deal. Any attempt of peace process by excluding more than half the population can hardly usher in peace and sustainability.

With the gradual evaporation of international interest in Afghanistan and the dwindling flow of resources, on-going negotiations with the Taliban minus the women, signing of the Shia Personal Status Law, President Karzai's endorsement of the Ulema Council statement, women in Afghanistan are likely to face a trying time once again and would remain vulnerable. Unless the women's voices are factored into the peace process and properly represented in all the decision making bodies, time is not far when all the achievements of the Afghan women will become history!

An alarming situation is regarding the law, which has recently been passed by the Afghan parliament and is now awaiting President Hamid Karzai's signature. This would prohibit authorities from questioning the relatives of a criminal suspect. The implications would effectively silence victims and undermine investigations into cases of sexual and domestic violence in a country where "honour killings" and forced marriages is the societal norm

(Berthiaume, 2014). The international community has repeatedly professed its support for women's rights, but are hesitant to speak out as the focus is on getting out of Afghanistan at the moment. Some nations from the west have also indicated a reluctance to raising the issue when the Afghan government and Taliban are negotiating a possible peace.

Conclusion and Way Forward

Although Japan's assistance has been consistent since 2001, and has touched upon majority of the sectors, including the security sector, political processes, infrastructure development, human resource development and humanitarian assistance, rural development, education and so on, women's cause would be completely defeated unless the international community comes forward in open confrontation against women's rights getting thwarted. Women need to be involved in the decision making bodies and any negotiation for peace essentially needs to imbibe the women themselves in the peace process. Such an initiative can only usher in sustainability in the programme and help in achieving the third Millennium Development Goal of Gender Equality and Empowerment of Women. Focused group discussions with women in the field displayed the need for opening up of more Polytechnic Educational Institutes in Afghanistan in collaboration with the National Solidarity Program under the Ministry of Rural Development. Soft Loans under the Islamic law proved to be a huge success that India had implemented in Balkh province (Dutta, 2010). Almost 100 per cent of the loan money was reimbursed and the same was used by others, having a rippling impact. Such scheme could be incorporated along with entrepreneurial training activity.

The following recommendations are being suggested particularly to ensure women's rights.

- Donor agencies need to factor in the concept of 'Gender budgeting' into all their assistance programs, particularly for education and health, for effective inclusion of women and girls. This would promote an active participation of women in the economy of Afghanistan.
- Provision of houses, drinking water, sanitation and health services in rural and urban areas need to be initiated on a war footing
- Training and capacity building measures, particularly for the women, needs to be a on-going continuous activity for empowering the women and creating a chain of master trainers to train other Afghan women back home.
- Care needs to be taken to in-build women's rights into the constitution and other Acts before any peace process is discussed and initiated.

REFERENCES

Afghan Women's Network (AWN), 2011, https://www.youtube.com/watch?v=FvglzLbC5ag

Afghanistan [PRT], Afghanistan Provincial Reconstruction Team Handbook, National and Provincial Data, Handbook 11-16, February 2011.

Amnesty International, Amnesty International Public Statement, Afghanistan: The Tokyo Mutual Accountability Framework and the Long Hard Road to Justice, 2 July 2013.

Berthiaume Lee, Canada sounds alarm over bill eroding women's rights in Afghanistan, 7 Feb, 2014, Canada.com, <http://www.canada.com/life/Canada+sounds+alarm+over+bill+eroding+women+rights+Afghanistan/9482897/story.html)>

Druzin Heath, *Afghanistan again at bottom of corruption index* in Stars and Stripes, Washington DC, 2013 <http://www.stripes.com/reporters/Heath_Druzin?author=Heath_Druzin>

Dutta Mondira, Initiatives for Afghan Women, A project Report sponsored by the Ministry of External Affairs, 2010.

HDI, Human Development Index, Afghanistan, 2012 (http://countryeconomy.com/hdi/afghanistan).

Human Rights Watch, World Report 2012 Afghanistan, <http://www.hrw.org/world-report-2012/world-report-2012-afghanistan>

Oxfam, 2009: <http://www.thestar.com/news/world/2011/10/02/afghan_women_risk_most_in_peace_talks_oxfam.html>

Oskarsson Katerina, Afghanistan in Transition, Second International Tokyo Conference on Afghanistan, 2012, <afghanistan@cimicweb.org >

Poole Lydia, Afghanistan, Tracking Major Resource Flow, 2002-2010, Briefing Paper, Jan 2011.

Rashid Ahmed, Taliban, I B Tauris & Company, 2013.

The Canadian Press, 2010, <http://o.canada.com/news/canada-pledges-another-227m-in-aid-to-afghanistan-at-tokyo-conference/>

UNDP, United Nations Development Fund for Women, Violence Against Women Primary Database Report, 2010.

UNDP, United Nations Development Fund for Women, Violence Against Women Primary Database Report, 2006.

Wikipedia.Org: http://en.wikipedia.org/wiki/Official_development_assistance.

Japan's Assistance in Afghanistan: Towards Self-Reliance, Ministry of Foreign Affairs, March 2013.

Japan's Contribution to Afghanistan—Working on the Frontline in the War on Terrorism, Ministry of Foreign Affairs, Japan, March 2007.

15

Buddhism: Japan's Soft Power Tool Towards India

Sushila Narsimhan

There is hardly any forum pertaining to India-Japan relations without a reference to India's glorious Buddhist heritage. While Buddha's birthplace Lumbini today forms part of southern Nepal, all the other places, namely Sarnath, Bodhgaya, and Kushinagar—where he first expounded *dharma*, attained enlightenment, and *mahaparinirvana* respectively, are located in India. However, despite the enormous goodwill, respect and admiration clustered around this rich reservoir of Buddhist heritage, the Indian policy-makers have been rather casual and indifferent in tapping the potential of Buddhism as a soft-power tool in its foreign policy and diplomacy.[1] In the process, India inadvertently lost the mantle of being the custodian of Buddhist heritage and its central role in the Buddhist world and the Buddhist legacy, which was quickly appropriated by countries like Japan and China. Thus, even though Buddhism originated in India, it has been an integral part of Japan's cultural and religious landscape for more than 1500 years. Today, compared to India's 0.8 per cent Buddhist population, Japan has more than 70 per cent Buddhists. Despite Japan's indigenous Shinto traditions, Japan has embraced, nurtured, and preserved this alien faith and the related-relics. Japan, of course, has a comprehensive network of legislation for protecting and preserving its cultural assets. In addition, Japan has also been, from time to time, taking steps to preserve and restore the Buddhist structures, wherever and whenever feasible, in countries having friendly diplomatic relations, such as India. The Indian policy-makers should actually be grateful to Japan for keeping alive this shared Buddhist heritage and waking them up to rediscover and utilize this asset favourably.

In the context of current interconnected and interdependent global society and the growing disquiet over the use of military power, countries have begun to rely more on soft-power diplomacy to achieve their foreign policy objectives. The term 'soft power' was first coined and popularized by Joseph Nye in the 1990s,[2] and since then the concept has been steadily gaining momentum. It has not only spurred scholarly debates but also motivated many countries to switch to the use of soft power and settle problems through peaceful coexistence and cooperation, rather than by military might and economic supremacy. The concept suits Japan's status as a country that is bound by constitutional restriction and mass pacifism, and is unable to carry out any international responsibilities involving military power, but is keen to carry out the other, non-military international cooperation. Tokyo's emphasis on soft approach, like foreign aid and power of Japanese culture overseas, is agreeable to most Japanese across the ideological spectrum: to the left, a non-militaristic approach to international relations is desirable; to the right, it is great for the world to appreciate various aspects of the Japanese culture. In short, there is a national consensus on the pursuit of 'soft power.'[3]

Instruments of Soft Power

Language Education and Traditional Art Forms

As a matter of fact, even before the notion of soft power came to limelight, countries like Germany and Japan, who had suffered defeats in the World War II, had already undertaken steps to set up specialized institutes for cultural promotion. While the then-divided West Germany had set up *The Goethe Institute* in 1951 to spread its culture and language, the post war Japan had established *The Japan Foundation* in 1972 with overseas branches in many countries under the supervision of Ministry of Foreign Affairs (MOFA), to promote Japanese language education overseas and facilitate art, cultural and intellectual exchanges with other countries.[4] Today it has 22 overseas branch offices in 21 countries—covering Asia, Oceania, the Americas, Europe, Middle East and Africa—providing financial aid foreign students and opportunities for field studies and study-in-Japan to generate goodwill towards the host country. In the 1970-80's, in quest for a sober and peaceful image for Japan, the Foundation's focus was on promoting the country's traditional art forms, like the austere *Noh* theatre, *Kabuki* opera, *Bunraku* puppet play, *chanoyu* (Zen-inspired tea ceremony), *shodo* (calligraphy), *ikebana* (stylized flower arrangement), *ukiyo-e* (woodblock prints), *suibokuga* (Zen-inspired black-ink painting) etc. These traditional art forms, without any shadow of doubt, are extremely exquisite, refined, elegant and aesthetic, but they have limited mass appeal. Japan's unique *sumo* wrestling, while popular at home, has no large international audience. Similarly, the Japanese martial arts such as *judo* and *karate*, have enormous appeal but only to small circles.

Pop Culture, Manga and Anime

In 2004, after the soft power concept gained worldwide attention, the MOFA launched a *Public Diplomacy Department* to promote various subcultures such as Japanese pop music, fashion, electronic gizmos and games (Sony Play Station 3 and *Nintendo*), comics (*manga*), and animated films (*anime*) etc., which would have a greater international outreach.[5] The aim was to project Japan a cool and beautiful country. Presenting his vision of "a beautiful country, Japan" (*utsukushii kuni, Nihon*), the then Prime Minister Shinzo Abe referred to Japan as "a country that values culture, tradition, history, and nature," and one "that is trusted, respected, and loved in the world, and which demonstrates leadership."[6] Elucidating grounds for this new public diplomacy direction, the then Foreign Minister Taro Aso, himself a die-hard *manga* fan,[7] seeking to project a 'cool' image[8] for Japan stated: "What is the image that pops up in someone's mind when they hear the name 'Japan'? Is it a bright and positive image? Warm? Cool? The more these kind of positive images pop up in a person's mind, easier it becomes for Japan to get its views across over the long term."[9]

The Japanese pop culture, *manga* and *anime* have achieved tremendous international prominence in recent years. The production, diffusion and consumption of *manga* and *anime* are driven as a commercial enterprise by market forces and consumer tastes. In India, they have built a substantial fan-base among both children and the adults. They have also filled the void in India-produced media outputs generally revolving around mythology and folklore which, though entertaining in their own right, do not quite satisfy younger generation's appetite for fantasy epics. However, the utility of pop culture, *manga* and *anime* is quite limited for Japan's foreign relations. It is like the allure of India's Bollywood culture which some may find quite frivolous and unappealing. These are superficial cultural tools which reflect unique Japanese identity and pride but lack the drive to function as a vehicle for strengthening bilateral relationships and produce the desired policy outcomes. Actually, much depends on what the recipient countries want and what soft attributes will make Japan an attractive as well as an enduring ally. Forcing values on others would only work against Japanese interests. It may well be desirable for the cultural contents embodied in the soft power tools to spread naturally through market forces or people's efforts. In a globalized world, the Asian consumer is barraged with multiple images and variety of cultural products from China, South Korea, and the West. In fact, in the northeast

India, it is the natural and spontaneous spread of *Hallyu*, or the Korean Wave,[10] which has enamoured the youth, and not the things 'Nippon'.

Buddhism as a Soft Power Tool

Why Buddhism?

Compared to the allure and one-way promotion of "Japan Brand" pop culture, Japan's pursuance of Buddhism as a soft power tool definitely holds more weight in public diplomacy. Although India does not bear any ill-will and enjoys cordial relations with Japan, it is aware of its pre-war and wartime wrong doings. In the context of prevailing international scenario tense on account of super-power rivalries and terrorist activities, Buddhism offers many advantages. In human history, Buddhism is perhaps the only faith system not linked to blood, racial, ethnic, or national groups. Some of the key Buddhist messages, such as equality, non-violence, as well as its dialogical approach hold universal appeal and are extremely conducive to its spread across different societies, cultures, and civilizations. These features make it a universal religion. Asia aside, Buddhism has been able to generate spiritual inspiration even among some Western countries where people are probing for a calmer and philosophical meaning to their lives. One of the most enduring and decisive elements of Buddhism as a "soft power" is that strikes a spiritual and an emotional chord not only with India and the Buddhist world but many other countries as well. It is precisely because of this reason that both India and China, who had almost abandoned Buddhism for other priorities, have now realized the 'power' of Buddha and are taking measures to correct this. So much so, that as part of their growing competition for influence in Asia, both India and China are vying to stake their claims with solid Buddhist credentials and make up for the lost opportunities by sponsoring conferences, financing religious sites, and displaying relics in Buddhist-predominant countries.

In the pursuit of foreign relations, it is customary for a country to employ its own soft power, or a tool where it has "native ownership." In the light of this argument, how do we posit or explain Japan's claim on Gautama Buddha and his teachings! In fact, the Buddhism that reached Japan was not the one which left India, or reached China, but a form that had been filtered and translated through several cultural lenses. It was adapted, modified, assimilated and indigenized in conformity with the customs and traditions of the Japanese people. In the light of this, we can say that the Japanese Buddhism represents a "Japanification" of Chinese and Korean Buddhism rather than Indian Buddhism.[11] Until the 19th century, religious link between Japan and India were minimal. India was cherished and venerated from afar as *Tenjiku*, a 'Heavenly Land of Paradise'.

Despite its alien trappings, Buddhism has been an integral part of Japan's cultural and religious landscape for more than 1500 years. Today, it is the most enduring pillar of Japan's soft power diplomacy. But it is not a sudden development. Rather, it can be traced to as early as 7th century AD when Prince Shotoku Taishi (547-622 AD), in his zeal to promote Buddhism, sent several goodwill missions to China to procure Buddhist texts and images.[12] Ever since its introduction into Japan in the 6th century AD, Buddhism has been on the centre-stage of Japan's spiritual and cultural thought.[13] Statistically, 60 per cent of its population today profess the Buddhist faith and 90 per cent of Japanese funerals are conducted according to Buddhist rites. There are about 75,000 Buddhist temples with over 100,000 priests. It is not surprising therefore for Japan to bandwagon on Buddhism and harness it as its "soft power" to disseminate an image of a peaceful and beautiful country and Japanese cultural values that would be useful to other countries. Buddhism offers both scope and opportunities whereby Japan can transcend parochial nationalism and assume a greater leadership role in the international community. Such a step would open avenues for trans-national dialogues and collaborations and make them even more receptive to Japanese soft power. The main objectives behind Japan's Buddhist diplomacy are: to restore the glory of Buddhist heritage; to assist in the socio-economic development of the Buddhist places and make them tourist-friendly; to promote Japanese tourism, which would facilitate people-to-people contacts and mutual exchanges; to engage with the Buddhist world, and more so with the 'Land of Buddha'; to foster better understanding and appreciation of Japan; and to seek greater integration with Asian community.

Restoring the Glory of Buddhist Heritage

Ever since the establishment of *The Japan Foundation* (1972) and the UNESCO-sponsored *The Japanese Funds-in-Trust for the Preservation of World Cultural Heritage* (1989), Japan has been, from time to time, funding many projects restoring world Buddhist relics, beautifying and developing the sites to make them tourist-friendly, showcasing Japanese Buddhist heritage to the world, promoting Indian Buddhist heritage, and engaging with the Buddhist world, including India. A shining example of the Indo-Japanese friendship is the $500,000 Sanchi and Satdhara project involving archaeological excavation at the sites and conservation of stupas and the two monasteries in Satdhara and Sanchi. The project carried out by the Archaeological Survey of India (ASI) in collaboration with UNESCO and the Japanese Trust Fund, which started in 1994, took ten years to materialize. Besides working on the sites, the project also had a training component to it. Micheal Jansen, a professor at the University of Aachen who has been associated with the project, helped train officials in the latest techniques of monument documentation.[14] While Sanchi is on the World Heritage list and manages to attract visitors from all over the world, this project helped put Satdhara, which is an important Buddhist site, on the tourist map and it has already become a popular destination for people interested in Buddhism. Behind all these initiatives, Japan's aim is not only to assist in the socio-economic development of the sacred Buddhist places but also foster goodwill, better understanding and appreciation of Japan, and promote tourism which would facilitate people-to-people contacts and mutual exchange.

Promotion of in-bound Japanese Tourism

For India, Japan is the most important tourist generating markets from East Asia, and contributes to 3.07 per cent to the total foreign tourist arrivals (FTA). In 2011, Japan ranked ninth among tourist generating countries in the world. The arrivals from Japan grew from 29,032 in 1981 to 193,525 in 2011 (a compounded annual growth rate of 6.5 per cent). Of these, 63.4 per cent were for business & professionals; 19.8 per cent for leisure, recreation, and holiday; 11 per cent for 'other' purposes.[15] For several decades, despite the cultural and religious legacy of Buddhism in Japan, it was the "Golden Triangle," namely Delhi, Agra, and Jaipur, which reigned as the most popular Japanese tourist destination. The sea-saw has now changed drastically. During the last decade, however, there is a major demographic change on account of Japan's aging population resulting in the sharp rise in the number of retirees. According to Japanese market survey, such a trend was bound to boost the prospects of Buddhist pilgrimage tourism among the growing leisure class thereby brightening the potential of the "Buddhist Circuit," namely Sarnath, Bodh Gaya, and Kushinagar, as an alternative to the "Golden Triangle."[16] The post war 'baby boom generation' (*dankai no sedai*) born in 1947-49 has already reached retirement age of 60 thereby giving rise to the aged population. The year 2012 alone witnessed a flood of retirements when, out of Japan's 127.72 million population, more than 7 million baby-boomers had reached 65 and retired.[17]

As estimated in the *Development of the Buddhist Sector for the Japanese Market* report (JMS), the increase in the number of retirees resulted in a drastic rise in the number of tourists visiting Buddhist destinations. As reported by the tourism minister of the Bihar State Government, more than 91 per cent of Japanese tourists coming to India visit Bihar.[18] In six months alone, between

January and June 2012, about 100 thousand Japanese visited the Buddhist Circuit in India.[19] According to the findings of *Japanese Market Survey* and *Japan Travel Bureau Foundation*, by and large, it is the elderly group that evinces maximum interest in Buddhist pilgrimage destinations. To them, the cultural, historical, and spiritual attributes of India "seem to be almost synonymous with the Buddhist sector."[20] For many including the Buddhist groups, the motivations for visiting India and the Buddhist sector were "spiritual." The consensual remarks included: "to reach a state of mind like which Buddha had attained" or "to feel as if one's soul was purified" or when one goes to India, he or she "becomes like a philosopher."[21] As pointed out by Amit Mitra, the former Secretary General of *Federation of Indian Chambers of Commerce and Industries* (FICCI), "The biggest advantage that we enjoy is that it is the land where Buddhism, Japan's major religion, was founded." The FICCI study outlines initiatives and strategies that could help India emerge as a major destination for Japanese tourists.[22] But, as per the report of the Japanese survey market, "to compete with the Golden Triangle it is vital for the Indian Tourism to ensure improvement in security and sanitary conditions because they are the key factors that determine travel destinations among Japanese consumers."[23]

As the first Asian country to successfully modernize and industrialize itself, Japan is also one of the first to employ Buddhism for diplomatic purposes and promote Buddhist tourism among modern Asian countries,[24] including India. An event that gave impetus to Japan's soft-power Buddhist diplomacy was the arrival of the royal Japanese guests—the Crown Prince Akihito and the Crown Princess Michiko—in India and their subsequent visit to Bodh Gaya on December 5, 1960. For the Buddhists, Bodh Gaya holds maximum significance as it was here that Gautama Buddha had attained enlightenment more than 2600 years ago. In the aftermath of the Royal visit, several public and private Japanese agencies, like the OECF and IBBA, came forward to contribute to the facelift of the Mahabodhi Mahavihara Temple Complex. The inclusion of the Mahabodhi Temple in the UNESCO World Heritage list in 2002 reinforced the cultural and historical significance of Bodh Gaya,[25] necessitating a befitting renovation and development not just of the temple complex but also the area by the Bihar State Government. To expedite the developmental tasks, the OECF and the JBIC came forward to lend a helping hand in sprucing up the place.

Two leading Buddhist associations, namely the *Mahabodhi Society of India* (MSI) formed in 1891, and an independent organization, namely the *Kokusai Bukkyo Koryu Kyokai* (International Buddhist Brotherhood Association or IBBA) formed in 1963 by several Japanese Buddhist sects, have played a pioneering role in the development of Bodh Gaya as a sacred pilgrim centre for the world Buddhists. The credit for making Bodh Gaya a global Buddhist destination goes to an Anglo-Sinhalese Don David Hewavitarne, who after converting to Buddhism changed his name to Anagarika Dharmapala. In 1884, he began a transnational campaign, went to Japan to seek support from Japan's Chief Priests belonging to various Buddhist sects in the renovation of the Mahabodhi Temple. A few eminent Japanese Priests, Kitabatake Doryu (1820-1907, Jodo Shin), Shaku Kozen (1849-1924, Shingon), and Shaku Soen (1859-1919, Rinzai), made a pilgrimage to Bodh Gaya in January 1891.[26] This was the first time that they had set their feet in *Tenjiku*, or the Heavenly Land of Paradise (Buddha) that they had so long cherished from afar! Undeterred by the poverty and the plight of the Indians under the oppressive British rule, these first-time Japanese travellers had created an increasing awareness about Sakyamuni (Buddha) and other pilgrimage sites associated with the life Buddha in Japan. This stimulated interest within the Japanese Buddhists community to undertake overseas travel to Buddhist sites in India and other parts of Asia.

In May 1891, Dharmapala together with a scholar-journalist Sir Edward Arnold (1832-1904) founded the Mahabodhi Society in Colombo, later shifted to Kolkata. Realizing the dire need for appropriate boarding and lodging facilities, the Mahabodhi Society, through good books of some Western Orientalists like Edward Arnold and Henry Steel Olcott, was able to procure land from Lord George Nathaniel Curzon, the British Viceroy of India between 1899 and 1904, and build a Rest House in 1901 to accommodate Japanese Buddhist monks, philosophers, and scholars visiting Bodh Gaya. The Society played an integral role in mobilizing pan-Asian Buddhist support in the development of Bodh Gaya. An event which precipitated its construction was the upcoming visit Swami Vivekananda and his Japanese guest Okakura Tenshin, scholar and an art curator from Japan.[27] Though the Mahabodhi Society Rest House was built with funds raised in Japan, the building reflects British colonial architecture. In addition to extending lodging facilities, the Rest House also facilitated mutual interaction and cultural exchanges among the international visitors and tourists. In due course of time, taking cue from this, the several other countries, like China, Thailand, Vietnam, Myanmar, Tibet, Bhutan, and Cambodia, also built temples, monasteries, and rest houses representing their unique aesthetic and architectural styles enriching the urban landscape of Bodh Gaya.

Similarly, the IBBA, with financial support provided by the Japanese government, has also played a significant role in beautifying the place and showcasing Japanese Buddhism by adding Peace Bell, Pagoda, a big meditation hall, building rest houses, Zen-style garden, etc. Several government agencies such as, *Overseas Economic Cooperation Fund* (OECF) created in 1961, and the Japanese *Bank for International Cooperation* (JBIC) set up in 1999, *Japan International Cooperation Agency* (JICA) formed in 2003, extended financial assistance to the respective state government for basic civic amenities, public conveniences, electricity substation, telephone exchange, transport system, piped water supply and tube-wells, drains and sewage lines, solid waste management, schools, fire station, airport, and town infrastructure and development in Bodh Gaya and also other Buddhist sites located all in various parts of India.[28] With aid from and in collaboration with the OECF, JBIC, and JICA, the IBBA has over the time constructed many temples, namely the Indosan Nippon Temple and the Daijokyo Buddhist Temple in Bodh Gaya, and Nichi Getsu San temple in Sarntah. The installation of a Kamakura's *Daibutsu*-like giant statue of Buddha within Daijokyo temple vicinity,[29] on November 18th 1989, has added to the charm of Bodh Gaya making it a major centre of tourist attraction and of the world Buddhism.

The development and beautification of Bodh Gaya has spurred new leisure and travel incentives and brought a large influx of relatively affluent Japanese pilgrims who look to India for spiritual inspiration. This corresponded with the growth of Japanese economy. The influx of foreign tourists has led to the mushrooming of hotels which coincided with a number of changes to the urban landscape. An interesting outcome of the flourishing Buddhist tourism is the emergence of Bodh Gaya as not only a global destination for the world Buddhists, but also a global hub for transnational marriages. It is believed there are more than 30 Bodh Gaya-men today who have foreign wives. Many of the successful hoteliers have Japanese wives. While some Japanese brides are living in Bodh Gaya, there are others who have returned to Japan with their Indian husbands, started hotel businesses, restaurants and travel agencies that cater to the Indo-Japanese traffic in tourism.[30] Bodh Gaya thus provides both marital bliss and spiritual fulfilment.

Revival of Nalanda University

A unique aspect of Japan's Buddhist diplomacy is that it is not confined only to the preservation, restoration and development of Buddhist structures and promotion of in-bound Buddhist tourism. Japan is now also seeking to harness opportunities thrown by India's pan-Asian plan to revive its historic *Nalanda Mahavihara*,[31] once-upon-a-time a major centre of Buddhist Studies. The renowned institution was a great centre of learning that operated for 800 years from 4th century onwards until its destruction in 1198 by the Turkish Muslim invaders led by Muhammad Bakhtyar Khalji. Though the idea of reviving the University was initiated in the 1990's, it picked up only after India's former President A.P.J. Abdul Kalam's vociferous backing in February 2006. The passage of the Nalanda University Act by the parliament on 21 September

2010 indicates India's commitment in reviving Nalanda's glorious heritage as a centre of cultural exchange and scholarship between East, Southeast and South Asia. India's mega multinational Nalanda project has thus opened avenues for transnational dialogues and collaborations.[32]

India's decision to share the idea with the members of the East Asia Summit, namely grouping of ten ASEAN Member States (i.e. Brunei Darussalam, Cambodia, Indonesia, Lao PDR, Malaysia, Myanmar, Singapore, Thailand, the Philippines and Vietnam), plus eight countries, namely Australia, China, India, Japan, New Zealand, Republic of Korea, Russian Federation and the USA, is an indication of India's ambition of unleashing its soft power through Nalanda on Asia and the world.[33] Nonetheless, the idea of using Nalanda as a soft power tool has evoked positive response and lot of euphoria and many have already committed their participation in the materialization of the project.

The project has thrown open so many opportunities and can further expand the scope for cooperative ventures. There are several push and pulls working from all sides. Lending support for India's ambitious Nalanda University project, a consortium led by Singapore and including China, India, Japan, and South Korea, has already initiated steps to raise $1 billion to meet the estimated cost for the construction of the University and development of necessary infrastructure. Seven member participating countries of East Asia Summit, namely Australia, Cambodia, Singapore, Brunei, New Zealand, Lao PDR, and Myanmar, have also signed inter-Governmental Memorandum of Understanding (MoU) with India pledged their support for the Nalanda cause. The enthusiasm with which the countries of South Asia, East Asia, Southeast Asia, and Asia-Pacific, have come forward to pledge their support in the execution of the Nalanda project reflects the growing desire of the participating countries to use soft power diplomacy while pursuing their foreign policy objectives. Nalanda, as an instrument of soft power, has become a conduit of international cooperation in the Asia-Pacific.

The involvement of so many players has brought to the fore the soft-power value of both Nalanda and Buddhism. The Buddhist element of Nalanda connects people culturally across Asia and offers a cause and a forum through which important powers in the Asia-Pacific can work together and promote regional peace and stability. Nalanda, it may be recalled, was a home to about 10000 students from distant lands, such as China, Korea, Japan, Tibet, Mongolia, Turkey, Sri Lanka, and Southeast Asia.[34] The project, therefore, wields enormous nostalgic and emotional appeal for all the Asians, who are now looking for an opportunity to re-discover their shared histories, cultures, and religions, and recover and restore the lost connections. Nalanda is the "voice of an enlightened Asia" As aptly put by India's then Foreign Minister Pranab Mukherjee, it "will rekindle ancient links between East and South Asia and will help us come closer together."[35]

Nalanda discourse has created a space where it represents not just a rising India but an ascendant Asia. In early twentieth century, Okakura Kakuzo (Tenshin)—a friend and contemporary of Rabindranath Tagore, summarized his views in a brief catch-phrase 'Asia is One,' arguing that Asian peoples from Arabia to Japan shared a unity of temperament: 'Arab chivalry, Persian poetry, Chinese ethics, and Indian thought, all speak of a single ancient Asiatic peace.'[36] The emphasis on Asian values is reinforced by Nalanda University's website which defines its plan as a confirmation of Asia's resurgence, forged on the common basis of 'peace and harmony' and 'Asian' values.[37] In short, Nalanda is envisaged as an icon of 'Asian Renaissance,' 'a centre for inter-civilization dialogue and inter-faith understanding.'[38]

Japan has expressed its keen interest in reviving Nalanda University and offered to invest approximately $100 million for the purpose, the highest amount offered by anyone so far. To help the local people and facilitate the construction work, the Japanese government has already built 42 tube wells to ensure regular water supply. There is no doubt that Japan's involvement in the development of Buddhist tourist circuits in South and Southeast Asia has been of long-standing. There is hardly any famous Buddhist place in these two regions which has not received Japanese funding. Thus, the Japanese eagerness to participate in the 'revive Nalanda' project is perfectly in tune with Japan's traditional policy, that is, to get connected to Buddhist world and more so with the land of Buddha. The influx of large numbers of Japanese tourists to Buddhist destinations in Bihar, further validates Japanese support for Nalanda.[39] As a matter of fact, the Japanese government had earlier offered to bear the entire expenses in the revival of Nalanda. This reveals Japan's ambition for a leading role in any regional initiative and for engaging India in a 'countering China' framework.[40] India's initiatives for the revival of Nalanda, however, are in tune with its 'Look East' policy directed towards greater integration with the East Asian community and attracting foreign investment for local development.

The Japanese interest in the 'revive Nalanda' project is motivated not only by its desire to reach out to the Buddhist world, but also in engaging India in the larger politico-strategic equation emerging in the Asia-Pacific. And, this includes the rise of both China and India as major players in the region, growing India-Japan strategic partnership and continued Sino-Japanese hostility. Japan played an important role in getting India its membership of the East Asia Summit, despite opposition from China, thereby, ensuring India's presence in any future East Asian community-building process and its active role in the strategic deliberations in the region. Nalanda offers both India and Japan a soft platform which could enable the two countries to engage in cooperative ventures in the Asia-Pacific.[41]

Conclusion

The complex structure of international relations prompt its actors to explore and employ various instruments, routes and approaches to deal with the new challenges and threats effectively. In the context of globalisation and the growing concern over the use of military power for achieving foreign policy objectives, the importance of soft power has increased considerably. Two examples will suffice to prove the importance of the soft power in the contemporary world. First, is the successful staging of the Beijing Olympics (2008) which has made China realize the importance of the soft power. This explains why China is promoting the study of the Chinese language and culture by establishing Confucius Institutes and investing $3 billion in developing Lumbini, the birth place of Gautama Buddha, now in Nepal. The other example is the United States' use of hard power in Iraq and Afghanistan which has generated worldwide anti-Americanism. These two examples make it crystal clear that instead of spending huge sums of resources and resort to 'hard power' to attain the foreign policy goals, it would be wiser to seek soft power options.

The use of soft power suits Japan's status as a country that is constitutionally unable to carry out international responsibilities involving military power, but is eager to carry out non-military international cooperation. However, even before Joseph Nye's concept of soft power came to the limelight, the post war Japan has been promoting its cultural products as vehicles of soft power to replace its post-war negative image with a new image of Japan being a cool and peaceful country. Since the formation of The Japan Foundation (1972), the focus has been on disseminating Japanese language education overseas, and providing aid to facilitate study-in-Japan programmes to foreign researchers and scholars; and showcasing Japan's traditional art forms and culture across the world. While the language program has gained considerable popularity, Japan's highly stylized traditional art forms, despite their exquisite elegance and aesthetic values, have failed to produce any lasting impact on the audience. From 2004 onwards, the focus shifted towards its pop culture. While the allure of Japan's popular culture, *manga*, and *anime* have the potential to familiarize Asia and the world with modern-day Japan, including its post war pacifist and democratic behaviour, it remains a superficial culture which lacks lustre in foreign relations.

Compared to the one-way promotion of a distinctive "Japan Brand" pop culture, Japan's pursuance of Buddhism as a soft power tool definitely holds more weight in public diplomacy. In the context of prevailing international scenario charged with conflict and terrorism, Buddhism offers many advantages. Some of the key Buddhist messages, such as equality, non-violence, as well as its dialogical approach hold universal appeal and are extremely conducive to its spread across different societies, cultures, and civilizations. And, for the countries of Asia who are spiritually aligned to Buddhism, there is no better soft power tool.

Despite its alien trappings, Buddhism has been an integral part of Japan's cultural and religious landscape for more than 1500 years. Today, it is the most enduring pillar of Japan's soft power diplomacy. Through several private and government agencies, Japan has been from time to time funding many projects restoring the Buddhist relics, developing the major Buddhist pilgrim sites in India. Japan has thus rendered a great service to Buddhism and the land of its birth by rediscovering, reclaiming, and keeping alive the 'wonder that was India.' India has finally woken up and is drawing world attention to its solid Buddhist credentials by making Buddhism as the core of its soft-power push in Asia. Japan has also brought several Buddhist sites and structures in India, known or hitherto unknown, on the world Buddhist tourist map. The Japanese presence is obvious to the tourists' eyes! There is no doubt that the primary objective is to cater to the needs and interests of the Japanese tourists, Japan has nonetheless done a great job by initiating steps to improve the infrastructure and the basic amenities for promoting in-bound Buddhist tourism, and using Buddhism as a means to promote bilateral political relations.

A unique aspect of Japan's Buddhist diplomacy is that it is backed by a conscious and systematic policy initiative, which extends beyond the restoration and development of Buddhist relics and sites, and is now directed towards harnessing India's classical educational linkages. A case in the point is India's upcoming 'revive Nalanda University' project, which has thrown open unlimited opportunities and brought to the forefront divergent and hostile players of the Asia-Pacific. The enthusiasm with which the countries of South Asia, East Asia, Southeast Asia, and Asia-Pacific, have come forward to pledge their support in the execution of India's mega Nalanda project reflects the growing desire of the participating countries to use soft power diplomacy while pursuing their foreign policy objectives. Nalanda, as an instrument of soft power, has become a conduit of international cooperation in the Asia-Pacific. Nalanda's Buddhist connection has also prompted Japan to make a magnanimous offer of $100 million to meet the cost. If materialized, the project would set the trend for the growing need of soft-power diplomacy in bringing together divergent and hostile players of the Asia-Pacific. It will spurt activities and processes that will rekindle shared histories, culture, shared interests; facilitate inter-civilization dialogue and inter-faith understanding, and contribute towards the building a harmonious Asian community.

The Buddhist themes of peace, harmony, tolerance, and nonviolence, are still relevant and hold worldwide appeal, but they have their own imitations. Firstly, although all Buddhists regard Gautama Buddha as the ultimate source of their faith, in reality, there exist different sects who use different texts and practice different forms of worship, and often there is little communication between them. Secondly, there is no doubt that Japan's Buddhist diplomacy is working very well with India where there is no historical baggage and where faith is considered as a soft power tool, but, whether it can play a constructive role in countries like China, which has a large Buddhist population and where faith is lately being actively employed as a form of statecraft to project its soft power, but the bitter historical legacy lingers on! Hence, one has to be extremely patient and cautious in the selection of soft power tools. Since they work indirectly, it could take years to produce the desired outcomes. They do not also guarantee absolute success. Much depends on what the recipient countries want otherwise it could provoke resistance towards the import of alien cultural values and products. In short, it is not a comprehensive 'one-fits-all' solution as there are limitations to its application and effectiveness.

END NOTES

1. S.D. Muni (2010), 'Nalanda: A Soft Power Project', *The Hindu Online* (30 August 2010).
2. Defining soft power as 'co-optive power' – the ability of a country to get others do what it wants – the Harvard University Professor Joseph S. Nye, Jr. identifies soft power as non-material or intangible resources of power, such as culture, ideology or institutions. Joseph S. Nye, Jr. "The Changing Nature of World Power," *Political Science Quarterly* (Summer 1990), 105: 2:177-192.
3. Peng Er Lam, "Japan's Quest for 'Soft Power': Attraction and Limitation" in *East Asia* (2007) 24:354-55.
4. Besides *The Japan Foundation*, the Japanese Government also set up *The Japan Exchange Teaching Program* (JET), *Japan Overseas Cooperation Volunteer Program* (JOCV), and *Official Development Assistance* (ODA).
5. *MOFA: Diplomatic Bluebook*, 2005:207. Popular *anime* shows, e.g., Doraemon, Ninja Hattori and Shin Chan, have been ruling the Indian viewership roosters ever since their introduction in 2008. The '*Manga* mania' has swept the adolescents and the merchandise relating to *manga* and *anime* has literally gone viral in the Indian market. 'Doraemon eggless cakes' (as most Indians are strict vegetarians), 'Pokemon Holi colours' (the Indian festival of colours) and Shin Chan *Raakhi* (Raakhi is a band made of silk thread and brocade which sisters tie on brothers' wrists as a token of their love on *Raksha Bandhan* festival in India) demonstrate how finely the Japanese cultural industry has penetrated the Indian cultural market.
6. Shinzo Abe's speech in the Diet (September 29, 2006). <www.kantei.go.jp> Shinzo Abe, as the 90th Prime Minister, was in office from 26 September to 26 September 2007, and

became the Prime Minster again on 26 December 2012.

7. Kazuo Ogura, "The Limits of Soft Power" in *Japan Echo* (2006), 33:5: 48-50.
8. The concept of '*Cool Japan*' was coined in 2002 by an American journalist Douglas McGray, who in an article "Japan's Gross National Cool" in *Foreign Policy* (1 May 2002), wrote that Japan despite its economic and political problems was pursuing its policy of advancing its cultural influence.
9. *MOFA, 2006.*
10. The Korean fixation in India is not just limited to music, drama, movies and TV. It is also seeping into kids' fashion, dress code, and hairstyles after popular Korean actors. The youngsters have even picked up Korean language which has become a popular mode of secret communication via SMS through mobile phones between lovers. The popularity of 'Korean Wave' is baffling as most of the shows, movies and songs are in Korean and not even dubbed in English.
11. Tachikawa Musashi, "On the Introduction of Buddhism of Buddhist Thought to Japan," *Japan in a Comparative Perspective*, International Symposium (1998), No.12: 63-75, International Research Center for Japanese Studies, Kyoto.
12. The missions that went to China between 607-18 AD comprised of young students and monks and carried Shotoku Taishi's letter addressed to the Chinese Emperor. It stated: "From the Son of Heaven in the Land where the Sun rises to the Son of Heaven where the Sun sets." The contents of the letter did not go down well with the Chinese Emperor who found it derogatory and humiliating and instructed his officials never to entertain people from the 'Eastern Barbarian' country.
13. Buddhism did suffer a set back during the Edo period (1600-1867), when the Tokugawa warrior regime patronized Confucianism, but it was not wiped out because as per the *Terauke* (Temple) Law, every Japanese was required to register birth at a Buddhist temple. Besides, the Buddhist temples also served as schools. At the same time, there has been no conflict but harmonious and peaceful co-existence between Buddhism and Shintoism.
14. "Restoring Old Glory" in *The Hindu* (Sunday February 8, 2004).
15. *Indian Tourism Statistics 2011*, Government of India, Ministry of Tourism, Market Research Division, New Delhi.
16. *Development of the Buddhist Sector for the Japanese Market, 1992*; cited in David Geary, *Destination Enlightenment: Buddhism and the Global Bazaar in Bodh Gaya*, Bihar, India, Unpublished Doctoral Dissertation submitted in The Faculty of Graduate Studies (Anthropology) The University of British Columbia, Vancouver (December 2009), p. 174.
17. Sakaiya Taichi, "The Baby Boomers Turn 60: A Great Decade to Come" in *Japan Echo*, 32:3 (June 2005), pp. 21-26.
18. "Japanese Tourism Magazine to Hard Sell Bihar," *The Tribune* (19 September, 2007); cited in Vibhanshu Shekhar, "Revival of Nalanda University: Key players and their soft power diplomacy" in the *IPCS Special Report: Institute of Peace and Conflict Studies*, no.48 (November 2007), p.8. <http://www.tribuneindia.com/2007/20070920/biz.htm#9>
19. Highlighting the newly excavated Buddhist site at Itkhori in Jharkhand's Chatra district, the Jharkhand Tourism Minister Ms. Vimla Pradhan during her visit to Japan, told the Japan National Tourism Organization (JNTO) that "one lakh Japanese had already visited Buddhist sites since the beginning of 2012." *The Hindu Business Line* (June 23, 2012).
20. *Japanese Market Survey Report* (JMS 25 & 38, 1992) in David Geary, *Destination Enlightenment*, p.175.
21. Ibid.
22. *Indian Express* (September 25, 2007).
23. *JMS 23*; cited in David Geary, *Destination Enlightenment*, p. 175.
24. *The Japan Foundation* and the *Japanese Funds-in-Trust for the Preservation of World Cultural*

Heritage have been involved in the restoration and preservation of Buddhist relics in many countries, such as China, India, Myanmar, Uzbekistan, Thailand, and Cambodia. Japan is also quick to align itself with Buddhists in its international affairs. For example, when the Taliban threatened in 2001 to destroy the Bamiyan Buddha statue in Afghanistan, the Japanese government engaged in active shuttle diplomacy trying to prevent the destruction. *MOFA* (March 21, 2001).

25. *UNESCO World Heritage Centre*, 2002.
26. Richard M. Jaffe, "Seeking Sakyamuni: Travel and the Reconstruction of Japanese Buddhism" in *The Journal of Japanese Studies*, 30:1 (Winter 2004), pp. 65-96.
27. Okakura Tenshin (1862-1913), had visited India in 1901-02. After spending few months with Rabindranath Tagore at Shantiniketan in Bengal, he also visited the Buddhist Circuit.
28. These include: Sarnath, Sravasti and Kushinagar (Uttar Pradesh); Gaya, Bodh Gaya, Rajgir, and Nalanda, (Bihar); Sanchi and Satdhara (Madhya Pradesh), and Ajanta-Ellora (Maharashtra). Of these, the renovation of Sanchi and Satdhara Buddhist Complex was undertaken by *The Japanese Funds-in-Trust for the Preservation of World Cultural Heritage* and the total budget of the project was $ 500,000. <www.unesco.emb-japan.go.jp/htm/mofaworld.htm> The JBIC has also funded Uttar Pradesh government for the construction of Sravasti-Kushinagar road.
29. The 82 feet tall statue carved out of pink chunar sandstone and red granite depicts the Buddha sitting in *dhyana mudra* on a lotus flower with his eyes half closed. It was designed by V. Ganapati Sathapati, a leading sculptor in India. For details, David Geary, *Destination Enlightenment*, pp. 79-83.
30. The Japanese women prefer Indian men in comparison to the Japanese men who supposedly have no time for the family and work like machines. The Indian men, according to the Japanese women, are good and give time to their wives and children. For details, Sanjay Kumar Jha, "Knot Uncommon" in *India Today* (March 31, 2003); David Geary, pp.136-38.
31. Primarily, a centre of Buddhist learning, Nakanda Mahavihara offered a vast range of academic curricula covering not just Buddhist philosophy but also art, mathematics, medicine, literature and several other streams of knowledge.
32. The new Nalanda University will be constructed at Rajgir, situated 12 km away from the ruins of ancient seat of learning, and 100 km away from Patna, Bihar.
33. India's decision to share the proposal with the leaders of East Asia Summit meet (held at Brunei on 10 October 2013) was largely dictated by its concern for a greater integration with the Asian community and to attract foreign investment for local developmental projects.
34. Some of the noted scholars who studies at Nalanda were: Hiuen-Tsang, I-Tsing, Nagarjuna, Aryadeva, and Padmasambhava (the founder of Buddhism in Tibet).
35. Statement by Dr. Pranab Mukherjee, at the *East Asia Summit Foreign Ministers' Lunch*, 31 July 2007. <http://meaindia.nic.in/pressrelease/2007/07/31pr01.htm>
36. Kakuzo Okakura (1904), *The Ideals of the East: With Special Reference to the Art of Japan*, New York, E.P. Dutton & Co., p. 10.
37. Nalanda University (2012), '*Our Vision*'. <http://nalandauniv.edu.in/abtvision.html>
38. George Yeo (Singapore Ex-Foreign Minister), "The Asian Renaissance," Speech at the Nalanda Buddhist Symposium (13 November 2006). <http://app.mfa.gov.sg/2006/press/view_press.asp?post_id=1881>
39. Vibhanshu Shekhar, "Revival of Nalanda University," p. 8.
40. Ibid., p. 9.
41. Ibid., p. 8.

16

India-Japan Relations: The Dividend of Cultural Affinity

Madhuchanda Ghosh

In the era of globalization cultural intercommunications seem to play a dominant role in inter-state relations. In India's evolving relationship with Japan, with the deepening of the Strategic and Global Partnership the focus of the mandarins of foreign policy is growing on the domain of bilateral cultural relations. There is high recognition of Japanese cultural soft power in India and vice-versa. The cultural, literary and religious linkages between the two countries prove the bedrock on which India-Japan relations are based. The importance of cultural intercommunications in widening and deepening mutual understanding between the populaces of India and Japan is vital to sustain the bilateral relations. This is because dearth of comprehensive knowledge and insights into each other's cultural orientation, value system, outlook and so on often become a breeding ground of misapprehensions that might lead to a psychological barrier. This paper will examine and analyse the impact of cultural variables in India-Japan relations.

Introduction

The rich cultural legacy existing between India and Japan has been referred to time and again by the leadership of the two states. Buddhism has been the most prominent link between the two countries which dates back to the 6th Century A.D. when the religion was introduced in Japan. Since then the cultural kinship between the two states have spanned centuries. During the early part of the 20th Century, significant exchanges between cultural luminaries of the two countries bolstered the bilateral relations and such direct proximities helped build bridges of understanding between India and Japan. Swami Vivekananda's visit to Japan in 1893 deserves mention in this regard.

While on his way to the Chicago Congress of World Religions Vivekananda visited cities of Yokohama, Osaka, Kyoto and Tokyo in Japan. He highly appreciated Japan's modernization efforts during the Meiji era.[1]

At the turn of the 20th century the meeting of the two great cultural ideologues, Rabindranath Tagore and OkakuraTenshin paved the way in promoting cultural relations between the two countries. The meeting of these two intellectuals started a bilateral dialogue that marked the beginning of an attempt to bring India and Japan closer. OkakuraTenshin emphasized the need to revive and rediscover the ancient religious and cultural unity which existed between India, China and Japan.

Amazed by the startling progress of Meiji Japan in science and technology, Rabindranath Tagore urged the Indians to learn from the Japanese work culture and harness their own skills. During his visits to Japan Tagore met Japanese intellectuals, cultural and political leaders and exchanged views with academicians, poets and artists. Tagore delivered an epoch-making speech at the Tokyo Imperial University on "The Message of India to Japan." In his speech Tagore pointed out that Japan has the capacity to bring about regeneration of Asia as it has absorbed modern civilization without compromising with its ancient culture. Interactions between Tagore and Okakura paved the way for Visva-Bharati University at Shantiniketan to become the hub of future cultural exchanges between the two countries.[2] Today Shantiniketan is the meeting ground of Japanese and Indian intellectuals, artists and scholars.

In the post-independent period India's cultural exchanges with Japan are governed by the Cultural Agreement signed between the two countries in October 1956. To promote mutual cultural and academic exchanges the India-Japan Mixed Cultural Commission was subsequently constituted in accordance with the Cultural Agreement. Since 1973 the Commission has been organizing regular meetings in New Delhi at the governmental level to promote intellectual exchange and thereby foster mutual understanding. With regard to the nature of cultural exchanges between India and Japan it needs to be noted that the flow of cultural exchanges between the two countries till the end of the 19th century had an overload of theological elements with India giving more than what it received. However, the trend underwent a sea change in the post World War II period as pointed out by scholars like Hajime Nakamura, P.A. Murthy, Tsuji Naoshiro and other experts of Indo-Japanese relations. In the post World War era a reverse flow of cultural influences from Japan to India could be identified which has been largely facilitated by the flow of technology, investment and goods from Japan. This post World War II phenomenon in India-Japan relations could be analysed as a case of culture following the movement of capital, technology, enterprises and personnel. Therefore, in comparison to the earlier phase of cultural exchanges, the bilateral cultural relationship in the post World War period has been characterized by an overload of material elements marked by heavy emphasis on technology, work ethics, techniques of organizing production and standardization.

Parameters of Cultural Exchange

The impact of the cultural variables in India-Japan relations could be comprehended by taking account of the various components of cultural exchanges between India and Japan which can be identified as: a) religion; b) tourism and art forms; and c) education.

Religion

Buddhism has been the most prominent link between the two countries which dates back to the 6th Century A.D. when the religion was introduced in Japan. The Mahayana (Great Vehicle) branch of Buddhism in the sinified form reached Japan from Korea in 552 A.D. Under the royal patronage of Prince ShotokuTaishi (574-622A.D.), who is sometimes described as the Ashoka of Japan, the new faith gained popularity. Buddhism subsequently acquired a distinct Japanese character through the independent study of Buddhist doctrines by Japanese savants and their interpretations and commentaries on the Buddhist texts. It is interesting to note that along with Buddhism many deities of the Sanskritic tradition also reached Japan and acquired Japanese names and forms. The Buddhist temples in Japan have idols of various Hindu gods and goddesses which are worshipped by the people along with Buddha. Though Buddhism was cultivated in Japan for centuries, it faced harsh treatment particularly during the Meiji era, because, it was erroneously judged to be turning people's minds away from this world.

During the Meiji period one of the most noted experts of Indian philosophy was Tetsujiro Inoue (1855-1944). He was a strong advocate of the promotion of Buddhist philosophy in Japanese society. In this context it worthwhile to note that like India, Japan has come under diverse religious influences at various historical junctures. Besides Shinto and Buddhism the philosophies of Confucianism, Taoism and Christianity have also made their forays into the Land of the Rising Sun. Shinto and Buddhism are the principal religions. It seems that after Shinto one of the most enduring influences on Japanese culture has been that of the Buddhist philosophy. The Buddhist principles of tolerance, peaceful co-existence, charity towards fellowmen are deeply embedded in the Japanese culture.

Japan and India have both drawn sustenance from Gautam Buddha's message of peace and compassion. In Japan there are various Buddhist groups like *Reiyukai* (Spiritual Friendship Society), *Rissho Koseikai* (Society of People of the Same Faith), *Soka Gakkai* (Value Creating Society) and the like that are engaged in cultivating and disseminating the Buddhist doctrines abroad. In India these organizations have their branches in Delhi, Mumbai, Kolkata, Agra, Jaipur and other cities. The followers of these spiritual organizations in India range from persons of culture, intellectuals and university students to bureaucrats and political leaders.

With regard to the preservation and restoration of cultural heritage sites in India, notably, the Ajanta Ellora caves and the Sanchi group of monuments, Japan has provided significant cooperation through Official Development Assistance (ODA) and the UNESCO/Japan Trust Fund. During the visit of the Indian Prime Minister Dr. Manmohan Singh to Japan in December 2006 the Indian side expressed its appreciation for Japanese assistance in the development of tourism-related infrastructure, including the Buddhist pilgrimage circuit in India. It was declared that the two states will enhance their ongoing cooperation in the development of infrastructure at Buddhist sites in India.[3] Modern stupas, temples and guest houses have been built along the Buddhist pilgrimage sites in Gaya, Rajgir and Varanasi. Japanese artists and painters have been making significant contribution with regard to restoring the Buddhist wall-paintings at Ajanta, Ellora and other places.

Tourism

Tourism is another important component of the cultural exchanges between India and Japan. It constitutes a potent medium of mutual understanding providing the people of the two states the opportunity to gain a firsthand knowledge about each other's cultures. Japan has a large pool of overseas tourists. It needs to be borne in mind that for an average Indian, Japan remains quite an expensive tourist destination while India is viewed as a popular tourist destination by Japanese tourists. This is evident from the annual visit by a sizeable Japanese tourist population to India in comparison with few Indian tourists visiting Japan. In this context it needs to be noted that the spiritual affinity between India and Japan has been a catalytic factor in the visit of Japanese tourists to India. India is perceived by the people of Japan as "*Tenjiku*" which means 'heaven'. The enduring spiritual appeal of India draws thousands of Japanese believers every year to the holy places of Buddhism. Besides the spiritual element, India's scenic beauty and cost-effective accommodations make it a popular tourist destination.

During the May 2013 visit of the Indian Prime Minister Dr. Manmohan Singh to Japan, the two countries underscored the importance of tourism in promoting greater understanding between the people of the two states. The

Joint Statement issued between Prime Minister Dr. Manmohan Singh and the Japanese Prime Minister Shinzo Abe includes various activities as part of promoting exchange between the people of the two countries and strengthening cooperation in the field of tourism.

Literature and Various Art Forms

During the early 20th century notable interactions between the Nobel laureate Indian poet Tagore and the famous Japanese poet Noguchi marked the dawn of a new era in literary exchanges between the two countries. The Indian epics Ramayana and Mahabharata as well as the works of noted Indian litterateurs have found their Japanese versions. Hajime Nakamura observed that some stories of ancient India were very influential in shaping Japanese stories. In order to propagate Hindi literature in Japan Professor Teiji Sakata has written some good volumes on introduction to Hindi folk tales from India.

In Japanese literature the influence of Buddhism has been profound. Bodhisena, a Buddhist monk is credited to bringing India and Japan together in the field of literature, education and art. He visited Japan on a special invitation from the Japanese emperor Shomu Tenno in 736 A.D. to teach Sanskrit. Bodhisena helped to provide Japan a simpler system of writing the Katakana script. The studies initiated by Bodhisena contributed to fixing the Japanese alphabet and for the classical literary revolution in Japan. Bodhisena received the honourable title – "*BrahmonSojo*" from the Japanese emperor.[4]

Buddhism has been the principal source of inspiration in Japanese traditional art, architecture, painting and sculpture. Nara period (725-794A.D.) was the golden era of Buddhist art in Japan. In *Horyuji* temple the wall painting is very similar to Ajanta painting of India. The mural painting representing scenes of Paradise, in the golden hall of *Horyuji* temple, which date from about 710 A.D. clearly owe their inspiration to Indian art. In the realm of painting notable exchanges have taken place between the artists of the two countries. In the early 20th century the Nobel Laureate Indian litterateur Rabindranath Tagore was instrumental in promoting interactions between the leading Indian and Japanese painters. The prolonged visits of the renowned Japanese painters Yokoyama Taikan and Hishida Shunso to Bengal and their interactions with painters like Abanindranath Tagore, Gagonendranath Tagore and others laid an indelible imprint on the Modern art Movement in Bengal. Yokoyama Taikan was successful in promoting Japanese fine arts in India. The genre of Bengal Art which developed under the leadership of Abanindranath Tagore had influences of the Japanese wash technique[5] which he acquired from Yokoyama Taikan and Hishida Shunso.

Education

Academic exchanges between India and Japan gained momentum following the Cultural Agreement of 1956. In India academic interest towards Japanese studies is, however, not a product of the Cultural Agreement. It could be traced back to the historical juncture when the two cultural ideologues Tagore and Okakura Tenshin initiated the Japanese language studies programme at the Visva-Bharati University at Shantiniketan in the early part of the 20th Century.

The post-independent period in India ushered in a renewed interest in the area of Japanese studies. With the initiation of training programmes and courses pertaining to Japanese studies in the premier universities like Jawaharlal Nehru University and Delhi University during the 1950s and 1960s the area study gradually gained currency in the Indian academic arena. The prospect for Japanese studies to emerge as a viable academic discipline in India, however, still remains obscure. Academic institutions in India are generally reluctant to propagate courses in a non-conventional area such as Japanese studies. Another veritable retarding factor is the limited scope of job opportunities for those who specialize in this field. The universities mostly recruit scholars, experts and researchers from traditional disciplines in the sense to which history, economics or political science belong. In comparison with India, Japan has had a long tradition of Indological studies. For aeons academics in Japan have studied philosophies of Buddhism, Jainism, Indian classical literature including languages like Sanskrit and Pali. Since the Meiji period Buddhist philosophy evolved as a core academic area study in institutions of higher learning. Research on Indian classical literature and Indian philosophy constituted the bulk of writings on India. In contemporary times, academic interest in Indian studies have been furthered by opuses of experts of Indological studies. One of the most noted savants of Indological studies was Dr. Hakuju Ui.

Increased interactions between academics and students of the two countries as well as easy access to research materials and funding for research have been catalytic in promoting academic exchanges between the two countries. It is interesting to note that Japan has an academic tradition of studying the Indian languages of Sanskrit and Pali. During the Meiji period a chair of Sanskrit and Pali was founded in the Tokyo Imperial University. The Buddhist doctrines written in Sanskrit and Pali texts have been preserved and cultivated by Japanese savants. Noted scholars like Junjiro Takakusu, Masaharu Anesaki, Daito Shimaji and others were the pioneers of Pali studies and established the academic tradition of Pali Buddhist studies in the Tokyo University. Presently, many Japanese universities offer courses in Sanskrit and Pali studies. These languages are taught in noted universities like Kyoto University, Osaka

University, Bukkyo University, universities of Kyushu, Hokkaido, Nagoya to name a few. Besides Sanskrit and Pali modern Indian languages are also taught in several universities. The National Institutes of foreign languages in Tokyo and Osaka have chairs of Hindi and Urdu. Apart from these languages Bengali and Tamil are also imparted in several Japanese academic institutions.

Till the early 1990s India-Japan cooperation in science and technology was not consistent compared to social sciences and humanities. While India continued to moot joint research and development proposals, covering earthquake prediction, pollution control protection, immunology, leprosy control, fermentation, engineering and the like, Japan's response was rather guarded and passive. The mire of inertia gradually gave way to active cooperation since the mid-1990s. For instance, the programme for leprosy elimination in India is receiving considerable support from the Nippon Foundation and Sasakawa Memorial Health Foundation apart from the World Bank, WHO and other international organizations.[6] Likewise, Japan has been a prominent and consistent partner in the countrywide Pulse Polio Immunization (PPI) campaign of the Indian government.[7] The Indo-Japanese Joint Committee for science and technology has opened new avenues for inter-governmental collaboration in the field of science and technology.[8] In the area of earthquake and tsunami prediction technology Japan has extended cooperation to India since the occurrence of the devastating tsunami in the Indian Ocean. Cooperation is significantly expanding, most notably, in the sphere of Information Technology.

Japanese Language Studies in India

India has been witnessing a boom in the study of Japanese language especially since the mid-1990s. There has been a growing interest among the Indians in the study of Japanese language. Since India embarked upon its economic liberalization programme, there has been a steady flow of Japanese investments in the Indian economy. With Japanese business firms making a foray into the Indian market, the need for Japanese speaking people has increased significantly. Accordingly, many universities have initiated Japanese language training programmes. Premier universities like Jawaharhal Nehru University, Delhi University, Jadavpur University, Visva-Bharati University of Shantiniketan and others offer courses in the Japanese language. Besides universities there are a large number of foreign language institutes in India which offer Japanese language courses.

A proliferation of centres offering instruction in Japanese language in all the major Indian cities bears testimony to the growing popularity of the language among the Indians. Delhi has many centres offering Japanese language training. In the other metropolitan cities like Kolkata, Mumbai and Chennai language centres have been established by the Japanese Consulate Generals. Since 1984 the Japan Foundation has introduced the *Nihongo no ryokushiken* (Japanese Language Proficiency Test) which is an examination system that is conducted world-wide.

To facilitate studies and research in the area of Japanese studies and Indian affairs the governments of both countries provide for educational funding in the form of scholarship and fellowship awards to promising students, scholars and researchers. The availability of scholarships and fellowships serves as an incentive to the students of both countries to undertake studies and research on India and Japan in the respective countries and thereby facilitates the exchange of scholars and publications. Following the Indo-Japanese Cultural Agreement the Ministry of Education of Japan (*Mombusho*) introduced scholarships to Indian students for undertaking study in Japan. Japanese studies scholars have access to well-structured organizations, the foremost in this regard being the *Mombusho* Scholars Association of India. Another significant organization is the Japanese Language Teachers Association of India (JALTAI) which includes members representing all the regions of India.

In the new millennium the growing need for Japanese language skills in the wake of widening economic engagement between India and Japan has pushed up the demand for Japanese language teachers in India. According to a survey by the Japanese Embassy, India would have to train about 30,000 teachers to impart Japanese language skills to higher secondary level students in India. In this context the Indian government's decision to introduce Japanese as an optional foreign language in the secondary school curriculum is important. The need has also been accentuated by the decision of the Central Board of Higher Secondary Education (CBSE) to adopt Japanese language as a second language in schools.[9] For the increasing number of young Indian IT professionals going to Japan sound knowledge of Japanese language is mandatory. Both the premiers of the two countries, Prime Minister Mr. Shinzo Abe and the Indian Prime Minister Dr. Manmohan Singh, have paid great importance to cultural and academic initiatives and strengthening of people-to-people contacts.

Conclusion

A careful study of the existing cultural intercommunications between India and Japan reveals some apparent inadequacies. The existing academic exchanges are still too small and inadequate and lack a long-term cooperative framework. Greater expansion and collaboration with regard to intellectual and academic activities are needed especially in the field of science and technology. In the 21st century as India is emerging as a regional power in Asia, studies pertaining to the contemporary Indian society, politics, economics, literature, culture and the like are gradually gaining attention in the Japanese academic circle.

For comprehensive development of India-Japan relations greater promotion of dialogues and discussions through conferences, seminars, workshops, youth fora and the like is imperative. Such interactions would help disseminate accurate information and at the same time facilitate more people-to-people contact. At the non-governmental level youth associations of students, scholars and researchers should play a more proactive role in this regard. At the governmental level the Ministry of Foreign Affairs of Japan (MOFA) has been organizing the South Asian Youth Forum on a regular basis to provide an effective platform for the purpose of enhancing youth exchanges between Japan and South Asia and disseminating knowledge about Japan to the South Asian youth.[10] Such youth exchange programmes play a crucial role in fostering mutual understanding between Japan and South Asia.

Apart from the youth exchanges India and Japan have also held joint symposia which have provided effective platforms in bringing together political leaders, business leaders and academia of the two states. This has enabled the two sides to voice their views, share ideas and information with their counterparts and thus, work cooperatively towards attaining common objectives. However, the number of such symposia needs to be increased to facilitate greater understanding between the two states. It is relevant to mention that Japan Foundation which was established in 1972 by the Japanese foreign ministry to promote and disseminate knowledge about Japan's culture overseas, opened its first South Asian office in India in 1993. However, over the years its commitment to South Asia has been quite low as pointed out by a personnel of Japan Foundation.[11] He pointed out that the Japanese government has allocated major funds for promoting its cultural exchanges with the East and the South East Asian countries in the coming years as compared to the South Asian region. Compared to East Asia and Southeast Asia only a miniscule proportion of Japan Foundation's allocations have been disbursed to South Asia over the years.

There is a lack of dissemination of accurate information on India and Japan to the populaces of the respective countries. Lack of sufficient and accurate information has precluded the development of adequate mutual understanding. Stereotype images tend to assert themselves even in knowledgeable writings. To the Japanese populace the general perception of India is stereotyped. Even in the 21st century the image of India in the minds of the average Japanese citizens is still that of a caste-ridden, impoverished and unenlightened country of teeming millions.[12]

While the 'caste-cattle-hot country' syndrome vis-à-vis India still continues to persist in the Japanese mind, the image of Japan in India also suffers from great limitations. How many Indians, barring a handful who specialise in Japanese studies, have knowledge of Japanese cultural heritage and tradition or for that matter about the fact that Japanese social life exemplifies the unique feature of striking a balance between preserving its age-old tradition and achieving modern technological prowess? To an average Indian knowledge about Japan is woefully limited to electronic goods and the Hiroshima and Nagasaki holocausts.

Optimum dissemination of accurate information is the *sine qua non* for the development of mutual understanding and appreciation between the peoples of the two countries and in this context, cultural intercommunications provides a crucial platform for the further build-up of India-Japan relations. To remove the stereo-typed images that have persisted over the years in the minds of the people of India and Japan vis-à-vis each other, cultural exchanges must to be enhanced. A sense of cultural affinity is often helpful in overcoming barriers and resistance to broader exchanges, including economic and technological. Greater flow of cultural exchanges would provide an edifice for deepening and expansion of India-Japan relations.

END NOTES

1. Vivekananda's visit to Japan paved the way for the establishment of Ramakrishna Vedanta Society in Zushi, near Tokyo.
2. Harish Chandra Tripathy, *Indo-Japanese relations:1901-1970* (Patna: Janaki Prakashan, 2001), pp.51-52.
3. For details see "Joint Statement towards India-Japan Strategic and Global Partnership," Tokyo, December 15, 2006, <http://pmindia.nic.in/visits/content.asp?id=147>.
4. For details on Bodhisena see Chapter 4 of Dr. S.R. Bhatt (ed.), *Buddhist Thought and Culture,* New Delhi: Low Price Publications, 2005.
5. http://www.chitralekha.org/yokoyama.htm
6. For further details, see WHO Special Ambassador's Newsletter No. 3, *The Nippon Foundation*, August, 2003, p. 5.
7. For further details, see *Japan Calling*, Embassy of Japan, May-July, 2001, p. 2.
8. The Committee identified the areas namely natural disaster reduction due to earthquake, landslides and cyclones; seismology and seismic structures; manufacturing technologies; computer hardware and software; accelerator based research as areas for Indo-Japanese cooperation. Joint seminars and workshops have been held and exchange of scientists has taken place.
9. "Demand for Japanese teachers rising in India," *Statesman*, February 6, 2007.
10. Author's personal experience in Japan as an Indian delegate in the 2002 South Asian Youth Forum, organised by the Japanese foreign ministry.
11. This point was raised by a personnel of the Japan Foundation in course of an interview with the author in May 21, 2013.
12. This point was revealed in course of some research interviews conducted with noted Japanese academic experts during 2012.

REFERENCES

Bhatt, S.R. (ed.), *Buddhist Thought and Culture* (New Delhi: Low Price Publications, 2005).

Cohen, Stephen P. *India: Emerging Power* (New Delhi: Oxford University Press, 2001).

Grant, Richard L. (ed.), *The Process of Japanese Foreign Policy: Focus on Asia* (London: The Royal Institute of International Affairs, 1997).

Hirabayashi, Hiroshi *Japan-India Relations—A Perspective,* Embassy of Japan (New Delhi, 2000).

Inoguchi, Takashi *Japan's International Relations* (Boulder: Westview, 1991).

Jain, Purnendra (ed.), *Distant Asian Neighbours* (New Delhi: Sterling Publishers, 1996).

Kesavan, K.V. (ed.), *Building a Global Partnership* (New Delhi : Lancers Books, 2002).

Peng Er Lam, Japan's Quest for "Soft Power": Attraction and Limitation, *East Asia* (2007) 24:349–363, DOI 10.1007/s12140-007-9028-6

Hanscom Smith, "Toward a Universal Japan: Taking a Harder Look at Japanese Soft Power", *Asia Policy* 15, January, 2013

17

Japanese Language as Soft Power

Janashruti Chandra

'Soft power' finds its first mention in a 1990 publication by Joseph Nye of Harvard University titled, "Bound to Lead: The Changing Nature of American Power" and has become a frequently used word today. Roughly defined as the country's ability to obtain the outcome it wants, not through coercion or rewards, but through its attractiveness. It is often used in contrast to 'hard power' which has its parameters based on military or economic might. Soft power stems from a country's culture ideals and policies.

In the 21st century, more than ever, it is widely accepted that 'Culture is power'. Culture can be effectively exploited to diffuse ethnic and religious prejudices and helps create a climate of tolerance. The era of globalization of economy has necessitated greater interactions with other countries. For smoother economic dealings many countries now realize the need for a peaceful stable international environment. Harnessing the potential of culture in the diplomatic arena has emerged to be an important tool. It is with such reason of national interest in the backdrop, that countries have set up their cultural institutes overseas. For example, Germany has its Goethe Institute; France its Alliance Francoise and China has its Confucius Institute. All these organizations serve in generating and cultivating interest about the country, so that some of the effort translates into some tangible results and ensures stronger relationships. If there is a certain level of knowledge and mutual goodwill, then nations can withstand the odds even if government ties break down. Much soft power is created through the available flow of information and the sense of awe instilled through knowledge dissemination.

The making of the soft power may be initiated by the government, but once set in motion; it lies outside the control of government. The United

Kingdom because of its Commonwealth past and media holds a strong appeal in the international arena, USA rose to a dominant global role with its ideals of freedom and openness to immigrants etc. There are attempts to measure soft power through indexing 50 odd factors such as number of cultural missions, business brands, architecture, as education destination etc.

Japan and Soft Power

Among the Asian countries Japan undoubtedly has more potential soft power resources. It is strong in the area of creativity but is weak to appraise and develop the overseas market. Of late, Korea has been riding high on the '*Hallyu*' wave and is engaging actively with the youth all over the world to 'sell' the Korea image well. The spillover effect of this trend contributed to Korean electronic items becoming household names and increased market share of Korean cars etc. Japan for long had projected its culture to be exclusive and unique focusing more on the classical arts such as the tea ceremony, flower arrangements, garden layout, drama with heavy input from classical literature etc. Japan took pride in being different and the entire thrust was in showcasing their uniqueness. Huntington doesn't hesitate to conclude that 'If economic integration depends on cultural commonality, Japan as a culturally lone country could have an economically lone future.' According to Nye, Japan's low birthrate, fast ageing population, and poor English skills are constraints to soft power.

It is only recently that it has embraced the concept of 'Cool Japan' and exporting popular culture of *anime*, *manga*, computer games, music, television drama etc. Through popular culture, Japan is reinventing itself and the cultural influence is said to have quietly grown. Napier (2007) states that the audience impressed by 'Cool Japan' is also inspired to know not only more about the product, but also its cultural origin. The number of foreigners learning the Japanese language despite the economic stagnation is an indicator.

In Japan, the concept of Soft Power became popular after the article titled, "Japan's Gross National Cool" by Mc Gray (2002). Japan's popular culture is being abundantly consumed by local populations worldwide and has exposed people to new images and ideas about Japan. The new image of Japan has helped to some extent in diffusing political hostilities in the region, but to have an impact on international competitiveness, it needs to develop a keener awareness of the value of soft power and strategize promotion of 'Cool Japan'. There are scholars who also argue that attraction to Japan's image may not help Japan's state policies. Japan's failure to secure a permanent seat in the UN Security Council is often cited as a limitation for soft power strategy.

It was only in the 1990s that the Cultural Agency of Japan started the use of the term 'cultural policy' in its official reports and cultural diplomacy to create a supportive climate for Japanese firms overseas to come to the forefront. Japan Foundation funded by the Japanese government and the Keidanren represents Japan's national interests and is the official organization to disseminate correct information about Japan. Their chief thrust area has been Japanese language teaching. Since the establishment of The Japan Foundations New Delhi office in 1994, most support has been extended to developing Japanese language education.

India and Soft Power

Let us consider the case of India before turning our focus back on Japan. Former Union Minister of State for External Affairs Tharoor notes that today it is not the size of the army or of the economy that matters, but instead it was the country that told the 'better story' which would qualify as the global player. India, though a slightly late player in showcasing soft power, has held the attention of the world because of her historical and cultural ties, philosophy, religious ethos, long lasting democracy, free press, entrepreneurial energy of India's people, yoga, ayurveda, Indian cuisine, Bollywood etc. These cultural products have made India more familiar and accessible. The Indian government has only recently incorporated the 'cultural element' into its foreign policy. Indian Council for Cultural Relations has set up centers in nineteen countries and has been active in creating goodwill for India, tapping and showcasing the potential that India has. To quote foreign policy analyst, C. Raja Mohan (2003)

> "The spiritualism of India has attracted people from all over the world, and its Gurus have traveled around the world selling yoga and mysticism. Bollywood has done more for Indian influence abroad than the bureaucratic efforts of the government. From classical and popular music to its cuisine, from the growing impact of its writers and intellectuals, India now has begun to acquire many levers of soft power."

Though India's soft power resources are multifaceted, India is still unable to wield her considerable variety of resources effectively. Perhaps it is necessary to recognize that certain soft power holds significance only if tailor-made to an audience in another culture. For example, when we talk of cricket as soft power, it will be only significant to those nations that understand cricket and not countries like Japan. Perceptions about India are varied. In India's immediate neighborhood, Pakistan and Nepal dislike India's 'big brother' attitude, Bangladesh and Sri Lanka complain of a 'trust deficit', while Afghanistan and Bhutan held positive perceptions.

Japan's Perception of India

Relations between the two countries have more or less been friendly and positive given their historical ties. The Japanese know it as the sacred '*Tenjiku,*' the land of philosophers and world leaders like Gandhi and Nehru, but unfortunately not much was known about life in India and Indians. A simple analysis of their school textbooks reveal this startling fact that opens up a psychological gap between the two countries. India was the first Asian country with which Japan signed its bilateral peace treaty in 1952. Japan deplored the 1974 and 1998 nuclear tests conducted by India, but this interlude too did not affect the people to people relations. At the government level too, the two countries have signed the Global Partnership Agreement that fosters cultural and academic initiatives and strengthens people to people contacts. Hopefully, these will correct some of the distorted images about India being caste ridden, a country of many religious conflicts and poverty. There is a renewed effort to raise the profile of India in Japan and promote Japanese language studies. From the economic angle as well, METI reports that focus should also be placed on India, as it is expected to become an enormous market during the medium term.

Language as a Soft Power

To the list of soft powers that India can boast about, 'language aptitude' could be suggested as a 'smart' power, for it cuts across all the fields and genres. In the multilingual milieu, Indians have a distinct advantage over countries where only one language is spoken. The learning ability, the comfort level with even foreign languages is heightened because of language sensibilities available. Learning Japanese will leverage bilateral relations between India and Japan by increasing people to people contact which will in turn contribute to greater understanding among the people of the cultures of both these countries.

Since the induction of Japanese language teaching at Shantiniketan, Japanese language education has come a long way. George (2009), Panda N. (2007) etc. have amply covered the institutions where it is taught and number of students engaged in learning the Japanese language. Some new institutions which have come forward with courses floated for Japanese are English and Foreign Languages University in Hyderabad, Doon University and Wardah University. Haldwani University is in the process of formulating a distance learning model and Manipal University in the South and Presidency University in the East are considering the teaching possibilities. In addition to the Central and State universities there are many private initiatives too. At the 2013 Japanese language speech contest, Embassy officials noted that the most remarkable aspect about Indo-Japan relationship is the growing number of students learning Japanese and the promise the Japanese language students offer to the two nations. In Jawaharlal Nehru University alone, the intake of students at the undergraduate level has doubled than say, a decade before. Indians themselves no longer undermine the future prospects of Japanese language education.

The number of candidates from India appearing for the Japanese Language Proficiency Test in the last three years as shown in the table, indicates the trend of rising numbers of students of the Japanese language.

Year/Month		Number of candidates	Year/Month	Number of candidates
2010	July	1435	2012 July	3068
	Dec	4987	Dec	4399
2011	July	2612	2013 July	3748
	Dec	3913		

Under the Global Partnership Agreement signed by Prime Ministers Koizumi and Singh, the projected number of Japanese language learners by 2010 was 30000. This goal was a bit too ambitious to be met, but steadily India has been trying to reach the target. Already, Central Board of Secondary Education has adopted Japanese as a third language to be taught at schools and the Japan Foundation's New Delhi office has supported the cause by producing textbooks for classes 6, 7 and 8 and in extending training to school teachers. Japanese is the first East Asian language to be included in the school education curriculum, to counter the West centric model. As a future project, the Japanese Language Teachers Association of India is also thinking on the lines of E-learning. Besides the script, given the language structure and cultural affinity it is not difficult for Indians to master the Japanese language.

If learning the Japanese language is given its due importance, interests of both Japan and India can be complemented. Japan hopes to increase the number of students attending Japanese universities to 3 million by 2020 under the Global 30 initiative. Indians learning Japanese can then be the potential students seeking higher education in Japan. It has been predicted that most of the higher studies on Japan will be contributed by Asian countries. India too will have its significant role. Original research on Japan is dependant on language training to some extent. With Japanese language skills in place Indians can also help promote Japan's soft powers such as *manga*, *anime*, music etc and create the Japan brand.

Last year, the number of Japanese companies in India crossed the 1000 mark and so, Japanese-knowing personnel are being sought for these work places too. If those joining the corporate world are proficient in the language and aware of Japanese practices it creates a supportive climate for Japanese businesses. Since the bubble economy burst at the beginning of 1990s, Japan's economic model has lost some of its sheen, but Japan can hope to join hands with the demographic advantage India offers besides its market potential to recover lost ground.

Interest in Japan as a tourist destination for Indians has been increasing too. In 2013 alone, Japanese National Tourism Organization records 60-70 thousand Indian tourists visiting Japan. Of late, Indian students are seriously considering Japan as an option for overseas studies too and Japan education fairs have become a regular feature. With professional courses like Japanese language having a focus on business, Japanese interpretation or specialized translations, Indian learners can benefit from the immense job prospects and higher salary packages a Japanese company offers. However, it is also important to maintain quality than only emphasize on numbers of Japanese language learners.

At the national level, through language India could learn some values and principles that propelled Japan to heights of economic development. Language is a carrier for value systems. Zeal for improvement, taking responsibilities, being sensitive to others are a few traits that come the mind when we speak of Japanese people. If BRICS report is to be believed then India is set to overtake Japan's economy by 2032 and it will be worthwhile to learn about Japan's experience so far and the role played by human capital. Interest in Japan will help India in taking lessons from Japanese industrialization, receptivity and assimilation of new ideas, technology, environment issues etc.

The scope of the Japanese language in India, if exploited well, can translate into strengthening SAARC relations as well. Japan in its Observer role in SAARC should also promote Japanese language in the region. It already strives to do so with programs such as JENESYS 2.0. Perhaps India could contribute as a network centre for Japanese language education. At present, a Japanese language speech contest is held at SAARC level, but the network of SAARC Japanese language teachers and scholars does not exist. For organized collaborative research it may be imperative to share resources, unify syllabus, bridge levels, and have cross cultural research and joint publications. If Japan actively pushes in this direction, it will support democratization and peace building measures via language. Such initiatives will be stepping stones to *kokusaika* or internationalization from the inward-orientation of its culture.

REFERENCES

George P.A. (2004), "Status of Japanese Language Teaching in India: Current and Future Trends", in Panda R. & Fukazawa Y. (eds.) India and Japan: Blossoming of a New Understanding, New Delhi, Lancer's Book, pp. 96-132.

Huntington S.A. (1996), The Clash of Civilization and the Remaking of World Order, New York: Touchstone, pp. 134-35.

Lam, Peng E. (2007), "Japan's quest for 'soft power': attraction and limitation," *East Asia* 24, pp. 349-363

Mac Gray, D. (2002), "Japan's Gross National Cool", Foreign Policy No.130, pp. 44-54

Mohan, C.R. (2003), "Indian diaspora and 'soft power'," *The Hindu*, January 5.

Napier, S. (2007), "Differing Destinations: Cultural Identification, Orientalism and 'Soft Power' in 21st Century Anime Fandom" in From Impressionalism to Anime: Japan as Fantasy and Fan Cult in the Mind of the West, London: Palgrave MacMillan, pp. 169-191

Nye, Joseph S. (1990), 'Bound to Lead: The Changing Nature of American Power', Basic books, New York.

Nye, Joseph S. (1990), Soft Power, Foreign Policy, No. 80, New York, pp. 153-171.

Panda N. (2007), "Language Learning Transcending Boundaries: the Japanese language in India and Indian languages in Japan", in Panda R. and Fukazawa Y. (eds), India and Japan in Search of Global Roles, New Delhi Promila and Co., pp. 421-444.

Panda R. (2010), "Soft Power as a Tool to Foster Cultural Diplomacy in India-Japan's Relations", in Japanese Studies, George P.A. (eds.), New Delhi, Northern Book Centre, pp. 34-64

Tharoor S. (2008), "India as a Soft Power", *IIC Quarterly*, Vol. 35, No.1, pp. 32-45

METI report "Tying together culture and its Industry". http://www.meti.go.jp/english/press/2011/pdf/0512_02b.pdf

http://www.jlpt.jp/statistics/pdf (Overseas data for JLPT exam candidates)

18

Japan's Influence on Sri Lankan Higher Education

Nanda Gunawardhana and Shanthini Shanmugarajah

Sri Lanka and Japan have a history that spans over centuries with a brilliant bilateral relationship that has been consistently cordial throughout, and since ancient times, the Japanese have had a marked influence on Sri Lankan Higher education, even in the periods before the University system was introduced to the country.

Japan has provided US$ 4697.4 million (or 25 per cent) of total foreign aid receipt of US$ 18820.8 million that Sri Lanka has received from all donor countries during the period 1960-2011. Its assistance has been significant across multiple sectors.

Various programs have been successfully conducted with over 12000 scholars and students being trained in various fields in Japan. Grant-in-aid was received to aid in institutional capacity building, such as the Dental Faculty of the University of Peradeniya. The latest addition has been the Sri Lanka Japan Study Centre launched earlier this year which operates as a streamlining portal for academics of both countries to find partners, pool data share resources and build a more vibrant collaborative research culture.

This paper aims at discussing the significant role that Japan has played in the development of the Educational Sector of Sri Lanka with emphasis on the Higher Education Sector and how we intend to further strengthen these ties and develop new programs; while discussing how the SAARC countries can create and strengthen ties with Japan as a region.

Background

Historical

Relations between Japan and Sri Lanka go far back into history tracing across many centuries. It began with Japanese traders who visited Sri Lanka as far back as the 17th century. The *Reverend Shaku Kohen* of the *Shigon* Sect was the first official Japanese national to set foot on the shores of *Serendib*, according to historic documents at the Tokyo University. The venerable Buddhist monk was reported to have landed in 1886 with financial assistance from the then Japanese Foreign Minister Hayashi Tadasu. Historical records show us that initially most exchanges were centred on Buddhism, leading to educational exchanges. Education plays a pivotal role in the life and culture of Sri Lanka and dates back to 543 BC. Higher education in Sri Lanka has been based on several prominent *Pirivenas* (Ancient Buddhist Monk Training Centers) in the local kingdoms. It is believed that numerous religious and educational exchanges took place over this period before the University system was introduced to Sri Lanka in 1921. Before this it is believed that higher education in Sri Lanka mostly consisted of apprenticed learning opportunities in various fields, and although no literature or records conclusively show it, it is believed that Japan had an influence in the education sector even during this time.

Official exchange between Sri Lanka and Japan commenced in the year 1952 with the establishment of the Japanese Embassy in Sri Lanka, closely followed by the establishment of the Sri Lankan Embassy in Japan in 1953. It is notable at this point that Sri Lanka was one of the first countries from the SAARC region to establish official ties with Japan. This was mostly due to the proceedings of the 1951 San Francisco Peace Conference, where late former President (then Minister for Finance) Mr. J.R. Jayawardane made a moving speech. He declared Ceylon's disclaim of war reparations from Japan and requested other representatives to accept Japan as a member of the international community. The speech was said to have moved some of the victor countries which had demanded severe sanctions on Japan, and this is remembered as a symbolic event in returning Japan to the international community later on. This formed the basis for the continued and more importantly consistently friendly and supportive bilateral relations between Sri Lanka and Japan independent of changes that have occurred over the years within each country individually.

Sri Lanka Higher Education

In Sri Lanka, education is considered to be a basic human right and since independence education from grade one to basic degree, is free and compulsory for age group 5-14 years. The Sri Lankan government encourages parents to send their children to schools by providing school text books and materials for uniforms. Even though facilities are not equally distributed over the country, today every 6 km^2 of the country has at least one school.

The concept of vocational education is still developing in Sri Lanka. There are 902 vocational education institutes registered under the Tertiary and Vocational Education Commission (TVEC) in Sri Lanka to train school leavers. While Primary and Secondary Education in Sri Lanka have developed exponentially over the years, the country's requirement today lies mostly in the area of Higher Education (tertiary Education).

The first step in tertiary education was taken with the establishment of the Ceylon Medical College in 1870. This expanded rapidly and lead to the founding of the Ceylon University College in 1921. In 1942 the first university was established as the University of Ceylon with several campuses island wide, Colombo (established 1942), Peradeniya (established 1949), Vidyodaya (established 1959), Vidyalankara (established 1959) and Katubedda (established 1972). It was dissolved in 1972 to establish the University of Sri Lanka. The Jaffna campus was added to the university in 1974. With the promulgation of the Universities Act. No 16 of 1978, state university status was restored to the 6 separate campuses. The University Grants Commission (UGC) was also created to plan and coordinate the state university education. After that, a number of state universities have been created. All these state universities are registered under the University Grants Commission, but a few come under the auspices of ministries other than the Ministry of Higher Education, in which the UGC is a part. Today we have 15 Universities and 3 campuses that come directly under the purview of the UGC.

The Higher Education system of Sri Lanka although it has grown rapidly since inception, still has much to be desired. Most of the state universities depend on funds given by the University Grants Commission, as it is their primary and sometimes only source of funding. However, Japan has been our key donor to the Educational Sector, especially since 1983. Japan's Official Development Assistance (ODA) allocation for the Education Sector of Sri Lanka has led to vast strides being made in the Higher Education Sector of Sri Lanka.

Japan's Higher Education

Formal education in Japan began with the adoption of Chinese culture in the 6th century. Buddhist and Confucian teachings as well as sciences, calligraphy, divination and literature were taught at the courts of *Asuka, Nara* and *Heian*. After the Meiji Restoration of 1868, the methods and structures of Western learning were adopted as a means to make Japan a strong, modern nation. Students and even high-ranking government officials were sent abroad to study, such as the Iwakura mission. Foreign scholars, the so-called '*oyatoi gaikokujin*', were invited to teach at newly founded universities and military academies. Compulsory education was introduced, mainly after the Prussian model. By 1890, only 20 years after the resumption of full international relations, Japan discontinued employment of foreign consultants.

Higher education in Japan, although inspired by countries like the United States and the United Kingdom, differs from higher education in most other developed countries in many significant ways. Key differences include the method of acceptance, which relies almost entirely on one or two tests, as opposed to Grade Point Average or GPAs or other methods of assessment.

Another major difference is graduate school, as very few non-science (Arts and Humanities) undergraduate students go to universities in Japan. This is because graduate schools for non-science students are generally considered useful only to those who want to work in academia.

Unlike higher education in some other countries, public universities are generally regarded as more prestigious than private universities, especially the Seven National Universities (University of Tokyo, Kyoto University, Tohoku University, Kyushu University, Hokkaido University, Osaka University, Nagoya University), which represents one university for each major region of Japan.

In 2010 more than 2.8 million students were enrolled in Japan's 778 universities. These figures clearly demonstrate that the higher education sector in Japan is advanced and well established in comparison to Sri Lanka and therefore there are numerous ways in which Sri Lanka can benefit from exchanges and collaborations with Japanese higher education institutes.

Fig. 1: Foreign Student intake in Japanese Institutions, Comparison Between Total and Sri Lankan Nationals (values for Sri Lanka x50 has been used for comparison purposes) [1]

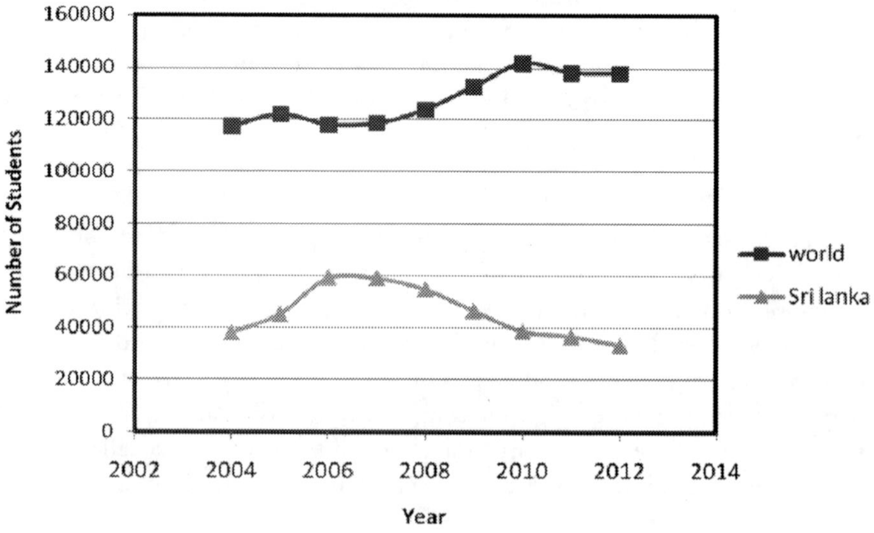

The trends seen in total foreign student intake into Japanese Institutions and intake of Sri Lankan students have been plotted in Figure 1. It is believed that the trend in Japanese intake was mostly influenced by the situation within the country and its rising popularity as a choice for higher education. While observing the trend in intake of Sri Lankan students in Japan, we feel that the peak following 2004 was mostly due to more scholarships being offered to Sri Lankan students following the tsunami that occurred that year.

Japans ODA Allocation to the Education Sector of Sri Lanka

Since the 1950s, Japanese ODA has mainly focused on the Asian region as a policy. Japan's assistance to Sri Lanka began under the Colombo Plan, with a US$ 50 000 loan in 1965. By 2000, Japan was Sri Lanka's largest aid donor, while Sri Lanka was Japan's 8th largest aid recipient. Japan's economic assistance to Sri Lanka through JICA has been one of Sri Lanka's biggest aid assistance.[2]

Japan, Asian Development Bank (ADB) and World Bank (WB) are the premier donors in Sri Lanka. Japan mainly supported economic and social infrastructure building during the last 50 years. At present, Japan's Country Assistance Program for Sri Lanka is divided between humanitarian and reconstruction support, assistance for institutional reforms, building economic infrastructure, enhancement of foreign currency earning capacity, and reduction of poverty.[3] As demonstrated by the data tabulated in Table 1, the assistance lent to Sri Lanka in the Education sector alone has been considerable and varied.

Table 1: Higher Education Related Assistance to Sri Lanka from Japan[1]

No.	Project	Year	Items donated
1.	University of Peradeniya, to improve facilities in the Faculty of Engineering	1983	Experimental and Educational Equipment
2.	Ruhunu University of Sri Lanka, to improve facilities of Medical and Science Faculties	1984	Equipment for Medical and Science Department
3.	Ministry of Education for the construction of a Teacher's Training College at Matara	1984	New Building (8.189M2)
		1985	A.V. System, Printers, Experimental Equipment, Agricultural Equipment
4.	Ministry of Youth Affairs and Sports for the National Youth Services Centre at Maharagama	1985	New Building (15.444M2) and Equipment
		1986	-do-
5.	Moratuwa University, to improve research facilities	1987	Measuring Apparatus, Computer, Spinning & Weaving Machine etc.

No.	Project	Year	Items donated
6.	Ministry of Youth Affairs and Sports to establish the Auto Mobile Engineering and Training Institute.	1987	Construction of Training Centre and Equipment
7.	Ministry of Education for the improvement of facilities for National Institute of Education, Maharagama	1989 1990	New Building (9.980M2) and training equipment -do-
8.	Open University of Sri Lanka for the establishment of Audio Visual Education Centre at Nawala Campus	1991	Construction of AV Educational Centre including Production Studio Editing Room, Maintenance Workshop etc. (1.871M2)
9.	University of Colombo Faculty of Science	1991 1992	Analytical Equipment, Experimental equipment etc. NMR, GC-MS, SEM Spectrophotometer etc.
10.	Ministry of Education & Higher Education	1995	Improvement of the Faculty of Dental Science
11.	Ministry of Education & Higher Education	1996	Improvement of the faculty of Dental Science
12.	Ministry of Education & Higher Education	1996	Improvement of the Education Equipment for the Faculty of Agriculture University Peradeniya
13.	Ministry of Higher Education and Education Sri Jayawardenapura University	1996	Improvement of the Educational Equipment for the faculty of Medical Science
14.	Ministry of Education & Higher Education Junior School Development	1998	Construction & Equipment Supply
15.	Ministry of Education & Higher Education	1998	Supply of Equipment to Faculty of Engineering

Since 1983, Japan ODA has contributed immensely towards developing the current formal education system in Sri Lanka. Japanese grant aid on education was focused on the following aspects.

- To build education infrastructure
- To supply materials and equipments
- Conducting of teachers' training programs and improving quality of education.

Japan's technical co-operation programme highlights the value of education and human resource development for economic advancement. Under this programme, over 12,000 Sri Lankan professionals and students have been trained in various fields in Japan. In addition to on-going scholarships programmes, a new programme entitled the Japanese Grant Aid for Human Resource Development Scholarship (JDS) has commenced since 2009.

Development Assistance from Japan Towards Higher Education in Sri Lanka

Inter-Institutional Support and Assistance

Most of the assistance that Sri Lankan Higher Educational Institutes have received from Japan are under this category. Inter-institutional support refers to the assistance provided by Japanese Universities and other institutions to those in Sri Lanka. This assistance has been mainly in knowledge transfer, providing of training and capacity building, equipment and instrument aid, and has mostly been individual collaboration based. The assistance provided thus by numerous Japanese institutions cannot be measured as no consolidated resources exist on the exchanges. However we believe that this is the most important type of exchange that Japan and Sri Lanka have had academically and which influenced the development of the Sri Lankan higher educational sector tremendously.

It has been observed for instance that during the course of a collaborative project, assistance from Japanese counterparts are always lent to the Sri Lankan counterparts to obtain instruments, and consumables such as chemicals that would be necessary for the research project. Also due to the strong institution to institution ties that exist, Memoranda of Understanding /student exchange agreements are signed and this results in more exchange and assistance from the particular institution. However, till date, these one on one exchanges haven't been fully brought together to identify the output, the reason being that it starts with a bottom up approach. In most cases, a scholar from Sri Lanka who visits Japan collaborates with a scholar there to begin a research project, and this slowly grows to become a research group consisting of both Sri Lankan and Japanese scholars, these scholars then involve administrative officials of the involved universities in their collaboration and visits ensue. This finally culminates in the signing of an official agreement thus ensuring that the exchange continues. In Sri Lanka most of the exchanges have been initiated thus, and therefore have contributed tremendously towards the development of higher education in Sri Lanka.

Assistance from JICA

Economic Cooperation between Japan and developing countries began in October 1954, when it joined the Colombo plan with a contribution of US $ 50,000. At this time, Japan was still a recipient of aid from the World Bank and the U.S. for the reconstruction of its own economy. Within a short period, Japan's ODA expanded to encompass all developing countries. From 1989 onwards, Japan was one of the world's biggest donors. According to available data, technical cooperation was aimed to provide developing countries with the necessary support for strengthening their self help efforts. In particular, this assistance attempted to facilitate foreign students, improve the higher educational institutions, facilitate administrators, develop and enhance vocational skills, improve occupational safety and health and strengthen industrial competitiveness.

Through the years JICA has given grants to improve educational facilities in Sri Lanka, some notable projects include the Peradeniya Teaching hospital, the Faculty of Dental Sciences Hospital in the University of Peradeniya and the Institute of Computer technology in the University of Colombo. In addition purchase and improvement of teaching equipment and facilities were funded in the Universities of Peradeniya, Colombo, Ruhuna, Sri Jayawardhanapura and Moratuwa.

JICA was also instrumental in establishing and developing a television station in the government sector to improve mass communication and telecast facilities in Sri Lanka, which along with the above mentioned points clearly demonstrates Japanese influence in the higher educational sector in Sri Lanka. In projects such as these and numerous other projects that JICA has initiated, even though the direct beneficiary was not the higher education sector of Sri Lanka, the projects have had an indirect impact on the sector. For example, projects held in recent times such as Assistance for Conflict – Affected people in the North and East, and contribution in the form of Japan's technical cooperation for tsunami disaster rehabilitation had vast indirect impact on the higher education sector, mostly because the projects would always involve scholars from around the country who were attached to higher education institutes and by bringing more opportunities to the students of said institutes. Even projects aimed at developing various industries in Sri Lanka, be it agricultural, textile etc. ultimately have an impact on the universities of Sri Lanka because of the new learning opportunities and scholar involvement that it incorporates.

Major JICA projects that directly influenced the development of the Higher Education sector of Sri Lanka[4]

The development of information technology through capacity building of University of Colombo, School of Computing (UCSC)

The School of Computing, University of Colombo (UCSC), is a centre of excellence in Sri Lanka for Information Technology. JICA extended its cooperation in ICT from 1987 to strengthen software development capacity and human development programs with the IT industry. Today the UCSC is a well recognized institute for IT not only in Sri Lanka but also overseas. The project for IT through capacity building which was concluded in June 2005 has been to enable the UCSC to enter the field of advanced media technology and make further advancements towards e-learning.

The project consisted of workshops and training courses on web based technology being conducted for over 200 participants from the Universities, IT training institutes and private companies in Sri Lanka. WBT modules such as Personal Computer Applications and Fundamentals of Programming were developed by counterparts and delivered on trial to UCSC international students and an external degree course of Bachelors of Information Technology (BIT) students. Five academic papers relating to Research and Development activities were presented at international conferences.

The dental education project in the University of Peradeniya

The dental hospital in Peradeniya is a grant of the Government of Japan and has excellent facilities for the practice of modern dentistry. It is the teaching hospital of the Dental Faculty, University of Peradeniya and is now recognized as a centre of excellence in South Asian region. Dissemination of the technical expertise was one of the main components and Japanese experts were dispatched to Sri Lanka and Sri Lankan medical and para-medical staff also received post graduate/training opportunities in Japan.

The project resulted in improvement of knowledge and skills of academic staff, capacity building of technical staff, capacity of general and dental nurses, improvement of management skills of administrative staff of the Dean's office and project management teams, and development of the capacity to conduct research and continuing education programmes for dental health personnel.

The project helped initiate collaborative relationships on an international level, organize joint clinical meetings and an academic cooperation agreement between the University of Peradeniya and Tsurumi University.

The establishment of Japan–Sri Lanka College of Technology to strengthen technical education and training in Sri Lanka

JICA has undertaken to extend technical cooperation to the Department of Technical Education and Training (DTET), which is towards the advancement of trained manpower among Mid-level technicians. The Project aims at strengthening the Managerial &Technical capacity of DTET and Maradana College of Technology by establishing three model courses, namely Mechatronics, IT and Metal Work, to upgrade to national vocational qualifications.

Major activities included establishing training infrastructure for conducting model courses, upgrading technical skill of teaching staff and teaching methods and improving training material.

Training under AOTS

The Association for Overseas Technical Scholarships (AOTS) was established in 1959 as the first technical cooperation institution organised on a private basis in Japan. Its main purpose was to promote international economic cooperation and to enhance economic development and friendly relations between other countries and Japan.

The main activities of the AOTS falls into three major categories according to the nature of its training programs: 1. Training programs in Japan to provide technical and management training for engineers and managers in developing countries; 2. Conducting group training programs overseas with instructors/ experts sent from Japan to provide technical and management training for engineers and managers in developing countries; 3. The management of *Kenshu* (training) Centres, which are four centres established in major cities in Japan that provide training facilities and accommodation for trainees who are away from their countries.

Japanese Government Scholarship Program

While financial and other assistance was provided to build colleges, to improve operation and management capabilities and enhance educational and training capabilities, Japan's considerable influence on the Sri Lankan Higher education sector was through the *Monbukagakusho* program—the Japanese government's sponsored scholarship programme for foreign students. These scholarships were made available to all nations and *Monbukagakusho* students from Sri Lanka constitute of 0.5 per cent of the total given. Of these, most students were postgraduates owing to the language barrier, and two thirds among them studied humanities and social sciences and one third were from science and engineering fields.

Japanese Language Teaching Centres and Courses

Three of the 15 universities in Sri Lanka teach Japanese Language courses. These degree and certificate courses were established with the assistance of Japan and contributed towards encouraging scholars and students wishing to pursue their higher education in Japan to do so, as in the country Japanese is the most widely spoken and understood language. Establishing the language courses in Sri Lanka helped improve relations between the two countries and to improve communication between scholars.

Other Scholarships available in Japanese Higher Educational Institutes

Private foundations also offer many opportunities for international students. There are over 115 scholarships provided by private foundations throughout Japan, of these Sri Lanka along with other SAARC region countries are eligible to apply for over 70. Through these scholarships students of various levels of expertise can apply for education in a range of fields.

The Strengths and Weaknesses of Sri Lanka Japanese Collaborations in Relation to the Higher Education Sector

The main strengths of collaborations have been, from Sri Lanka's point of view, access to higher technology and technology transfer in various scientific fields, the opportunities to access Japanese post graduate facilities, development in areas of research which may not have been funded nor able to be undertaken in Sri Lanka if not for the collaboration, development of inter disciplinary teams for research projects and the scientific infrastructure development.[2]

Even during the early 1990s there was a general reluctance among scholars in Sri Lanka to pursue their higher education in Japan; this was mostly because countries such as the United Kingdom, USA, and Australia etc. were considered to be more prestigious and more beneficial. However this line of thought has shifted and today we see more scholars keen on learning in Japan. It has also been suggested that education alone cannot guarantee economic growth and development,[5] as seen in countries like Sri Lanka, the Philippines and Indian States of Kerala and West Bengal.[6] In many ways Japan offers a unique experience to foreign students coming in, not only in excellence in education but also in an attitude shift especially by helping implant group consciousness. Group consciousness refers to things such as punctuality, morning meetings, uniform and discipline. This attitude shift has been one of the foremost reasons for scholars valuing the role Japan plays in influencing the Higher Education Sector in Sri Lanka.

Other unique offerings of Japanese education are habits such as reading, preservation of notes, easy to understand textbooks and the prevalence of libraries that are widely practiced and more of a routine in Japan.

The data plotted in Figure 2 demonstrates the major identified limitations that foreign students face when pursuing their higher education in Japan.[2] The seven major areas have been identified in the legend of Figure 2, the category of others, include among others factors, such as Japanese Culture, food, winter climate, strict regulations of the Japanese Government and Universities, unavailability of religious facilities, work load etc. These mostly

Fig. 2: Limitations Foreign Students Face in Japanese Higher Education[2]

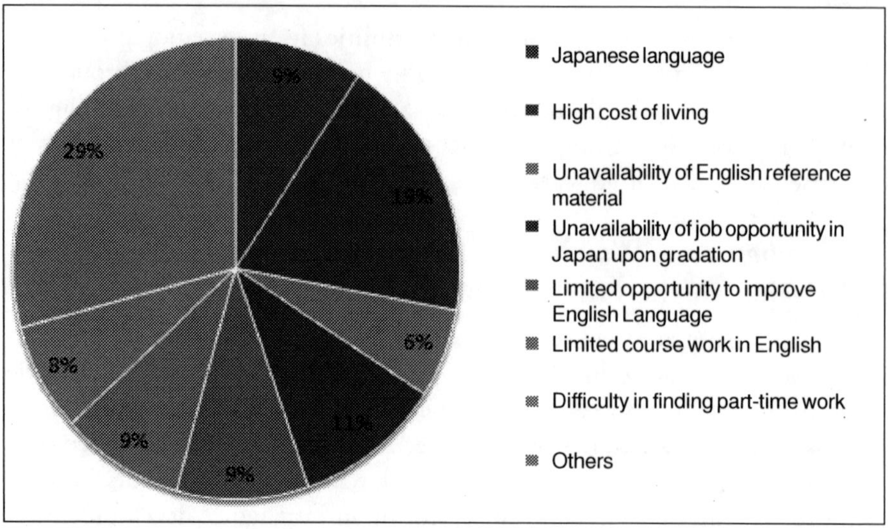

demonstrate the key difficulties students face while pursuing their higher education in Japan.

One of the major weaknesses of the collaborations so far has been failures in collaboration and organizational systems, including difficulties among Sri Lankan Institutions to collaborate with each other. The collaborations could have benefited more if the Sri Lankan Government or beneficiary institutions had showed greater commitment. Another weakness that has been observed is non prioritization of research in Sri Lanka.

Limitations in the Development of the Higher Education Sector using Japanese Assistance

While Sri Lanka has received a significant amount of aid from Japan for the development of the higher education sector, the assistance received was not always processed smoothly and therefore resulted in its non optimal utilization.

One of the key problems faced in regard to this matter is the poor organizational and administrative arrangements. In assessing the organization and administrative arrangements it is very clear that most projects funded through Japanese Institutions/Government experienced delays, difficulties in procuring staff and equipment owing to the procedural complexities and in some cases perhaps due to inefficiencies. In most cases whenever bottlenecks or red-tape arose in the implementation process, they were eventually resolved and the project coordinators always strived to ensure that there was minimal adverse impact on the project. However, it still remains that poor organizational and administrative arrangements present in the 'Sri Lankan Higher Education Sector' in particular, are major drawbacks when it comes to receiving and utilizing assistance in the form of foreign aid.

The University of Ceylon since its inception in 1942 experienced a phase of impressive growth in many respects, but not much in the area of administrative processes. Due to the minimal reform in the university administration and the ad hoc manner in which things are done on a necessity influenced basis, this has resulted in a twofold effect,

1. Stakeholders not being fully aware of the correct procedure/process that certain actions require
2. Stakeholders not being able to do things according to the laid out procedure, due to time/resource constraints.

Another commonly encountered limitation while receiving assistance is that the procurement guidelines of Sri Lanka do not match those of the Japanese system. This has once again led to many unnecessary delays in procurement of equipment and resources. Once again this is a problem that has been frequently encountered and dealt with on a case by case basis. It is very clear that due to the lack of Institutional Capacity Building initiatives and the outdated procurement guidelines enforced in Sri Lanka, any aid received from Japanese institutions along with all foreign aid will continue to experience delays and discrepancies.

The Japanese Embassy in Sri Lanka: Role in Development of Higher Education in Sri Lanka

One factor that has greatly influenced the receiving of aid and assistance from Japan has been the relationship between Sri Lankan stakeholders and the Embassy of Japan in Sri Lanka. The embassy and in turn the Ambassador of the time marks a very important focal point of contact for any country where it is based. Since it was established in 1952, the Japanese Embassy and Ambassador have always been held in high regard, and are kept constantly updated regarding the most important exchanges between the two countries, whether undertaken by institutions or individuals.

When undertaking any international venture, the embassy's support becomes vital, as it facilitates the process and expedites the receiving/sending of aid and assistance. In Sri Lanka, due to the numerous projects that have received Japanese aid and the excellent relations that were maintained over time, the proposal to establish the Sri Lanka Japan Study Centre was expedited due to monumental support offered by the Japanese Embassy in Colombo.

Once sufficient justification was offered to make the case for the University of Peradeniya, it was decided that the centre would be physically located in The University of Peradeniya while maintaining a network with all Sri Lankan institutions and being the focal point in Sri Lanka for all Japanese Institutions and scholars who wished to exchange ideas or initiate collaborations. The involvement of the embassy ensured that all hitches in the implementation process were dealt with expeditiously and that the centre was given its due importance in the international arena.

This resulted in the Centre being recognised in the Joint statement released in March 2013 when the President of Sri Lanka and the Prime minister of Japan met in Tokyo to discuss matters of state.

In all projects where aid has been received from Japan, one feature that has been consistent is the support and assistance offered from the embassy by playing a critical role in the implementation processes in the country. In order for assistance and support to be obtained from Japan one of the first steps that is required to be taken by any country is to develop a good link with the Japanese Embassy with a good flow of communication and involvement.

The general functions of an embassy involve consular services and representing the home country's interests and contribution. What we do not realize is that, in the carrying out of its routine activities the embassy plays an important role indirectly. The assistance lent by the Japanese embassy in this regard has been invaluable towards the development of Sri Lankan higher education. Most of the government sponsored scholarships from Japan come through the embassy.

Role of Sri Lanka Japan Study Centre for the Development of Higher Education Sector Institutions

While there have been numerous exchanges between Sri Lanka and Japan due to the reasons described earlier they have occurred in a very ad hoc manner, with a bottom up approach and no streamlining of the exchanges. While assistance from Japan has been substantial they were not optimally utilized or regulated. This gave rise to the need for a streamlining body, one that would mediate all research and academic related exchanges between the two nations. As one of the largest and oldest University in the country with an ideal setting for multi disciplinary research and playing host to one of the largest bodies of staff who have received their higher educational qualifications from Japan, the University of Peradeniya was identified as the ideal host for the centre which would then maintain a network with all higher educational institutions and related bodies to streamline all educational exchanges with Japan.

The Sri Lanka-Japan Study Centre of the University of Peradeniya was launched on the 29th of March 2013 by holding a conference on Sri Lanka Japan Collaborative Research to signify the landmark of the completion of 60 years of diplomatic relations between the two countries. The study centre aims at enhancing academic exchanges, collaborative research and goodwill between universities of Sri Lanka and universities in Japan. The study centre will promote and disseminate collaborative research carried out between scholars of universities in Sri Lanka in collaboration with universities in Japan, foster communication among diverse disciplines, and encourage new approaches in understanding the relationship of Sri Lanka and Japan, and its place in the world.

"The objectives of the centre are:

i) To further strengthen the academic and research cooperation between Sri Lankan and Japanese Universities.
ii) To further strengthen the student exchange programmes between University of Peradeniya and Japanese Universities.
iii) To build human capital on research methodologies and modern technological tools for research in different disciplines through finances secured from join submission of proposals with Japanese Universities.
iv) To improve physical capacity for collaborative research takes place between the universities of two countries.
v) To facilitate coordination of research and training activities between two countries.
vi) To facilitate and strengthen the existing linkages between different Faculties of University of Peradeniya with universities in Japan.
vii) To host and organize joint academic and research conferences between the two countries."

(Sri Lanka Japan Study Centre Website, As per the senate paper of the University of Peradeniya)

It is expected that the Sri Lanka Japan Study Centre will grow and eventually form strong formal links not only with Japanese Universities but also institutions such as JICA, JSPS, JST, JASSO etc. It is also expected that with time the centre will be renown as a centre for excellence and will initiate and facilitate multi disciplinary research between the two countries and work towards fulfilling its other objectives.

Future Plans in relation to Sri Lanka–Japan Higher Education

1. One of the activities to be undertaken in the near future is the introducing of sandwich/double degrees. A sandwich degree, typically, is a four year undergraduate degree offered by a Sri Lankan higher

educational institute with a one year industrial internship in Japan and vice versa. A double degree would be one where student works in parallel for two university degrees; one from a Sri Lankan institution and one from a Japanese institution. We believe that this is a vital part of building strong bonds and will result in effective knowledge transfer and initiation of collaborative research between the staff and scholars of both countries.

2. Initiation of multidisciplinary research projects will be encouraged and the process for implementing some such projects has already started. In the future more attention is to be given to the initiation of multidisciplinary projects as opposed to collaborative research projects that encompass a single discipline as is the usual trend. Most Sri Lankan Institutions have varying disciplines being taught within the University itself and will provide the ideal setting for the initiation of multi disciplinary research. It must also be noted that it is through such multi disciplinary research that we can make a severe impact on the development and advancement of the two countries and that the output will benefit the masses.
3. Another plan that is to soon to be implemented is the initiation of true student exchange programs. Up until now most student exchange programs that Sri Lankan higher educational institutes have had with Japanese Institutions have been of a relatively short term and they have not always been reciprocal. Initiation of new student exchange programs in a well structured way that would ensure students being sent from Sri Lanka to Japan and vice versa for a significant length of time to follow a structured course would aid them in accomplishing their goals and completing their degrees.
4. While knowledge exchange between Sri Lanka and Japan has been an ongoing process, it lacks structure and consolidation. It is necessary that knowledge exchange, and that too web based knowledge exchange in particular, be developed so that our scholars can be provided access to the forum and be able to locate and obtain the data that they are in need of. A virtual platform encouraging knowledge exchange that will facilitate the researchers of the two countries and provide the scholars, especially of Sri Lanka, with data that they would not have access to otherwise is to be created by the Sri Lanka Japan Study Centre.
5. Till date we have had many conferences and workshops on international levels, and have learned that they are always full of opportunities for scholars to meet resource persons and collaborators.

In the future more such workshops and conferences will be organized where cutting edge research will be presented and young scholars are provided with the chance to develop collaborations and receive advice from the experts in their field.

6. Another area that so far has not been given much attention is the publicity of research programs. To develop a webpage specifically for Sri Lankan staff and students to be kept informed of opportunities available in the higher education sector in Japan and give them due publicity would be an important step to be undertaken. Also, most scholars and potential students are not aware of scholarships available from the Sri Lankan government, both for Sri Lankan students who wish to study in Japan and Japanese Students wishing to come to Sri Lanka. Knowledge about the available opportunities should be widespread and be given more publicity.
7. Introducing public-private partnership among Sri Lankan Higher Education Sector and the Japanese industry and vice versa is another future plan. This is vital to the maintaining of the momentum in research and development in both countries. The encouragement of the partnerships between institutions and industry gives the unique opportunity for the students and scholars of the institution to get much required hands-on experience and will provide the industry with fresh and innovative ideas. The development of this kind of partnerships would result in a spike in the research and development of all stakeholders. It will result in the students getting updated knowledge in regard to technology and understanding current trends.
8. Sri Lanka and Japan share certain social concerns such as aging population.[7] This opens up the avenue where Sri Lanka and Japan have shared interests to initiate collaborative research. This will be an important undertaking that would be mutually beneficial to both nations and can be undertaken with great implications to this and other social issues.

Japan and the SAARC Region—Higher Education Sector

The South Asian Association for Regional Cooperation (SAARC), founded in 1985, is dedicated to improving the welfare of the people of South Asia through economic growth, social progress and cultural development in the region. SAARC's seven founding members are Bangladesh, Bhutan, India, the Maldives, Nepal, Pakistan, and Sri Lanka. Afghanistan joined the organisation in 2007. Australia, China, European Union, Iran, Japan, Mauritius, Myanmar, the Republic of Korea and United States are the

Observers to SAARC. In terms of population, the SAARC region covers nearly 1,600 million people, and is one of the largest such regional organizations. The SAARC countries have common features including geographic and climatic conditions and share issues concerning the socioeconomic, cultural and educational advancement of their people. Common issues related to education that are shared among most member countries include, low literacy rates, poor infrastructure, substandard quality of education, heavy dropout rates and inadequate funding.[8]

All SAARC countries have a similar higher education structure including entry qualifications and age, duration of courses and instructional management system. The pressing demands for higher education and a strong desire for foreign qualification by youth are common issues.

Japan places importance on South Asia, with which it shares the basic values of continued economic development, democracy, freedom, and the rule of law, and supports cooperation within the region based on a history of good relations with each country. Viewing SAARC as an association significant for its ability to provide a platform for the stability and development of the South Asia region, Japan established the Japan-SAARC Special Fund in 1993 to reinforce the Association's activities and foundation, and has implemented a variety of support and exchange programs. Support from Japan for the SAARC region has mainly been centred on organizing conferences and in providing support to individual countries.

The numbers of students from selected SAARC countries who pursue their higher education in Japan are plotted by year in Figure 3. One point that is consistently seen across all data is that despite the contribution of various factors such as population and economic development, Sri Lanka and Nepal

Fig. 3: Students from Selected SAARC Countries who Pursued their Higher Education in Japan[9]

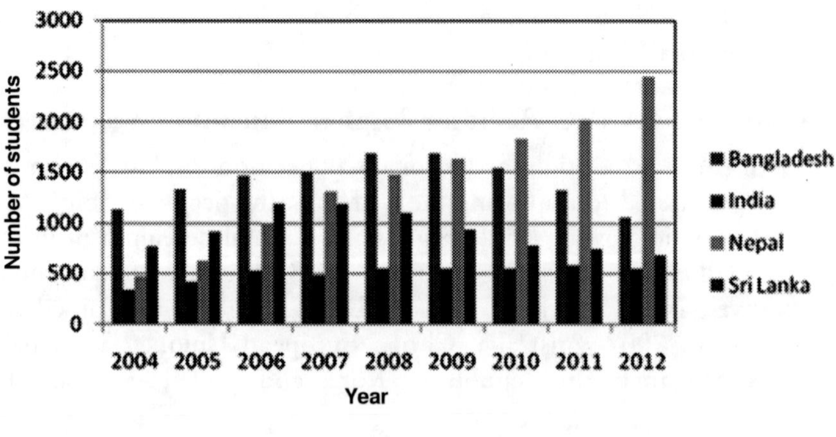

have noticeably better relations with Japan in regard to education than other SAARC countries when the above data is normalized according to population. This may be influenced by Sri Lanka and Nepal being predominantly Buddhist countries. Another general distinguishing feature of Sri Lanka-Japan Relationship has been their consistently positive and cordial relation that has carried on unperturbed over the years. It can also be inferred that the total number of SAARC region students studying in Japan has increased over the years.

Recommendation for SAARC–Japan Relations

1. **Establishing of Study Centres in the SAARC countries.**
   The establishment of the Sri Lanka Japan Study Centre turned a new page in the relationship between Sri Lanka and Japan and it is believed that the establishing of such centres in all SAARC countries would provide a much needed focal point in each nation. The centres can coordinate their efforts among themselves to ensure maximum benefit, optimum utilization and amplified results from Japanese Assistance. The Centre established in Sri Lanka has been specifically established in order to facilitate collaborative research. If such centres are established in other SAARC countries, international multidisciplinary research will come to the forefront and in turn will contribute towards the cumulative development of the region.
2. **SAARC Higher Education Coordination Desk at Embassy**
   It would be very useful to have a separate desk to handle higher education related matters in the embassies in various countries, especially in Japan. This would help in coordinating and facilitating educational exchanges and efforts and would definitely help in establishing more coordinated relations among the SAARC countries when it comes to educational and research exchanges, and would facilitate multilateral relationships.
   A designated desk for SAARC countries would ensure a more streamlined coordination within the region that will certainly contribute toward its overall relationship with Japan and in turn other regions and countries.

END NOTES

1. Japan International Cooperation Agency Retrieved January, 2014. [Online] Available from: http://www.jica.go.jp/english/index.html [Accessed Jan 2014].
2. Ratnayake, P., & Silva, De S., (2013). Human Capital Development with Japanese Assistance, Saga, Japan, Saga University Economic Society.
3. ODA white paper JICA, 2008.
4. Karunathilaka C.P.A (2009) Human Capital Development and Resource Allocation: The case in Sri Lanka, Central Bank of Sri Lanka.

5. Pritchett Lant (March 1996), "Where Has All the Education Gone", Policy Research Working Paper 1581, The World Bank, Policy Research Department.
6. Lopez Ramon, Thomas Vinod and Wang Yan (December 1998) Addressing the Education Puzzle: The Distribution of Education and Economic Reform, Policy Research Working Paper 2031, The World Bank, Economic Development Institute, USA.
7. Yokuo Murata, The influence of Japanese Education on Asian Countries – Opinion Analysis of the Former university Students and Trainees in Japan.
8. Chauhan, C.P.S, Higher Education: Current Status and Future Possibilities in Afghanistan, Bangladesh, Bhutan, India, Maldives, Nepal, Pakistan and Sri Lanka; 2008, Analytical Reports in international Education, Vol. 2, No. 1.
9. Japan Student Services Organization (JASSO), 2013. Online] Available from http://www.jasso.go.jp/about_jasso/index_e.html [Accessed Jan 2014].

Appendix I

China in the SAARC

Period	Remarks
Nov. 12–13, 2005	13th SAARC Summit at Dhaka agreed in principle to admit China as an Observer
April 3-4, 2007	14th SAARC Meeting at New Delhi; Foreign Minister Li Zhaoxing attends
August 1-3, 2008	Vice Foreign Minister Wu Dawei attend the 15th SAARC meeting in Sri Lanka
April 28-29, 2010	Deputy Foreign Minister Wang Guangya attended the 16th SAARC meeting in Bhutan
Nov. 10-11, 2011	Vice Foreign Minister Zhang Zhijun attended the 17th summit at Addu in Maldives.
June 2012	China appointed Yang Houlan, Ambassador to Nepal as Ambassador to SAARC

Source: Department of Policy Planning, Ministry of Foreign Affairs, PRC China's Foreign Affairs (various years)

Appendix II

China and the SAARC

Period	Remarks
May & Oct. 2007	China organised two "Understanding Modern China" workshops for South Asian diplomats
June 2007	China organised the "Seminar on Poverty Policy and Practice" for South Asian government officials
Sept. 2007	China invited a high-level delegation of diplomats from South Asia
2008	China hosted a workshop for SAARC officials, Seminar on China-SAARC relations, China-South Asia Business Forum and South Asian Countries Commodity Fair
2009	The first China-South Asia forum on radio and TV; an international seminar on China-SAARC relations; China-South Asia Business Forum and South Asian Commodities Fair, press delegation, etc conducted. Diplomats from South Asia taken to Hubei province
March 2010	Communist Party's International Department hosted a workshop for party officials from South Asian countries on rural development and poverty alleviation
May 2010	All China Federation of Trade Unions held a seminar of trade union leaders from South Asia
June 2010	5th China-South Asia Business Forum & 3rd South Asia Commodity Fair held at Kunming
2011	6th China-South Asia Business Forum; 4th South Asian Countries trade fair; Seminar on Agriculture Cooperation; Seminar for Cadres from South Asian Political Parties; China-SAARC seminar, etc.
2012	7th China-South Asia Business Forum; 5th South Asian Countries Trade Fair; Regional Workshop for Countries of SAARC on upgrading National Biodiversity Strategies and Action Plans; Seminar for Cadres from political parties of South Asia; exchange program for diplomats from SAARC

Source: Department of Policy Planning, Ministry of Foreign Affairs, PRC China's Foreign Affairs (various years)

Appendix III

Trade between China-South Asia, 2011-12

(Unit: $10,000)

Country	2011 Total	Exports	Imports	2012 Total	Exports	Imports
Afghanistan	23441	23001	440	46924	46405	519
Bangladesh	825921	781057	44864	844984	796991	47992
Bhutan	1746	1738	8	1562	1560	1
India	7390824	5053709	2337115	6647333	4767751	1879582
Maldives	9726	9712	14	7667	7649	19
Nepal	119509	118123	1386	199768	196816	2952
Pakistan	1055833	843971	211862	1241365	927539	313825
Sri Lanka	314161	298872	15289	316305	300109	16196

Source: China's National Bureau of Statistics accessed at <http://www.stats.gov.cn/tjsj/ndsj/2013/indexeh.htm>

Appendix IV

Recommendations of the 3rd SAARC-Japan Symposium on *"Promoting Energy Cooperation in South Asia"*, *New Delhi, 7-8 January 2010*

While appreciating the growing energy requirement for socio-economic development in the region, increasing regional demand for energy security and cooperation among the SAARC Member States and their deep concerns on the issues of global warming and climate change, the participants of the 3rd Japan-Symposium on "Promoting Energy Cooperation in South Asia" held on January 7-8, 2010 recommended that:

1. Enhancing energy supplies is essential to accelerate economic and social developments and to improve the Human Development Indices of the SAARC Member States. Providing access to affordable energy supplies to the teeming millions living below the poverty line is the way forward to alleviate poverty in the SAARC region. This can be achieved through the optimal utilization of the indigenous energy resources for the SAARC Member States and sharing these resources through cross border energy infrastructure.
2. Recognizing the need for collaboration among the SAARC Member States in harnessing the indigenous energy resources and procuring energy supplies from other regions to meet their increasing energy needs, a "SAARC Regional Energy Framework Agreement", be put in place. Promoting cross border investments in energy sector among the SAARC Member States, investment protection and arbitration mechanisms, sharing of technology, experiences and best practices should form an integral part of this Agreement. Policies that involve the private sector as strategic partners should also be evolved. The existing regional policy development mechanisms need to be effectively utilized for coordination and harmonization of SAARC Member States' energy policies.
3. The SAARC Member States should promote renewable energy projects, such as wind, solar and biomass using the latest technology, to reduce the dependence on imported fuel.
4. Energy efficiency and demand side management in the electricity sector

are the other two important areas that merit attention of the SAARC Member States.

5. A regional forum should be established where the professionals engaged in energy sector including those in regulatory bodies, generation, transmission, distribution and exploration utilities could regularly meet and exchange views, ideas, technologies and success stories. This will promote institutional networking and linkages within the SAARC region, which is essential to operationalize the regional level programs. To start with, the Sikkim University may initiate the concept of establishing a South Asian energy club, as a forum for engaging energy sector professionals to exchange views, ideas, technologies and success stories.
6. The SAARC Development Fund (SDF) should be increasingly utilized for regional energy projects. Besides the commitments from the SAARC Member States the SDF could draw the financial support from international financial institutions to finance regional projects.
7. Cross border energy trade is taking place between India, Nepal, Bhutan and Sri Lanka and also between Pakistan and Afghanistan. This has to be consolidated by broadening the scope and coverage including through regional power and gas interconnections. Establishing a regional power trading mechanism would be beneficial in this context and help in promoting regional power trade, as in Southern African Power Pool.
8. There is an imperative need to assess global warming led climate change and its impact on the energy resources in the region. Scientific studies should be carried out with the assistance of environment and glaciology experts to assess the extent of erosion and melting of glaciers which feed the main river systems in South Asia. Help of energy experts be sought to study, strategize and address the energy security concerns of the SAARC Member States.
9. The role of civil society including academics and media in discussions, debate and analysis on issues of energy in the context of regional cooperation/development in South Asia has been very critical and crucial. This has led to many regional cooperation and development projects and ideas in the past. This South Asian tradition has to be consolidated further by organizing regional symposia, workshops and conferences more frequently in the different SAARC Member States.
10. The SAARC Member States may consider incorporating a chapter each on Energy Efficiency to reduce energy consumptions and use of renewable energy technologies for reducing the dependence on fossil fuels as part of the school curriculum.
11. Japan may actively facilitate intra and inter-regional dialogue and cooperation through continuing SAARC Japan Symposia.

Appendix V

Charter of the South Asian Association for Regional Cooperation

We, the Heads of State or Government of BANGLADESH, BHUTAN, INDIA, MALDIVES, NEPAL, PAKISTAN and SRI LANKA;

1. Desirous of promoting peace, stability, amity and progress in the region through strict adherence to the principles of the UNITED NATIONS CHARTER and NON-ALIGNMENT, particularly respect for the principles of sovereign equality, territorial integrity, national independence, non-use of force and non-interference in the internal affairs of other States and peaceful settlement of all disputes;

2. Conscious that in an increasingly interdependent world, the objectives of peace, freedom, social justice and economic prosperity are best achieved in the SOUTH ASIAN region by fostering mutual understanding, good neighborly relations and meaningful cooperation among the Member States which are bound by ties of history and culture;

3. Aware of the common problems, interests and aspirations of the peoples of SOUTH ASIA and the need for joint action and enhanced cooperation within their respective political and economic systems and cultural traditions;

4. Convinced that regional cooperation among the countries of SOUTH ASIA is mutually beneficial, desirable and necessary for promoting the welfare and improving the quality of life of the peoples of the region;

5. Convinced further that economic, social and technical cooperation among the countries of SOUTH ASIA would contribute significantly to national and collective self-reliance;

6. Recognizing that increased cooperation, contacts and exchanges among the countries of the region will contribute to the promotion of friendship and understanding among their peoples;

7. Recalling the DECLARATION signed by their Foreign Ministers in NEW

DELHI on August 2, 1983 and noting the progress achieved in regional cooperation;

8. Reaffirming their determination to promote such cooperation within an institutional framework;

DO HEREBY AGREE to establish an organization to be known as SOUTH ASIAN ASSOCIATION FOR REGIONAL COOPERATION hereinafter referred to as the ASSOCIATION, with the following objectives, principles, institutional and financial arrangements:

Article I

OBJECTIVES

The objectives of the ASSOCIATION shall be:

a) to promote the welfare of the peoples of SOUTH ASIA and to improve their quality of life;
b) to accelerate economic growth, social progress and cultural development in the region and to provide all individuals the opportunity to live in dignity and to realize their full potentials;
c) to promote and strengthen collective self-reliance among the countries of SOUTH ASIA;
d) to contribute to mutual trust, understanding and appreciation of one another's problems;
e) to promote active collaboration and mutual assistance in the economic, social, cultural, technical and scientific fields;
f) to strengthen cooperation with other developing countries;
g) to strengthen cooperation among themselves in international forums on matters of common interests; and
h) to cooperate with international and regional organizations with similar aims and purposes.

Article II

PRINCIPLES

1. Cooperation within the framework of the ASSOCIATION shall be based on respect for the principles of sovereign equality, territorial integrity, political independence, non -interference in the internal affairs of other States and mutual benefit.
2. Such cooperation shall not be a substitute for bilateral and multilateral cooperation but shall complement them.
3. Such cooperation shall not be inconsistent with bilateral and multilateral obligations.

Article III

MEETINGS OF THE HEADS OF STATE OR GOVERNMENT

The Heads of State or Government shall meet once a year or more often as and when considered necessary by the Member States.

Article IV

COUNCIL OF MINISTERS

1. A Council of Ministers consisting of the Foreign Ministers of the Member States shall be established with the following functions:
   a) formulation of the policies of the ASSOCIATION;
   b) review of the progress of cooperation under the ASSOCIATION;
   c) decision on new areas of cooperation;
   d) establishment of additional mechanism under the ASSOCIATION as deemed necessary;
   e) decision on other matters of general interest to the ASSOCIATION.

2. The Council of Ministers shall meet twice a year. Extraordinary session of the Council may be held by agreement among the Member States.

Article V

STANDING COMMITTEE

1. The Standing Committee comprising the Foreign Secretaries shall have the following functions:
   a) overall monitoring and coordination of programme of cooperation;
   b) approval of projects and programmes, and the modalities of their financing;
   c) determination of inter-sectoral priorities;
   d) mobilization of regional and external resources;
   e) identification of new areas of cooperation based on appropriate studies.
2. The Standing Committee shall meet as often as deemed necessary.
3. The Standing Committee shall submit periodic reports to the Council of Ministers and make reference to it as and when necessary for decisions on policy matters.

Article VI

TECHNICAL COMMITTEES

1. Technical Committees comprising representatives of Member States shall

be responsible for the implementation, coordination and monitoring of the programmes in their respective areas of cooperation.

2. They shall have the following terms of reference:
   a) determination of the potential and the scope of regional cooperation in agreed areas;
   b) formulation of programmes and preparation of projects;
   c) determination of financial implications of sectoral programmes;
   d) formulation of recommendations regarding apportionment of costs;
   e) implementation and coordination of sectoral programmes;
   f) monitoring of progress in implementation.
3. The Technical Committees shall submit periodic reports to the Standing Committee.
4. The Chairmanship of the Technical Committees shall normally rotate among Member States in alphabetical order every two years.
5. The Technical Committees may, inter-alia, use the following mechanisms and modalities, if and when considered necessary:
   a) meetings of heads of national technical agencies;
   b) meetings of experts in specific fields;
   c) contact amongst recognised centres of excellence in the region.

Article VII

ACTION COMMITTEES

The Standing Committee may set up Action Committees comprising Member States concerned with implementation of projects involving more than two but not all Member States.

Article VIII

SECRETARIAT

There shall be a Secretariat of the ASSOCIATION.

Article IX

FINANCIAL ARRANGEMENTS

1. The contribution of each Member State towards financing of the activities of the ASSOCIATION shall be voluntary.
2. Each Technical Committee shall make recommendations for the apportionment of costs of implementing the programmes proposed by it.
3. In case sufficient financial resources cannot be mobilized within the region

for funding activities of the ASSOCIATION, external financing from appropriate sources may be mobilized with the approval of or by the Standing Committee.

Article X

GENERAL PROVISIONS

1. Decisions at all levels shall be taken on the basis of unanimity.2. Bilateral and contentious issues shall be excluded from the deliberations.

IN FAITH WHEREOF We Have Set Our Hands And Seals Hereunto. DONE In DHAKA, BANGLADESH, On This The Eighth Day Of December Of The Year One Thousand Nine Hundred Eighty Five.

Hussain Muhammad Ershad
PRESIDENT OF THE PEOPLE'S REPUBLIC OF BANGLADESH

Jigme Singye Wangchuk
KING OF BHUTAN

Rajiv Gandhi
PRIME MINISTER OF THE REPUBLIC OF INDIA

Maumoon Abdul Gayoom
PRESIDENT OF THE REBUPLIC OF MALDIVES

Birendra Bir Bikram Shah Dev
KING OF NEPAL

Muhammad Zia-ul-Haq
PRESIDENT OF THE ISLAMIC REPUBLIC OF PAKISTAN

Junius Richard Jayewardene
PRESIDENT OF DEMOCRATIC SOCIALIST REPUBLIC OF SRI LANKA

Index